THE
Multicultural Classroom

THE
Multicultural Classroom

Readings for Content-Area Teachers

Edited by

Patricia A. Richard-Amato
University of Nevada, Reno

and

Marguerite Ann Snow
California State University, Los Angeles

Longman

**The Multicultural Classroom: Readings
for Content-Area Teachers**

Longman, 10 Bank Street, White Plains, N.Y. 10606

Associated companies:
Longman Group Ltd., London
Longman Cheshire Pty., Melbourne
Longman Paul Pty., Auckland
Copp Clark Pitman, Toronto

Distributed in the United Kingdom by Longman Group
Ltd., Longman House, Burnt Mill, Harlow, Essex CM20
2JE, England and by associated companies, branches,
and representatives throughout the world.

Executive editor: Joanne Dresner
Development editor: Penny Laporte
Production editor: Linda W. Witzling
Cover design: Anne M. Pompeo

Library of Congress Cataloging-in-Publication Data
Richard-Amato, Patricia A.
    The multicultural classroom : readings for content-area teachers /
  by Patricia A. Richard-Amato and Marguerite Ann Snow.
        p.   cm.
    Includes bibliographical references and index.
    ISBN 0-8013-0511-X
    1. English language—Study and teaching—Foreign speakers.
  2. Interdisciplinary approach in education. I. Snow, Marguerite
Ann. II. Title.
PE1128.A2R475   1992
428.007—dc20   90-25876
                                                        CIP

3 4 5 6 7 8 9 10-DO-95949392

*For **Jay** and **Rich***

Contents

Acknowledgments

We wish to thank all those people who have so generously contributed their time and talents to help us bring this book to you. Acknowledgments first go to our many contributors who have shared their insights and expertise in the areas of second language education and multicultural teaching. We are particularly grateful to Donna Christian and to our other readers for their thoughtful reviews and many valuable suggestions: Leslie Jo Adams, Helena Anderson Curtain, Carol Enseki, and Cynthia Park. In addition, we wish to thank Dr. Charles Leyba, our Division Chair at California State University, Los Angeles, for his encouragement and support; our editors at Longman, Joanne Dresner, Penny Laporte, Linda Witzling, and others who advised us along the way; and the staff of the John F. Kennedy Library at California State University, Los Angeles, who helped us track down sources.

Introduction

Our society is becoming increasingly more culturally diverse. No longer can we speak of one culture, that is, the Anglo-American culture, as the embodiment of all things "American." Manifested also are the values, life-styles, and traditions of Mexican Americans, African Americans, Laotian Americans, Chinese Americans, Vietnamese Americans, Central Americans, Native Americans, Korean Americans, and many more. It is evident, too, that as our society becomes more and more pluralistic, so do our classrooms.

This metamorphosis within our schools, especially in urban areas, presents a multitude of challenges for content-area teachers (Kindergarten to adult) in math, science, social studies, literature, art, and so forth. It is essential to have classrooms that foster cultural understanding of and sensitivity to immigrant students and others belonging to nondominant groups within our society. Effective teaching skills must be developed across the content areas to meet the sociocultural, cognitive, and language needs of this burgeoning population.

One of our greatest challenges is presented by recently arrived immigrants and refugees who are struggling simultaneously to master subject matter and to learn a second language. Some of these students have escaped war; others have experienced persecution in their homelands because of their political, ethnic, or religious backgrounds. Still others have fled from poverty and are seeking job and educational opportunities to improve their daily lives and those of their families. Many have been attracted by the same basic freedoms that brought our own predecessors here during earlier periods of substantial immigration.

Among these recent arrivals are many individuals already educated within the parameters of their own cultural needs and aspirations. In some cases their education may equal or surpass that associated with comparable grade levels within American society. In other cases individuals may not be literate in their native languages. With adequate preparation, both groups are capable of learning English and functioning effectively in our schools and in the greater society. It is important throughout the acculturation process that these students be encouraged not only to take on a second language to enable them to operate in a second culture, but that they also maintain their native languages and cultures as much as possible so that these important resources are not lost

1

to future generations. One's native language and culture are too valuable to lose and, if cherished, can bring about feelings of self-esteem, inner joy, and a measure of security.

Other language minority students who present challenges in our classrooms are international students on student visas who have learned English as a foreign language in their native countries. At first these students usually have great difficulty understanding interpersonal and academic English spoken at normal speeds. They often need extensive listening and speaking experiences to ease them into the mainstream.

Other challenges to us come from those students who immigrated to this country at an early age or who were born in this country and who in fact may be English dominant. Many have not yet acquired the academic English language skills necessary for success in school. For them, remediation as we know it has not worked. What they require from us, in addition to the tools of learning, is a nonthreatening place where they can be encouraged to develop an increased pride in their cultures and in themselves that will enable them to rise above the poverty, prejudice, and degradation that often accompany membership in nondominant groups in any society.

Although many of the students just described come into our classrooms with great anticipation and ardent faith in the system, they are often disappointed to find that their needs are not recognized, much less addressed. Unfortunately, many teachers, already overwhelmed with challenges at all levels, are too ill-prepared and too frustrated to provide the kinds of classrooms that will adequately identify and meet the needs of these students. Moreover, the teachers typically find themselves unfamiliar with issues in second language (L2) learning, yet they must shoulder much of the responsibility for promoting such learning through content instruction. This book is an attempt to fill the gap by providing both conceptual and practical ideas to assist teachers in meeting this responsibility. Ultimately, by making classrooms better places for students who represent nondominant cultures, teachers will be making the classrooms better for all students.

Intended primarily for preservice and in-service teachers, this book includes edited readings selected from the work of experienced content-area and language teachers, applied linguists, and researchers. Part I lays down a strong theoretical foundation for successful teaching in multicultural classrooms. Part II focuses on the cultural considerations that must be taken into account. Part III discusses pedagogical strategies and management issues across the content areas, and Part IV relates many of these strategies and issues to specific content areas. Ending each chapter are questions and activities suitable for individual reflection and work or for whole-class or small-group work in teacher-training programs. Not all the readings will be appropriate for every teacher and every classroom. It is expected that teachers will select those techniques and practices with which they feel most comfortable and that are most appropriate for their students.

PART I

Theoretical Foundations

In meeting the needs of students in multicultural classrooms, particularly those of the language minority student in content-area classes, it is important to consider the many theoretical issues that have an impact on teaching and learning. The selections included here all offer different pieces of the theoretical puzzle—from theories of second language (L2) acquisition to research associated with learner grouping strategies. The aim of Part I is to provide the theoretical underpinnings for the practical issues of classroom application that come later in the book.

We begin with an introduction to the language minority student in Chapter 1 by Donna Brinton, Linda Sasser, and Beth Winningham, who also describe the kinds of educational programs into which these students are typically placed. The chapter provides an overview of L2 acquisition theory to guide us as we try to understand the processes by which language minority students expand their linguistic repertoire. In Chapter 2, Jim Cummins presents a theoretical framework for conceptualizing language proficiency, offering a distinction between social and academic language. Ann Snow, Mimi Met, and Fred Genesee call for the integration of language and content instruction in Chapter 3 as one approach to helping students develop academic language skills. In Chapter 4, Anna Uhl Chamot and Michael O'Malley expand on this theme in their description of a model that aids language minority students in the transition to mainstream classes. Chapter 5 by Mary McGroarty concludes Part I with a discussion of the rationale and research supporting cooperative learning as an important tool in promoting second language development and content-area learning.

1

Language Minority Students in Multicultural Classrooms

DONNA BRINTON *University of California, Los Angeles*

LINDA SASSER *Alhambra, California, School District*

BETH WINNINGHAM *Los Angeles Unified School District*

EDITORS' INTRODUCTION

A first step in meeting the needs of language minority students in multicultural classrooms is understanding who they are and what their needs might be. In this chapter, we hear directly from language minority students of their experiences in adjusting to a new language and culture. To help us better understand the second language (L2) learner, Donna Brinton, Linda Sasser, and Beth Winningham provide an overview of the L2 acquisition process and discuss the kinds of programs currently used to teach English to language minority students. The authors stress academic skill development as way to empower language minority students so that they may accomplish their goals and benefit fully from what schooling has to offer.

> When my teacher asked me what's my name, where do I come from, etc., I can hardly answered his questions. One of his questions was very hard for me to answer, especially in front of class. So I answered his question wrong. Everybody laughed at me because they think is so funny. I never felt so embarrassed in my whole life before. That was the worst memory on my life. My face was blushed when they laughed and giggled at me.
>
> *Susan, 14, Indonesia*

Who are the language minority students who make up an increasing percentage of the public school population in the United States?

From "The Limited English Proficient Student" by D. Brinton, L. Sasser, and B. Winningham, 1988, in G. Gadda, F. Peitzman, & W. Walsh (Eds.), Teaching Analytical Writing *(pp. 95–133). Copyright 1988 by the California Academic Partnership Program. Adapted by permission.*

It was a cold summer morning, and it was also my first day of school in United States. The school start at eight, but I was waked up at six. I felt pressure on me, because I don't know how to spoke English at all. So it was push me to do my best on everything at that day.

Sherman, 15, Korea

Eager students like Sherman enter our schools everyday. Although we may not yet know these newest Americans, our task is to prepare them for their futures. As we accumulate both information and experience, we can help these young people attain parity in multicultural America. It is an important responsibility. These students may be urban or rural; schooled or unschooled; literate, nonliterate, or preliterate; and they may be legal immigrants, refugees, or undocumented aliens.

These students will have differing learning styles: Some will learn to speak English quickly, while others will not; some will learn to read and write with great proficiency, but others will not even graduate from our high schools.

May 27, 1982

Principal
XXX High School

Dear Mr. XXX,

According to my opinions, the rule is unfair. I have taken the proficiency test about 6 times. Since I was in 9 grade but I can't pass it even I'd tried my best. I'm care about it so much because the rule is so hard. . . . Why is the rule so difference between this school and others? Some schools led the students get the multiple choice test instead of writing a paragraph. This school has a special program for foreigners, why doesn't it have a special test for them to graduate? If you were in my situation, how would you feel and think about it?

Phong, 19, Vietnam

These new arrivals come from intact nuclear families, extended families, shattered families. Many of them live in crowded apartments where people sleep in shifts and the lights are always burning. Some of them reside in neighborhoods where there is no place to go but out and nothing to do when they get there.

When our family came to United States, we had rented a very tiny apartment, it just had a kitchen, a restroom and a bedroom, but they are four people in our family so it was really crowed. There are a lots of little kids around the neighborhood, and one of the little kids came up to me and hit me. I had do nothing to him, so I hit him too and stare to cry. Few minutes later his father bring him and asked me why I hitted him, but at that time I don't speak any English, so I was speechless. He took me to my father and told him I hitted his son, so my father didn't ask me what was all happened and just stare to blame me. So I was very angry of that, and I never going to forget this. And at that time I also decided I want to learn English as fast as I could. It's not for anyone else. It's just a protection to myself.

Su-Chin, 14, Taiwan

Unfortunately, racial and ethnic tensions exist among and between the many ethnic groups. Many school campuses suffer from misunderstandings and occasional violence as language minority students adapt, with varying degrees of success, not only to the culture of the United States but to the cultures of one another.

One day when I was at home alone I felt bored and unhappy, so I decided to go to a very famous chinese restaurant that was at the corner of the street I was living. When I get there I felt a lttle strange because there were only chinese people that were wearing expensive clothes. I didn't understood anything of what they were talking about because their language was different. At that time I just knew a little english, almost nothing. They were all looking at me like if I were an ugly ghost. I kept walking until I get to the place where I buy the food. When I get there I ask for a hamburger but the man didn't understood me, so I went outside and look for a person who speak english well, and told him to buy me a hamburger, but he told me that there were no hamburgers, ''there are only chine food,'' he said. I felt scare to go in again and I just go back home and watch television.

Francisco, 15, Mexico

The feelings that these students from different countries share are both negative and positive. Those who arrive in desperate circumstances from war-torn nations are often preoccupied by the need to survive emotionally and economically. Such needs take precedence over expending energy on school tasks. Yet many such students are motivated to succeed: They persist and work diligently to surmount the double hurdles of language and culture. These language minority students have a fresh perspective to offer that can energize the classroom and challenge both curriculum and teacher. If we facilitate their growth, we can extend their horizons and enable them to reach their full potential as visible and vocal citizens.

To do so, we must take the time to meet second language students in our classrooms halfway as they attempt to contribute their understanding and prior knowledge.

My second period is Math class. Though I didn't understand what the teacher was talking about, but those signs and numbers are familiar to me. I took this class because my brain could not translate the word "Trigonometry" to my own language even though I have studied it before. One day, I was in this class as usual. My teacher was doing a question on the board. She made a mistake and no one knew it except me, but I eyed it until the bell rang. I was making, too, a BIG mistake. I walk to her after most students had left and I show her where the mistake was. But she just said very loud and angry to me that she didn't understand what I was telling to her. I feel that I wasn't exist in the world. Then I left the classroom. I said to her "I won't talk to you again! very loudly in my mind.

Jeau, 17, China

We must also be careful not to confuse the limitations of language with limitations of cognition. When students with limited English-speaking skills enter school, it is necessary to assess their levels of English proficiency before assigning class schedules. Because these assessments vary, students labeled fluent in one system may be designated limited in another. Some schools retain students in English as a second language (ESL) classes longer than necessary, while others hurry them out before they are ready. In other schools, limited English proficient (LEP) students are even thought to be in need of linguistic remediation. As a consequence, they may be placed in remedial classes intended for native English speakers to make up for what is thought to be their cognitive deficiencies. The end result is not surprising: Bright and capable students may graduate from high school with little exposure to the demands of a college preparatory curriculum because their continuing need for English language development has been confused with a limited ability to think.

THE CHALLENGES OF LITERACY

Filled with ug, the younghede Tenderis groped his way along the downsteepy path toward the cosh wherein dwelled the feared spirit-person. Squint-a-pipes that he was, Tenderis found negotiating his way through the eileber and venerated dway-berries very teenful in the nyle. He tripped over zuches spiss with maily malshaves that made him quetch at their touch. (S. K. Sperling, Poplollies and Bellibones: A Celebration of Lost Words, pp. 33, 35.)

Imagine this as an assigned text and answer the comprehension questions that follow: What was Tenderis's emotion as he approached the cosh? Why was it difficult to go through the eileber and dway-berries? Further suppose that your teacher is aware of the archaic and difficult vocabulary and suggests that you use your dictionary to define these terms: *younghede, teenful,* and *maily.* Even if you do this assignment perfectly, overall comprehension might elude you.

Such is the situation that often faces language minority students in school. Using syntax and context clues, they are able to answer fact and knowledge questions correctly, yet they cannot paraphrase the main ideas or analyze passages to apply their ideas to new situations.

According to Goodman (1982), ''The two most important resources that any learners bring to learning to read and write are their competence in the oral language and their undiminished ability to learn language as it is needed for new functions. The role of literacy instruction in school is to facilitate the use by learners of these resources'' (p. 246). For students who lack full competency in the second language, this means that they need class time to sort out and talk through the complex process of responding to many kinds of academic tasks. Carefully structured activities will help them acquire new concepts and specialized vocabulary. The teacher who engages students in interactive dialogue will not be limiting instruction to a series of low-level comprehension questions that do little to prepare them for the cognitively demanding tasks of content-area instruction.

As we have indicated, the language minority students enrolled in schools in the United States are extremely diverse. They differ, for example, not only in such outwardly evident characteristics as ethnicity, age, gender, and language background but also in their communicative needs, their opportunities to use the second language, their attitudes toward it, their cognitive styles, their personalities, and so on. All these characteristics influence their language learning strategies at all proficiency levels. (See Chapter 10 for a detailed discussion of the typical language behaviors associated with different levels.)

THE SECOND LANGUAGE ACQUISITION PROCESS

Despite very large differences in the second language (L2) population we encounter, there are some universal characteristics that can help us better understand these learners as they travel along the language learning continuum. First, it should be stressed that each second language student progresses independently, though rather predictably, toward a target form of the language that contains fewer and fewer errors. Most second language learners will pick up such features as negation and certain grammatical morphemes (e.g., the verb ending -ing) relatively early in the L2 acquisition process, while other features (e.g., prepositional usage, the article system) may require much longer exposure and more fine tuning. Second, this language acquisition sequence appears to be relatively independent of the learner's first language, and can thus be likened to the natural sequence of a child's first language (L1) acquisition. However, there is evidence that the first language mainly facilitates the acquisition of certain features, and thus the sequence of L2 acquisition can be said to be colored by the learner's first language.

Brown (1987) sheds some light on this sequence of language development by dividing acquisition into four stages: random errors, emergent interlanguage, the systematic stage, and the stabilization stage. In other words, the learner progresses from stage one, presystematic guessing, to the second stage in which there is growing consistency in the use of a given language item. At this stage, the learner is typically unable to correct errors even when they are pointed out. In the third stage, although the learner's version of the rules may not yet be entirely well formed, the learner is able to correct errors when they become salient. It is at this point that conscious knowledge of rules may have maximum benefit. And finally, in the stabilization stage, the learner's application of rules (either conscious or subconscious) is entirely consistent.

To understand the variation that occurs among learners, we should remember that learners acquire the second language very much according to their own internal timetable; this is sometimes referred to as the *internal syllabus*. This fact can help to explain why some learners acquire rules more readily than others, and it can help explain many a teacher's frustration with students who continue to make errors that have been painstakingly explained in class. Thus, it must be kept in mind that individual variables will influence the amount of time needed to acquire a rule, and that although some learners appear to be slower than others, this does not mean they will not eventually acquire the rule.

Just as much variability can be observed in the ability and readiness of the learner to produce the target language. Krashen and Terrell (1983) hypothesize that comprehension of the target language precedes production, and that production can be divided into naturally occurring stages, including nonverbal responses, single-word responses, two- or three-word responses, phrase production, sentence production, and finally the production of more complex discourse. While this rubric is certainly a useful one for charting many students' interlanguage, it does not account for the student who, due to cognitive or personality factors, undergoes an unusually long silent period before speaking in the target language, or the student at the opposite extreme of the spectrum who seems willing, despite minimal proficiency in the target language, to utter long streams of semi-intelligible phrases. In short, though we can find some system in the language learning behavior of these diverse individuals, we need as well to keep in mind the tremendous influence of the many individual variables, both cognitive and affective, on L2 acquisition. (See especially Chapters 2 and 6.)

UNDERSTANDING SECOND LANGUAGE ERRORS

Some of the findings gained from research on the process of L2 acquisition help to set priorities for the instruction of language minority students. (See specific strategies in Chapters 9 and 10 for dealing with student errors.) When working with these students, it is important to keep in mind that L2 acquisition is a developmental process. It can thus be helpful to think of a child acquiring his or her own first language, and the stages that this child goes through before attaining adultlike speech. Above all, it is important to view the errors that these learners make as natural products of the language acquisition process and as a phenomenon that is likely to disappear gradually as these learners are exposed to more comprehensible input—that is, meaningful language used in communication by native speakers that challenges the learner and therefore allows an opportunity for acquisition (Krashen, 1982).

Some insight into the sources of L2 errors can help provide guidance in dealing effectively with speech and writing. An ongoing controversy in the field of applied linguistics has involved the question of whether errors are caused by interference (i.e., overreliance on the forms of the native language) or whether they are the product of an independent, developmental sequence of acquisition. According to the bulk of the L2 research (Hatch, Gough & Peck, 1985), interference from the native language appears to play only a minimal role in the learner's overall acquisition of the L2 and is probably primarily restricted to interference on the phonological level—such as when a French speaker substitutes the phonemes $\setminus s \setminus$ or $\setminus z \setminus$ for the English "th" sounds, which are nonexistent in French, or when a Korean speaker experiences difficulty distinguishing between English $\setminus p \setminus$ and $\setminus f \setminus$ or $\setminus b \setminus$ and $\setminus v \setminus$ due to the different point and manner of production of the corresponding sounds in Korean.

Most researchers today concur that there is a usual pattern of acquisition and that errors are generally the result of an incomplete progression along that path. This theory, which is founded on observations of the subjects of L2 acquisition research, states that at any stage in the acquisition process, the learners may or may not be "ready" to internalize certain aspects of the new language. Depending on the stage of development in the interlanguage process, they may accept the nativelike form or create alternate forms of their own via the processes of overgeneralization or simplification. For example, it is not uncommon for learners to overgeneralize the rule for forming the past tense of regular verbs and to produce an ungrammatical form such as "teached" instead of producing the correct form "taught," or for them to simplify the grammatically redundant formation of the present continuous tense and produce an utterance such as "I going" in place of "I am going." Language acquisition researchers postulate that these patterns are, though not invariant, strikingly similar across age and native language groups.

PROGRAMS FOR THE LIMITED ENGLISH PROFICIENT STUDENT

As educators working with language minority students, we attempt to devise, write, and teach curricula that prepare our students to communicate in their new language. Our long-term aim is to move our students toward "communicative competence" in English. Proposed by Canale and Swain (1980), communicative competence includes the following components.

Linguistic competence: Mastery of grammar (both at the subconscious level and at the conscious level in the case of learned rules)

Discourse competence: Knowledge of how language functions above and beyond the sentence level (for example, the ability to recognize a logical sequence or to pose a persuasive argument)

Sociolinguistic competence: Ability to use language appropriately in a variety of situations depending on the topic, status of participants, and the purpose of the interaction

Strategic competence: Ability to employ a variety of coping strategies (e.g., repetition, request for clarification) to avoid breakdowns in communication

Throughout the United States, there is a variety of program types that have been designed to teach communicative competence as well as academic skills to language minority students. In earlier times, such students were often "submersed" into regular classes where little accommodation to their L2 learning needs was made. Fortunately, educators now realize that this sink-or-swim approach is detrimental to language minority students. The following are the most common programs currently in place.

ESL Classes: Students from non-English-speaking home backgrounds attend ESL classes taught by trained language development specialists. All instruction is in English, using ESL methods and techniques. Once a specified level of proficiency is reached (exit criteria vary from district to district), students may be transitioned into another kind of program for language minority students or mainstreamed into regular classes.

Bilingual Classes: Content-area instruction (i.e., reading, math, social studies) is provided in the student's native language. Concurrently, students receive ESL instruction.

Sheltered Content Classes: Language minority students (often from a variety of home language backgrounds) are grouped together and taught by a content teacher (e.g., math, social studies) who uses a variety of instructional strategies to make content instruction comprehensible. (See Chapter 10 for a detailed discussion of effective instructional strategies for content instruction.)

Adjunct Classes: Students are enrolled in paired language and content classes in which instruction is coordinated between ESL teachers and content-area teachers.

School districts may offer one, all, or a combination of these programs. In many areas, bilingual classes exist side by side with ESL classes. As mentioned, there is a great variety of program configurations, depending upon local resources, student demographics, and commitment to the needs of language minority students. For example, in some districts language minority students are mainstreamed into classes with native English speakers after only one or two semesters, while students in other districts stay in the ESL program for much longer periods of time. Regardless of the type of program, it is not uncommon for language minority students to be mainstreamed without ever having been exposed to analytical thinking or writing in the second language. In fact, many teachers of language minority students find that students are generally successful at the beginning and intermediate levels of acquisition and quickly develop basic interpersonal communication skills; however, they lack the cognitive academic language that is critical to their success in secondary and postsecondary education. (See Chapter 2 for an in-depth discussion of cognitive academic language proficiency.) It is at these transitional and advanced stages in particular that the curriculum and teaching strategies for language minority students must aim to strengthen their performance.

In general, programs for language minority students around the country appear to lack standardized curricular guidelines. Some districts operate with little or no curriculum, and the responsibility for developing instructional guidelines falls to the individual school or even to individual teachers. Teachers in other districts, in contrast, feel the burden of overly restricted guidelines that often adhere to a traditional grammar-based approach that does not allow enough focus on the integration of all skills and on the development of higher-order thinking skills. Given the tremendous growth in the number of language minority students in this country and the increasing demand for guidance in curriculum design, there is a pressing need for continuity in instruction, and for a recognition of the responsibility of state and national governments vis-à-vis this need.

The impact of population demographics in the large urban areas of the United States is undeniable. In many language minority communities, the high school dropout rate approaches 50 percent. At the same time, language minority students comprise an ever-increasing segment of the undergraduate population of American universities. The history of this country is, in many ways, a history of immigration, and thus this shift in demographics alone is certainly no cause for concern. That these students' needs are not being met is a concern, however.

In addition, there seems to be a growing educational gap between the levels of academic preparation provided by our high schools and the expectations of universities. This gap impacts especially heavily on language minority students and their chances for academic success. These students, like their native English-speaking counterparts, need to be taught advanced-level reading and writing skills. They need to be able, for example, to read critically and to incorporate information from secondary sources into their own writing, that is, to paraphrase, summarize, and quote effectively from background texts. Furthermore, a focus on helping these students to develop analytical thinking abilities should be a top priority from the earliest levels of elementary school.

CONCLUSION

An understanding of some of the factors impacting the acquisition of English as a second language has implications not only for the ESL/language arts teacher but for all instructors because language minority students are often expected to perform competently in the content areas while their English skills are still developing. Research in L2 acquisition suggests that learners acquire control over aspects of English—vocabulary, syntax, word forms and endings, linguistic appropriateness—at different rates but simultaneously. There is no reason to assume that second language learners cannot grapple with cognitively demanding content until they control all or most of the features of English grammar and usage. However, because the students are still acquiring English proficiency, it is incumbent upon content-area teachers to be supportive of the efforts of language minority students and to equip themselves with effective instructional strategies. By understanding the affective and academic needs of language minority students, content-area teachers can enhance their students' chances for success both in school and in their lives ahead.

FOLLOW-UP QUESTIONS AND ACTIVITIES

1. It is clear from the short vignettes at the beginning of the chapter that many language minority students go through a very difficult adjustment period after arriving in this country. What can you as a teacher do to promote a classroom environment that is sensitive to the language minority students' sociopsychological needs?

2. Many language minority students live in crowded conditions that are not conducive to studying. With a small group, brainstorm ways in which teachers and the school administration might compensate for the lack of study opportunities at home.

3. Define the term *interlanguage* on the basis of the discussion in Chapter 1. Does this term help you conceptualize the L2 acquisition process? How are errors viewed in this perspective on L2 learning? What implications might this knowledge have for error correction?

4. Have you ever studied a foreign language? If so, characterize your language-learning experience. What was positive or negative about it? To what extent were you successful? To what do you attribute your success or lack thereof? Did you require a ''silent period,'' or were you uninhibited about using the foreign language right away? How might your own language-learning experience help you relate to your language minority students?

5. Note the components of communicative competence described by Canale and Swain on page 12. Think of an example in English for each of the four components. If you have studied a foreign language, were you able to develop skills in all four components of communicative competence, or did you mainly learn grammar? How did this influence your language development?

6. In this chapter, a variety of programs for language minority students was mentioned. Which programs were you already aware of? In the school with which you are most familiar, what kinds of programs for language minority students exist? If possible, find out more about these programs by interviewing the principal, program coordinator, and classroom teachers. Gather information about funding sources, teacher qualifications, student identification and placement, exit criteria, curriculum and materials, and any other information you would like to know. Report your findings to your class, and discuss your reactions.

2

Language Proficiency, Bilingualism, and Academic Achievement

Jim Cummins *Ontario Institute for Studies in Education*

Editors' Introduction

In this chapter, Jim Cummins proposes a distinction between two levels of language proficiency: surface-level conversational proficiency and the deeper level of cognitive academic language proficiency. His work in second language (L2) education is an elaboration of the earlier contributions of theorists in a variety of settings (e.g., Skutnabb-Kangas & Toukomaa (1976) with Finnish immigrants in Sweden, and Donaldson's (1978) studies of child language acquisition in Scotland). The distinction proposed by Cummins has far-reaching implications for both teaching and testing and bears careful consideration for its relevance to content-area instruction.

EVOLUTION OF A THEORETICAL FRAMEWORK FOR CONCEPTUALIZING LANGUAGE PROFICIENCY

Skutnabb-Kangas and Toukomaa (1976) initially drew attention to the distinction between "surface fluency" in a language and academically related aspects of language proficiency. They noted that Finnish immigrant students who were either born in Sweden or who immigrated at a relatively young (i.e., preschool) age appeared to converse in peer-appropriate ways in everyday face-to-face situations in both first language (L1) and second language (L2), despite literacy skills that were very much below age-appropriate levels in both languages. Following Skutnabb-Kangas and Toukomaa (1976), a distinction was introduced between "surface fluency" and "conceptual-linguistic knowledge" (Cummins, 1979b) and was later (Cummins, 1979a, 1980) formalized in terms of basic interpersonal communicative skills (BICS) and cognitive/academic language

From "Bilingualism and Special Education: Issues in Assessment and Pedagogy" by J. Cummins, 1984 (pp. 136–151). San Diego, CA: College-Hill. Reprinted by permission.

proficiency (CALP). The former was defined in terms of "the manifestation of language proficiency in everyday communicative contexts," whereas CALP was conceptualized in terms of the manipulation of language in decontextualized academic situations.

This distinction was applied to a broad range of theoretical and educational situations; for example, it was used to dispute Oller's (1979) theoretical claim that one global dimension could account for all individual differences in "language proficiency" as well as to emphasize the consequences of extrapolating from L2 BICS to L2 CALP in psychological assessment and bilingual education situations.

The distinction between BICS and CALP was expressed in terms of the "iceberg" metaphor adapted from Roger Shuy (1978, 1981). Shuy used the iceberg metaphor to highlight the distinction between the "visible," quantifiable, formal aspects of language (e.g., pronunciation, basic vocabulary, grammar) and the less visible and less easily measured aspects dealing with semantic and functional meaning ("pragmatic" aspects of proficiency in Oller's [1979] terms). He pointed out that most language teaching (whether L1 or L2) attempted to develop functional or communicative proficiency by focusing on the surface forms despite the fact that the direction of language acquisition was from deeper communicative functions of language to the surface forms.

Shuy's (1978, 1981) analysis can be seen as elaborating some of the linguistic realizations of the BICS/CALP distinction. Chamot (1981) and Skinner (1981) have suggested that the cognitive aspects can be elaborated in terms of Bloom's taxonomy of educational objectives (Bloom & Krathwohl, 1977). Specifically, the surface level would involve knowledge (remembering something previously encountered or learned); comprehension (grasp of basic meaning, without necessarily relating it to other material); application (use of abstractions in particular and concrete situations); while the deeper levels of cognitive/academic processing would involve analysis (breaking down a whole into its parts so that the organization of elements is clear); synthesis (putting elements into a coherent whole); and evaluation (judging the adequacy of ideas or material for a given purpose).

The conceptualization of language proficiency to which these notions gave rise is depicted in Figure 2.1. Clearly what is suggested here is not a precise model of proficiency but rather a series of parallel distinctions that are generally consistent with research evidence and appear to have important heuristic value. The major points embodied in the BICS/CALP distinction are that some heretofore neglected aspects of language proficiency are considerably more relevant for students' cognitive and academic progress than are the surface manifestations of proficiency frequently focused on by educators, and that educators' failure to appreciate these differences can have particularly unfortunate consequences for language minority students.

However, any dichotomy inevitably oversimplifies the reality, and it became clear that the terms "BICS" and "CALP" had the potential to be misinterpreted

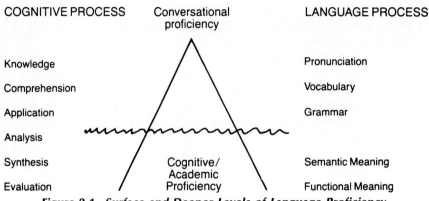

Figure 2.1. *Surface and Deeper Levels of Language Proficiency*

(see, e.g., Edelsky et al., 1983; Rivera, 1984). Consequently, the theoretical framework was elaborated in terms of the contextual and cognitive dimensions underlying language performance while still maintaining the essential aspects of the BICS/CALP distinction.

The framework in Figure 2.2 proposes that "language proficiency" can be conceptualized along two continuums. First is a continuum relating to the range of contextual support available for expressing or receiving meaning. The extremes of this continuum are described in terms of "context-embedded" versus "context-reduced" communication. They are distinguished by the fact that in context-embedded communication the participants can actively negotiate meaning (e.g., by providing feedback that the message has not been understood), and the language is supported by a wide range of meaningful paralinguistic and situational cues; context-reduced communication, on the other hand, relies primarily (or at the extreme of the continuum, exclusively) on linguistic cues to meaning, and thus successful interpretation of the message depends heavily on knowledge of the language itself. In general, context-embedded communication is more typical of the everyday world outside the classroom, whereas many of the linguistic demands of the classroom (e.g., manipulating text) reflect communicative activities which are closer to the context-reduced end of the continuum.

The upper parts of the vertical continuum consist of communicative tasks and activities in which the linguistic tools have become largely automatized (mastered) and thus require little active cognitive involvement for appropriate performance. At the lower end of the continuum are tasks and activities in which the communicative tools have not become automatized and thus require active cognitive involvement. Persuading another individual that your point of view is correct and writing an essay are examples of quadrant B and D skills respectively. (See strategies in Chapter 10 for adding contextual support in content-area instruction.)

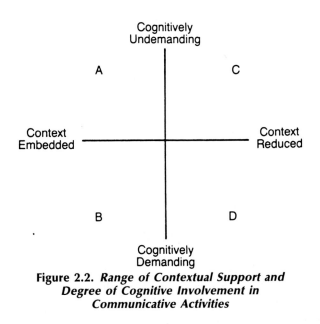

Figure 2.2. *Range of Contextual Support and Degree of Cognitive Involvement in Communicative Activities*

The framework is compatible with several other theoretical distinctions elaborated to elucidate aspects of the relationships between language proficiency and academic development: for example, Bruner's (1975) distinction between communicative and analytic competence, Olson's (1977) distinction between utterance and text, Donaldson's (1978) embedded and disembedded thought and language, and Bereiter and Scardamelia's (1981) distinction between conversation and composition (see Cummins, 1981, 1983b). The current framework owes most to Donaldon's distinction and thus it is briefly considered here.

Embedded and Disembedded Thought and Language

Donaldson (1978) distinguishes between embedded and disembedded cognitive processes from a developmental perspective and is especially concerned with the implications for children's adjustment to formal schooling. She points out that young children's early thought processes and use of language develop within a "flow of meaningful context" in which the logic of words is subjugated to perception of the speaker's intentions and salient features of the situation. Thus, children's (and adults') normal productive speech is embedded within a context of fairly immediate goals, intentions, and familiar patterns of events. However, thinking and language that move beyond the bounds of meaningful interpersonal context make entirely different demands on the individual, in that it is necessary to focus on the linguistic forms themselves for meaning rather than on intentions.

Donaldson (1978) offers a reinterpretation of Piaget's theory of cognitive development from this perspective and reviews a large body of research that supports the distinction between embedded and disembedded thought and language. Her description of preschool children's comprehension and production of language in embedded contexts is especially relevant to current practices in assessment of language proficiency in bilingual programs. She points out that:

> The ease with which preschool children often seem to understand what is said to them is misleading if we take it as an indication of skills with language *per se*. Certainly they commonly understand us, but surely it is not our words alone that they are understanding—for they may be shown to be relying heavily on cues of other kinds. (p. 72)

She goes on to argue that children's facility in producing language that is meaningful and appropriate in interpersonal contexts can also give a misleading impression of overall language proficiency:

> When you produce language, you are in control, you need only talk about what you choose to talk about. . . . The child is never required, when he is himself producing language, to go counter to his own preferred reading of the situation—to the way in which he himself spontaneously sees it. But this is no longer necessarily true when he becomes the listener. And it is frequently not true when he is the listener in the formal situation of a psychological experiment or indeed when he becomes a learner at school. (pp. 73–74)

The relevance of this observation to the tendency of psychologists and teachers to overestimate the extent to which ESL students have overcome difficulties with English is obvious.

Donaldson provides compelling evidence that children are able to manifest much higher levels of cognitive performance when the task is presented in an embedded context, or one that makes "human sense." She goes on to argue that the unnecessary "disembedding" of early instruction in reading and other academic tasks from students' out-of-school experiences contributes significantly to educational difficulties.

Application of the Theoretical Framework

How does the framework elaborated in Figure 2.2 clarify the conceptual confusions that have been considered above? The framework has been applied to a variety of issues which will be only briefly noted here.

First, the context-embedded/context-reduced distinction suggests reasons why ESL students acquire peer-appropriate L2 conversational proficiency sooner than peer-appropriate academic proficiency, specifically the fact that there are considerably more cues to meaning in face-to-face context-embedded situations than in typical context-reduced academic tasks. The implications for psychological assessment and exit from bilingual programs have already been noted.

A *second* application of the framework relates to language pedagogy. A major aim of schooling is to develop students' ability to manipulate and interpret cognitively demanding context-reduced text. The more initial reading and writing instruction can be embedded in a meaningful communicative context (i.e., related to the child's previous experience), the more successful it is likely to be. The same principle holds for L2 instruction. The more context-embedded the initial L2 input, the more comprehensible it is likely to be, and paradoxically, the more successful in ultimately developing L2 skills in context-reduced situations. A central reason why language minority students have often failed to develop high levels of L2 academic skills is because their initial instruction has emphasized context-reduced communication insofar as instruction has been through English and unrelated to their prior out-of-school experience.

A *third* application concerns the nature of the academic difficulties experienced by most children characterized as ''learning disabled'' or ''language disordered.'' These students' language and academic problems are usually confined to context-reduced, cognitively demanding situations (see, e.g., Cummins & Das, 1977; Das & Cummins, 1982). For example, children with ''language learning disabilities'' (Stark & Wallach, 1980) have extreme difficulty acquiring French in typical French as a second language classes where the language is taught as a subject, yet acquire fluency in French in context-embedded French immersion programs (Bruck, 1984). This suggests that it may be especially important for these children to experience instruction that is embedded in a meaningful context.

The framework is also relevant to theories of communicative competence (see, e.g., Oller, 1983a), in that it provides a means for carrying out a task analysis of proficiency measures and predicting relationships among them. For example, it is immediately apparent why the issue of the relationship between ''oral'' language and reading is so confused. Measures of ''oral'' language can be located in any one of the four quadrants, and consequently they often have very low correlations with each other (compare, for example, the Wechsler Intelligence Scale for Children [WISC-R] vocabulary subtest with a measure of conversational fluency).

In conclusion, the framework proposed above has the advantage of allowing the academic difficulties of both language minority students and students characterized as ''learning disabled'' to be conceptualized in terms of more general relationships between language proficiency and academic achievement. The context-embedded/context-reduced and cognitively undemanding/cognitively demanding continuums are clearly not the only dimensions that would require consideration in a theoretical framework designed to incorporate all aspects of language proficiency or communicative competence. However, it is suggested that these dimensions are directly relevant to the relationships between language proficiency and educational achievement and that they facilitate the interpretation of research data on the linguistic and academic progress of language minority students. In the next section, the cross-lingual dimensions of language proficiency are considered.

CONCEPTUALIZING BILINGUAL PROFICIENCY

On the basis of the fact that in bilingual program evaluations little relationship has been found between amount of instructional time through the majority language and academic achievement in that langauge, it has been suggested that L1 and L2 academic skills are interdependent, i.e., manifestations of a common underlying proficiency. The interdependence principle has been stated formally as follows (Cummins, 1981):

> To the extent that instruction in Lx is effective in promoting proficiency in Lx, transfer of this proficiency to Ly will occur provided there is adequate exposure to Ly (either in school or environment) and adequate motivation to learn Ly. (p. 29)

In concrete terms what this principle means is that in a Spanish-English bilingual program, Spanish instruction that develops L1 reading skills for Spanish-speaking students is not just developing Spanish skills; it is also developing a deeper conceptual and linguistic proficiency that is strongly related to the development of English literacy and general academic skills. In other words, although the surface aspects (e.g., pronunciation, fluency) of, for example, Spanish and English or Chinese and English are clearly separate, there is an underlying cognitive/academic proficiency that is common across languages. This "common underlying proficiency" makes possible the transfer of cognitive/academic or literacy-related skills across languages. Transfer is much more likely to occur from minority to majority language because of the greater exposure to literacy in the majority language and the strong social pressure to learn it.

Continuing with the iceberg metaphor, bilingual proficiency is represented in Figure 2.3 as a "dual iceberg" in which common cross-lingual proficiencies underlie the obviously different surface manifestations of each language. The interdependence or common underlying proficiency principles implies that experience with *either* language can promote development of the proficiency underlying both languages, given adequate motivation and exposure to both either in school or in the wider environment.

What are some of the literacy-related skills involved in the common underlying proficiency? Conceptual knowledge is perhaps the most obvious example. An immigrant child who arrives in North America at, for example, age fifteen, understanding the concept of "honesty" in his or her L1 has only to acquire a new *label* in L2 for an already existing concept. A child, on the other hand, who does not understand the meaning of this term in his or her L1 has a very

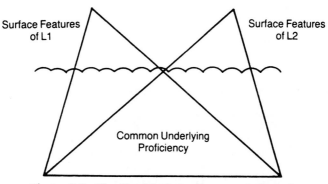

Figure 2.3. *The Dual Iceberg Representation of Bilingual Proficiency*

different, and more difficult, task to acquire the *concept* in L2. By the same token, subject matter knowledge, higher-order thinking skills, reading strategies, writing composition skills, developed through the medium of L1 transfer or become available to L2 given sufficient exposure and motivation.

Common experience also indicates the existence of some form of common underlying proficiency. For example, as John Macnamara (1970) has pointed out, if L1 and L2 proficiencies were separate (i.e., if there were *not* a common underlying proficiency), this would leave the bilingual in a curious predicament in that "he would have great difficulty in 'communicating' with himself. Whenever he switched languages, he would have difficulty in explaining in L2 what he had heard or said in L1" (pp. 25–26).[1]

Comprehensive reviews of the extremely large amount of data supporting the common underlying proficiency principle have been carried out. The supporting evidence is derived from (1) results of bilingual education programs (see Baker & de Kanter, 1981; Cummins, 1983a), (2) studies relating both age on arrival and L1 literacy development to immigrant students' L2 acquisition (see Cummins, 1983b), (3) studies relating bilingual language use in the home to academic achievement, (4) studies of the relationships of L1 and L2 cognitive/academic proficiency (Cummins, 1979a), and (5) experimental studies of bilingual information processing (Katsaiti, 1983).

---

[1] Research data (Cummins et al., 1984) suggest that some aspects of context-embedded language skills are also interdependent across languages. Specifically, it was found that Japanese immigrant students in Canada manifested similar interactional styles in both Japanese and English and that these styles in L1 and L2 were related to personality variables. On the basis of these results, Cummins et al. suggest a distinction between "attribute-based" and "input-based" aspects of language proficiency: the former are cross-lingual in nature and reflect stable attributes of the individual (e.g., cognitive skills, personality) while the latter are largely a function of quality and quantity of exposure to the language in the environment.

CONCLUSION

In this chapter, research findings on how long it takes language minority students to acquire English proficiency were reviewed and interpreted within a theoretical framework concerned with the nature of language proficiency and its cross-lingual dimensions. The fact that immigrant students require, on the average, five to seven years to approach grade norms in L2 academic skills, yet show peer-appropriate L2 conversational skills within about two years of arrival, suggests that conversational and academic aspects of language proficiency need to be distinguished. It is apparent that, as a result of failure to take account of these two dimensions of language proficiency, many of the psychological assessments underestimated children's academic potential by assessing students whose academic functioning still reflected insufficient time to attain age-appropriate levels of English proficiency.

Some of the reasons why language minority children acquire L2 conversational skills more rapidly than age-appropriate L2 academic skills are apparent from the dimensions hypothesized to underlie the relationships between language proficiency and academic development. Considerably less knowledge of the L2 itself is required to function appropriately in conversational settings than in academic settings as a result of the greater contextual support available for communicating and receiving meaning.

A large amount of data suggests that L1 and L2 context-reduced, cognitively demanding proficiencies are interdependent or manifestations of a common underlying proficiency. This theoretical principle accounts for the fact that instruction through the medium of a minority language does not result in lower levels of academic performance in the majority language.

Thus, there is little justification for the frequent scepticism expressed by educators about the value of bilingual or heritage language programs, especially for students with potential language or learning difficulties. It is this type of student who appears to need and to benefit most from the promotion of L1 literacy skills and the development of an additive form of bilingualism.

These same findings also suggest how ill-advised it is for educators to encourage parents of bilingual children with learning difficulties to switch to English in the home. This is not only unnecessary in view of the common underlying proficiency principle, but it will often have damaging emotional and cognitive effects as a result of the lower quality and quantity of interaction that parents are likely to provide in their weaker language.

Finally, it is clear on the basis of the data supporting the common underlying proficiency principle that policy in regard to the education of minority students is not as bereft of research evidence as most educators and policymakers appear to believe. Although the causes of minority students' underachievement are not yet fully understood, we do have a partial theoretical basis for policy in that we can predict with confidence the academic outcomes of bilingual programs implemented in a variety of societal contexts; specifically, we can predict that students instructed through a minority language for all or a part of the school day will perform in majority language academic skills as well as or better than equivalent students instructed entirely through the majority language. For minority students academically at risk there is evidence that strong promotion of L1 proficiency represents an effective way of developing a conceptual and academic foundation for acquiring English literacy.

FOLLOW-UP QUESTIONS AND ACTIVITIES

1. In Figure 2.1, Cummins places language process on the right-hand side and cognitive process on the left-hand side. How do you think the components of each reflect his notions of surface versus deep processing levels? What do you think he means by semantic and functional meaning? How might they relate to the cognitive processes of analysis, synthesis, and evaluation? Do you agree with his interpretation of the relationship between Bloom's taxonomy and BICS/CALP? Explain.

2. Take a look at the quadrants represented in Figure 2.2 that indicate the range of contextual support and the degree of cognitive involvement. Into which quadrant would you place the following activities? Be prepared to explain your decisions.
   a. Listening to a lecture
   b. Conducting a science experiment
   c. Talking on the telephone
   d. Taking standardized achievement tests
   e. Introducing someone to another person
   f. Reading a chapter in the textbook and answering comprehension questions at the end of the chapter

3. According to Cummins, research shows that immigrant students require, on the average, five to seven years to approach grade level in L2 academic skills. What are the implications of this finding for program planning and development? Consider the different program types discussed in Chapter 1. To what extent is each designed with this finding in mind?

4. Recall Cummins's notion of a Common Underlying Proficiency (CUP), which refers to his contention that a student's L1 provides a strong conceptual and academic foundation for acquiring literacy skills in L2. What theoretical support for bilingual education is provided by this notion? Think about the array of backgrounds from which language minority students come when they enter school. According to the principle of CUP, which students would you expect to succeed quite easily in content-area classes? Which students would have more difficulties?

5. Now that you have read this chapter and thought about some of the educational implications of Cummins's theories, what is your reaction to his distinction between BICS and CALP? Does it make theoretical sense to you? Cummins himself says in the chapter that any dichotomy tends to oversimplify reality and that the terms have potential for misinterpretation. What do you think he means? Do you think the concepts will be useful in guiding your instructional decisions and practices? If so, in what ways?

3

A Conceptual Framework for the Integration of Language and Content Instruction

Marguerite Ann Snow   *California State University, Los Angeles*

Myriam Met   *Montgomery County, Maryland, Public Schools*

Fred Genesee   *McGill University, Montreal*

Editors' Introduction

Ann Snow, Myriam Met, and Fred Genesee propose a conceptual framework for the integration of language and content teaching in the public schools. In this model, language and content teachers work together to determine teaching objectives which derive from two considerations: (1) content-obligatory language, or language that is essential to an understanding of content material and (2) content-compatible language, or language that can be taught or reinforced naturally within the context of a particular subject. The framework requires collaboration across language arts and English as a second language (ESL) and content-area curricula, and across grade levels. Implied in the framework is a reconceptualization of the role of the content-area teacher in relation to language minority students.

There is growing interest in a model of language education that integrates language and content instruction. This approach contrasts with many existing methods, in which language skills are taught in isolation from substantive content. Several theoretical rationales underlie this shift in perspective.

For young children, cognitive development and language development go hand in hand; language is a tool through which the child comes to understand the world. In first language (L1) acquisition, these processes are paired

From "A Conceptual Framework for the Integration of Language and Content in Second/Foreign Language Instruction" by M. A. Snow, M. Met, and F. Genesee, 1989, TESOL Quarterly, 23, pp. 201–217. Copyright 1989 by Teachers of English to Speakers of Other Languages. Adapted by permission.

naturally. For children who are second language learners, however, traditional methods for teaching second languages often dissociate language learning from cognitive or academic development. In contrast, an integrated approach brings these domains together in instruction.

A second rationale behind integrating language and content teaching is that language is learned most effectively for communication in meaningful, purposeful social and academic contexts. In real life, people use language to talk about what they know and what they want to know more about, not to talk about language itself. What school children know and need to know more about is the subject matter of school. In the typical school setting, however, language learning and content learning are often treated as independent processes. Mohan (1986) notes: ''In subject matter learning we overlook the role of language as a medium of learning. In language learning we overlook the fact that content is being communicated'' (p. 1). Cantoni-Harvey (1987) further underscores this point: ''When the learners' second language is both the object and medium of instruction, the content of each lesson must be taught simultaneously with the linguistic skills necessary for understanding it'' (p. 22).

Another underlying rationale is that the integration of content with language instruction provides a substantive basis for language teaching and learning. Content can provide both a motivational and a cognitive basis for language learning. Content provides a primary motivational incentive for language learning insofar as it is interesting and of some value to the learner and therefore worth learning. Language then will be learned because it provides access to content, and language learning may even become incidental to learning about the content (e.g., in immersion classes).[1]

Content also provides a cognitive basis for language learning in that it provides real meaning that is an inherent feature of naturalistic language learning. Meaning provides conceptual or cognitive hangers on which language functions and structures can be hung. In the absence of real meaning, language structures and functions are likely to be learned as abstractions devoid of conceptual or communicative value. If these motivational and cognitive bases are to be realized, then content must be chosen that is important and interesting to the learner. In the case of language learning in school, the focus of our concern here, this is achieved by selecting content that is part of the mainstream curriculum.

A fourth rationale concerns the intrinsic characteristics of language variation. It is increasingly recognized that language use in school differs in some important general ways from language use outside of school and, moreover, that different subject areas are characterized by specific genres or registers (see

---

[1] The immersion model is a foreign language program in which English-speaking students receive the majority of their elementary school education through the medium of a foreign language (e.g., Spanish, German, Chinese).

Heath, 1983b; Wells, 1981). Thus, learning the school register or specific subject-area registers may be a prerequisite to mastery of specific content or to academic development in general. This is of particular concern to teachers of limited English proficient (LEP) students. (See Chapter 8 for a more detailed discussion of school register.)

What is called for in the model proposed here is a recognition of the importance of language structures, skills, or functions that are characteristic of different content areas. These skills can be identified by (a) informed speculation about what kinds of language skills or functions are called for in specific content areas, (b) informal observation of the language requirements of specific content areas, or (c) systematic analysis of students' actual language needs in content classes. In contrast to mainstream content classes, where the teacher assumes students have the requisite language skills, an integrated content class does not make such assumptions. The primary objective of such classes remains content mastery, but it is recognized that content classes have great language-teaching potential as well.

There are several other reasons for the shift from teaching language alone to content-based approaches. The success of immersion as a model of foreign language education has provided strong evidence for the effectiveness of language learning through subject-matter learning. Extensive research has revealed that immersion students learn the academic content specified in the school curriculum and at the same time develop significant levels of language proficiency (Genesee, 1987; Lambert & Tucker, 1972). Furthermore, concern for the education of language minority students in the United States has prompted a reexamination of the methodologies appropriate for teaching English to LEP students in the public schools.

Cummins's (see Chapter 2 of this volume) work (1980, 1981) provided theoretical impetus for considering the integration of language and content instruction. He posited a paradigm in which language tasks may be characterized as context reduced or context embedded and in which the tasks addressed through language may be cognitively demanding or undemanding. In context-embedded language tasks, support for meaning is readily available through the immediate communicative situation, whether through background knowledge or through visual or other contextual cues. In contrast, context-reduced tasks offer little available contextual support for the learner to derive meaning from the immediate communicative setting.

However, as language teachers try to make language meaningful by providing contextual cues and supports, too often their attempts bring the learner into cognitively undemanding situations. Thus, although it is easy for children to learn to label colors and shapes, for example, activities in the language class rarely require students to use this new language knowledge in the application of higher-order thinking.

In contrast, when language and content are integrated, it is possible to practice language (e.g., colors and shapes) by applying such labels to more sophisticated tasks, such as sorting geometric shapes by those that differ from one another by one attribute (color or shape only) or by two attributes (color and shape).

For these reasons, then, content-based language instruction is receiving increasing attention. Yet, if such an orientation is to be effective, language teaching must be carefully considered and planned. It is unlikely that desired levels of language proficiency will emerge simply from the teaching of content through a second language. The specification of language-learning objectives must be undertaken with deliberate, systematic planning and coordination of the language and content curricula.

THE CONCEPTUAL FRAMEWORK

Consider the following two scenarios. Scenario 1: The ESL teacher teaches a twenty-minute lesson on weather terms—a lesson completely devoid of any connection to what the class is doing that day or week in its other subjects. Scenario 2: The chemistry teacher asks her students to write up the steps in the laboratory experiment just conducted, without ever considering that LEP students may not know the vocabulary or rhetorical mode for describing a process. In these scenarios, both teachers have their respective priorities and perceived responsibilities: The content teacher is responsible for subject matter; the language teacher is responsible for the language curriculum. In the traditional model, the teachers' responsibilities do not overlap.

In this chapter, we propose an alternative model that calls for a reconceptualization of the roles of teachers working in schools where L2 education is a primary goal. In this model, the language and content teachers maintain their respective priorities. However, their areas of responsibility are expanded so that by working in tandem, they will be able to maximize the language development of second language learners.

According to the model, language-learning objectives in a content-based program are derived from three sources: (a) the ESL curriculum, (b) the content-area curriculum, and (c) assessment of the learners' academic and communicative needs and ongoing evaluation of their developing language skills. From these sources, two types of language objectives can be specified: content-obligatory language objectives and content-compatible language objectives. This conceptual framework is displayed graphically in Figure 3.1.

Content-obligatory language objectives specify the language required for students to develop, master, and communicate about a given content material. For every topic or concept, certain language is essential or obligatory for understanding and talking about the material. Content-obligatory language objectives are both structural (i.e., specification of verbs, nouns, rhetorical devices, etc.) and functional (e.g., study skills such as note taking; language functions such as requesting/giving information, narrating, persuading, etc.). For instance,

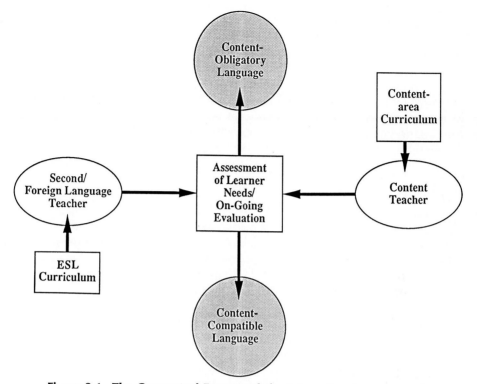

Figure 3.1. *The Conceptual Framework for Integrating Language and Content Instruction*

a lesson on gravity in a fourth-grade science class would require that students know the vocabulary *to rise, to pull,* and *force;* similarly, a math lesson on measurement would require students to know the vocabulary for systems of measurement, whether inches and feet, or metric terms.

These examples may seem rather obvious, but needs assessment to determine the essential vocabulary, structures, and so on is typically not part of the curriculum-planning process in the public schools. By working as a team, the content and language teachers can pool their respective expertise: The content teacher knows the key concepts to be imparted, and the language teacher knows how to teach the pertinent language skills.

For content-compatible language objectives, the content teacher and the language teacher ask: What other language skills are compatible with the concept or information to be taught? Content-compatible language objectives *can* be taught within the context of a given content but are *not required* for successful content mastery. Whereas content-obligatory objectives derive directly from the linguistic needs for communicating the information in the content area, content-compatible language objectives derive from the ESL curriculum and ongoing assessment of learner needs and progress.

Traditionally, ESL curricula have been fairly standard both in content and sequencing. Learners acquire vocabulary related to classroom procedures, the weather, parts of the body, colors, and numbers, to name some typical topics taught early on in the language-learning sequence. The present tense is taught before the past; agreement of number and gender precedes indirect object pronouns. These topics and structures may or may not have any relationship to the language skills students need in their content classes. They exist as autonomous objectives within the ESL curricula.

In an integrated approach, on the other hand, the language curriculum is altered so that language objectives and content objectives compatible with each other are taught concurrently. For example, the skills to describe weather may best be taught when students pursue a unit on meteorology in their science class. In this way, students learn not only appropriate language, but also how to apply this language to useful skills such as charting rainfall and temperatures in cities where the target language is spoken. A natural outcome of such activity is cultural learning as well: Students learn the geographic and climatic diversity of the places where the target language is spoken.

Ongoing evaluation of students' difficulties with the second language also provides a rich source of information for specifying content-compatible objectives. Research on the oral proficiency of immersion graduates, for example, indicates that despite achieving very high levels, these students do not approximate native-speaker norms in the productive skills of speaking and writing (see Genesee, 1987, and Swain & Lapkin, 1982, for reviews of studies). One result of such findings has been an overemphasis on incorporating traditional forms of grammar instruction into the immersion language arts curriculum. An alternative is to use analysis of students' language or communication difficulties to determine appropriate content-compatible language objectives. These objectives could then be used by teachers to provide for increased input of correct structures and for extended output through student practice.

A fifth-grade social studies lesson can be used to illustrate the role of content-compatible language. In discussing the route taken by a famous explorer, Cabrillo, for instance, the teacher can incorporate review or reinforcement of the past tense forms into the activities of the lesson. Although accurate production of the past tense is not essential for understanding the chronology of Cabrillo's travels, such a lesson presents an ideal opportunity for contextualized focus on a troublesome verb tense.

Similarly, science experiments provide a natural context for discussing cause-and-effect relationships. Cause and effect may be expressed simply by using *because* or more elaborately through *if-then* clauses. Either of these cause-and-effect language structures may be emphasized as content-compatible language objectives, depending on the proficiency level of the learners and their communicative needs.

Once persistent errors are identified, instructional activities can be designed that are either integrated into the subject-matter lesson or taught directly in the ESL class. If, for example, evaluation reveals student weaknesses in the use of the conditional, teachers may design content activities requiring its use. In a fifth-grade unit on explorers of the New World, teachers may ask students to complete the sentence, ''If Columbus had been from France . . .'' Such an exercise not only has the advantage of providing meaningful and contextualized grammar practice, it also requires students to use critical thinking skills in applying known facts (the impact of Spanish discovery of the New World) to a hypothetical situation. On an ongoing basis, language and content teachers provide feedback to each other and to students. Thus, students' errors provide indicators of areas in which additional instruction or practice is needed.

The next section illustrates the conceptual framework just described in two different instructional settings designed for LEP students learning English as a second language. The principles of the model just discussed are applied differently depending upon the instructional context and the division of instructional responsibilities.

APPLICATION OF THE CONCEPTUAL FRAMEWORK

Setting 1: The Mainstream Class

The first application is to the mainstream classroom, in which LEP students generally spend a good part of their day. Typically, this class is taught by a teacher whose primary focus is to develop students' skills in the objectives stated in the standard school curriculum.

In our conceptual framework, the mainstream teacher works closely with the ESL teacher. First, the team identifies which content areas are to be taught in the coming weeks. The content teacher identifies those language skills that will be new for all students and those that will be new only for the LEP students.

For example, in a science demonstration on the evaporation/condensation cycle, it is likely that the terms *evaporate, condense,* and *cycle* will be new for all students. Perhaps some students will know *moisture;* most will not. Typically, the English-speaking students will have the functional skills to ask for and give information, to describe, to generate hypotheses. More than likely, the LEP students will need assistance with some or all of these functions, particularly as they relate to this topic. Furthermore, the English-speaking students will experience few difficulties in reading the procedural discourse required to follow directions for an experiment or in writing expository prose to report the results. In contrast, the LEP students will need considerable assistance with the reading and writing tasks related to the content demands.

Working cooperatively, the mainstream teacher and language teacher thus pinpoint the linguistic needs of the learner and plan jointly to meet them. Some preparatory activities in the ESL classroom will facilitate the task of the content teacher. At the same time, the content teacher takes on the responsibility of ensuring that language skills are taught as part of the content lesson.

Planning carefully to ensure that language is acquired through experience, the mainstream teacher uses concrete materials, realia, manipulatives, and a variety of activities to provide opportunities for students to match language to its referents. Definitions, paraphrasing, and additional oral examples of the science concepts can be used to reinforce the acquisition of both the language functions and vocabulary associated with key concepts. Written materials are designed that facilitate comprehension of the content text. The mainstream teacher uses prereading strategies so that students will have the necessary background knowledge of both concepts and language with which to make sense of the text. Written assignments are structured so that not only are students' limited language skills taken into account, but language growth is planned as an outcome as well. (See Chapter 10 for further treatment of instructional strategies.)

In this model, the content determines the language objectives. The content teacher shares in the planning in two major ways: (a) by ensuring that content is accessible to students, despite their limited language skills, through the identification of content-obligatory language objectives and (b) by planning for and implementing strategies that will address demonstrated language needs through content-compatible language study in the mainstream class.

Setting 2: The ESL Class

The second application of the conceptual framework is to the ESL pullout setting. In this type of instructional program, LEP students, usually from heterogeneous language backgrounds, are "pulled out" of mainstream classrooms for special instruction in English. An actual classroom example from Hawkins (1988) illustrates the principles of the framework. In her study, Hawkins was interested in documenting cases of "scaffolding," or assisted instruction, in which the teacher and learner engage in a series of interactions that ultimately lead to instances of actual learning. She looked at the classroom language use of fourth-grade LEP children in Rosemead, California. What is relevant for our discussion here is the context in which these successful interactions were produced.

In this pullout program, the ESL teacher integrated language instruction with the content of the students' social studies lessons in a very interesting way. She knew that the students were just starting a unit on the California mission system but did not know the specifics of the content to be covered. Each day in the ESL class, she asked the students to tell her about what they had learned in social studies. Different students volunteered answers. At times, there was confusion about certain facts, but usually this was resolved with the teacher and students arriving at a common understanding of the facts or events.

After the question and answer session, the students practiced working with the information in different ways, such as writing short summaries or describing the chronology of events to their partners. Occasionally, however, the class could not reach an agreement about the details or events described in the social studies lesson. In these cases, the ESL class collectively developed a list of questions, wrote the questions down in their notebooks, and sought clarification of the information during the next social studies class. The following day, the ESL students used the notes they had taken in the social studies class and discussed the information in question.

This example illustrates the principles of the conceptual framework for integrating language and content instruction in a setting where language is typically taught in isolation from the subject matter of LEP students' regular classes. The content of the mission unit provided a meaningful context in which to practice a variety of language and academic skills. The ESL teacher reinforced certain content-obligatory language and concepts (e.g., vocabulary such as *mission, priest, to explore,* and the cause-and-effect concept of bringing a new way of life to the Indians).

Content-compatible language was also introduced and reinforced in a variety of ways. Students practiced asking and answering questions, taking notes, and summarizing information in written form. In addition, the students used a variety of language types, such as logical connectors or seriation, and language functions, such as agreeing and disagreeing, guessing, and arriving at a group consensus. Furthermore, the ESL teacher could diagnose both language and content deficiencies in a very direct way and incorporate this information into on-the-spot activities or reserve them for future lessons.

The ESL students were motivated to learn the material because it was important in their mainstream class. They were not talking about language per se in the ESL class but were using language to make sense of information they had learned in their social studies class. Moreover, the information gap that existed between the students and ESL teacher provided an authentic, natural context for interaction. The students became the possessors of knowledge, knowledge that the ESL teacher wanted, thereby creating a real purpose for communication.

These two examples are intended to illustrate practical applications of our conceptual framework. We believe that the model is equally applicable to other instructional settings where L2 learning is one of the goals of instruction. The common ground of the instructional situations described is reconceptualizing the role of teachers—both language teachers and content teachers—to recognize the value of integrating language and content. Such an integration will assist language minority students in mastering English and achieving in school.

IMPLICATIONS OF AN INTEGRATED APPROACH

Clearly, the integration of language and content teaching carries with it a number of broad implications, the first of which is that ESL teachers and content teachers must collaborate. Such collaboration requires a reciprocal relationship between instructors. Thus, the language instructor may consult with the classroom teacher about what is being taught, with particular attention given to content that has specific or special language requirements. The language instructor is then able to incorporate into language instruction meaningful and important content that has evident language-related value in the rest of the curriculum.

Likewise, the classroom teacher can consult with the language teacher regarding what can be done in the content areas to promote the learning of language skills requisite to particular content areas. Since content teachers may be ill-prepared to ''teach'' language or even to recognize students' language-learning needs because of lack of training in language-teaching pedagogy, language teachers become pedagogical resources for mainstream teachers who are willing to assume some responsibility for treating students' language needs.

The artificial and rigid distinctions between the roles of the language teacher and the content teacher are broken down in this model. For sheltered English teachers, these roles are fused, requiring them to plan consciously for language growth as an integral part of content instruction.

A corollary implication of this perspective concerns the formal integration and coordination of the language arts and academic curricula. Accordingly, the content areas of the school program are cross-referenced with language-learning objectives, and the ESL curriculum is cross-referenced with subject areas that provide particularly suitable vehicles for teaching language objectives. This language-across-the-curriculum perspective has been advocated for some time for native speakers of English (see Anderson, Eisenberg, Holland, Weiner, & Rivera-Kron, 1983; Department of Education and Science, 1975). Such an integrated approach ensures that language skills learned in the ESL class will be useful and usable in content classes, since it effectively obviates the need for transfer.

Full integration of language and content instruction also implies integration of instruction across grade levels so as to achieve a coherent developmental program. There is some evidence from evaluations of immersion programs that language development may reach a plateau in the middle or late elementary grades (Genesee, 1987). It appears that students are able to make do with a relatively limited set of language skills beyond the primary grades, despite the fact that the content itself is more demanding. In immersion, it is assumed that students' language develops as a function of unsystematic and unknown changes in the communicative requirements of academic instruction. If the curriculum is not developmental from a language-learning point of view and/or if language use by the teacher for academic instruction is not developmental in that it does not make increasingly greater demands on the students, then students' language skills will not continue to develop. Concerted measures are called for in this model in order to promote continuous language growth across grade levels. This may be achieved by consciously and systematically incorporating increasingly advanced levels of language into the content areas at successively higher grades.

It follows that the integration of content and language instruction may also entail integration of differentially difficult language structures, skills, or functions that are required for effective communication about the content in question. For example, students may need to learn conditionals as well as present tense verb forms early on in order to comprehend or participate in discussions about science or history. Or written language may need to be taught along with spoken language. Whereas the ESL curriculum has traditionally been orgranized around a hierarchy of syntactic structures from the simple to the complex, an integrated approach eschews distinctions that are artificial from a communication point of view. The communicative needs of the learner and/or the communicative requirements of particular content inform the teachers as to what and when particular language elements are to be taught.

Furthermore, the integration of content and language instruction implies the integration of higher-order thinking skills into the classroom. As discussed in the preceding point, this is particularly likely in cases in which the content is based on the academic curriculum. Use of higher-order thinking is desirable because it can stimulate learners' interest in the content and therefore in language, precisely because it is somewhat beyond their level of competence. In contrast, nonintegrated language instruction may be of little interest to learners, since the limited concepts and content embodied in such instruction may be simplified to match the more limited language objectives of these approaches. Use of higher-order thinking skills is also desirable as a means of promoting higher-order language skills or, as discussed above, as a means of promoting advanced levels of language proficiency. This will obtain to the extent that higher-order thinking skills require more complex or elaborate language skills in more cognitively demanding tasks.

A final implication of the integration of content and language instruction concerns the relationship between learning and teaching. Ellis (1984) has argued that language use, or "doing discourse," and language learning are the same thing. That is to say, "the procedures that the learner employs in using L2 knowledge are also the means by which new L2 knowledge is internalized" (p. 52). Few researchers or educators would disagree that frequent opportunities to use language can facilitate language learning. Thus, an integrated approach to content and language instruction aims to engage students fully with teaching activities and pedagogical materials. Teaching serves to provide opportunities for students to engage themselves in learning about content through language.

CONCLUSION

In sum, the conceptual framework proposed here offers language and content teachers a systematic approach to the identification and instruction of language aims within content teaching. Although the mainstream class and the ESL class were selected to illustrate the practical application of the framework, we believe the framework also applies to other types of L2 teaching settings. Finally, we believe that the implications of integrating language and content teaching must be considered seriously if content-based instruction is to be implemented effectively.

FOLLOW-UP QUESTIONS AND ACTIVITIES

1. Evaluate the proposed conceptual framework in terms of what you know about the traditional structure of the public schools. With a small group, develop a list of potential hurdles that must be overcome to implement such an approach. Come up with a list of strategies that might be useful in developing a collaborative program (e.g., incentives for teachers).

2. Select a concept or topic you might be likely to teach and apply the conceptual framework. What content-obligatory language would you identify? What content-compatible language? Develop a lesson plan around these objectives. Include the age level for which the unit is intended, the procedure, and what your follow-up lesson might be to reinforce the concepts. Present it to your group or class for feedback.

3. If you were actually able to teach the lesson you designed in the second activity, how would you evaluate its effectiveness in teaching content and language? For example, what criteria would you use for making determinations about content-obligatory language? How would you know if these were valid criteria? What kinds of sensitivities might you have to develop?

4

The Cognitive Academic Language Learning Approach: A Bridge to the Mainstream

ANNA UHL CHAMOT AND J. MICHAEL O'MALLEY

Georgetown University

EDITORS' INTRODUCTION

Because of the typical lack of coordination existing between the English as a second language (ESL) and content-area curricula, language minority students are often unprepared for the academic and cognitive demands of content-area classes. In this chapter, Anna Uhl Chamot and J. Michael O'Malley make an important contribution to increased articulation of language and content instruction. They propose the Cognitive Academic Language Learning Approach (CALLA), which is designed to assist upper elementary and secondary school ESL students make the transition from ESL classes to content classes by providing English language development through content-area instruction. CALLA draws theoretical support from cognitive psychology and first language (L1) reading. It also relies heavily on the work of Cummins (see Chapter 2). Although their work focuses primarily on the ESL class, many of Chamot and O'Malley's insights and strategies are applicable to all classrooms where language minority students are present.

The major objective of ESL programs at the elementary and secondary levels in the United States is to prepare students to function successfully in classrooms where English is the medium of instruction for all subject areas. The approaches used to achieve this objective vary considerably, despite their common intent. A recent national survey (Chamot & Stewner-Manzanares, 1985) of the state of the art in ESL in public schools, for example, found that of thirteen different instructional approaches currently in use, the most widely cited by a sample of school districts, Bilingual Education Multifunctional Support Centers, and teacher trainers in representative universities were the audiolingual method, the Natural Approach, Total Physical Response, communicative approaches, and eclectic or combination approaches. None of these approaches, whatever their other merits or deficiencies, focuses specifically on developing the English language skills used in content-area subjects, such as science, mathematics, and social studies.

Students in ESL programs develop many important skills in English and may become quite proficient in day-to-day survival in English. At the conclusion of one or more years of ESL instruction, language minority students may perform satisfactorily on language proficiency assessment measures and be judged by their teachers as proficient in English communicative skills. They are then mainstreamed into the all-English curriculum, where typically they encounter severe difficulties with the academic program. This problem has been attributed to the increased language demands made by the academic curriculum, particularly as students move beyond the primary grade level. Various researchers have found that the development of these academic language skills lags behind the development of social communicative language skills, often by as much as five to seven years (Cummins, 1983c, 1984a; Saville-Troike, 1984; see also Chapter 2).

Before entering the mainstream curriculum, language minority students should be able to use English as a tool for learning subject matter. This ability becomes particularly acute from the middle elementary grades onward because in these upper grades the language of subjects such as social studies, science, and mathematics becomes more academic and less closely related to the language of everyday communication than is the case at the primary grade level. By the middle elementary grades, students are expected to have mastered basic skills in reading, writing, and computation and to understand and use increasingly abstract language. At this level, and increasingly at higher grade levels, the curriculum requires that students listen and read to acquire new information, speak and write to express their understanding of new concepts, use mathematics skills to solve problems, and apply effective strategies for learning to all areas of the curriculum. For the minority-language student, these requirements of the upper elementary and secondary school entail additional language demands. Language proficiency, which may have previously focused on communicative competence, must now focus on academic competence.

A DESCRIPTION OF THE COGNITIVE ACADEMIC LANGUAGE LEARNING APPROACH

This chapter describes the Cognitive Academic Language Learning Approach (CALLA), an instructional method for limited English proficient (LEP) students who are being prepared to participate in mainstream content instruction.

CALLA (pronounced \ kalá \ ) combines English language development with content-based ESL and with instruction in special learner strategies that will help students understand and remember important concepts. Richards (1984) has pointed out that second language (L2) methods can be based on a syllabus (or curriculum) or on a theory of learning processes and instructional procedures and that many current methodological approaches reflect one assumption but not the other. CALLA makes these two approaches to language teaching methods interdependent by integrating language learning and teaching theory and the specification of content to be taught.

Richards (1984) has also indicated the importance of addressing the needs of second language learners in program planning. CALLA is designed to meet the educational needs of three types of LEP students: (a) students who have developed social communicative skills through ESL or exposure to an English-speaking environment but who have not developed academic language skills appropriate to their grade level; (b) students exiting from bilingual programs who need assistance in transferring concepts and skills learned in their native language to English; and (c) bilingual, English-dominant students who are even less academically proficient in their native language than in English and need to develop academic English language skills.

The bridge that CALLA provides between special language programs and mainstream education is illustrated in Figure 4.1. LEP students in ESL and bilingual programs develop initial skills in understanding, speaking, reading, and writing in English, and they practice the essentials of communication for mainly social purposes. CALLA is intended for students at the intermediate and advanced levels of English proficiency who need additional experiences in English language development specifically related to three academic areas: science, mathematics, and social studies. The intent is to introduce vocabulary, structures, and functions in English by using concepts drawn from content areas. CALLA is not intended to substitute for mainstream content-area instruction or to teach the basic content expertise required in school district curricula, as is the intention of immersion and sheltered English programs.

The three content areas addressed by CALLA can be phased into the intermediate-level ESL class one at a time. We recommend beginning with science, since by using a discovery approach to science, teachers can capitalize on experiential learning opportunities that provide both contextual support and language development. The next subject to be introduced is mathematics, which has less contextual support and a more restricted language register than science. Social studies is the third subject introduced in the CALLA model, since of the three, it is the most language and culture dependent; in addition, it includes many topics that are not easily amenable to experiential learning activities. A fourth subject area, English language arts, is a planned addition to the model. Because language is the focus of study as well as the medium through which lessons in literature and composition are taught, this subject is the most language dependent of all, and it is also probably at least as culture dependent as social studies.

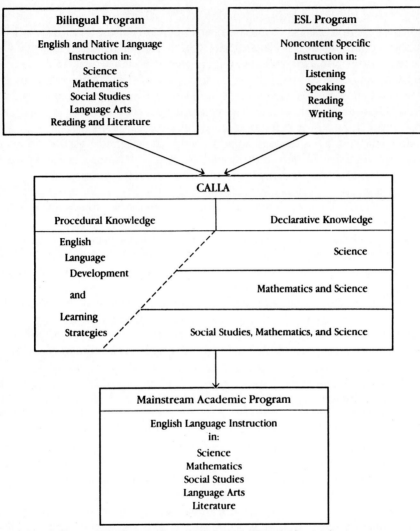

Figure 4.1. *The CALLA Model: A Bridge to the Mainstream*

The CALLA model has three components: (a) a curriculum correlated with mainstream content areas, (b) English language development integrated with content subjects, and (c) instruction in the use of learning strategies. Each of these components is examined separately, following a discussion of the theoretical framework underlying CALLA. The final section of this chapter provides guidelines for integrating these components into a single instructional approach.

THEORETICAL BACKGROUND

A brief examination of the theoretical base for CALLA illustrates the relationship between this instructional approach and current developments in cognitive psychology. Recent efforts to describe both L2 acquisition and learning strategies within the cognitive theory proposed by Anderson (1981, 1983, 1985) provide the necessary theoretical foundation (O'Malley, Chamot & Walker, 1987).

In Anderson's view, information is stored in memory in two forms: *declarative knowledge*, or what we know about a given topic, and *procedural knowledge*, or what we know how to do. Examples of declarative knowledge include word definitions, facts, and rules, including our memory for images and sequences of events. This type of knowledge is represented in long-term memory in terms of meaning-based concepts rather than precisely replicated events or specific language. The concepts on which meaning is based are represented in memory as nodes that are associated with other nodes through connecting associations or links. These interconnected nodes may be organized into propositions, which show the relationships of arguments in sentences; into hierarchies, which show classification relationships with similar concepts in memory; or into larger units of memory called *schemata*, which reveal a configuration of interrelated features that define a concept. In any of these representations, the strength of associations in the link between nodes is largely due to prior learning experiences.

Procedural knowledge underlies our ability to understand and generate language. According to Anderson's theory, procedural knowledge is represented in memory by production systems, which are the basis for explaining how complex cognitive skills such as language are learned and used. Production systems are rule-based conditional actions (*if-then* relationships), which are initially represented like declarative knowledge but which may become automatic through repeated practice. Production systems have been used to describe procedural knowledge in reading, mathematical problem solving, and chess, as well as language comprehension and production. Production systems have been used by Anderson (1983) to represent linguistic rules and by O'Malley, Chamot, and Walker (1987) to represent sociolinguistic, discourse, and strategic competence (see Chapter 1).

Whereas declarative knowledge of factual information may be acquired quickly, procedural knowledge such as language skill is acquired gradually and only with extensive opportunities for practice. Anderson indicates that language is a complex cognitive process that requires explicit or implicit knowledge about language as a system and extensive practice to reach an autonomous stage. This theoretical distinction is a familiar one to second language teachers, who tend to alternate between teaching language as declarative knowledge (grammar, rules, pronunciation, vocabulary) and language as procedural knowledge (communicative competence, functional proficiency, fluency).

What is most important about Anderson's theory is that an interplay between declarative and procedural knowledge leads to the refinement of language ability. Anderson discusses ways in which new information is processed in working memory and accessed to long-term memory, from which it can be retrieved at a later date. He identifies three empirically derived stages that describe the process by which a complex cognitive skill such as language is acquired: (a) a cognitive stage, in which learning is deliberate, rule based, and often error laden; (b) an associative stage, in which actions are executed more rapidly and errors begin to diminish; and (c) an autonomous stage, in which actions are performed more fluently and the original rule governing the performance may no longer be retained. Thus, because the same procedure is used repeatedly, access to the rules that originally produced the procedure may be lost.

Although he does not mention learning strategies, Anderson's description of these cognitive processes is congruent with the types of learning strategies that have been identified in research with LEP students (Cohen & Aphek, 1981; Naiman, Fröhlich, Stern & Todesco, 1978; O'Malley, Chamot, Stewner-Manzanares, Küpper & Russo, 1985; O'Malley, Chamot, Stewner-Manzanares, Russo & Küpper 1985). A number of the mental processes Anderson discusses serve to explain how strategies are represented, how they are learned, and how they influence L2 acquisition. O'Malley, Chamot, and Walker (1987) have suggested that learning strategies are declarative knowledge that may become procedural knowledge through practice. Learning strategies are conscious and deliberate when they are in the cognitive and associative stages of learning but may no longer be considered strategic in the autonomous stage, since the strategies are applied automatically and often without awareness (Rabinowitz & Chi, 1987). As with other complex cognitive skills, the strategies are acquired only with extensive opportunities for application.

Viewing L2 acquisition as a cognitive skill offers several advantages for research on language learning strategies. Anderson's model provides a comprehensive and well-specified theoretical framework for L2 learning and can be adapted to provide a detailed process view of how students acquire and retain a new language. This model can also help to identify and describe the existence and use of specific learning strategies for different types of learners at various stages in L2 development. Finally, a cognitive-skill model of L2 acquisition can provide guidance in the selection and application of learning strategies in the instruction of second language students.

We have applied Anderson's theoretical principles to the CALLA model in the following preliminary way:

1. The content component of the CALLA model represents declarative knowledge. This includes the concepts, facts, and skills underlying science, mathematics, and social studies at the student's grade level. An extension of these content areas to include English language arts would add grammatical knowledge, rhetorical knowledge, and knowledge about literary themes, plots, and story grammars to this store of declarative knowledge.

2. The language development component of CALLA aims to teach the procedural knowledge that students need to use language as a tool for learning. In this component, students are given sufficient practice in using language in academic contexts so that language comprehension and production become automatic and students develop the ability to communicate about academic subjects.

3. The learning-strategies instruction component of the CALLA model builds on Anderson's theory and suggests ways in which teachers can foster autonomy in their students. Many of the learning strategies identified in previous research (O'Malley, Chamot & Küpper, 1986; O'Malley, Chamot, Stewner-Manzanares, Küpper & Russo, 1985; O'Malley, Chamot, Stewner-Manzanares, Russo & Küpper, 1985; Rubin, 1981; Wenden, 1985) can be used as powerful learning tools.

COMPONENTS OF THE MODEL

The Content-Based Curriculum

The importance of integrating language learning with content learning has been stated by Mohan (1986):

> Regarding language as a medium of learning naturally leads to a cross-curriculum perspective. We have seen that reading specialists contrast learning to read with reading to learn. Writing specialists contrast learning to write with writing to learn. Similarly, language education specialists should distinguish between language learning and using language to learn. Helping students use language to learn requires us to look beyond the language domain to all subject areas and to look beyond language learning to education in general. Outside the isolated language classroom students learn language and content at the same time. Therefore we need a broad perspective which integrates language and content learning. (p. 18)

The purpose of CALLA is to provide a broad framework for using language to learn through the integration of language and content.

Content-based English language development is not only important for developing academic language skills, but it is also inherently more interesting to many students than ESL classes that focus on language only. Content areas such as science, mathematics, and social studies present numerous topics related to a variety of personal interests. LEP students can be motivated not only by the topics presented but also by knowing that they are developing the concepts and skills associated with these subjects—in other words, that they are actually doing ''real'' school work instead of merely learning a second language for applications that have yet to be revealed.

LEP students making the transition from a special language program such as bilingual education or ESL need systematic and extensive instruction and practice in the types of activities they will encounter in the mainstream class. An occasional, randomly selected ESL lesson on a topic in social studies or science will not adequately prepare students. This is especially true in the middle- and upper-grade levels, where the curriculum in the content areas becomes progressively more demanding, both in terms of information load and language demands. To be most effective, a content-based ESL curriculum should encompass the sequence and major-scope areas of the mainstream curriculum. The topics incorporated should be authentic and important topics for the grade level of the student.

In a beginning-level ESL class, for example, middle- and upper-grade (as well as primary-grade) students learn to count and do simple arithmetic computation in English. But this is not an appropriate content-based, English language development curriculum for older students because it is not sufficiently challenging. A curriculum that merely reviews concepts and skills already developed in the first language can rapidly become a series of exercises in translation of vocabulary and skills from L1 to L2 and may not stimulate students to begin to use the second language as a tool for learning. Instead, students who already have a background in a content area and who have already developed English proficiency through ESL instruction need a content-based curriculum in which they use English to solve problems and develop additional concepts that are appropriate for their grade and achievement level.

For these reasons, it is important that the content component be based on the mainstream curriculum for the grade level of the students who will participate in the program. This does not mean that it should be identical to the mainstream program (which would make it a submersion model) or that it should replace the mainstream program (as in immersion and "sheltered English" programs). Rather, a CALLA curriculum includes a sample of high-priority content topics that develop academic language skills appropriate to the subject area at the student's grade level. Of course, adjustments will need to be made in the case of students whose previous schooling has been interrupted and who are therefore not at grade level in their native language. As with any instructional program, teachers should discover what students already know about a subject and then build on this previous knowledge by providing them with experiences that develop new concepts and expand previous ones.

To select content topics for CALLA lessons, ESL teachers can coordinate with classroom teachers and consult subject-area textbooks for the grade level concerned. Classroom teachers can identify the most important concepts and skills taught in the content areas they teach. Science, mathematics, and social studies textbooks can be used as a source of specific information to be presented. Having used these resources to identify lesson topics, the ESL teacher can build language development activities onto the content information selected.

To sum up, the CALLA content-based curriculum is based on authentic subject matter from the mainstream curriculum that has been selected as central to the concepts and skills that are developed at particular grade levels.

English Language Development

The purpose of English language development, the second component of the CALLA model, is to provide students with practice in using English as a tool for learning academic subject matter. Reading and language arts can be taught as part of content-area subjects such as social studies, mathematics, and science. The language demands of the different content subjects, which include the language of curriculum materials and of classroom participation, need to be analyzed so that students can be taught the actual language functions, structures, and subject-specific vocabulary that they will need when they enter the mainstream content class. These language demands, which are different from those of the beginning-level ESL class or the type of language used for social interaction, need to be specifically taught and practiced in the context of actual subject-matter learning.

Cummins (1982, 1983c) indicates that two dimensions can be used to describe the language demands encountered by LEP students. The first dimension concerns contextual cues that assist comprehension, and the second concerns the complexity of the task. Language that is most comprehensible is contextualized and rich in nonverbal cues such as concrete objects, gestures, facial expressions, and visual aids. Language that is least comprehensible is language in which context cues have been reduced to such a degree that comprehension depends entirely on the listener's or reader's ability to extract meaning from text without assistance from a nonverbal context.

The second dimension, task complexity, suggests that comprehension is affected by the cognitive demands of the task. Examples of less demanding language tasks are vocabulary, grammar drills, and following directions. More cognitively demanding tasks call on the use of language for higher-level reasoning and for integrative language skills (e.g., reading and listening comprehension, speaking or writing about academic topics). By combining these two dimensions, tasks involving language use can be classified into one of four categories: easy and contextualized, difficult but contextualized, context reduced but easy, and context reduced and difficult (see Chapter 2).

Although context-reduced language is commonly associated with written language, oral language can also vary along the context-embedded to context-reduced continuum. Davidson, Kline, and Snow (1986) define contextualized oral language as conversational, interactive, and supported by shared knowledge and experiences. Decontextualized oral language, on the other hand, is characterized as language that is not interactive and concerns a topic on which no shared knowledge exists. This seems a fair description of much of the content and presentation style in typical subject-area instruction.

Figure 4.2 is based on Cummins's (1982) model of two intersecting continua for L2 tasks. Allen (1985) has pointed out that ESL classes generally stress activities in quadrant I and that students are then mainstreamed directly into quadrant IV activities. The sample activities listed in each quadrant can provide the teacher with information about activities appropriate to the English proficiency level and age or grade placement of LEP students. The activities listed in quadrant I might be used in beginning-level ESL classes. LEP students' first experiences with decontextualized language could be planned around the activities listed in quadrant II. Some of these activities relate to personal or social communication, and others relate to school activities involving mainly rote learning. Academic content is included in the activities listed in quadrant III, but context needs to be built into the activities to assist comprehension. Activities in this quadrant require hands-on experiences and concrete referents. Finally, the activities listed in quadrant IV represent those of the mainstream classroom at the upper elementary and secondary levels. These are the kinds of activities that LEP students have most difficulty with because they are cognitively demanding and because the language associated with them is reduced in context. Although ESL students probably need to begin with quadrant I activities and must eventually be able to perform quadrant IV activities, some teachers may prefer that activities in quadrants II and III take place concurrently rather than sequentially.

An important objective of the English language development component of the CALLA model is to provide students with extensive transitional language activities in quadrant III and gradually initiate some practice with the context-reduced and cognitively demanding activities of quadrant IV. Although some language activities may be integrated with mainstream content-area instruction in the typical school curriculum, these may consist primarily of reading for information. LEP students need to develop not only content-area reading skills, but also the listening, speaking, and writing skills associated with each subject. The number and variety of language activities in a content-based curriculum for LEP students should provide many opportunities for the development of academic language proficiency.

The following aspects of language should be included in the language development component of the CALLA model (Chamot, 1985): development of the specialized vocabulary and technical terms of each content area; practice with the language functions used in academic communication, such as explaining, informing, describing, classifying, and evaluating; development of the ability to comprehend and use the language structures and discourse features found in different subject areas; and practice in using the language skills needed in the content classroom, such as listening to explanations, reading for information, participating in academic discussions, and writing reports. By integrating these types of language activities with grade-appropriate content, a curriculum based on the CALLA model can provide LEP students with the conceptual

Nonacademic or cognitively undemanding activities	Academic and cognitively demanding activities
I	**III**
Developing survival vocabulary	Developing academic vocabulary
Following demonstrated directions	Understanding academic presentations accompanied by visuals, demonstrations of a process, etc.
	Participating in hands-on science activities
Playing simple games	Making models, maps, charts, and graphs in social studies
Participating in art, music, physical education, and some vocational education classes	Solving math computation problems
	Solving math word problems assisted by manipulatives and/or illustrations
Engaging in face-to-face interactions	Participating in academic discussions
Practicing oral language exercises and communicative language functions	Making brief oral presentations
	Using higher level comprehension skills in listening to oral texts
	Understanding written texts through discussion, illustrations, and visuals
	Writing simple science and social studies reports with format provided
Answering lower level questions	Answering higher level questions
II	**IV**
Engaging in predictable telephone conversations	Understanding academic presentations without visuals or demonstrations
	Making formal oral presentations
Developing initial reading skills: decoding and literal comprehension	Using higher level reading comprehension skills: inferential and critical reading
Reading and writing for personal purposes: notes, lists, recipes, etc.	Reading for information in content subjects
Reading and writing for operational purposes: directions, forms, licenses, etc.	Writing compositions, essays, and research reports in content subjects
	Solving math word problems without illustrations
Writing answers to lower level questions	Writing answers to higher level questions
	Taking standardized achievement tests

Context-embedded (I, III) — *Context-reduced* (II, IV)

Figure 4.2. *Classification of Language and Content Activities within Cummins's (1982) Framework*

knowledge and language skills they will need to participate successfully in the mainstream classroom.

Learning-Strategy Instruction

The CALLA model uses learning-strategy instruction as an approach to teaching the content-based language development curriculum described in the preceding sections. Learning-strategy instruction is a cognitive approach to teaching that helps students learn conscious processes and techniques that facilitate the comprehension, acquisition, and retention of new skills and concepts. The use of learning-strategy instruction in L2 learning is based on four main propositions (see Chipman, Sigel & Glaser, 1985; Derry & Murphy, 1986; Weinstein & Mayer, 1986):

1. Mentally active learners are better learners. Students who organize new information and consciously relate it to existing knowledge should have more cognitive linkages to assist comprehension and recall than do students who approach each new task as something to be memorized by rote learning.
2. Strategies can be taught. Students who are taught to use strategies and provided with sufficient practice in using them will learn more effectively than students who have had no experience with learning strategies.
3. Learning strategies transfer to new tasks. Once students have become accustomed to using learning strategies, they will use them on new tasks that are similar to the learning activities on which they were initially trained.
4. Academic language learning is more effective with learning strategies. Academic language learning among students of ESL is governed by some of the same principles that govern reading and problem solving among native English speakers.

While research evidence supports the first two propositions, the transfer of strategies to new learning requires extensive instructional support. We have attempted to make learning-strategy instruction a pervasive part of the CALLA program in response to this need, not only to encourage use of strategies while the students are in CALLA, but also to encourage strategy use when the students exit to the mainstream curriculum.

The fourth proposition is based in part on our own observation that strategies for language learning are similar to strategies for learning content (O'Malley, Chamot, Stewner-Manzanares, Küpper & Russo, 1985) and in part on our positive experiences with the effects of learning strategy instruction on integrative language tasks among ESL students (O'Malley, Chamot, Stewner-Manzanares, Russo & Küpper, 1985). While strategies for learning language and content are very similar, LEP students may have difficulty in discovering the application of strategies to content because their attention is focused on figuring out and comprehending the English language. In CALLA, the blending of language and content results in unified learning tasks to which students can apply learning strategies that facilitate the comprehension and retention of both declarative and procedural knowledge.

Strategy instruction, we believe, is necessary to provide LEP students with extra support in learning language and content, especially when they are in the process of making the transition from the simplified language of the beginning-level ESL class to the more authentic language of the intermediate and advanced level. This is not a new notion. Honeyfield (1977), in arguing against simplification of text after the beginning ESL level, suggests an alternative approach in which we would help intermediate and advanced students to ''cope earlier with unsimplified materials by giving training in such skills as *inferring unknown meanings from context, giving selective attention to material in accordance with realistic reading purposes, recognizing communicative structure* [italics added], and others'' (p. 440). The italicized skill descriptions are precisely what we understand as conscious learning strategies, as defined in the cognitive psychology literature.

Studies in learning-strategy applications indicate that students taught to use new strategies can become more effective learners (O'Malley, 1985). In a recent experimental study, second language learners were taught to use learning strategies for vocabulary, listening comprehension, and formal speaking tasks using academic content (O'Malley, Chamot, Stewner-Manzanares, Russo & Küpper, 1985). The results showed that learning-strategy instruction was most effective for the more integrative language tasks that involved the use of academic language skills to understand or produce extended text.

Our original list of learning strategies (see O'Malley, Chamot, Stewner-Manzanares, Russo & Küpper, 1985) was derived from research on learning strategies in L1 reading and problem solving, research in L2 learning, and our own initial research. This initial list has undergone adaptations based on later research (O'Malley, Chamot & Küpper, 1986) and on our experiences in training teachers on the CALLA model. The three major categories of learning strategies, however, have continued to be useful in differentiating groups of strategies and in showing teachers how to integrate strategy instruction into their daily lessons. These major categories are as follows:

1. *Metacognitive strategies:* These involve executive processes in planning for learning, monitoring one's comprehension and production, and evaluating how well one has achieved a learning objective.
2. *Cognitive strategies:* The learner interacts with the material to be learned by manipulating it mentally (as in making mental images or relating new information to previously acquired concepts or skills) or physically (as in grouping items to be learned in meaningful categories or taking notes on or making summaries of important information to be remembered).
3. *Social-affective strategies:* The learner either interacts with another person in order to assist learning, as in cooperation or asking questions for clarification, or uses some kind of affective control to assist learning.

We have selected a smaller number of strategies from the original list of those reported by ESL students (see O'Malley, Chamot, Stewner-Manzanares, Russo & Küpper, 1985) for teachers to use as the principal instructional approach for CALLA. These, we believe, are strategies that are easy to teach, useful for both discrete and integrative language tasks, and applicable to both content and language learning.

Learning strategies for CALLA are listed and defined in the Appendix (page 55). Some of these strategies may be known to teachers by the term of *study skills*. Study skills describe overt behavior, such as taking notes, writing summaries, or using reference materials. Learning strategies, on the other hand, generally refer to mental processes that are not observable. Although this distinction between learning strategies and study skills is important theoretically, we do not believe that it is always necessary to differentiate them in practice.

Some learning strategies are particularly powerful because they can be used for many different types of learning activities. For example, metacognitive strategies that can be applied to any type of learning are selective attention, self-monitoring, and self-evaluation. Students can use selective attention to assist comprehension by attending to the linguistic markers that signal the type of information that will follow. Some examples of phrases that serve as linguistic markers are discussed in Chamot and O'Malley (1986b):

> "Today we're going to talk about . . ." indicates the main topic of the presentation. Markers such as "The most important thing to remember about . . ." indicate that a main idea is about to be presented. When students hear markers such as "For instance . . ." or "An example of . . .", they know that they can expect an example or a detail. And when students hear a marker such as "Finally, . . ." or "In conclusion, . . .", they can expect a concluding summary of the main points. (p. 11)

Self-monitoring is a metacognitive strategy that has been linked to productive language, in which students correct themselves during speaking or writing. We have discovered that effective ESL listeners also use self-monitoring to check on how well they are comprehending an oral text (O'Malley, Chamot & Küpper, 1986). The consequence of self-monitoring is that students spend more time being actively involved in the comprehension and learning task. Self-evaluation assists learning by helping students decide how well they have accomplished a learning task and whether they need to relearn or review any aspects of it.

A number of cognitive learning strategies can be used by ESL students to assist learning. Elaboration is one of the most powerful strategies and can be applied to all four language skills and to all types of content. When students elaborate, they recall prior knowledge, consciously interrelate parts of what they are learning, and integrate new information to their existing knowledge structure, or schemata. The following example (Chamot & O'Malley, 1986a) illustrates elaboration:

> The learner thinks, ''Let's see. I have to read some information about the early history of California. What do I already know about California history? Well, the Spanish were there first, and then it belonged to Mexico, then there was a war between Mexico and the U.S., and now it's an important state. . . .'' The student goes on to read the assigned text, confirms previous knowledge, and also learns some new facts. During or after reading, the student may think, ''Well, I didn't know that there were Russians in California too. Let's see, how does this fit in with what I already know about the Spanish in California?'' The student uses elaboration in relating new information to previous knowledge and by incorporating it into an existing conceptual framework. (p. 18)

School tasks often require students to learn new information on topics on which they do not possess existing knowledge, so that elaboration may not be possible. It is important for students in this case to organize the new information effectively so that the information can be retrieved and future efforts to use elaboration will be fruitful. Grouping is a strategy that students without prior knowledge on a topic can use to organize or classify new information. In this way, a network, or schema, is established that will make the new knowledge accessible in the future. Grouping is particularly important in science and social studies content areas, where students need to understand classification systems and cause-and-effect relationships. To facilitate comprehension of groups or sets, students may use the strategy of imagery as a way of making mental or actual diagrams of the structure of new information. Grouping and imagery may be particularly effective in conveying knowledge structures to students whose prior education has been interrupted.

The social-affective learning strategies listed in the Appendix can be helpful for many types of learning activities. Cooperation is a strategy that has been shown to have positive effects on both attitude and learning. It is particularly useful for LEP students because by working cooperatively on a task, they practice using language skills directly related to an academic task. Questioning for clarification is also important because students need to learn how to ask questions when they do not understand. Some LEP students may not know how or when to ask appropriate questions, or even that U.S. teachers expect students to ask questions. Self-talk is an affective strategy in which students allay their anxiety by reassuring themselves about their own abilities. It has been used as a way of helping students overcome test anxiety and could be used in any situation in which students feel anxious about a learning task.

We believe that teachers can help their LEP students become more effective learners in general by showing them how to apply a variety of learning strategies to different activities that they may encounter in learning English as well as other subjects in the curriculum. Suggestions for learning-strategy instruction include showing students how to apply the strategies, suggesting a variety of different strategies for the language and content tasks of the curriculum, and providing many examples of learning strategies throughout the curriculum so that students will be able to generalize them to new learning activities in other classes and even outside the classroom (Chamot & O'Malley, 1986a). Effective transfer of strategies to other classes also requires that students be made aware of the strategies they are using and be able to verbalize the conditions under which strategies can be used.

A DESCRIPTION OF A CALLA LESSON PLAN MODEL

To integrate the three components of CALLA, we have developed a lesson plan model that incorporates content-area topics, language development activities, and learning-strategy instruction. In this plan, learning-strategy instruction is embedded into daily lessons so that it becomes an integral part of the regular class routine, rather than a supplementary activity. In this way, students have opportunities to practice the strategies on actual lessons, and use of the strategies becomes part of the class requirements. At first, the teacher shows the students how to use the strategies and provides reminders and cues so that they will be used. Later, teachers should diminish the reminders to allow students to use strategies independently.

CALLA lessons identify both language and content objectives, so that teachers can specify both procedural and declarative tasks for their ESL students. The lessons are divided into five phases: Preparation, Presentation, Practice, Evaluation, and Follow-Up Expansion. In the Preparation phase, teachers provide advance organizers about the lesson and students identify what they already know about a topic, using elaboration as a strategy. In the Presentation phase, teachers provide new information to students, using techniques that make their input comprehensible. Teachers can use advance organizers and encourage the use of selective attention, self-monitoring, inferencing, summarizing, and transfer. In the Practice phase, students engage in activities in which they apply learning strategies, often in cooperative small-group sessions. During this phase, the teacher should encourage the use of strategies such as grouping, imagery, organizational planning, deduction, inferencing, and questioning for clarification. In the Evaluation phase, students reflect on their individual learning and plan to remedy any deficiencies they may have identified. Finally, in the Follow-Up Expansion phase, students are provided with opportunities to relate and apply the new information to their own lives, call on the expertise of their parents and other family members, and compare what they have learned in school with their own cultural experiences.

CONCLUSION

The Cognitive Academic Language Learning Approach, an instructional method for LEP students at the intermediate and advanced levels of English proficiency, is intended to be a bridge between bilingual or ESL instruction and academic mainstream classes. It focuses on English language development through cognitively based content-area instruction in science, mathematics, and social studies. CALLA teaches students the academic language skills and learning strategies they need to succeed in content areas and can also help the English-dominant but still LEP bilingual student acquire these types of language skills. The approach addresses the need for English language development in the four language skill areas of listening, reading, speaking, and writing. CALLA is designed to supply added support for English language development among LEP students and is not a replacement for experience in mainstream classes.

CALLA is the result of an interdisciplinary effort to improve the education of LEP students in U.S. schools. We plan to continue developing, refining, adapting, and testing our model in the hope that CALLA can make a significant contribution to the present and future needs of our growing language minority school population.

APPENDIX: LEARNING STRATEGY DEFINITIONS

Learning strategy	Definition
Metacognitive strategies	
1. Advance organization	Previewing the main ideas and concepts of the material to be learned, often by skimming the text for the organizing principle
2. Organizational planning	Planning the parts, sequence, main ideas, or language functions to be expressed orally or in writing
3. Selective attention	Deciding in advance to attend to specific aspects of input, often by scanning for key words, concepts, and/or linguistic markers
4. Self-monitoring	Checking one's comprehension during listening or reading or checking the accuracy and/or appropriateness of one's oral or written production while it is taking place
5. Self-evaluation	Judging how well one has accomplished a learning activity after it has been completed
Cognitive strategies	
1. Resourcing	Using target language reference materials such as dictionaries, encyclopedias, or textbooks
2. Grouping	Classifying words, terminology, or concepts according to their attributes
3. Note taking	Writing down key words and concepts in abbreviated verbal, graphic, or numerical form during a listening or reading activity
4. Summarizing	Making a mental, oral, or written summary of information gained through listening or reading
5. Deduction/induction	Applying rules to understand or produce the second language or making up rules based on language analysis

APPENDIX: LEARNING STRATEGY DEFINITIONS (continued)

Learning strategy	Definition
Cognitive strategies (continued)	
6. Imagery	Using visual images (either mental or actual) to understand and remember new information
7. Auditory representation	Playing back in one's mind the sound of a word, phrase, or longer language sequence
8. Elaboration	Relating new information to prior knowledge, relating different parts of new information to each other, or making meaningful personal associations with the new information
9. Transfer	Using previous linguistic knowledge or prior skills to assist comprehension or production
10. Inferencing	Using information in an oral or written text to guess meanings, predict outcomes, or complete missing parts
Social-affective strategies	
1. Questioning for clarification	Eliciting from a teacher or peer additional explanation, rephrasing, examples, or verification
2. Cooperation	Working together with peers to solve a problem, pool information, check a learning task, model a language activity, or get feedback on oral or written performance
3. Self-talk	Reducing anxiety by using mental techniques that make one feel competent to do the learning task

FOLLOW-UP QUESTIONS AND ACTIVITIES

1. Anderson's theory of cognitive psychology states that information is stored in memory in two forms: declarative knowledge and procedural knowledge. Consider your subject area in terms of this dichotomy. What kinds of information in your field can be classified as declarative knowledge? What kinds can be considered procedural knowledge? Do you think these types of material should be taught differently? If so, how? If not, why not?

2. Using the four quandrants shown in Figure 4.2, where do activities you might typically employ fall? Think of other language and content tasks not listed that are common in your subject area, and classify them in terms of the quandrants.

3. Which of the learning strategies discussed by Chamot and O'Malley seem most appropriate for your particular teaching situation? Recall your own academic training in your subject area. Did you use any of the learning strategies listed in this chapter? Are there any other learning strategies you used when you studied your subject in college that you think might be useful to your students?

4. If you are currently teaching (or doing supervised teaching), interview the ESL teacher at your school. How does the ESL teacher view his or her role in content-area instruction? Does the ESL curriculum overlap in any systematic way with instruction in any of the content areas? Is there any attempt made to bridge the ESL and mainstream classes?

5

Cooperative Learning:
The Benefits for
Content-Area Teaching

MARY McGROARTY   *Northern Arizona University*

EDITORS' INTRODUCTION

DeAvila, Duncan, and Navarrete (1987), as rationale for their cooperative learn-
ing curriculum entitled Finding Out/Descubrimiento, *observe that although*
unsuccessful students may not have academic strategies, it is a question of inex-
perience and not ability. In this chapter, Mary McGroarty carefully lays out and sup-
ports with empirical research the linguistic, curricular, and social benefits that can
accrue through the use of cooperative learning. Hence, language minority students
are able to gain the repertoire of strategies necessary for effective functioning in
academic settings. In addition to the overall cognitive advantages associated with
cooperative learning, she points to the pedagogical advantages that accrue when
teachers let go of their traditional authority and become facilitators in the learning
process.

THE BENEFITS OF COOPERATIVE
LEARNING ARRANGEMENTS IN
SECOND LANGUAGE INSTRUCTION

Observers and critics of education have long noted that competitive classroom
environments do not promote learning for all students equally; where only
those perceived as most academically able consistently meet traditional achievement goals and, thus, further confirm their own sense of competence, other
students may well then lose interest and withdraw from the intellectual exchange
in the classroom (Cohen, 1986; Kagan, 1986, 1980). In classrooms marked by

From ''The Benefits of Cooperative Learning Arrangements in Second Language Instruction'' by
M. McGroarty, 1989, NABE Journal, 13, pp. 127–143. Copyright by the National Association for
Bilingual Education. Reprinted by permission.

linguistic heterogeneity, competitive learning approaches run the further risk of rewarding mainly those students who know English best, native speakers, and those who have close to nativelike abilities. The competitive classroom atmosphere, reliance on transmission of knowledge through teacher presentation, and instruction in English only may thus retard the academic progress of students who learn best through other group settings and other approaches to knowledge where they can draw on their ability to interact with each other and with curriculum materials and use both first (L1) and second language (L2) skills.

To provide a framework that offers more equitable access to knowledge than that available in competitive classrooms, scholars concerned about education have developed theoretical foundations and practical strategies for encouraging the use of cooperative learning groups as one means of diversifying the paths that lead toward academic mastery (cf., Cohen, 1986; Kagan, 1986; Slavin, 1983). In *Beyond Language: Social and Cultural Factors in Schooling Language Minority Students* (California State Department of Education, 1986), a group of social scientists and educators described the social conditions that have sometimes hindered the educational progress of language minority students and presented some innovative approaches, prominent among them the use of cooperative learning, to improve the level of student engagement with the curriculum. A nationwide review by researchers at the Center for Applied Linguistics has also found cooperative learning methods of growing importance in the instruction of language minority students (Jacob & Mattson, 1987).

In this chapter I discuss some of the benefits of cooperative learning arrangements for multicultural content-area instruction. Research on cooperative learning in settings of linguistic diversity corroborates the advantages of cooperative instruction shown in settings where all students speak the same language: increase in student exposure to and practice of relevant skills; improved interaction and language development; feasibility of use in several content areas; greater possibilities for task variety, and improved affective relationships for all in the classroom.

First a Definition

There is a variety of cooperative learning methods that differ in types of academic and social outcomes emphasized. Overall, the academic outcomes of cooperative learning include three potential results directly relevant to language development: (1) more, and (2) more complex language input for students; and (3) more opportunities to refine communication through natural talk, or production of "comprehensible output" (Swain, 1985). Three additional results pertain to learning in all academic skill areas: (1) increased frequency and type of practice; (2) better differentiation of the learning task through clearer definition and greater subdivision of component processes; and (3) an evaluation structure that rewards improvement and is, thus, equally accessible to all students, not just high achievers (Kagan, 1986). The social outcomes particularly relevant for L2 instruction include: (1) provision of a more democratic, less competitive classroom environment; (2) improved race relations; and (3) development of the prosocial skills involved in seeking and offering peer assistance and learning to maximize group as well as individual strengths (Kagan, 1986).

The five major models of cooperative learning differ in their focus on each of these outcomes. Peer tutoring emphasizes mutual assistance in the mastering of predetermined consent. In jigsaw, the second principal type of cooperative method, students are divided into teams with each member having responsibility for a single part of the learning task. Cooperative projects, the third type, require groups to work together to produce a final collective project. In cooperative/individualized methods, a student's individual progress contributes to a team grade. In the last type, cooperative interaction, students work on individual assignments requiring interaction although no group grade is given.[1] All methods are similar, however, in the "division of the class into small teams whose members are positively interdependent" (Kagan, 1986, p. 241). Cooperative methods require that the whole class be subdivided into groups that work together to accomplish academic tasks. Webb (1982) shows that cooperative activities can best be analyzed in terms of component processes such as giving help, receiving or not receiving help, and being passive or off-task; successful cooperative arrangements are those that maximize provision of assistance adequate to the tasks at hand. Because completion of the activity requires all members of the group to participate in achieving the goal, it creates peer motivation to use and develop the component skills such as reading an activity card, weighing a block, or drawing a map that are needed to conclude the activity. Students must thus learn to identify the skills of group members and assume responsibility for asking questions and explaining things to each other, thus creating a "norm of cooperation" (Cohen, 1986; Cohen & Lotan, 1987; Kagan, 1986). By building skills in inquiry and interaction, cooperative learning addresses the academic and social dimensions of classroom experience so that all can participate in the acquisition of knowledge. While it does not entirely eliminate differences in levels of student performance, it has been shown to be more effective than traditional large-group instruction in guiding students to discover a variety of ways to experience new concepts and develop academic and interactional skills, particularly when groups are balanced on relevant dimensions such as ethnic diversity (González, 1983a) and student ability level (Webb, 1982).

Many of the processes central to cooperative learning occur in the group give-and-take as students negotiate their group's solution to the task at hand. The issue of language proficiency is clearly of major importance in being able to carry out one's participation in the group. Can coopertive learning approaches be used with students who do not share a common language or whose levels

---

[1] See Kagan (1986) for a more expanded discussion of the five major types and Cohen (1986, Chapter 5) for considerations in choosing a model.

of mastery of the language of the classroom are as yet incomplete? Since participation in group deliberation is vital to successful implementation of cooperative work, these questions are critical ones for educators in all content classes serving limited English proficient (LEP) students.

Research conducted in settings of linguistic diversity offers some answers here, and it is valuable to examine results in order to appreciate the potential of cooperative learning in content-area classes. Many of these insights will not appear new to teachers attuned to language-teaching techniques that stress communication among students as an integral part of instruction; indeed a short review of the linguistic, curricular, pedagogical, and social benefits achieved through cooperative models shows how these approaches parallel current trends in L2 instruction. Nearly all cooperative learning approaches include the ''combination of spontaneous conversational activities and exposure to natural language'' characteristic of ''communication centered instruction'' now widely recommended in professional literature for language teachers (Horwitz, 1986). For content-area teachers, however, it is valuable to review the potential benefits of cooperative instruction for language development and instruction.

I have identified six major benefits of cooperative work in settings of linguistic heterogeneity. The number is arbitrary and could be revised depending on one's focus of interest. Nonetheless, although the number is arbitrary, the areas selected represent the main linguistic, pedagogical, and social outcomes that can emerge when cooperative learning is used appropriately and are thus helpful in assessing its applicability to multicultural settings.

Benefit 1

In multicultural classrooms, cooperative learning as exemplified in small-group work provides frequent opportunity for natural L2 practice and negotiation of meaning through talk.

This is a main point in Long and Porter's (1985) review of the pedagogical and psycholinguistic rationale for group work in L2 learning. This advantage occurs through diversifying the opportunities for language use; when students can talk with each other, not only with the teacher, the possibilities for practice in both comprehension and production of the L2 increase dramatically in both actual time and interactional variety. When English as a second language (ESL) students at various proficiency levels are given an interesting problem to solve through discussion with each other or with native speakers, they work to communicate in language that is, to the best of their ability, conceptually accurate, even if not always grammatically well formed (Long & Porter, 1985). Students frequently speak with each other rather than waiting for the teacher to initiate and regulate verbal exchange, and so they have many more opportunities to produce ''comprehensible output'' (Kagan, 1986; Swain, 1985).[2] Only through

---

[2] Comprehensible output here refers to language correctly expressed in terms of appropriate syntactic form as well as basic lexicon (Swain, 1985).

continued active efforts to make their meaning clear by using the complete range of grammatical and syntactic patterns available will students develop extensive rather than minimal communicative skills. Such structural control of a language grows increasingly important as students advance on the proficiency continuum and is essential in attaining nativelike capability.

Furthermore, the nature of the interaction in cooperative learning arrangements includes a greater range of verbal skills than that typically found in teacher-centered instruction, where student responses are often constrained by time and teacher concern for "right" answers. The tasks and group structures used in cooperative learning foster many different types of verbal exchange, so there are more possibilities for fluent speakers to tailor speech and interactions to the communicative needs of the less proficient, thus facilitating L2 acquisition (Gaies, 1985; Long, 1981). A recent study of a cooperative learning task using the jigsaw method in a beginning university Dutch class sheds some light on the processes involved (Deen, 1987). While in a cooperative setting, all students asked a number of questions and engaged in frequent self- and other-correction regardless of proficiency level, thus attempting to check comprehension and adjust communication strategies to interlocutor competence. Working together, the students provided the verbal "scaffolding," or framing, that models and supports target language use (Hawkins, 1988). In task-oriented groups, students correct each other and attempt to fill in the gaps of their understanding by repairing and rephrasing what their partners say in order to come to consensus (Long & Porter, 1985). The necessity of providing and clarifying information and opinion creates the motivation for less proficient students to persist in conveying meanings accurately in English and to attempt many strategies to do so. University ESL students prompted each other much more than they did native speaker conversational partners, thus practicing more varied means of verbal clarification in coming to conclusion of a task (Porter, 1983). In English as a foreign language (EFL) classes, too, cooperative learning has proven successful in diversifying opportunities for L2 practice (Bejarano, 1987). Limited English proficient (LEP) students at the elementary level have also been observed to assist each other effectively in English during small-group instruction (Cohen & Lotan, 1987; Hawkins, 1988). Additionally, other research has shown that repair sequences, where learners negotiate meaning between themselves, were frequent for all ESL learners studied, particularly among pairs of students at different proficiency levels who did not share a first language (Varonis & Gass, 1983). Most available evidence, then, confirms that cooperative learning tasks expand the possibilities for frequency and variety of appropriately tailored interaction and practice in verbal skills, even when student proficiency in the second language is limited.

Benefit 2
In multicultural classrooms, cooperative learning can help students draw on primary language resources as they develop second language skills.

Cooperative learning is effective in multicultural classrooms when learning groups include bilingual students, who serve as crucial links in providing information to all group members, some of whom may be monolingual in either of the languages involved (Cohen, 1986). When participants must understand a task in order to carry out the appropriate activity, even if activities are visual or manipulative in nature, there is powerful incentive for the bilingual students to convey necessary information to other students who are less proficient in English and who can then extend or clarify their comprehension through discussions in their primary language. The press to figure out an interesting task can lead students to use as much of their pertinent L1 competence and their developing L2 repertoire as possible, with native speakers or bilingual peers, thus creating many opportunities for natural language practice. In this way, the peer interaction so important to successful L2 learning is encouraged in cooperative settings by the use of bilingual students as intermediaries (Wong-Fillmore, Ammon, McLaughlin & Ammon, 1985).

Furthermore, cooperative learning arrangements in multicultural classrooms can encourage use of the first language in academic domains, which will facilitate student understanding of concepts and efficient acquisition of L2 skill. In one study where elementary students with different degrees of proficiency in Spanish and English were observed while working in cooperative groups, it was found that the frequency of task-related talk, even if in Spanish, was proportionately related to student gains in English (Neves, 1983, cited in Cohen, 1986). Although these students were in groups where English was used along with Spanish, this finding suggests that academic use of the primary language help students master English, perhaps by consolidating their conceptual knowledge in settings that allow them to use the first language while being naturally exposed to appropriate L2 labels during group work. Use of L1 discussions to clarify meaning and reveal the extent of reading comprehension in the second language has also been reported in other bilingual elementary classrooms, where student discussion of a reading lesson in Spanish showed much more complete comprehension of the material than they were allowed or expected to demonstrate in English (Díaz, Moll & Mehan, 1986). Once aware of the discrepancy, teachers were able to draw on the students' comprehension in order to make the English reading instruction more challenging, as befitted the students' conceptual level.

The results from the university-level Dutch class shed further light on the roles of the two languages: In a jigsaw task involving ''expert'' groups who then reported information back to ''project team'' members, more English questions were used in the expert portion of the task as students clarified the information to be conveyed while more Dutch questions were used as the project teams put the pieces of the activity (a cartoon sequence) in order (Deen, 1987, 1986). The first language again served as the initial channel of understanding so that accurate communication in the second language was consequently possible. It is clear that cooperative learning can provide teachers with a possible way to use the primary language as a bridge rather than a barrier to academic knowledge and L2 mastery. Again, although these investigations took place in elementary and postsecondary classrooms respectively, the results are persuasive and bear investigation in instructional programs at all levels.

Benefit 3

In multicultural settings, cooperative learning offers additional ways to incorporate content areas into language instruction.

This is the principal curricular benefit of cooperative learning approaches, for they can be used in many subjects. Interest in the relationship between L2 instruction and other content areas continues to grow as educators search for ways to help students master academic content while they improve language skills (see, for example, Brinton, Snow & Wesche, 1989; Kessler & Quinn, 1988; Milk, 1985; Mohan, 1986). In research reviewed so far, the role of the content used to generate cooperative activities was central. For communication to be sparked by genuine student interest and desire to find things out, successful topics were those with intrinsic interest, with a variety of solutions or paths to solutions, and with no single right answer (Cohen, 1986, provides additional guidelines for topic selection). In math, for example, students can generate and evaluate their own word problems illustrating concepts like subtraction or multiplication and see how many different ways there are to arrive at solutions. In science, students can develop several different hypotheses related to the phenomena under study and, through classroom experimentation, determine which are most accurate.

Optimal topics for cooperative L2 experiences can be generated in several content areas, many of those which incorporate various kinds of world knowledge that students can bring to bear on a task through verbal and non-verbal interaction. For example, determining solutions to such problems as which weights are equivalent in volume to different shapes or which survivors on a desert island should be saved requires both conceptual and linguistic knowledge. . . . In using provocative content to stimulate negotiation, cooperative learning models allow students and teachers to draw on cognitive and experiential skills in addition to grammar as they exchange ideas.

These findings reflect in microcosm what the large body of literature on immersion models of L2 education has shown on a larger scale: Elementary school students who learn content through a second language, be it French or Spanish, also acquire a level of communicative proficiency in the second language far superior to students who simply study the second language as a school subject (California State Department of Education, 1984). Students master grade-appropriate cognitive skills as they develop a high level of competence in the language of instruction. Content courses taught in the second language are powerful vehicles for L2 mastery at the postsecondary level as well. Canadian research has shown that Anglophone university students studying psychology in French scored as well as controls in the subject matter and significantly better in comprehension and willingness to use French than similar students who had taken a French language course instead (Edwards, Wesche, Krashen, Clément & Kruidenier, 1984; Hauptman, Wesche & Ready, 1988). A related instructional model, the Adjunct Approach, which combines a content course with a related writing class, has been used with ESL students about to enter a U.S. university and has been effective in demonstrating linguistic and subject-area achievement (Snow & Brinton, 1988). Educators concerned with ESL instruction in U.S. elementary and secondary schools have also turned their attention to the possibilities of language development through content-area instruction (Crandall, 1987).

It is clear from these examples that teaching interesting content via a second language can provide students with the means to develop a high level of functional language ability and the confidence needed to persist in communicating in the second language. Indeed, the integration of language and academic instruction through a stimulating curriculum that requires considerable negotiation of meaning is a hallmark of both effective immersion and bilingual instruction (Genesee, 1986, 1987). While the feasibility of different approaches such as bilingual, immersion, or adjunct instruction varies not only according to student level and subject area but also according to the social context, the use of different content areas as foundations for L2 instruction offers promise to educators concerned with both. (See Chapters 1 and 10 for further discussion of program models.)

Benefit 4
Cooperative learning tasks require a variety of group activities and materials to support instruction; this whole array of changes in traditional classroom technology creates a favorable context for language development.

The curriculum materials used in cooperative learning fulfill an essential role: They must embody the concepts to be learned through several channels and require more diverse pedagogical techniques. To engage all the students and offer each a way to demonstrate competence relevant to the task, activities and materials must tap spatial, visual, and manual abilities as well as verbal ones (Cohen, 1986; Kagan, 1986). Science activities, for instance, should include visual estimation and manipulation of quantities, not just calculation. For example, to establish the concept of relative weight and volume, lessons could involve measuring the same amount of sand, water, or other material into different size containers, or determining the appropriate amount of various ingredients to prepare a certain quantity of food, and then actually making it. The differentiated group structure, the different media used, and the discovery orientation of the tasks together create a complex instructional situation that requires teachers to clarify task structure and delegate responsibility to students, who then must determine how to work out their individual and collective solutions (Cohen & Lotan, 1987). Both processes are realized in large part through verbal interaction.

Although cooperative tasks using only text-based materials can be designed, their use is problematic in settings where students show a considerable range of literacy skills (as is often the case in classrooms serving second language learners). Materials that rely only on mastery of literacy skills for successful completion will appeal only to students whose literacy skills are already established (Cohen, 1984); to foster growth in oral and written language as well as content-area knowledge, tasks or projects for cooperative learning should embed literacy tasks in sequences that include nonverbal, visual, tactile, and manipulative information (Cohen & DeAvila, 1984; Cohen, 1986). After measuring out similar quantities of material into different containers several times, for example, students as a group could produce as many written statements as they can describing the relationship between the amount of material and the container size. In social studies, students might together build a model of a typical dwelling from any historical period, look for related pictures, hear stories related to the period and discuss them together before contributing to a written class summary, and, if appropriate, creating their own stories or summaries.

Teachers aware of the interest in "sheltered" language teaching (Parker, 1986), or teaching that controls complexity of language while providing additional support for understanding, will find this emphasis on a rich array of concrete anchors for language and literacy development familiar. It parallels current instructional methods emphasizing language acquisition activity, such as content-based instruction (Crandall, 1987) and the Natural Approach (Krashen & Terrell, 1983). Like cooperative learning, current approaches to language learning encourage learners to use a variety of sensory information as they determine how to accomplish group projects or demonstrate comprehension of a lesson. By furnishing diverse instructional materials, then, cooperative learning creates an environment that supports L2 and literacy acquisition through nonlinguistic as well as verbal means, a situation much more typical of everyday learning outside school (Resnick, 1987; Tharp & Gallimore, 1988).

Benefit 5

Cooperative learning models require redefinition of the role of the teacher in ways that allow teachers to expand general pedagogical skills and emphasize meaning as well as form in communication.

Any learning arrangement that requires the teacher to become a facilitator rather than a direct supervisor of learning implies a great change in the way most teachers usually behave (Cohen, 1986; Kagan, 1986). Hence all systematic efforts to implement cooperative learning have incorporated teacher training in practical and philosophical foundations as a critical first step. The teacher's role becomes one of letting go of traditional authority to a degree, creating teams of students whose strengths complement each other (Cohen, 1986) and learning to monitor the students' adherence to tasks and norms (Cohen & Lotan, 1987). For most teachers, long accustomed to being the main authority in the classroom, this change can be a difficult one; yet, because sharing responsibility for learning with the students frees teachers to concentrate on other aspects of instruction such as creating well-balanced student teams and identifying new approaches to curricular areas, it offers teachers a way to add to their pedagogical repertoire and gain additional competencies that can enhance professional skills and build morale.

For sheltered content-area teachers, there is an additional concern to be addressed; besides being the main authority figure in the classroom, they may also be the sole (or one of the few) native language models available to the students and may hence be reluctant to use group work since they fear it might expose students to an inordinately large proportion of errors. However, research indicates that learners produce no more errors when speaking with each other than they do when conversing with native speakers (Porter, 1983) or with the teacher (Deen, 1987). Altogether, the analyses summarized above suggest that interaction with classmates, even if classmates are nonnative speakers, does not induce students to commit more errors than they otherwise would and, in fact, creates abundant natural contexts for self- and other-correction of errors that affect meaning, both semantic and syntactic. Hence, teachers need not be the only monitors of linguistic accuracy because students can check each other as they talk; teachers can then turn their attention to establishing conditions for meaningful exchanges where grammar and lexicon serve a larger purpose. Cooperative approaches to language learning need not, and possibly ought not to supplant formal grammatical instruction in every setting, but they can give teachers and students the chance to deal with the meanings as well as the forms of the second language through natural exchange of information.

Benefit 6
Cooperative learning approaches encourage students to take an active role in acquisition of knowledge and language skills and to encourage each other as they work on problems of mutual interest.

Preparing the students to be resources for each other in accomplishing a shared goal, rather than competitors to best each other, is a cardinal point of cooperative instruction. Like the pretraining of teachers, the pretraining of students is vital for effective cooperative experiences. Systematic efforts to implement this approach require considerable time to developing the norm of cooperation and the understanding of such roles as leader, facilitator, and recorder so that students realize the different roles and functions they will play (Cohen & Lotan, 1987; Cohen, 1986; Kagan, 1986).

In addition to making these roles clear to students, content-area teachers must also model the emphasis on meaning and selective tolerance for grammatical and lexical errors, so that students place importance on meaningful communication. In cooperative learning arrangements, the students determine the meaningfulness of an activity together with others and clarify things in their own terms to come to consensus or solve a problem; hence, they become the judges of the adequacy of information conveyed and the tutors for each other. This offers one way of creating a classroom community that promotes language acquisition through positive relationships among the students (Holt, 1986). Furthermore, such arrangements give students practice in discerning different meanings, asking questions, constructing and defending various solutions to learning tasks, and eliciting each other's strengths, thus developing skills in social management as well as language. From a psychological standpoint, then, cooperative language learning experiences are one way to empower language minority students (Cummins, 1986) and other second language learners through a reciprocal interaction model of instruction emphasizing student control of classroom discourse and discovery processes.

Such interaction and student control can have positive individual as well as social consequences. In a study comparing cooperative learning (specifically, a jigsaw method requiring individual experts to contribute to group solutions), bilingual, and regular third- and fourth-grade classrooms serving linguistically and ethnically mixed groups in northern California, González (1983b) found that students in both the jigsaw and the bilingual classes grew slightly in self-esteem, while students in traditional classrooms declined. Moreover, there was evidence of different levels of preference for cooperative activities based on language background. In seven out of eight trials, Spanish-dominant students made more cooperative choices than either bilingual or English-dominant students. Hence, it appears that in classrooms like these, cooperative learning is conducive to positive psychological outcomes for all involved and may be clearly preferred by many students from some language groups.

In summary, these insights from research show some of the possibilities of cooperative learning for improving the learning experiences of second language students. There is no question that more research directed at identifying the types of cooperative tasks and group structures best suited to different instructional settings and school subjects is needed, as is additional specification of other influences such as gender and level of student achievement that may come into play in cooperative activities (Webb & Kenderski, 1985). Nevertheless, the strong general agreement shown in disparate research settings indicates that cooperative language learning facilitates functional L2 proficiency; does not retard formal mastery of the language; allows for creative integration of primary language skills, content areas, and materials; and gives teachers and students experience with new roles that enhance social climate as well as linguistic skills. Teachers and researchers can now take up the challenge of discovering which cooperative approaches will best serve them and their students in attaining the full communicative competence relevant to broader educational goals.

RECOMMENDED READINGS

Andrini, B. (1989). *Cooperative learning and mathematics: A multi-structural approach.* San Juan Capistrano, CA: Resources for Teachers.

Cohen, E. (1986). *Designing group work: Strategies for the heterogeneous classroom.* New York: Columbia University, Teachers College Press.

Johnson, D. W., & Johnson, F. P. (1987). *Joining together: Group theory and group skills*. Englewood Cliffs, NJ: Prentice Hall Regents.

Kagan, S. (1986). Cooperative learning and sociocultural factors in schooling. In California State Department of Education, *Beyond language: Social and cultural factors in schooling language minority students*. Los Angeles: Evaluation, Dissemination and Assessment Center, California State University.

Slavin, R. E. (1983). *Cooperative learning*. White Plains, NY: Longman.

Stone, J. (1989). *Cooperative learning and language arts: A multi-structural approach*. San Juan Capistrano, CA: Resources for Teachers.

FOLLOW-UP QUESTIONS AND ACTIVITIES

1. McGroarty contends that in cooperative learning, the student's first language serves as ''. . . a bridge rather than a barrier to academic knowledge and second language mastery (p. 63).'' Explain how this occurs. Refer also to Chapter 2.

2. Of the six main benefits mentioned, which do you feel make the strongest case for cooperative learning? Can you think of any other possible benefits? What about possible drawbacks? How might these be overcome?

3. Kagan (1986) describes cooperative learning as a highly structured system offering rewards based on a fairly complex system of points. To provide motivation, points are given to individuals and/or groups after specific tasks have been completed. Others claim that extrinsic rewards such as points are not necessary when the responsibility for learning is shared (see Richard-Amato, 1988). What are your feelings on this matter? Discuss them.

4. Describe ways in which cooperative learning (or some version thereof) can be used in a specific content area. Share your ideas with a small group to receive their feedback.

PART II

Cultural Considerations

Language minority students in American classrooms represent a rich cross-section of cultural groups. As part of our effort to design an educational environment that is maximally effective, we must not only have a background in issues of language development but must also understand something of the cultural context of teaching language minority students. This necessarily involves a reciprocal process: As we learn more about the complex cultural issues with which language minority students must struggle to become both bilingual and bicultural, we must also examine our own attitudes and systems of cultural belief. Consideration of these sociocultural issues is an important step toward understanding and appreciating the rich linguistic and cultural diversity that language minority students bring into our classrooms.

The four chapters in Part II consider cultural issues from a number of different perspectives. In Chapter 6, H. Douglas Brown defines culture and provides an interesting overview of a variety of sociocultural issues, including attitudes, stereotypes, acculturation, and the relationship between language, thought, and culture. The stages of ethnic identity and their curricular implications are discussed by James Banks in Chapter 7. Shirley Brice Heath, in Chapter 8, broadens the scope of our investigation by comparing the types of language used in school with those of the homes and communities of language minority students. In Chapter 9, Robin Scarcella provides many helpful tips for giving culturally sensitive feedback in the content-area classroom.

6

Sociocultural Factors in Teaching Language Minority Students

H. Douglas Brown *San Francisco State University*

Editors' Introduction

In the teaching of language minority students, becoming aware of our own attitudes and behavior is part of the foundation on which we can build an understanding of and respect for our students. In this chapter, H. Douglas Brown addresses sociocultural factors from the perspective of both the teacher and the learner. He cautions us about the dangers of cultural stereotyping and emphasizes the powerful role of attitudes on language learning. From his detailed description of culture shock, we gain a greater appreciation of the difficult adjustment often faced by second language (L2) students who are learning not only a new language but a new culture. The chapter concludes with a discussion of the relationship between language and thought, including some interesting cross-cultural examples of how varying cultural patterns, customs, and ways of life are expressed in language. Brown's chapter provides much information for reflection as we work to create instructional environments that are both linguistically and culturally sensitive to language minority students.

Culture is a way of life. Culture is the context within which we exist, think, feel, and relate to others. It is the ''glue'' that binds a group of people together. John Donne wrote: ''No man is an island entire of itself; every man is a piece of the continent, a part of the main'' (*Devotions*, XVII). Culture is our continent, the collective identity of which each of us is a part.

Larson and Smalley (1972) described culture as a blueprint that:

> guides the behavior of people in a community and is incubated in family life. It governs our behavior in groups, makes us sensitive to matters of status, and helps us know what others expect of us and what will happen if we do not live up to their expectations. Culture helps us to know how far we can go as

From H. Douglas Brown, Principles of Language Learning and Teaching *(2nd ed.), © 1987, pp. 122–145. Adapted by permission of Prentice Hall, Inc., Englewood Cliffs, New Jersey.*

individuals and what our responsibility is to the group. Different cultures are
the underlying structures which make Round community round and Square
community square. (p. 39)

Culture might be defined as the ideas, customs, skills, arts, and tools that
characterize a given group of people in a given period of time. But culture is
more than the sum of its parts. "It is a system of integrated patterns, most
of which remain below the threshold of consciousness, yet all of which govern
human behavior just as surely as the manipulated strings of a puppet control
its motions" (Condon, 1973, p. 4). The fact that no society exists without a
culture reflects the need for culture to fulfill certain biological and psychological
needs in human beings. Consider the bewildering host of confusing and contra-
dictory facts and propositions and ideas that present themselves every day to
any human being; some organization of these facts is necessary to provide some
order to potential chaos, and therefore conceptual networks of reality evolve
within a group of people for such organization. The mental constructs that
enable us thus to survive are a way of life that we call *culture*.

These constructs are infinitely diverse, and therefore cultures have widely
differing characteristics. Nevertheless, such patterns for living have, in the view
of some anthropologists, universal characteristics. George Peter Murdock (1961,
pp. 45–54) cites seven universals of cultural patterns of behavior: (1) They
originate in the human mind; (2) they facilitate human and environmental
interactions; (3) they satisfy basic human needs; (4) they are cumulative and
adjust to changes in external and internal conditions; (5) they tend to form
a consistent structure; (6) they are learned and shared by all the members of a
society; and (7) they are transmitted to new generations.

Culture thus establishes for each person a context of cognitive and affective behavior, a blueprint for personal and social existence. But we tend to
perceive reality strictly within the context of our own culture; this is a reality
that we have created, not necessarily objective reality, if indeed there is any
such thing as objectivity in its ultimate sense. "The meaningful universe in
which each human being exists is not a universal reality, but 'a category of
reality' consisting of selectively organized features considered significant by
the society in which he lives" (Condon, 1973, p.17). Although the opportunities
for world travel in the last quarter of this century are increasing, there is still
a tendency for us to believe that our own reality is the "correct" perception.
Perception, though, is always quite subjective. Perception involves the filtering
of information even before it is stored in memory, resulting in a selective form
of consciousness. What appears to you to be an accurate and objective perception of a person, a custom, an idea, is sometimes jaded or stilted in the view of
someone from another culture. Misunderstandings are therefore likely to occur
between members of different cultures. We will probably never be able to
answer the question of how perception came to be shaped in different ways by
different cultural groups; it is another chicken-or-egg question. But differences

are real, and we must learn to deal with them in any situation in which two cultures come into contact.

It is apparent that culture, as an ingrained set of behaviors and modes of perception, becomes highly important in the learning of a second language (L2). A language is a part of a culture and a culture is a part of a language; the two are intricately interwoven such that one cannot separate the two without losing the significance of either language or culture. The acquisition of a second language, except for specialized, instrumental acquisition (as may be the case, say, in "Indian" English), is also the acquisition of a second culture. Both linguists (see Lado, 1957) and anthropologists (see Burling, 1970) bear ample testimony to this observation.

The sections of this chapter attempt to capture some of the important aspects of the relationship between learning a second language and learning the cultural context of the second language. An examination of the notion of cultural stereotypes and attitudes will precede a discussion of what it means to "learn" another culture, followed by a section on the relationship among language, thought, and culture.

CULTURAL STEREOTYPES

Mark Twain gave us a delightfully biased view of other cultures and other languages in *The Innocents Abroad.* In reference to the French language, Twain comments that the French "always tangle up everything to that degree that when you start into a sentence you never know whether you are going to come out alive or not." In *A Tramp Abroad,* Twain notes that German is a most difficult language: "A gifted person ought to learn English (barring spelling and pronouncing) in 30 hours, French in 30 days, and German in 30 years." So he proposed to reform the German language, for "if it is to remain as it is, it ought to be gently and reverently set aside among the dead languages, for only the dead have time to learn it."

Twain, like all of us at times, has expressed caricatures of certain languages. Such caricatures are not unlike linguistic and cultural stereotypes. In the bias of our own culture-bound world view, we picture other cultures in an over-simplified manner, lumping cultural differences into exaggerated categories, and then we view every person in a culture as possessing corresponding stereotypical traits. Thus Americans are all rich, informal, materialistic, and overly friendly. Italians are passionate and demonstrative. The British are reserved, polite, thrifty, and drink tea. Germans are stubborn, industrious, methodical, and drink beer. Orientals are reserved, wise, cunning, and "inscrutable." François Lierres, writing in the Paris newsmagazine *Le Point,* gave some tongue-in-cheek advice to French people on how to get along with Americans: "They are the Vikings of the world economy, descending upon it in their jets as the Vikings once did in their *drakars.* They have money, technology, and nerve. . . . We would be wise to get acquainted with them." Upon which he offered some *do's* and *don't's*. Among the *do's:* Greet them, but after you have been introduced once, don't shake hands, merely emit a brief cluck of joy—"hi." Speak without emotion, with self-assurance, giving the impression you have a command of the subject even if you haven't. Check the collar of your jacket—nothing is uglier in the eyes of an American than dandruff. Radiate congeniality and show a good disposition—a big smile and a warm expression are essential. Learn how to play golf. Then, among the *don't's:* Don't tamper with your accent—Maurice Chevalier is well liked in America. And don't allow the slightest smell of perspiration to reach the offended nostrils of your American friends.

How do stereotypes form? Our cultural milieu shapes our world view—our *Weltanschauung*—in such a way that reality is thought to be objectively perceived through our own cultural pattern, and a differing perception is seen as either false or "strange" and is thus oversimplified. If people recognize and understand differing world views, they will usually adopt a positive and open-minded attitude toward cross-cultural differences. A closed-minded view of such differences often results in the maintenance of a *stereotype*—an oversimplification and blanket assumption. A stereotype is a category that singles out an individual as sharing assumed characteristics on the basis of his or her group membership. The stereotype may be accurate in depicting the "typical" member of a culture, but it is inaccurate for describing a particular person, simply because every person is a unique individual and not all of a person's behavioral characteristics can be accurately predicted on the basis of cultural norms.

Cross-cultural research has shown that there are indeed characteristics of culture that make one culture different from another. Condon (1973) concluded from cross-cultural research that American, French, and Hispanic world views are quite different in their concept of time and space. Americans tend to be dominated by a psychomotor view of time and space that is dynamic, diffuse, and nominalistic. French orientation is more cognitive with a static, centralized, and universalistic view. The Hispanic orientation is more affectively centered with a passive, relational, and intuitive world view. It is from these general but reasonably accurate descriptions that stereotypes emerge.

Are cultural stereotypes "bad"? Not necessarily, if a person recognizes positive effects of stereotyping. All human beings organize the environment by means of systematic and meaningful storage. Having developed one particular world view—one set of tools for storing experiences and for reacting to others in our culture—we place incongruous or different world views into categories for meaningful understanding. Since one person is not an integral part of another world view, that other world view is simplified. Sometimes these perceptions are accurate. To say that Americans think of distances in relatively broad categories (60 miles is an easy jaunt) and that the French view distances in narrower categories (60 miles, or 100 kilometers, is a considerable travel distance) is reasonably accurate. So the cautious accumulation of stereotyped images can help a person to understand another culture in general and the differences between that culture and his or her own.

But there are obvious negative connotations of stereotyping. One is the idea that all persons in a culture fit neatly into a group of rigid categories. Clearly not all Americans are rich, friendly, and materialistic, even though that may be a fairly accurate stereotype of an American in general. And to judge a single member of a culture by overall traits of the culture is both to prejudge and to misjudge that person. The most destructive aspect of stereotyping is that which is derogatory or falls short of valuing and prizing people from different cultures. Mark Twain's comments about the French and German languages, while written in a humorous vein and without any malice, could be interpreted by some to be insulting.

False stereotyping is another negative aspect of cultural stereotyping. Sometimes our oversimplified concepts of members of another culture are downright false. Americans sometimes think of Japanese as being unfriendly because of their cultural norms of respect and politeness. The false view that members of another culture are "dirty" or "smelly"—with verbal and non-verbal messages conveying that view—in fact usually stems merely from different customs of so-called cleanliness. Muriel Saville-Troike (1976) notes that "Middle-class whites may objectively note that the lower socioeconomic classes frequently lack proper bathing facilities or changes of clothing, but may be surprised to discover that a common stereotype blacks hold of whites is that they 'smell like dogs coming in out of the rain.' Asians have a similar stereotype of Caucasians" (p. 51).

Both learners and teachers of a second language need to understand cultural differences, to recognize openly that not everyone in the world is "just like me," that people are *not* all the same beneath the skin. There are real differences between groups and cultures. We can learn to perceive those differences, appreciate them, and above all to respect, value, and prize the personhood of every human being.

ATTITUDES

Stereotyping usually implies some type of *attitude* toward the culture or language in question. I recently happened upon an incredible example of a negative attitude stemming from a stereotype; the following passage is an excerpt from an item on "Chinese literature" in the *New Standard Encyclopedia* published in 1940:

> The Chinese Language is monosyllabic and uninflectional. . . . With a language so incapable of variation, a literature cannot be produced which possesses the qualities we look for and admire in literary works. Elegance, variety, beauty of imagery—these must all be lacking. A monotonous and wearisome language must give rise to a forced and formal literature lacking in originality and

interesting in its subject matter only. Moreover, a conservative people . . . ,
profoundly reverencing all that is old and formal, and hating innovation, must
leave the impress of its own character upon its literature. (Volume VI)

Fortunately, one would probably not find such views expressed in encyclo-
pedias today. Such biased attitudes are based on insufficient knowledge, misin-
formed stereotyping, and extreme ethnocentric thinking.

Attitudes, like all aspects of the development of cognition and affect in
human beings, develop early in childhood and are the result of parents' and
peers' attitudes, contact with people who are different in any number of ways,
and interacting affective factors in the human experience. These attitudes form
a part of one's perception of self, of others, and of the culture in which one
is living.

Gardner and Lambert's (1972) extensive studies were systematic attempts
to examine the effect of attitudes on language learning. After studying the
interrelationships of a number of different types of attitudes, they defined
motivation as a construct made up of certain attitudes. The most important
of these is group-specific, the attitude learners have toward the members of
the cultural group whose language they are learning. Thus, in Gardner and
Lambert's model, an English-speaking Canadian's positive attitude toward
French-Canadians—a desire to understand them and to empathize with them—
will lead to high integrative motivation to learn French. That attitude is a factor
of learners' attitudes toward their own native culture, their degree of ethnocentrism, and the extent to which they prefer their own language over the one
they are learning as a second language. Among the Canadian subjects Gardner
and Lambert distinguished between attitudes toward French-Canadians and
attitudes toward people from France.

John Oller and his colleagues (see Chihara & Oller, 1978; Oller, Baca &
Vigil, 1978; Oller, Hudson & Liu, 1977) conducted several large-scale studies
of the relationship between attitudes and language success. They looked at
the relationship of Chinese, Japanese, and Mexican students' achievement in
English to their attitudes toward self, the native language group, the target
language group, their reasons for learning English, and their reasons for travel-
ing to the United States. The researchers were able to identify a few meaningful
clusters of attitudinal variables that correlated positively with attained proficiency. Each of the three studies yielded slightly different conclusions, but for
the most part, positive attitudes toward self, the native language group, and the
target language group enhanced proficiency. There were mixed results on the
relative advantages and disadvantages of integrative and instrumental motivation. For example, in one study they found that better proficiency was attained
by students who did not want to stay in the United States permanently. All
of these attitude studies, however, now need to be viewed in the light of Oller's
(1981, 1982) more recent remarks, which cast some shadows of doubt on the
validity of any study that relies on self-report measures of affective variables.

It seems intuitively clear, nevertheless, that second language learners benefit from positive attitudes and that negative attitudes may lead to decreased motivation and in all likelihood, because of decreased input and interaction, to unsuccessful attainment of proficiency. Yet the teacher needs to be aware that everyone has both positive and negative attitudes. The negative attitudes *can* be changed, often by exposure to reality—for example, by encounters with actual persons from other cultures. Negative attitudes usually emerge either from false stereotyping or from undue ethnocentrism. The quotation from the encyclopedia might lead one to stereotype Chinese incorrectly and therefore to develop a negative attitude toward learning a language that reportedly lacks "elegance, variety, beauty of imagery." Teachers can aid in dispelling what are often myths about other cultures and replace those myths with a realistic understanding of the other culture as one that is different from one's own, yet to be respected and valued. Learners can thus move through the hierarchy of affectivity as described by Bloom and Krathwohl (1977), through awareness and responding, to valuing, and finally to an organized and systematic understanding and appreciation of the foreign culture.

ACCULTURATION

Second language learning in some respects involves the acquisition of a second identity. Guiora (1981) introduced the concept of language ego to capture the deeply seated affective nature of L2 learning, stressing the necessity for permeable ego boundaries in order to successfully overcome the barriers to L2 learning. Others have placed strong emphasis on affective characteristics of L2 learning because of the highly *social* context of language. Second language learning is often second culture learning. In order to understand just what second culture learning is, one needs to understand the nature of acculturation, culture shock, and social distance.

If a French person is primarily cognitive-oriented and an American is psychomotor-oriented and a Spanish speaker is affective-oriented, as claimed by Condon (1973), it is not difficult on this plane alone to understand the complexity of *acculturation*, the process of becoming adapted to a new culture. A reorientation of thinking and feeling, not to mention communication, is necessary. As Condon (1973) says:

> For instance, to a European or a South American, the overall impression created by American culture is that of a frantic, perpetual round of actions which leave practically no time for personal feeling and reflection. But, to an American, the reasonable and orderly tempo of French life conveys a sense of hopeless backwardness and ineffectuality; and the leisurely timelessness of Spanish activities represents an appalling waste of time and human potential. And, to a Spanish speaker, the methodical essence of planned change in France may

seem cold-blooded, just as much as his own proclivity toward spur-of-the-moment decisions may strike his French counterpart as recklessly irresponsible. (p. 25)

The process of acculturation runs even deeper when language is brought into the picture. To be sure, culture is a deeply ingrained part of the very fiber of our being, but language—the means for communication among members of a culture—is the most visible and available expression of that culture. And so a person's world view, self-identity, and systems of thinking, acting, feeling, and communicating can be disrupted by a change from one culture to another.

Culture shock is a common experience for a person learning a second language in a second culture. Culture shock refers to phenomena ranging from mild irritability to deep psychological panic and crisis. Culture shock is associated with feelings in the learner of estrangement, anger, hostility, indecision, frustration, unhappiness, sadness, loneliness, homesickness, and even physical illness. Persons undergoing culture shock view their new world out of resentment, and alternate between being angry at others for not understanding them and being filled with self-pity. Edward Hall (1959) describes a hypothetical example of an American living abroad for the first time:

> At first, things in the cities look pretty much alike. There are taxis, hotels with hot and cold running water, theatres, neon lights, even tall buildings with elevators and a few people who can speak English. But pretty soon the American discovers that underneath the familiar exterior there are vast differences. When someone says ''yes'' it often doesn't mean yes at all, and when people smile it doesn't always mean they are pleased. When the American visitor makes a helpful gesture he may be rebuffed; when he tries to be friendly nothing happens. People tell him that they will do things and don't. The longer he stays, the more enigmatic the new country looks. (p. 59)

This case of an American in Japan illustrates the point that initially persons in a foreign culture are comfortable and delighted with the ''exotic'' surroundings. As long as they can perceptually filter their surroundings and internalize the environment in their *own* world view, they feel at ease. As soon as this newness wears off, and the cognitive and affective contradictions of the foreign culture mount up, they become disoriented.

Peter Adler (1972) describes culture shock in more technical psychological terms:

> Culture shock, then, is thought to be a form of anxiety that results from the loss of commonly perceived and understood signs and symbols of social intercourse. The individual undergoing culture shock reflects his anxiety and nervousness with cultural differences through any number of defense mechanisms: repression, regression, isolation and rejection. These defensive attitudes speak, in behavioral terms, of a basic underlying insecurity which may encompass loneliness, anger, frustration and self-questioning of competence. With the familiar props, cues, and clues of cultural understanding removed, the individual

becomes disoriented, afraid of, and alienated from the things that he knows and understands. (p. 8)

The anthropologist George M. Foster (1962) described culture shock in extreme terms: "Culture shock is a mental illness, and as is true of much mental illness, the victim usually does not know he is afflicted. He finds that he is irritable, depressed, and probably annoyed by the lack of attention shown him" (p. 87).

It is feasible to think of culture shock as one of four successive stages of acculturation. The first stage is the period of excitement and euphoria over the newness of the surroundings. The second stage—culture shock—emerges as individuals feel the intrusion of more and more cultural differences into their own images of self and security. In this stage individuals rely on and seek out the support of their fellow countrymen in the second culture, taking solace in complaining about local customs and conditions, seeking escape from their predicament. The third stage is one of gradual, and at first tentative and vacillating, recovery. This stage is typified by what Larson and Smalley (1972) call *culture stress:* some problems of acculturation are solved while other problems continue for some time. But general progress is made, slowly but surely, as individuals begin to accept the differences in thinking and feeling that surround them, slowly becoming more empathic with other persons in the second culture. The fourth stage represents near or full recovery, either assimilation or adaptation, acceptance of the new culture and self-confidence in the "new" person that has developed in this culture.

Wallace Lambert's (1967) work on attitudes in L2 learning referred often to Durkheim's (1897) concept of *anomie*—feelings of social uncertainty or dissatisfaction—as a significant aspect of the relationship between language learning and attitude toward the foreign culture. As individuals begin to lose some of the ties of their native culture and adapt to the second culture, they experience feelings of chagrin or regret, mixed with the fearful anticipation of entering a new group. Anomie might be described as the first symptom of the third stage of acculturation, a feeling of homelessness, where one feels neither bound firmly to one's native culture nor fully adapted to the second culture. Lambert's research has supported the view that the strongest dose of anomie is experienced when linguistically a person begins to master the foreign language. In Lambert's (1967) study, for example, when English-speaking Canadians became so skilled in French that they began to think in French, and even dream in French, feelings of anomie were markedly high. For Lambert's subjects the interaction of anomie and increased skill in the language sometimes led persons to revert or to regress back to English—to seek out situations in which they could speak English. Such an urge corresponds to the tentativeness of the third stage of acculturation—periodic reversion to the escape mechanisms acquired in the stage of culture shock. Only until a person is well into the third stage do feelings of anomie decrease as the learner is over the hump in the transition from one culture to another.

In keeping with these bleak descriptions of culture shock, Mark Clarke (1976) likened L2 learning and second culture learning to *schizophrenia,* where "social encounters become inherently threatening, and defense mechanisms are employed to reduce the trauma" (p. 380). Clarke cited Gregory Bateson's (1972) description of the "double bind" that foreigners in a new culture experience:

1. The individual is involved in an intense relationship; that is, a relationship in which he feels it is vitally important that he discriminate accurately what sort of message is being communicated so that he may respond appropriately.
2. The individual is caught in a situation in which the other person in the relationship is expressing two orders of message and one of these denies the other.
3. The individual is unable to comment on the messages being expressed to correct his discrimination of what order of message to respond to, i.e., he cannot make a metacommunicative statement. (p. 208)

Clarke then goes on to note that virtually every encounter with people in a foreign culture is an "intense relationship" in which tremendous effort is expended to keep communication from breaking down. For example, "Getting a taxi driver to understand where you want to go; attempting to discover if he has indeed understood you, given that he says he has, but continues to drive in the wrong direction; and searching frantically all the while for the proper phrases to express yourself so that you don't appear stupid or patronizing; all of this combines to give a simple ride across town Kafkaesque proportions which cannot be easily put in perspective by the person who has suffered through them" (p. 380). That such behavior can be compared with schizophrenia is clear from Bateson's (1972) description of alternatives commonly adopted by a schizophrenic to defend himself:

1. He might . . . assume that behind every statement there is a concealed meaning which is detrimental to his welfare. . . . If he chooses this alternative, he will be continually searching for meanings behind what people say and behind chance occurrences in the environment, and he will be characteristically suspicious and defiant.
2. He might . . . tend to accept literally everything people say to him; when their tone or gesture or context contradicted what they said he might establish a pattern of laughing off these metacommunicative signals.
3. If he didn't become suspicious of metacommunicative messages or attempt to laugh them off, he might choose to ignore them. Then he would find it necessary to see and hear less and less of what went on around him, and do his utmost to avoid provoking a response in his environment. (p. 211)

The schizophrenic period of culture shock and of language learning is therefore indeed a crucial period during which time the learner will either sink or swim.

The description I have given of culture shock paints a rather severe picture of an unwitting and helpless victim of an illness, and an illness for which there is no clearcut cure. Peter Adler (1972) points out that culture shock, while surely possessing manifestations of crisis, can also be viewed more positively as a profound cross-cultural learning experience:

> a set of situations or circumstances involving intercultural communication in which the individual, as a result of the experiences, becomes aware of his own growth, learning and change. As a result of the culture shock process, the individual has gained a new perspective on himself, and has come to understand his own identity in terms significant to himself. The cross-cultural learning experience, additionally, takes place when the individual encounters a different culture and as a result (a) examines the degree to which he is influenced by his own culture, and (b) understands the culturally derived values, attitudes and outlooks of other people. (p. 14)

While certainly not every learner will find a cross-cultural experience to be totally positive, many do derive positive values from the experience, and for those for whom learning a second culture might otherwise become a negative experience, or an illness, teachers can help that experience to become one of increased cultural awareness and self-awareness for the learner. Stevick (1976) cautioned that learners can feel alienation in the process of learning a second language, alienation from people in their home culture, the target culture, and from themselves. In teaching an ''alien'' language we need to be sensitive to the fragility of students by using techniques that promote cultural under-standing. Numerous materials and techniques—readings, films, simulation games, role-plays, culture assimilators, ''culture capsules,'' and ''culture-grams''—are now available to teachers to assist them in the process of accultura-tion in the classroom (McGroarty & Galvan, 1985).

While these techniques and materials are valuable to us, no one would say that culture shock can be prevented with ''affective vaccinations.'' But teachers can play a therapeutic role in helping learners to move through stages of acculturation. If learners are aided in this process by sensitive and perceptive teachers, they can perhaps more smoothly pass through the second stage and into the third stage of culture learning, and thereby increase their chances for succeeding in both L2 learning and second culture learning.

It is exceedingly important that teachers allow learners to proceed into and through that second stage, through the anomie, and not to force a quick bypass of the second stage. We should not expect learners to deny the anger, the frustration, the helplessness and homelessness they feel. Those are real feelings and they need to be openly expressed. To smother those feelings may delay and actually prevent eventual movement into the third stage. A teacher can enable learners to understand the source of their anger and frustration, to express those feelings, and then gradually to emerge from those depths to a very powerful and personal form of learning.

SOCIAL DISTANCE

The concept of *social distance* has emerged as an affective construct to give explanatory power to the place of culture learning in L2 learning. Social distance refers to the cognitive and affective proximity of two cultures that come into contact within an individual. "Distance" is obviously used in an abstract sense, to denote dissimilarity between two cultures. On a very superficial level one might observe, for example, that Americans (people from the United States) are culturally similar to Canadians, while Americans and Chinese are, by comparison, relatively dissimilar. We could say that the social distance of the latter case exceeds the former.

John Schumann (1976) described social distance as consisting of the following parameters:

> In relation to the TL [target language] group, is the 2LL [second language learning] group politically, culturally, technically or economically dominant, non-dominant, or subordinate? Is the integration pattern of the 2LL group assimilation, acculturation, or preservation? What is the 2LL group's degree of enclosure? Is the 2LL group cohesive? What is the size of the 2LL group? Are the cultures of the two groups congruent? What are the attitudes of the two groups toward each other? What is the 2LL group's intended length of residence in the target language area? (p. 136)

Schumann used these factors (dominance, integration pattern, cohesiveness, congruence, attitude, and length of residence) to describe hypothetically "good" and "bad" language learning situations, and illustrated each situation with two actual cross-cultural contexts. Two hypothetical "bad" language learning situations were described:

1. One of the bad situations would be where the TL group views the 2LL group as dominant and the 2LL group views itself in the same way, where both groups desire preservation and high enclosure for the 2LL group, where the 2LL group is both cohesive and large, where the two cultures are not congruent, where the two groups hold negative attitudes toward each other, and where the 2LL group intends to remain in the TL area only for a short time.
2. The second bad situation has all the characteristics of the first except that in this case, the 2LL group would consider itself subordinate and would also be considered subordinate by the TL group. (p. 139)

The first situation is typical, according to Schumann, of Americans living in Riyadh, Saudi Arabia. The second situation is descriptive of Navajo Indians living in the southwestern part of the United States.

A "good" language learning situation, according to Schumann's model:

> would be one where the 2LL group is non-dominant in relation to the TL group, where both groups desire assimilation (or at least acculturation) for the 2LL

group, where low enclosure is the goal of both groups, where the two cultures are congruent, where the 2LL group is small and non-cohesive, where both groups have positive attitudes towards each other, and where the 2LL group intends to remain in the target language area for a long time. Under such conditions social distance would be minimal and acquisition of the target language would be enhanced. (p. 141)

Schumann cites as a specific example of a ''good'' language learning situation the case of American Jewish immigrants living in Israel.

Schumann's hypothesis is that the greater the social distance between two cultures, the greater the difficulty the learner will have in learning the second language, and conversely, the smaller the social distance (the greater the social solidarity between two cultures), the better will be the language learning situation.

PERCEIVED AND OPTIMAL SOCIAL DISTANCE

One of the difficulties in Schumann's hypothesis of social distance is the measurement of actual social distance. How can one determine *degrees* of social distance? By what means? And how would those means be quantifiable for comparison of relative distances? So far the construct has remained a rather subjectively defined phenomenon that, like empathy, self-esteem, and so many other psychological constructs, defies definition even though one can intuitively grasp the sense of what is meant.

William Acton (1979) proposed a solution to the dilemma. Instead of trying to measure *actual* social distance, he devised a measure of *perceived* social distance. His contention was that it is not particularly relevant what the actual distance is between cultures, since it is what learners perceive that form their own reality. We have already noted that human beings perceive the cultural environment through the filters and screens of their own world view and then act upon that perception, however biased it may be. According to Acton, when learners encounter a new culture, their acculturation process will be a factor of how they perceive their own culture in relation to the culture of the target language, and vice versa. For example, objectively there may be a relatively large distance between Americans and Saudi Arabians, but an American learning Arabic in Saudi Arabia might for a number of reasons perceive little distance, and in turn act on that perception.

By asking learners to respond to three dimensions of distance, Acton devised a measure of perceived social distance—the Professed Difference in Attitude Questionnaire (PDAQ)—which characterized the ''good'' or successful language learner (as measured by standard proficiency tests) with remarkable accuracy. Basically the PDAQ asked learners to quantify what they perceived to be the differences in attitude toward various concepts (''the automobile,'' ''divorce,'' ''socialism,'' ''policemen,'' for example) on three dimensions: (1) distance (or difference) between themselves and their countrymen in general; (2) distance between themselves and members of the target culture in general; and (3) distance between their countrymen and members of the target culture. By using a semantic differential technique, three distance scores were computed for each dimension. Acton found that in the case of learners of English who had been in the United States for four months, there is an *optimal* perceived social distance ratio (among the three scores) that typifies the "good" language learner. If learners perceived themselves as either too *close* to or too *distant* from either the target culture or the native culture, they fell into the category of "bad" language learners as measured by standard proficiency tests. The implication is that successful language learners see themselves as maintaining some distance between themselves and *both* cultures. Unfortunately, Acton's PDAQ did not *predict* success in language. However, this is no great surprise since we know of no adequate instrument to predict language success or to assess language aptitude. But what the PDAQ did was to describe empirically, in quantifiable terms, a relationship between social distance and L2 acquisition.

Acton's theory of optimal perceived social distance supports Lambert's (1967) contention that mastery of the second language takes place hand in hand with feelings of anomie or homelessness, where learners have moved away from their native culture but are still not completely assimilated or adjusted in the target culture. More importantly, Acton's model leads us closer to an understanding of culture shock and the relationship of acculturation to language learning by supplying an important piece to a puzzle. If you combine Acton's research with Lambert's, a rather interesting hypothesis emerges—namely, that mastery or skillful fluency in a second language (within the second culture) occurs somewhere at the beginning of the third—recovery—stage of accultura-tion. The implication of such a hypothesis is that mastery might not effectively occur before that stage or, even more likely, that learners might never be successful in their mastery of the language if they have proceeded beyond early Stage 3 without accomplishing that linguistic mastery. Stage 3 may provide not only the optimal *distance*, but the optimal cognitive and affective *tension* to produce the necessary *pressure* to acquire the language, yet pressure that is neither too over-whelming (such as that which may be typical of Stage 2 [culture shock]) nor too weak (which would be found in Stage 4, adaptation/assimilation). Language mastery at Stage 3, in turn, would appear to be an instrument for progressing psychologically through Stage 3 and finally into Stage 4.

According to my hypothesis (for further details, see Brown 1980), a learner who fails to master a second language in a second culture may for a host of reasons have failed to synchronize linguistic and cultural development. Learners who have achieved nonlinguistic means of coping in the foreign culture will pass through Stage 3 and into Stage 4 with an undue number of *fossilized* forms of language, never achieving mastery.[1] They have no reason to achieve

---

[1] Fossilized forms occur when L2 development is arrested. Common fossilized patterns in English are lack of article use (the, a, an) and third person singular -s (e.g., "He talk" instead of "He talks").

mastery since they have learned to cope without sophisticated knowledge of the language. They may have acquired a sufficient number of functions of a second language without acquiring the correct forms. What I have suggested in this *optimal distance* model might well be seen as a culturally based critical-period hypothesis, that is, a critical period that is independent of the age of the learner. While the optimal distance model applies more appropriately to adult learners, it could pertain to children, although less critically so. Because they have not built up years and years of a culture-bound world view (or view of themselves), children have fewer perceptive filters to readjust and, therefore, move through the stages of acculturation more quickly. They nevertheless move through the same four stages, and it is plausible to hypothesize that their recovery stages are also crucial periods of acquisition.

I am suggesting a hypothesis that of course needs further research and refinement. But previous research on sociocultural variables in language learning seems to bear out the hypothesis. Teachers could benefit from a careful assessment of the current cultural stages of learners with due attention to possible optimal periods for language mastery.

LANGUAGE, THOUGHT, AND CULTURE

No discussion about cultural variables in L2 acquisition is complete without some treatment of the relationship between language and thought. We saw in the case of L1 acquisition that cognitive development and linguistic development go hand in hand, each interacting with and shaping the other. It is commonly observed that the manner in which an idea or "fact" is stated affects the way we conceptualize the idea. Words shape our lives. The advertising world is a prime example of the use of language to shape, persuade, and dissuade. "Weasel words" tend to glorify very ordinary products into those that are "unsurpassed," "ultimate," "supercharged," and "the right choice." In the case of food that has been sapped of most of its nutrients by the manufacturing process, we are told that these products are now "enriched" and "fortified." A foreigner in the United States once remarked that in the United States there are no "small" eggs, only "medium," "large," "extra-large," and "jumbo." Euphemisms—or "telling it like it isn't"—abound in American culture where certain thoughts are taboo or certain words connote something less than desirable. We are persuaded by industry, for example, that "receiving waters" are the lakes or rivers into which industrial wastes are dumped and that "assimilative capacity" refers to how much of the waste you can dump into the river before it starts to show. Garbage men are "sanitation engineers"; toilets are "rest rooms"; slums are "substandard dwellings." Even a common word like "family" has for some social scientists been replaced by "a microcluster of structured role expectations."

Verbal labels can shape the way we store events for later recall. In a classic study, Carmichael, Hogan, and Walter (1932) found that when subjects were briefly exposed to figures like those in Figure 6.1 and later asked to reproduce them, the reproductions were influenced by the labels assigned to the figures.

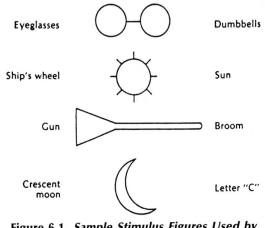

Eyeglasses   Dumbbells

Ship's wheel   Sun

Gun   Broom

Crescent   Letter "C"
moon

Figure 6.1. *Sample Stimulus Figures Used by Carmichael, Hogan, and Walter (1932)*

For example, the first drawing tended to be reproduced as something like this:

if subjects had seen the "eyeglasses" label, and on the other hand like this:

if they had seen the "dumbbells" label.

Words are not the only linguistic category affecting thought. The way a sentence is structured will affect nuances of meaning. Elizabeth Loftus (1976) discovered that subtle differences in the structure of questions can affect the answer a person gives. For example, upon viewing a film of an automobile accident subjects were asked questions like "Did you see *the* broken headlight?" in some cases, and in other cases "Did you see *a* broken headlight?" Questions using *the* tended to produce more false recognition of events. That is, the presence of the definite article led subjects to believe that there *was* a broken headlight, whether they saw it or not. Similar results were found for questions like "Did you see some people watching the accident?" versus "Did you see any people watching the accident?" or even for questions containing a presupposition: "How fast was the car going when it hit the stop sign?" (presupposing both the existence of a stop sign and that the car hit a stop sign, whether the subject actually saw it or not).

On the discourse level of language we are familiar with the persuasiveness of an emotional speech or a well-written novel. How often has a gifted orator swayed opinion and thought, or a powerful editorial moved one to action or change? These are common examples of the influence of language on our cognitive and affective organizations.

Culture is really an integral part of the interaction between language and thought. Cultural patterns, customs, and ways of life are expressed in language; culture-specific world views are reflected in language. Cultures have different ways of dividing the color spectrum, for example, illustrating differing world views on what color is and how to identify color. Gleason (1961) noted that the Shona of Rhodesia and the Bassa of Liberia have fewer color categories than speakers of European languages and they break up the spectrum at different points. Of course, the Shona or Bassa are able to perceive and describe other colors, in the same way that an English speaker might describe a "dark bluish green," but the labels that the language provides tend to shape the person's overall cognitive organization of color and to cause varying degrees of color discrimination. Eskimo tribes commonly have as many as seven different words for *snow* to distinguish among different types of snow (falling snow, snow on the ground, fluffy snow, wet snow, and so forth), while certain African cultures in the equatorial forests of Zaire have no word at all for snow.

But even more to the point than such geographically conditioned aspects of language are examples from the Hopi language (Whorf, 1956). Hopi does not use verbs in the same way that English does. For example, in English we might say "he is running," but in Hopi we would have to choose from a number of much more precise verbal ideas, depending upon the knowledge of the speaker and the validity of the statement. A different form of the verb expresses: "I know that he is running at this very moment," "I know that he is running at this moment even though I cannot see him," "I remember that I saw him running and I presume he is still running," or "I am told that he is running." Also, *duration* and *time* are expressed differently in Hopi. Time, for example, is not measured or wasted or saved in Hopi. Time is expressed in terms of events, sequences, and development. Plant a seed and it will grow; the span of time for growth is not important. It is the development of events— planting, germination, growth, blossoming, bearing fruit—that is important.

A tantalizing question emerges from such observations. Does language *reflect* a cultural world view, or does language actually *shape* the world view? Drawing on the ideas of Wilhelm von Humboldt (1767–1835), who claimed that language shaped a person's *Weltanschauung*, Edward Sapir and Benjamin Whorf proposed a hypothesis that has now been given several alternative labels: the *Sapir-Whorf hypothesis*, the *Whorfian hypothesis*, *linguistic relativity*, or *linguistic determinism*. Whorf (1956) sums up the hypothesis:

> The background linguistic system (in other words, the grammar) of each language is not merely a reproducing instrument for voicing ideas but rather is itself the shaper of ideas, the program and guide for the individual's mental

activity, for his analysis of impressions, for his synthesis of his mental stock in trade. Formulation of ideas is not an independent process, strictly rational in the old sense, but is part of a particular grammar and differs, from slightly to greatly, as between different grammars. We dissect nature along lines laid down by our native languages. The categories and types that we isolate from the world of phenomena we do not find there because they stare every observer in the face; on the contrary, the world is presented in a kaleidoscopic flux of impressions which has to be organized by our minds—and this means largely by the linguistic systems in our minds. We cut nature up, organize it into concepts, and ascribe significances as we do, largely because we are parties to an agreement to organize it in this way—an agreement that holds through our speech community and is codified in the patterns of our language. The agreement is, of course, an implicit and unstated one, but its terms are absolutely obligatory; we cannot talk at all except by subscribing to the organization and classification of data which the agreement decrees. (pp. 212–214)

Ronald Wardhaugh (1976) expresses the antithesis of the Whorfian hypothesis:

The most valid conclusion to all such studies is that it appears possible to talk about anything in any language provided the speaker is willing to use some degree of circumlocution. Some concepts are more ''codable,'' that is, easier to express, in some languages than in others. The speaker, of course, will not be aware of the circumlocution in the absence of familiarity with another language that uses a more succinct means of expression. Every natural language provides both a language for talking about every other language, that is, a metalanguage, and an entirely adequate apparatus for making any kinds of observations that need to be made about the world. If such is the case, every natural language must be an extremely rich system which readily allows its speakers to overcome any predispositions that exist. (p. 74)

The Whorfian hypothesis has unfortunately been misinterpreted by a number of linguists and other scholars. In one case, Guiora (1981) criticized Whorf's claim that the influence of language on behavior was ''undifferentiated, all pervasive, permanent and absolute'' (p. 177). Guiora called these claims ''extravagant.'' It would appear that it was Guiora's interpretation that was extravagant, for he put ideas into Whorf's writings that were never there. Clarke, Losoff, McCracken & Rood (1984), in a careful review of Whorf's writings, eloquently demonstrated that the Whorfian hypothesis was not nearly as monolithic or causal as some would interpret it to be. ''The 'extravagant claims' made in the name of linguistic relativity were not made by Whorf, and attributing to him simplistic views of linguistic determinism serves only to obscure the usefulness of his insights'' (p. 57).

The language-teaching profession today has actually attended to a more moderate view of the Whorfian hypothesis, if only because of the intuitive evidence of the *interaction* of language and culture. Aspects of language do indeed seem to provide us with cognitive mind sets. In English, the passive voice, our verb system, and numerous lexical items already referred to in this section all contribute to influencing our thinking. But we can also recognize that through both language and culture, some universal properties bind us all together in one world. The act of learning to *think* in another language may require a considerable degree of mastery of that language, but a second language learner does not have to learn to think, in general, all over again. As in every other human learning experience, the second language learner can make positive use of prior experiences to facilitate the process of learning by retaining that which is valid and valuable for second culture learning and L2 learning.

RECOMMENDED READINGS

There are a number of classic references in the field of cultural anthropology that can serve as excellent background material for this chapter. Hall (1959) and Hall (1966) are both excellent sources written for the layperson. Slightly more technical, but still a very readable source is Burling (1970), an introduction to the relationship between language and culture. Lado (1957) is dated, but if time permits it can give you an appreciation of a historical perspective in relating linguistics to culture, especially Chapters 1 and 6.

You can get some valuable insights from reading one or all of Oller's studies on attitudes (Oller, Hudson & Liu, 1977; Oller, Baca & Vigil, 1978; Chihara & Oller, 1978). Those articles provide a picture of the type of instrumentation that is used to measure attitudes and also give more technical information supporting their conclusions on the relationship between attitudes and language learning. Gardner and Lambert (1972) is also a good background resource for this chapter.

A most interesting trilogy of works can be found in Clarke (1976), Schumann (1976), and Acton (1979).

McGroarty and Galvan (1985) offer a concise summary of culture and L2 learning, including a summary of teaching techniques.

Ostrander and Schroeder's (1979) fascinating book on ''superlearning'' is written for the lay public. If read with a grain of salt, it can provide some stimulating ideas for language teaching.

FOLLOW-UP QUESTIONS AND ACTIVITIES

1. Think of everyday examples of the subjectivity of perceiving people and behavior through the eyes of your own cultural viewpoint. Refer to eating customs, daily work patterns, family life, marriage customs, politeness patterns, and the like. Does your own pattern somehow seem more reasonable or sensible than that of some other culture with which you are familiar?

2. Consider some of the cultures with which you are familiar and list various stereotypes of those cultures. Share your stereotypes with those of a class-mate or friend and compare your perceptions. How might those stereotypes *help* you to understand someone from another culture? How might they *hinder* your understanding?

3. Discuss sensitive cross-cultural differences (religious, political, social, or personal issues) with someone from another culture. Can you empathize with those differences? In your discussion, what attitudes were reflected toward your culture? What attitudes do you think you expressed toward the other culture?

4. Try to think of some area of your affective or cognitive self in which you feel some prejudice toward members of another culture or even a subculture within your own cultural group. What may be the deeply seated causes of this prejudice? Have you tried to overcome this prejudice? If so, how? What advice might you give to a person desiring to overcome a prejudice?

5. If you have ever lived in another country, can you now identify some of the stages of acculturation in your own experience? Describe your feelings. Did you move through all four stages? Did you reach assimilation? Or adaptation? Did you experience anomie?

6. Is Clarke pushing matters a little too far in likening culture shock to schizophrenia?

7. In your second language, find examples that support the contention that language (specific vocabulary items, perhaps) seems to shape the way the speaker of a language views the world. In what way does the Whorfian hypothesis present yet another chicken-or-egg issue?

7

The Stages of Ethnicity

JAMES A. BANKS *University of Washington*

EDITORS' INTRODUCTION

In multicultural teaching, an understanding of key conceptual issues and problems related to education, ethnicity, and cultural diversity is vital. In this chapter, James Banks discusses the complexity of ethnic identity. He describes several hypothesized stages that members of ethnic groups may experience in the development of ethnicity and considers the curricular implications for instruction at each stage. This chapter takes a different perspective from the other chapters in this section in that it focuses on designing multiethnic experiences for students in classrooms across the content areas. Although the guidelines are general, we as teachers in culturally diverse teaching settings may find them useful not only in instruction but also in developing a greater understanding of our own ethnic identity.

ETHNIC GROUPS ARE COMPLEX AND DYNAMIC

Many of our curriculum development and teacher education efforts are based on the assumption that ethnic groups are static and unchanging. However, ethnic groups are highly diverse, complex, and changing entities. Ethnic identity, like other ethnic characteristics, is also complex and changing among ethnic group members.

Effective educational programs should help students explore and clarify their own ethnic identities. To do this, such programs must recognize and reflect the complex ethnic identities and characteristics of the individual students in the classroom. Teachers should learn how to facilitate the identity quests among ethnic youths and help them become effective and able participants in the common civic and national culture.

Adapted from James A. Banks, "The Stages of Ethnicity: Implications for Curriculum Reform," in Multiethnic Education: Theory and Practice, *Second Edition. Copyright © 1988 by Allyn and Bacon. Used with permission.*

THE STAGES OF ETHNICITY: A TYPOLOGY

To reflect the myriad and emerging ethnic identities among teachers and ethnic youths, we must attempt to identify them and to describe their curricular and teaching implications. The description of a typology that attempts to outline the basic stages of the development of ethnicity among individual members of ethnic groups follows. The typology is a preliminary ideal-type construct in the Weberian sense and constitutes a set of hypotheses based on the existing and emerging theory and research and on the author's study of ethnic behavior.

This typology is presented to stimulate research and the development of concepts and theory related to ethnicity and ethnic groups. Another purpose of the typology is to suggest preliminary guidelines for teaching about ethnicity in the schools and colleges and for helping students and teachers to function effectively at increasingly higher stages of ethnicity. Ford (1979) developed an instrument to measure the first five of these six stages of ethnicity and administered it to a sample of classroom teachers. She concluded that her study demonstrated that teachers are spread into the five stages that I had hypothesized. The sixth stage of the typology was developed after the Ford study was completed.

Stage 1: Ethnic Psychological Captivity

During this stage the individual absorbs the negative ideologies and beliefs about his or her ethnic group that are institutionalized within the society. Consequently, he or she exemplifies ethnic self-rejection and low self-esteem. The individual is ashamed of his or her ethnic group and identity during this stage and may respond in a number of ways, including avoiding situations that bring contact with other ethnic groups or striving aggressively to become highly culturally assimilated. Conflict develops when the highly culturally assimilated psychologically captive ethnic is denied structural assimilation or total societal participation.

Individuals who are members of ethnic groups that have historically been victimized by cultural assaults, such as Polish Americans and Australian Aborigines, as well as members of highly visible and stigmatized ethnic groups, such as African Americans and Chinese Canadians, are likely to experience some form of ethnic psychological captivity. The more that an ethnic group is stigmatized and rejected by the mainstream society, the more likely are its members to experience some form of ethnic psychological captivity. Thus, individuals who are members of the mainstream ethnic group within a society are the least likely individuals to experience ethnic psychological captivity.

Stage 2: Ethnic Encapsulation

Stage 2 is characterized by ethnic encapsulation and ethnic exclusiveness, including voluntary separatism. The individual participates primarily within his or her own ethnic community and believes that his or her ethnic group is superior to other groups. Many individuals within Stage 2, such as many Anglo-Americans, have internalized the dominant societal myths about the superiority of their ethnic or racial group and the innate inferiority of other ethnic groups and races. Many individuals who are socialized within all-white suburban communities in the United States and who live highly ethnocentric and encapsulated lives can be described as Stage 2 individuals.

The chacteristics of Stage 2 are most extreme among individuals who suddenly begin to feel that their ethnic group and its way of life, especially its privileged and ascribed status, are being threatened by other racial and ethnic groups. This frequently happens when African Americans begin to move into all-white ethnic communities. Extreme forms of this stage are also manifested among individuals who have experienced ethnic psychological captivity (Stage 1) and who have recently discovered their ethnicity. This new ethnic consciousness is usually caused by an ethnic revitalization movement. This type of individual, like the individual who feels that the survival of his or her ethnic group is threatened, is likely to express intensely negative feelings toward outside ethnic and racial groups.

However, individuals who have experienced ethnic psychological captivity and who have newly discovered their ethnic consciousness tend to have highly ambivalent feelings toward their own ethnic group and try to confirm, for themselves, that they are proud of their ethnic heritage and culture. Consequently, strong and verbal rejection of outgroups usually takes place. Outgroups are regarded as enemies, racists, and, in extreme manifestations of this stage, are viewed as planning genocidal efforts to destroy their ethnic group. The individual's sense of ethnic peoplehood is escalated and highly exaggerated. The ethnic individual within this stage of ethnicity tends to reject strongly members of his or her ethnic group who are regarded as assimilationist oriented and liberal, who do not endorse the rhetoric of separatism, or who openly socialize with members of outside ethnic groups, especially with members of a different racial group.

The Stage 2 individual expects members of the ethnic group to show strong overt commitments to the liberation struggle of the group or to the protection of the group from outside and "foreign" groups. The individual often endorses a separatist ideology. Members of outside ethnic groups are likely to regard Stage 2 individuals as racists, bigots, or extremists. As this type of individual begins to question some of the basic assumptions of his or her culture and to experience less ambivalence and conflict about ethnic identity, and especially, as the rewards within the society become more fairly distributed among ethnic groups, he or she is likely to become less ethnocentric and ethnically encapsulated.

Stage 3: Ethnic Identity Clarification

At this stage the individual is able to clarify personal attitudes and ethnic identity, to reduce intrapsychic conflict, and to develop clarified positive attitudes toward his or her ethnic group. The individual learns self-acceptance, thus developing the characteristics needed to accept and respond more positively to outside ethnic groups. Self-acceptance is a requisite to accepting and responding positively to other people. During this stage, the individual is able to accept and understand both the positive and negative attributes of his or her ethnic group. The individual's pride in his or her ethnic group is not based on the hate or fear of outside groups. Ethnic pride is genuine rather than contrived. Individuals are more likely to experience this stage when they have attained a certain level of economic and psychological security and have been able to have positive experiences with members of other ethnic groups.

Stage 4: Biethnicity

The individual within this stage has a healthy sense of ethnic identity and the psychological characteristics and skills needed to participate successfully in his or her own ethnic culture as well as in another ethnic culture. The individual also has a strong desire to function effectively in two ethnic cultures. We can describe such an individual as *biethnic*. Levels of biethnicity vary greatly. Many African Americans, in order to attain social and economic mobility, learn to function effectively in Anglo-American culture during the formal working day. The private lives of these individuals, however, may be highly black and monocultural.

Non-white minorities in the United States are forced to become biethnic to some extent in order to experience social and economic mobility. However, members of mainstream groups, such as Anglo-Americans, can and often do live almost exclusive monocultural and highly ethnocentric lives.

Stage 5: Multiethnicity and Reflective Nationalism

The Stage 5 individual has clarified, reflective, and positive personal, ethnic, and national identifications; has positive attitudes toward other ethnic and racial groups; and is self-actualized. The individual is able to function, at least beyond superficial levels, within several ethnic cultures within his or her nation and to understand, appreciate, and share the values, symbols, and institutions of several ethnic cultures within the nation. Such multiethnic perspectives and feelings, I hypothesize, help the individual live a more enriched and fulfilling life and formulate creative and novel solutions to personal and public problems.

Individuals within this stage have a commitment to their ethnic group, an empathy and concern for other ethnic groups, and a strong but *reflective* commitment and allegiance to the nation state and its idealized values, such as human dignity and justice. Thus, such individuals have reflective and clarified ethnic and national identifications and are effective citizens in a democratic pluralistic nation. Stage 5 individuals realistically view the United States as the multiethnic nation that it is. They have cross-cultural competency within their own nation and commitment to the national ideals, creeds, and values of the nation-state.

The socialization that most individuals experience does not help them attain the attitudes, skills, and perspectives needed to function effectively within a variety of ethnic cultures and communities. Although many people participate in several ethnic cultures at superficial levels, such as eating ethnic foods and listening to ethnic music, few probably participate at more meaningful levels and learn to understand the values, symbols, and traditions of several ethnic cultures and are able to function within other ethnic cultures at meaningful levels.

Stage 6: Globalism and Global Competency

The individual within Stage 6 has clarified, reflective, and positive ethnic, national, and global identifications and the knowledge, skills, attitudes, and abilities needed to function within ethnic cultures within his or her own nation as well as within cultures outside his or her nation in other parts of the world. The Stage 6 individual has the ideal delicate balance of ethnic, national, and global identifications, commitments, literacy, and behaviors. This individual has internalized the universalistic ethical values and principles of humankind and has the skills, competencies, and commitment needed to take action within the world to actualize personal values and commitments.

CHARACTERISTICS OF THE STAGE OF ETHNICITY TYPOLOGY

This typology is an ideal-type construct (see Figure 7.1) and should be viewed as dynamic and multidimensional rather than as static and linear. The characteristics within the stages exist on a continuum. Thus, within Stage 1, individuals are more or less ethnically psychologically captive; some individuals are more ethnically psychologically captive than are others.

The division between the stages is blurred rather than sharp. Thus, a continuum also exists between as well as within the stages. The ethnically encapsulated individual (Stage 2) does not suddenly attain clarification and acceptance of his or her ethnic identity (Stage 3). This is a gradual and developmental process. Also, the stages should not be viewed as strictly sequential and linear. I am hypothesizing that some individuals may never experience a particular stage. However, I hypothesize that once an individual experiences a particular stage, he or she is likely to experience the stages above it sequentially and developmentally. I hypothesize, however, that individuals may experience the stages upward, downward, or in zigzag pattern. Under certain conditions, for example, the biethnic (Stage 4) individual may become multiethnic (Stage 5); under new conditions the same individual may become again biethnic (Stage 4), ethnically identified (Stage 3), and ethnically encapsulated (Stage 2).

Figure 7.1 illustrates the dynamic and multidimensional characteristics of the development of ethnicity among individuals. Note especially the arrowed lines that indicate that continua exist both horizontally and vertically.

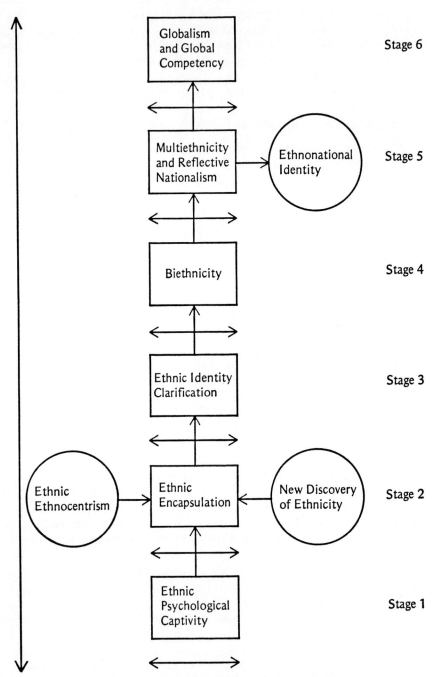

Figure 7.1. *The Stages of Ethnicity: A Typology*

PRELIMINARY CURRICULAR IMPLICATIONS OF THE STAGES OF ETHNICITY TYPOLOGY

The discussion that follows on the curricular implications of the stages of ethnicity typology should be viewed as a set of tentative hypotheses that merit testing by educators and researchers interested in ethnicity and education. The reader should keep foremost in mind the tentative and exploratory nature of the following discussion.

Curricular Implications of Ethnicity: Stage 1

The student within this stage of ethnicity can best benefit from monoethnic content and experiences that will help him or her to develop ethnic awareness and a heightened sense of ethnic consciousness. Such monoethnic experiences should be designed to help the individual come to grips with personal ethnic identity and to learn how his or her ethnic group has been victimized by the larger society and by institutions, such as the media and the schools, which reinforce and perpetuate dominant societal myths and ideologies. Courses in African American studies, Chinese Canadian studies, and Australian Aboriginal studies conceptualized in *interdisciplinary* and *humanistic* ways, and other monoethnic experiences can help the individual within this stage to raise his or her level of ethnic consciousness. Strategies that facilitate moral development and decision-making skills should be an integral part of the curriculum for the ethnically psychologically captive individual (Banks & Clegg, 1985).

Curricular Implications of Ethnicity: Stage 2

Individuals within this stage can best benefit from curricular experiences that accept and empathize with their ethnic identities and hostile feelings toward outside groups. The teacher should accept the individual's hostile feelings and help him or her express and clarify them. A strong affective curricular component that helps students clarify their negative ethnic and racial feelings should be a major part of the curriculum. The students should be helped to deal with their hostile feelings toward outside groups in constructive ways. The teacher should help the individual begin the process of attaining ethnic identity clarification during the later phases of this stage.

Curricular Implications of Ethnicity: Stage 3

Curricular experiences within this stage should be designed to reinforce the student's emerging ethnic identity and clarification. The student should be helped to attain a balanced perspective on his or her ethnic group. A true acceptance of one's ethnic group involves accepting its glories as well as its shortcomings. The individual in this stage of ethnicity can accept an objective view and analysis of his or her ethnic group, whereas an objective analysis is often very difficult for Stage 1 and Stage 2 individuals to accept. Value clarification and moral development techniques should be used to enhance the individual's emerging ethnic identity clarification.

Curricular Implications of Ethnicity: Stage 4

Curricular experiences should be designed to help the student master concepts and generalizations related to an ethnic group other than his or her own and to help the student view events and situations from the perspective of another ethnic group. The student should be helped to compare and contrast his or her own ethnic group with another ethnic group. Strategies should also be used to enhance the individual's moral development and ability to relate positively to his or her own ethnic group and to another ethnic group.

Curricular Implications of Ethnicity: Stage 5

The curriculum at this stage of ethnicity should be designed to help the student develop a global sense of ethnic literacy and to master concepts and generalizations about a wide range of ethnic groups. The student should also be helped to view events and situations from the perspectives of different ethnic groups within the United States as well as within other nations. The student should explore the problems and promises of living within a multiethnic cultural environment and discuss ways in which a multiethnic society may be nurtured and improved. Strategies such as moral dilemmas and case studies should be used to enable the individual to explore moral and value alternatives and to embrace values, such as human dignity and justice, that are needed to live in a multiethnic community and global world society.

Curricular Implications of Ethnicity: Stage 6

At this stage, the student his acquired three levels of identifications that are balanced: an ethnic, national, and global identification and related cross-cultural competencies. Since the typology presented in this chapter constitutes a continuum, the process of acquiring an effective balance of ethnic, national, and global identifications and related cross-cultural competencies is a continuous and ongoing *process*. Thus, the individual never totally attains the ideal ethnic, national, and global identifications and related cross-cultural skills for functioning within his or her ethnic group, nation, and world. Consequently, a major goal of the curriculum for the Stage 6 individual is to help the student function at Stage 6 more effectively.

Knowledge, skills, attitudes, and abilities that students need to function more effectively within their ethnic group, nation, and world should be emphasized when teaching students at Stage 6. This includes knowledge about the individual's own ethnic group, other ethnic groups, the national culture, and knowledge about other nations in the world. Valuing strategies, such as moral dilemmas and case studies that relate to the individual's ethnic group, nation, and world, should also be effectively used at this stage to enhance the student's developing sense of ethnic, national, and global identifications. A major goal of teaching students within this stage is to help them understand how to determine which particular allegiance—whether ethnic, national, or global—is most appropriate within a particular situation. Ethnic, national, and global attachments should be given different priorities within different situations and events. The student within Stage 6 should learn how to determine which identification is most appropriate for particular situations, settings, and events.

When planning multiethnic experiences for students and teachers, we need to consider the ethnic characteristics of individuals. In designing curricula related to ethnicity, we often assume that ethnic groups are monolithic and have rather homogeneous needs and characteristics. However, students differ greatly in their ethnic identities and characteristics just as they differ in their general cognitive and affective development (Kohlberg & Mayer, 1972; Piaget, 1968). Consequently, some attempt should be made to individualize experiences for students within the multiethnic curriculum.

FOLLOW-UP QUESTIONS AND ACTIVITIES

1. Read again the stages of ethnicity described by Banks and privately think about your own ethnicity as it relates to your current values and beliefs.

2. In your opinion, what are the attitudes, skills, behaviors, and other characteristics needed to become an effective teacher in a multicultural instructional setting? Share your ideas with your classmates.

3. Consider the curricular implications of ethnicity at Stages 1 through 3. Design activities that reinforce students' emerging ethnic identities. How might these activities help to gradually attain a balanced perspective of ethnic groups?

4. Share a cross-cultural experience, either positive or negative, with your classmates. What did you learn from the experience?

8

Sociocultural Contexts of Language Development: Implications for the Classroom

SHIRLEY BRICE HEATH   *Stanford University*

EDITORS' INTRODUCTION

In this chapter, Shirley Brice Heath provides a provocative account of the influences of the home and community on the development of literacy skills by language minority students. Offering an anthropological perspective, she views all language learning as cultural learning; thus, as teachers, we must be aware of the sociocultural contexts of language development. Heath's major premise is that there is a poor fit between the kinds of language uses to which many language minority students are exposed at home and in the community and mainstream uses of language characteristic of the school. To support this premise, Heath provides brief case studies of three language minority communities: Chinese American, Mexican American, and Indo-Chinese American. In probing the sociocultural influences of these communities on children's language development, she examines parental assumptions about their roles as teachers, genres of uses of oral and written language, and links between the home, community, and other institutions. She believes that success in school for language minority students depends ultimately on exposure and participation in the widest possible range of oral and written uses of language. As teachers, we are challenged to create classrooms that give language minority students such opportunities in all content areas and at all age levels.

This chapter considers how children from some of the different language minority groups learn ways of using language in their homes and communities. The two-part message of this chapter is simple:

From "Sociocultural Contexts of Language Development" by S. B. Heath, 1986, in Beyond Language: Social and Cultural Factors in Schooling Language Minority Students *(pp. 143–182). Sacramento, CA: Bilingual Education Office, California State Department of Education. Adapted by permission.*

1. For all children, academic success depends less on the specific language they know than on the ways of using language they know.
2. The school can promote academic and vocational success for all children, regardless of their first language (L1) background, by providing the greatest possible range of oral and written language uses.

This chapter opens by contrasting two views: first, the social science view that language learning is cultural learning and thus variable across sociocultural groups; and second, the educator's view that language learning for all children follows the single developmental model that schools reflect in the scope and sequence approach of the curriculum. Ethnographers have helped answer the question of how we can gain knowledge about how children of different language minority groups learn to use language and have identified three major factors in language socialization: (1) parents' assumptions about child rearing and their role in teaching language; (2) range of types of language uses available to children at home; and (3) extent of exposure young children have in their communities to a diversity of speakers, languages other than their own, and ways of using language that differ from those of their homes. The chapter closes with suggestions for ways in which increased knowledge about the sociocultural contexts of language learning in the homes and communities of language minority children can enable school personnel to promote and sustain children's facility in the widest possible range of using oral and written language to share and build knowledge.

LANGUAGE LEARNING AS CULTURAL LEARNING

Educators know relatively little about how children from families and communities of language minorities learn to use language. It is not possible to generalize to these children the findings of current research on children from middle-class English-speaking families which posit a unilinear developmental path of language acquisition for all children. Yet, behind language arts curricula in schools stands an image of a "natural" path of development in language learning for all children. Educators' ideas about the pace and direction of children's movement along this path have depended heavily on studies reporting the language learning of mainstream middle-class first-born children, either interacting at home with their parents or in a laboratory setting with props provided by researchers. These scholars have given much more attention to how children learn the structures of their language than to ways in which they learn to use language to accomplish social and cognitive goals (Fletcher & Garman, 1979; Snow & Ferguson, 1977). In recent years, however, the research of ethnographers in language minority communities has expanded our knowledge about not only the structures of different languages but also the variation of language socialization patterns and the wide range of language uses different communities enjoy and foster in their children's early learning.

The sociohistorical, religious, and socioeconomic contexts of families and communities of language minorities often differ markedly from the home life derived from mainstream patterns that dominate the thinking of school and human services personnel, such as social workers and guidance counselors. I argue in this chapter that all language learning is cultural learning: Children do not learn merely the building blocks of their mother tongue—its sounds, words, and order; they learn also how to use language to get what they want, protect themselves, express their wonderings and worries, and ask questions about the world. The learning of language takes place within the political, economic, social, ideological, religious, and aesthetic web of relationships of each community whose members see themselves as belonging to a particular culture. Thus, as children learn their language and how to use it, they learn also about the roles people, who are given certain names—such as mother, father, oldest, youngest—play in their lives. They learn how decisions are made and enforced, what to eat and drink, how to define and respect that which is called beautiful or good, and how to identify, ignore, avoid, or destroy that which is called ugly, bad, or worthless.

Cultural learning includes all the learning that enables a member of a family and community to behave appropriately within that group, which is critical to one's self-identification and whose approval is necessary for self-esteem. The family and others, such as friends who interact face-to-face on a regular basis with the child, form the primary social group from whom a sense of "who am I and what am I worth?" initially derive. It is little wonder, then, that care givers' ways of using language guide children's fundamental language performance for accomplishing successful and satisfying social interactions.

For some children, the primary group provides the major learning environment for the preschool years. For other children, contexts for learning language extend beyond the family and immediate community into secondary social groups or institutions, which provide educational, medical, religious, and recreational services. In these secondary networks, children find uses of language—oral and written—that differ to a greater or lesser degree from those that sustain their daily life at home. For some children, these settings provide occasions for using a language other than their home language and for using language to exchange information drawn from written sources or authorities who are not intimately known to the children. For all children, these settings introduce the kinds of encounters that permeate much of formal schooling and allow individuals to obtain the attention, services, and evaluations of the teacher (Merritt, 1982).

Most of these secondary social groups, such as churches, day care programs, and neighborhood libraries and recreational programs, expect to provide services in English and to use a certain number of written materials to support their daily operations. For example, registering a child for day care, obtaining a doctor's appointment, clearing a parking ticket, requesting pastoral visits, and signing out library books require oral communication that is linked in part to some written materials. Just as important as the written language of these documents are the uses of oral language that surround them and underlie the daily activities of these secondary social groups (Shuy, 1984). Successful handling of the forms, instructions, and informational texts these institutions give out requires certain ways of talking. Individuals must know, for example, how to ask for clarification about content and procedures and must understand that written texts are often given with the assumption that their readers will take certain actions after reading them. Furthermore, individuals have to learn to recognize the importance of some written materials as permanent records either to be kept by the owner or passed on to others.

The smooth operation of secondary institutions depends on certain uses of oral and written language; and the more frequent and intense the occasions for young children to participate in such institutions, the greater the chance that they will learn before they begin school many of the uses of language that help ensure academic success. Some of these uses are compatible with the habits of talk that surround written materials within primary institutions, such as the home; and certainly, some families practice uses of language that are highly compatible with some of those valued in school, work, and bureaucratic negotiations. However, an underlying premise of language use in secondary institutions is that the interactions of individuals are not based on intimate knowledge, extensive shared backgrounds, or the expectation of a long and sustained relationship. Thus, oral and written language must be depersonalized and able to stand somewhat autonomously from certain types of extensive knowledge that are not stated explicitly.

Some primary groups are open—admitting and even encouraging the involvement of secondary or outside social institutions in the child's early socialization; others open themselves less to outsiders and depend on familiar institutions and closely linked community members for almost all daily support. It is often the case that language minorities, particularly those in low or threatened socioeconomic positions, such as migrant workers, illegal aliens, or refugees, neither seek extensive interactions with outside or mainstream institutions nor create and manage analogous institutions within their own communities. Hence, the children from these groups often come to school bringing language uses and cultural beliefs supporting ways of using language that differ greatly from those of the classroom.

USING LANGUAGE IN SCHOOL

Strangely enough, although the common expectation is that the school prepares the young for life in the "real world" gradually and with compassion, school personnel rarely recognize that some fundamental notions that lie behind the language arts curriculum represent harsh demands for language minority children (Heath, 1982a). Not only is there the general expectation that all children will learn to speak English but also the assumption that they have internalized *before* they start to school the norms of language used in academic life. Schools expect all children to have learned how to do, at least, the following with language before they begin their formal schooling:

1. Use language to label and describe the objects, events, and information that nonintimates present them. The most common form of request for such labels and descriptions is the "known information" question, one for which the teacher already knows the answer ("Can anyone tell me today's date?" "What's the name of the main character in the story?").

2. Use language to recount or recast past events or information shared with or given by nonintimates in a predictable order and format. Teachers request such recountings by questions ("Where have we heard this term before?" "What happened the other day when someone didn't follow the rules for putting books away?") and shape answers by correcting facts and their ordering as the student offers the recount ("Did Ann really make her book from construction paper, or was it something else? Think hard for a minute." "But wait, tell us about what happened when we were leaving the playground; don't jump ahead so fast.").

3. Follow directions from oral and written sources without needing sustained personal reinforcement from adults or peers ("Let's get ready for lunch." "Turn to page 65.").

4. Use language to sustain and maintain the social interactions of the group. Individual or personal goals or desires are acceptable only so long as they do not disrupt the harmony and balanced working relations of other group members ("If you want to use the scissors, Jenny, ask Tammy politely.").

5. Use language to obtain information from nonintimates. Children should know how to request and to clarify information, and they should view such information as extending beyond the authority of a particular person or specific occasions to either general use or transfer to similar situations ("Why didn't you ask?" "Remember the other day when we worked a problem like this one on the board? If not, open your books, and find the example.").

6. Use language on appropriate occasions to account for one's unique experiences, to link these to generally known ideas or events, and to create new information or to integrate ideas in innovative ways ("My uncle has geese on his farm; I could bring some feathers" —said in response to teacher's query in a science lesson about why goose down repels water and provides such a warm covering; "Somebody once gave my mom an African violet; now they're all over the house. Is that propagation?''—said in response to introduction of biology unit on plant propagation.).

Those students who achieve academic success either bring to school all of these language uses, and the cultural norms that lie behind them, or they learn quickly to intuit the rules of these language uses for both speaking and writing. Those who ultimately succeed in the highest academic lanes acquire or bring with them the facility for using oral and written language for multiple purposes and in varying styles; those who would go on to higher education must learn to use not only English but at least one other language as well in their academic pursuits. (For a full review of the studies of classroom discourse from which these genres were derived, see Cazden [1985]; since the seminal work of Sinclair & Coulthard [1975], and Mehan [1979], studies have consistently demonstrated the narrow range of language uses rewarded in classrooms. This narrowness is especially evident for producing written language; see Applebee [1981] and Langer [1986]; see Heath [1985a] for discussions of the relation of genre uses to academic success.)

School personnel depend on these uses of language because they believe they promote learning and ensure harmonious classroom interactions. In general, schools expect those who do not come to school fluent in these language uses to learn them in the developmental order given above; for example, learning to label and describe is expected before learning to use language to seek out or test information, and certainly before offering orally or in writing integrated or innovative ideas. Moreover, as students move higher in grade levels or advance in the study of a particular subject, they find more opportunities for using language to obtain, test, and create information than they had in their early years of schooling or in their introductions to subject matter. The curricula of both primary and secondary levels of schooling are based on the assumption that both the range of occasions for these language uses and their sequencing, in oral and written forms, represent a ''normal'' pattern of development for all children.

A SINGLE DEVELOPMENTAL MODEL

The primary social groups of working-class English-speaking groups and language minorities may not share the school's expectations about when, where, and how children learn language. (This chapter will discuss only language minority groups; however, native English-speaking groups may, as a result of historical, racial, or class factors, as well as separate cultural identities, develop sociocultural patterns that differ from those of the mainstream and the school. See Heath [1983b] for a full-length discussion of the widely different language socialization patterns of African American and white working-class communities in the Piedmont Carolinas.) The school expects children to follow a single developmental model in acquiring uses of language. Yet, educators' developmental models have, in large part, come from psychologists or linguists who have either studied their own children or children of

similar primary social group membership. Much of the research of those who
have described language acquisition and posited universals has been carried
out with what we term *mainstream children* whose families are school-oriented,
nuclear, and open to numerous types of involvement with secondary social
groups such as Boy Scouts, Sunday school, camps, swimming clubs, and
nursery schools. These mainstream homes offer toys and books bought and
used by caregivers, usually parents, with young children. Parents surround
their children with a future orientation and encourage the development of a
self-image, which is reinforced as the child grows older by fellow members
of secondary social groups, such as Scouts, athletic coaches and team members,
and fellow summer campers. Fundamental to developmental models is the
expectation that children have experience in such future-oriented groups both
before and during the school years and that they absorb norms for listening,
following rules, asking clarification questions, and expecting adults to lead them
in their activities (Heath, 1983b). Developmental models assume a linear progression for learning in which earlier stages will not normally be repeated,
and behaviors characteristic of later stages will not precede or appear in the
place of those behaviors judged as simpler or more fundamental than others.

Those scholars who argue against a single developmental model and set
learning in sociocultural contexts admit a universal base of potential for all
neurologically normal human beings. However, they argue that an individual's
potential will be played out in different patterns in accordance with factors in the
language socialization of an individual's primary social group (Leiderman,
Tulkin & Rosenfeld, 1977; Schwartz, 1976; Wagner & Stevenson, 1982). Interactions with members of the primary social group; the extent of involvement
outside this group; the number and types of toys, books, and other objects
especially designed for children in the home; and expectations of appropriate
roles for children will heavily influence the order and combination of language
skills and uses the child learns (Schieffelin & Ochs, 1986).

Certain aspects of the grammar of the native tongue may even condition
certain perceptual or meaning categories children create for themselves. For
example, children whose first language contains morphemes that mark objects
as long, flat, rigid, or flexible, will choose shapes over color before children
whose first language does not contain morphemes marking such refined
categories of shape. However, if a language group whose native tongue did
not mark such categories were to train their children to attend to shape before
color, their children could learn to select out and name such properties. We
must bear in mind that the cultural learning of each primary social group is
only a relatively small and arbitrary selection of the possible sets of behaviors
(including ways in which language is used) of which the human infant is
capable. Similarly, developmental models endorsed by schools represent an
arbitrary and limited set of choices that can match the choices made by primary
social groups to greater and lesser extents. For many language and culture
groups, there is little fit between the kinds of language uses chosen by the
school and those developed in the family and community.

ETHNOGRAPHY AND THE STUDY
OF LANGUAGE DEVELOPMENT

Applied anthropologists often use information gathered through ethnographies —long-term studies of the daily habits of a particular social group in which researchers both observe and participate in the lives of those they are studying. These ethnographic studies can be used to help national or regional institutions that are planning social change for such groups. The goal behind the sharing of ethnographic information with social planners is to adjust plans for social change to local conditions, expectations, and cultural habits, so that change can occur with as little disruption as possible to the daily habits of the group (see Díaz, Moll & Mehan, 1986).

There are several dangers in the localized work that social scientists such as ethnographers do; the greatest is the overgeneralization of their work. The public at large uses inclusive labels for groups of people: Chicanos, Native Americans, Indo-Chinese, Asians, African Americans, Hispanics, and so on. Little attention is given to historically or socially accurate definitions of such terms, or to the fact that members of some social groups do not agree on names for themselves (Lampe, 1984 on Mexican Americans). The report of a study on one group of recently arrived migrants from Mexico is overgeneralized to all those of Mexican origin, regardless of their period of residence within the United States or of their sense of self-identification. A research finding reported for one group of African Americans is erroneously extended to all African Americans. A newspaper account of the academic prowess or gang organization of one Asian group is overextended to all who even ''look like Asians.''

Human beings have an overwhelming tendency to generalize information about social groups other than their own; stereotypes, ethnic jokes, racism, national pride, and denigrations of the language of others are all forms of this kind of generalization. Every social group is ethnocentric—and ''linguacentric''—viewing its own ways of behaving and talking as better than all others and as appropriate for establishing the standards by which all others will be judged.

It is important, therefore, to recognize that patterns reported for one group of African Americans of one neighborhood of Spanish speakers or one Chinese American community may not occur in other communities that may, on the surface, seem to be similar. Historical background, socioeconomic class, regional location, religion membership, and the extent of racial prejudice a group encounters are only some of the major influences that lead to different patterns of behavior and language use for groups speaking the same language or coming from the same national origin. The school and many other institutions within the United States have the goal of changing people's values, skills, and knowledge bases. Hence, teachers, social welfare agents, policemen, doctors, and ministers overlook group differences and urge people to change in the direction of the majority or the mainstream. The question is, then, ''How might information from local communities, which may be generalized only with caution to similar communities, be used by the school and other institutions of social change?'' (We will return to this question again after discussion of language development in three language minority groups.)

FIRST- AND SECOND-LANGUAGE DEVELOPMENT IN A COMMUNITY PERSPECTIVE

The immediate primary social group—the family and intimate friends—judge a speaker's L1 competence and may also facilitate second language (L2) competence. For example, if a primary social group uses Spanish as the language of everyday interactions, family members and friends will judge young children as linguistically competent on the basis of skills exhibited in Spanish. If, by the age when other children are talking clearly and transmitting content accurately, an individual child is still not communicating needs and desires effectively, community members will assess the child as linguistically incompetent. Similarly, if the child uses language in ways that are inappropriate within certain situations of that cultural group—picks up swear words and insults and flings these at adults, for instance—parents and other caregivers will assess the child as socially incompetent.

The primary social group can often also facilitate L2 competence. In an environment in which the learning of English is seen as part of the skills the language minority child will need, adults may provide models and occasions for exposure to English. The distribution of English-speaking models may vary widely across language minority communities and families (see Sawyer [1976] and Laosa [1980] for discussion of these varieties for Spanish-speaking families). In some households, adults may, in the desire to have their children learn English, speak only English to the children, though the adults' knowledge of English may not be such that they can handle the language for a wide variety of topics or occasions. In other families, the parent who is more proficient in English than the other may choose to speak only English at home, while the other parent speaks a minority language. In still other cases, while the parents retain the minority language, the older children who have learned to play games, exchange taunts, and talk about school and their social concerns in English may speak English among themselves and their native tongue to their elders.

Children growing up in communities in which such models are available within the family may have few occasions for hearing English spoken by intimates for a wide variety of purposes and in a range of styles. Their knowledge of the uses of English may then be said to be ''limited,'' or ''limited English proficient'' (LEP). For example, they may hear enough English to gain only a receptive knowledge and to understand what is being said. Later, they may develop a productive knowledge of English, but the extent of their productive knowledge will depend on the degree to which they have been exposed to models who use English for a full range of uses. If they hear English used in limited functions, such as in play or for talk on only some topics by a few models in their primary group, they are likely first to learn set phrases or chunks of language, such as greetings or the language of play (''time out,'' etc.), and only later to manipulate the components of the language system productively (Wong-Fillmore, 1976). In particular, the range of uses of English associated with written materials, or the exchange of information not directly related to daily interactions, is likely to be narrower than that found in families using English for multiple purposes in writing and speaking.

Individuals need not be the only direct channel for the introduction of English in language minority communities. Institutions, such as the church, health clinic, library, Scout groups, or nursery schools, may create situations in which English speakers interact with non-English speakers. If the language minority community is not large enough to support its own grocery stores, small shops, and services such as laundries, adults must leave the community and negotiate with English speakers to maintain their daily home life. Pre-schoolers who accompany parents on these excursions outside their community learn English from these exchanges, though initially a receptive knowledge only. Later, when they are old enough to go for errands on their own, they must have productive skills or recruit someone who does. Perhaps as important as these occasions for hearing English is the fact that language minority speakers come to know directly (rather than simply through the media) that there is a range of occupations in which English speakers work. There are English-speaking shopkeepers, grocery clerks, and postal clerks, just as there are English speakers in what are often more threatening occupations—such as medicine, law enforcement, and schooling.

Later, school success need not depend on preschool exposure to English; the child's exposure to and participation in the widest possible range of oral and written uses of any language is more critical than the particular language of this exposure and participation. Children who live in communities large enough to support their own shops and a range of job types in a language other than English can provide direct models of a wide range of language uses for children. The language of negotiation in the corner laundry, community health clinic, church nursery school, and legal aid office differs in structure, vocabulary, and intent from that generally used in the home. The greater the opportunities for experiencing language uses across a variety of contexts, the greater the language repertoire the children of the language minority community will learn. To the extent that this repertoire includes uses of language similar to those of schools, workplaces, and bureaucratic agencies, children will have in place knowledge that will facilitate their learning these functions in English when they get to school. All occasions that demand explanation of facts and assumptions not shared by others provide practice in the kind of decontextualized impersonal language that the school and other mainstream institutions value. For instance, a child who listens to a bank teller tell his mother the rules for opening a savings account learns something about how to present information to someone who does not share it.

But what of events and occasions for language learning in the homes of language minority communities? Let us become more specific and consider some of the work that is available on the primary social groups in such communities. Because full ethnographies of communication in language minority communities in the United States are very rare, we must draw from research by psychologists sensitive to cultural differences, general anthropological and historical accounts, and ethnographic research now in progress, as well as interviews with spokespersons for some of these language groups. For communities of Chinese Americans, Mexican Americans, and Indo-Chinese Americans, we will consider: (1) parental assumptions about their role as teacher, (2) genres of uses of oral and written language, and (3) links between the home and community and outside institutions. Researchers now see these as the major sociocultural influences on children's language development.

Parental Assumptions

Parents can relate to their children in many different ways, and some communities promote certain relationships over others. Some parents may believe they are responsible not only for nurturing their children but also for training them and acting as their primary teachers. In this view, the responsibility for the child's development rests with the parent as an active force in the child's training. Yet another parental view is one that sees the child as having the greatest active role in his or her development; self-development is expected so long as parents provide basic nurturing and caregiving for the very young. Yet another view is that which emphasizes communal responsibility for the young. Infants belong to their families as well as their communities, and child rearing is too precious a task to be given over completely to two individuals, the physical parents. Thus, the social, moral, and religious development of the child rests with the community; parents provide basic needs and reinforce the communal values in the home. Other variants of parental assumptions of responsibility depend on the family structure—extended or nuclear, the segregation of tasks according to age or sex, and the presence of dysfunctional influences, such as alcoholism, drug abuse, and severe poverty. Fundamental in examining cross-cultural patterns of language socialization, however, is the acknowledgment that parents can and do play widely varying roles in their children's language learning.

Chinese American Families

Within those Chinese American families for which we have data derived from historical accounts, interviews, or ethnographies, parental roles are closely linked with communal membership and values. Historical studies of traditional Chinese family life reinforce this view and document the long-standing esteem for age, authority, perfection, restraint, and practical achievements (Hsu, 1949). (For a comparison of the mainstream ''American'' family and Chinese family norms, see Hsu, [1983]; and Ogbu & Matute-Bianchi, 1986). Every individual in the Chinese American family is expected to fulfill his or her role, regardless of personal characteristics. The family and community have a strong commitment to maintaining role relations and hierarchical status categories; rights and duties are unequally distributed because individuals are expected to conform to particular role and status duties. Role behaviors, along sex and age lines especially, are predictable because members of the community have a high degree of consensus and reinforce required behaviors through rituals and other established systems of interaction, such as family business parties (Cheng, 1948; Hsu, 1955; Ogbu & Matute-Bianchi, 1986; Stover, 1962).

Children are expected to learn to acknowledge these guiding mandates for behavior and to assume responsibilities according to their age and sex. Moreover, they are expected to play roles and perform duties independently of their personal feelings or goals. Parents see themselves as primary agents in directing children to assume in appropriate fashion the roles that the community expects of boys and girls, and later young men and women. Children must defer to adults, who determine what their children can do and tell them when they should do it. Children are encouraged to model themselves after authorities, to listen to authorities and watch what they do, and finally to practice again and again to achieve perfection. Learning is centered on the situation rather than the individual, because the individual must center on the situation in order to adjust to both the familiar environment and new circumstances. The attention to role autonomy and to situation rather than self as individual encourages mutual adaptation and dependence among those sharing a situation (Hu, 1960; Mead, 1951; Stover, 1962).

In conversational exchanges, parents control topics, length of time for talk by children, and the direction of the conversation. Parents initiate conversation with children, ask them factual questions, talk about steps they are following as they go about tasks, and monitor their children's talk and activities through verbal correction, explication, and evaluation. (Compare Hu [1944] and Liu [1959] with Stover [1962]. The latter study is based on participant observations of families in the United States and show strong continuities in verbal and other face-to-face behaviors with forms described in earlier literature.)

Parents have the goal of providing the very young with a secure environment that meets physical and emotional needs. They monitor their children's behavior with attention and follow up by punishment or praise to reinforce children's behaviors regarded as acceptable and proper for children of a particular age. Parents and other family members provide children with special toys and books, expect them to take care of these items, to learn to use them appropriately, and to read to learn. The extent of reinforcement of school norms and the provision at home of books and other items that support school activities vary along class lines. However, families across classes see their role as complementing that of the school; and they tell their children to listen to the teacher, to obey, and to recognize that practicing habits rewarded by the school will help ensure their future job opportunities. Particularly in middle- or upper-class families, specific practical skills at school—such as writing, reading, mathematics, and science—exceed in important areas of study, which they may regard as having no value for occupational or personal goals of the future. Within the family and the community, however, these same parents may emphasize aesthetic and historical skills and knowledge, as well as perfection in the practice of more mundane activities. In short, Chinese American parents see themselves as active agents in their children's language learning; and it is not at all unusual for them to expect their children to continue speaking Chinese along with English because of the practical values of both languages and the communal identification values of Chinese. Children who leave aside their native tongue as they grow older may also feel they have to leave behind strong identity linkage to the roots of their community.[1]

Mexican American Families

We have laid out reasons why generalizations across communities, regions, and historical periods for any language minority often bear little resemblance to specific actual realities. This warning about overgeneralization applies especially in the 1980s to Hispanic populations—the fastest growing and perhaps most diverse language minority group in the United States. Descriptions of the number and variety of Hispanics in the United States abound, and there is growing public recognition of the variation among Hispanics (Ford Foundation, 1984) and their diverse attitudes, and approaches toward acculturation or assimilation (Montgomery & Orozco, 1984). Scholarly research must acknowledge this variability and admit that far too many studies still report information about only impoverished or lower-class Hispanics, regional representatives of certain

---

[1] Discussion of language socialization in the homes of Chinese American and Mexican American children in this chapter have benefited greatly from research-in-progress and unpublished research carried out by students at both the University of California, Berkeley, and Stanford. All errors of fact and interpretation remain, of course, my own. Of particular help has been the research of Lucinda Alvarez, who has studied two bilingual preschoolers of working-class families at home and at school. Her research (1986) documents the kinds of speech events available to children and the nature of the language uses of their parents who migrated to the United States from rural Mexico. Davida Desmond, Ann Eisenberg (1982), Eli Pardo (1984), and Cynthia Prince have taken part in discussions of the materials presented here on Mexican Americans and provided complementary and substantiating data. Olga Vasquez and Yolanda de la Cruz, Mexican American teachers of bilingual children, have read portions of this chapter to assess accuracy and relevance. Christinia Cheung has provided substantial data on the language learning environments of mainstream and working-class Chinese American families. Genevieve Lau, a Chinese American teacher and school administrator, has not only provided data but has also assessed the chapter's account of Chinese American families and their children. Within the next few years, the publications of research currently underway by these and other scholars will, no doubt, both alter and greatly augment these beginning efforts to describe the sociocultural foundations of language development among the language minorities of California.

groups, or Hispanics of a certain national origin, drawing broad, sweeping conclusions about Hispanics in general. (For a critique of current research, see Peñalosa [1975] and Heath [1985c].)

The discussion following here focuses only on communities of those Mexican American families of relatively recent (within the past two decades) arrival in the United States. These families, though comparatively more economically stable in the United States than they were in Mexico, are lower- or working-class and may not have access to regular routes to upward socioeconomic mobility and occupational choice. Many are confined to work in service jobs (hospitals, hotels, restaurants, and large office buildings), factory work in the garment and electronics industries, and agribusiness. (See Chavez [1984], Connor [1986], and Heath [1985c] for discussions of patterns of identification, occupational choice, and movement out of the migrant stream for Mexican Americans, as well as comparisons between the patterns of choice for recent Mexican migrants to the United States and earlier waves of immigrants from Mexico.)

Among families of recent migrants from Mexico, parents have been able, in their years before migration, to depend on extended family members to share responsibility for child rearing; circumstances after migration to the United States often alter these family patterns somewhat. The ideal remains, however, that parents, especially mothers, have primary caregiving responsibility while children are young; but the entire extended family accepts the child as a member at birth, and parents may therefore expect other family members to share some responsibilities for childrearing (Laosa, 1984). Seasonal rituals that accompany baptism, choice of godparents, confirmation, and reaching the age of fifteen reinforce the membership of any child in the extended family, which includes not only kin but also close family friends.

Parents model behaviors their children are to learn, and children observe and repeat actions others have demonstrated. Adults do not usually accompany their actions with step-by-step directions, nor do they monitor children's actions by giving sequential orders or asking children to verbalize what they are doing as they work. They seldom ask questions that require children to repeat facts, rehearse the sequence of events, or foretell what they will do. Children ask questions of parents primarily when they seek information relevant to a task or decision at hand. Parents and older siblings tell young children what to do, and as they carry out tasks, adults reinforce good behaviors by evaluating them as "good" or "right" or denounce inappropriate responses as "bad" or "wrong." Older children are expected to entertain younger ones and see that when they have needs, the mother or some other maternal figure is informed.

Interpersonal behaviors in these families can perhaps be characterized as divided into a public world when members from outside the family are present, and a private world reserved only for family members and occasionally for close and trusted friends. The social and linguistic content of interactions in each of these worlds appears to be quite different (Sanchez, 1984). Though researchers in such homes and communities can report only language behaviors—such as those noted—that may be more public than private, they do note that older children talk about times such as bedtime, when parents come into their rooms to bless them and talk, or when young children climb into bed with their parents for periods of quiet accounts or eventcasts. These occasions are surely times when children tell their parents about things they have learned to do, places they have been, victories and frightening experiences they have had, and plans they have for tomorrow, next weekend, or next summer. Because of strong norms of politeness and respect that may cause these families to appear to be authoritative or ''neutral'' with respect to their children's language contributions in the presence of outsiders, researchers must be alert for sources of information that suggest that there are some extended occasions for children to report their feelings, knowledge, and plans to adults (Alvarez, 1986; Delgado-Gaitan, 1982; Pardo, 1984).

It is impossible to generalize about the views of either Mexican American families or communities regarding whether or not their children should keep their Spanish and learn English. Some families, who have come from Mexico to find temporary work that will enable them to return to Mexico with cash for purchasing their own land or paying off debts, may not see English as a definite part of the future of their children. Others who plan to remain in the United States, with frequent visits to Mexico, assume their children will keep their Spanish, but recognize that they must learn enough English to meet school expectations and to have a wider choice of job opportunities. Still other families link Spanish symbolically and instrumentally to their self-identification and daily survival, and they promote Spanish, while encouraging their children to learn English as well. Within families who have older children, both Spanish and English may be used on a daily basis—parents and younger children speaking Spanish, and older children using English among themselves but Spanish with their parents and younger siblings.

The reasons and patterns for retaining Spanish and acquiring English are infinitely varied, and their attitudes toward one or the other language or the use of both not only are different across communities of different regional origin, occupational level, and location after migration, but also can be highly unstable. Return migration, the constant supply of new migrants, and the existence of models of Spanish and English bilinguals in the mainstream institutions of education, law, and medicine change attitudes rapidly.

Recent Mexican American arrivals usually choose to settle in communities where there are either family members or close friends who share responsibilities for caregiving. Younger children are almost never alone with only one adult; they are surrounded by adults and children. Adults intervene in children's play when there are major disruptions, to praise or scold certain behaviors or language uses, and to tease children. Teasing requests from adults usually ask children about the personal names or qualities of those around them (e.g., "You're my little mama, aren't you?"). Nicknames, songs, and rhymes affectionately call attention to particular characteristics of little girls and boys and are often subtle invitations from adults for play with young children (Schieffelin and Ochs, 1986). Playful exchanges are accompanied with strong positive reinforcement by the teaser and by the audience. Young children grow up in a rich verbal environment filled with talk from a wide variety of speakers, and though relatively little of this talk is directed specifically to preschoolers, they hear language from old and young used for many functions; and they are pulled into adult talk through directives, correctives, teasing language play, and occasions when adults want to teach them to do something. Visits to relatives and participation in festivals and celebrations of holidays bring these children into contact with family and friends from distant communities.

Before children become adolescents, the dictum that children are not equal conversational partners with adults is played out in daily interactions as well as special social occasions. To the extent possible, adults talk together, and children and young people talk to each other; gatherings rarely include children and adults talking together. Adults tell children to offer food or drink to guests, not to interrupt adults when they are talking, and to be responsive to the calls of adults or older children. Good manners require that children be respectful of their elders, answer talk directed to them, and not initiate social conversations with elders. Adolescents in the presence of adults are expected to listen; on such occasions, adults may tell stories about themselves, other individuals known to all present, or characters remembered by a particular adult. These stories sometimes are accounts of behaviors that are unacceptable, and stories may end with a value-laden summary statement that assesses the wrongdoer. Stories may also tell of fictional or real-life heroes and heroines, "old times," and escapades of relatives or friends. A favorite theme of such stories is the wayward behavior of the young, but children who are present are not addressed directly; indirectly, they hear admonishments and warnings regarding their possible future actions.

In short, Mexican American working-class families of relatively recent arrivals to the United States seem to consider their children active agents in their own language learning. Adults see themselves as teachers of only specific types of language uses—especially those through which children show their respect for and politeness toward elders. In general, however, adults expect children to learn to use the language of most everyday interactions without specific instruction from their elders. Adults are models in a supportive social community. Though primary nurturing responsibilities rest with mothers, the extended family carries broad moral and social obligations. Adults expect children to go further in life than they have gone, but they rarely suggest specific future careers for their children or seek out opportunities for their children to observe, talk with, or be apprenticed to adults in particular careers.

Indo-Chinese American Families

Generalizations about Indo-Chinese refugee groups are especially untrust-
worthy, because almost no long-term social science research has been carried
out in their communities. From the few descriptions involving intensive interactions with family and community members, we can glean only bits and pieces
about parent responsibilities in language development (Reder, 1981; Reder,
Green & Sweeney, 1983). Across all the Indo-Chinese refugee groups, including
Vietnamese, Hmong, Laotians, and Cambodians, fairly strict age and sex divisions of labor and role expectations exist (Finnan, 1980). Men and women carry
out different tasks and serve different roles with outsiders, and the young are
expected to respect age and look to their elders as models for their future development. The linguistic and cultural adaptation by these groups seems to be
conditioned by: (1) their prior social class membership and urban experience,
(2) the period of time spent in refugee camps before arrival in the United States,
and (3) conditions of initial entry into the United States.

The earliest groups of Vietnamese refugees were from the middle and upper
classes, who had had extensive experience with cross-national business, urban
life, and formal schooling. Many were fluent in French, were highly literate,
and brought institutions with them (or adopted American ones) to provide
mutual support for their group members. They developed organizations similar
to chambers of commerce or other business support groups, created family
businesses, and built a secure network and firm financial base for the academic
efforts of their young. Those who came later were, in some cases, helped by
those who had become established, and the intact community has been a stable
support unit for the return of individual students after the pressures of trying
to adapt to new academic settings. (See Hume [1985]; compare these descriptions with those of Tepper [1980].)

Other groups, such as the Hmong, Laotians, and Cambodians, have come
from refugee camps in Thailand; have had considerably less experience in urban
settings; and are often unfamiliar with institutions such as the school, factory,
public hospital, and employment office. Many of the Hmong had little or no
experience with written forms of their language, and though some had learned
basic reading and writing skills in the refugee camps in Thailand, they had
few literates among them who could lead their adaptation to American life.
However, within the camps, some had begun to learn English; and those who
had sufficient English served as cultural brokers with representatives of federal
and state agencies when they arrived in the United States. The Hmong, organized through a traditional clan membership, have an acknowledged leader
within the United States, and distantly scattered communities have kept in
touch through audiocassettes. Their members have preferred argicultural occupations and have worked as cooperative groups to secure large blocks of land
to establish their own farms from Minnesota to California.

Early language learning opportunities for many of the Indo-Chinese refugees
came in their initial sponsorship by individual families or churches. In their

first months in the United States, they lived in close contact with mainstream American families who modeled not only the sounds, lexicon, and sentence structures of English but also ways of using language with children to reinforce those habits valued in schools. In some locations, the adoption of Christianity and participation in church life have provided occasions not only for using English in a wide variety of functions but also for seeing firsthand the teaching strategies that surround written texts.

In short, though we do not have the data to allow analysis of specific parental assumptions about learning among Indo-Chinese refugees, we can outline the extent to which these families have had compatible support systems helping them acquire English and habits of using English that would be acceptable in school. Adoption by churches and individual families helped provide extended, intense, and immediate observation and participation with academic and social uses of English. The prior adaptation by earlier families of Vietnamese and the establishment of support institutions helped facilitate knowledge about English language classes, business opportunities, and services available from state and federal agencies. Strong tendencies both to accept guidance from those among their own members who could act as cultural brokers and to work cooperatively to pool resources and labor have enabled most of these groups to build stable supportive communities for their young. Most Indo-Chinese groups entertain little or no hope of returning to their homeland, and they are thus driven by a future mental image of life in the United States. Therefore, occupational choices, self-identification as family and community members, and expectations of sustaining strong links between their communities and outside institutions drive them to learn English and to see the school as essential in their success.

Genres of Language Uses

The term *genres* is one we usually think of in association with written forms of language. However, we use the term here to refer to the first level of discourse for language learners; genre refers to the type or kind of organizing unit into which smaller units of language, such as conversations, sentences, lists, or directives may fit. Each cultural group has fundamental genres that occur in recurrent situations; and each genre is so patterned as a whole that listeners can anticipate by the prosody or opening formulas what is coming— a joke, a story, or a recounting of shared past experiences. Moreover, each sociocultural group recognizes and uses only a few of the total range of genres that humans are capable of producing.

Within the bureaucratic world and workplaces of every society, institutions require expertise in only some arbitrarily chosen genres. We may think of genre as synonymous with form, schema, or mold; we recognize each distinctive genre because it contains organized patterns for combining speech acts (such as requests, directives, etc.) and signaling what is to come within the stretch of discourse identifiable as a particular genre. Each genre is governed by its own set of rules. Though there may be certain fragments (such as questions, affirmations, declarations, and evaluations) existing outside the frame of genres, all genres that we can identify are internally organized to accommodate these fragments.

Before discussing patterns from language minority groups, we will review the patterns existing in mainstream school-oriented communities and in school activities. Linguists, sociologists, psychologists, and anthropologists have provided data that support the following school patterns; the first two—label quests and meaning quests—are language activities that ground school learning; the latter four are genres in which these activities become integrated as the learner becomes fully skilled in a repertoire of genres.

1. *Label quests.* These are language activities in which adults either name items or ask for their names. With very young children, adults name the item, usually pointing to it or holding it in front of the child. As children learn to say words, adults ask "What's this?" "Who's that?" Label quests include not only the names of items but their attributes as well. While feeding a young child, the mother may say "potato, hot potato," as she prepares to feed the child. When the child can talk, he or she is asked questions about clothes, foods, toys, and books: "What color is that?" "Where is the big spoon?"

Throughout school, but particularly in the primary grades, teachers ask students to give them the names and attributes of items used in the classroom, read about in books, and discussed in class. Textbooks rank questions that ask "what" and "what kind of" as their easiest. Throughout schooling, teachers and curriculum designers assume knowledge of labels and attributes precedes higher-order knowledge, such as that required to answer "why," "how," and "when" questions.

2. *Meaning quests.* Within this language activity, adults either infer for the young child what he or she means, interpret their own behavior or that of others, or ask for explanations of what is meant or intended. The mother may say of the baby's cry "You're hungry," or may explain away an action by saying "Mother didn't mean to . . .," or may speak of a book's character as intending to be good or bad, secretive or open. Adults make inferences about the meaning of children's statements as they restate, "Up, mama, up," into "You want to get up on my lap, don't you?"

In school, teachers and tests ask students to explain the meanings of words, pictures, combinations of events, and their own behaviors. It is not sufficient to say what something is; one must also learn to say what it means—how it was intended, what action will be its result, and how it is to be interpreted or valued. From basal readers to twelfth-grade Shakespeare classes, teachers ask the meaning of passages and require students to infer from a written text what an author meant.

3. *Recounts.* Within this genre, the speaker retells experiences or information known to both teller and listener. As children retell, they may be questioned

by the listener who wants to scaffold the telling in a certain way. For example, adults ask children to repeat stories they have heard read to them or to tell third parties about an outing they have gone on with a parent. The prompt for such recounts is usually a question—"Can you tell Daddy what happened to you and Mommy today?"—and questions correct the recount when it begins to veer off the chronological path.

Teachers ask children to provide summaries of material known to teacher and fellow students, to recount facts known to all class members, and to display their knowledge through oral and written recounts almost daily. Tests ask questions that depend upon a strict recounting of the passage the student has read.

4. *Accounts.* Unlike recounts, which depend upon a power differential, one party asks another to retell or perform for the sake of performance; accounts are generated by the teller. Thus, power resides initially in the teller rather than in another person who serves as judging audience. Accounts provide information that is new to the listener or new interpretations of information that the listener already knows (e.g., a reinterpretation of why the hot water heater is leaking again). Examples include children telling parents about an afternoon spent at a friend's birthday party or at a neighborhood backyard swimming pool. Accounts are judged not only by their truth value—"Could this have happened?"—but also by the organization of the telling. If the teller follows what the audience expects as a "logical" telling, the account will be accepted; if the organization of the telling seems chaotic and unpredictable, the listener will discount the event and the teller (Michaels, 1981).

Schools allow the general stream of students few occasions for accounts. Show-and-tell in the primary grades and creative writing in the upper grades are the major occasions in which students may tell about their own experiences and be held accountable to the content and the form of the telling. However, at the highest levels of ability grouping and in higher education, teachers ask students for their interpretations, their valuation of events or materials read on the basis of their experiences, their integration of the knowledge of others, or their creation of knowledge (initially in creative writing and later in reports of experiments and other types of research).

5. *Eventcasts.* In this genre, individuals provide a running narrative on events currently in the attention of the teller and listeners (as in sportscasts or in giving directions), or they forecast events to be accomplished in the future (as in developing plans). The narrative may be simultaneous with the events or precede them. A mother may narrate as she changes a child's diaper the events that will ensue: "We'll get dressed, then we'll have our bottle, and then we'll go see if we can take a ride to pick Daddy up from work." As children grow older, they provide eventcasts during their solitary play, talking aloud to themselves about what they are doing, and in dramatic play, as they tell their friends who will play certain roles, what identities certain objects will assume, and how the script for the dramatic play in the pretend kitchen, battlefield,

or doctor's office will go. Adults model eventcasts as they talk about plans for the future and the sequenced steps they will take on a family trip. Making Jell-O in the kitchen or changing a tire are accompanied by running narratives that detail steps being taken in the process.

In school, teachers often begin the day or the class hour by telling students what will take place. Mathematics and science teachers explicate for students the steps they are to take as they work out problems and experiments; eventually, they expect students to be able to explain these steps themselves. The outline for an essay or the study plan for a group project are eventcasts—explication of sequential steps to be taken to accomplish a current or future goal.

6. *Stories.* This is perhaps the most familiar genre, because of our customary associations with the written stories read to children and requested of children's imagination. The mold of these fictional accounts is such that they must include some animate being who moves through a series of events with goal-directed behavior (Stein, 1982). Children hear their parents tell stories about their youth, have stories read to them, and listen to Bible stories at church. Parents elaborate factual accounts to make them fictional stories that will entertain young children at bedtime or cajole them into taking foul-smelling medicine. Peers create and elaborate on ghost tales, and parents embellish real events or possible events to teach lessons.

In mainstream homes and in school, much of the activity surrounding these genres is focused on books or the accomplishment of particular tasks. For example, adults reading a child's book that has only pictures and no storyline may ask children to label items and then to tell the meaning of actions taking place in the pictures. Once they have read a book, children are asked to recount its contents or to compare it with accounts they have given of their own experiences. As children draw, they are asked to provide eventcasts of their drawing; when they build with blocks, Tinkertoys, or other combinations of objects, they become accustomed to questions such as, "What are you making?" "What are you going to do when you run out of blocks?" (For a review of mainstream families' language behaviors surrounding book reading and play, see Heath [1982b, 1983a].)

In language minority homes, some or all of these language activities and genres, as well as others, can and do occur; many others, besides those valued by the school, also occur. Critical to school success, however, is the extent to which all of these school-valued genres occur in the home—in either the minority language or in English—repeatedly, around written materials, and with strong positive reinforcement. It is important that members of the child's primary and secondary social groups model these genres, ask questions about them, and guide their elaboration and extension. The frequency and intensity of occasions both within and outside the home that call for these genres is critical. In mainstream communities, voluntary associations, church schools, nursery schools, and baseball teams support these genres; and language minority children need similar repeated reinforcement and occasions for practice both within and outside their homes.

Links between the Home and Community

We have argued that students who come from homes in which English is not the native language must have—in either their mother tongue or English—multiple, repeated, and reinforced access to certain language uses that match those of the school. The language activities (label quests and meaning quests) and genres (recounts, accounts, eventcasts, and stories) noted here function as the primary language uses through which students demonstrate the academic, cognitive, and linguistic proficiency required by the school. It is through these language uses that students in school display their knowledge. The extent to which children have access to these uses of language and to which such occasions of access revolve around written texts determine, in large part, success in school and in many mainstream institutions beyond the school (see Chapter 2).

In homes that continue to use their native tongue, there is a strong likelihood that there will be a wide range of genres, including some or all of those valued in school as well as others valued within the primary group but not in institutions beyond the family and community. These children will have had multiple, repeated, and reinforced occasions to practice naming, describing, explaining, planning, summarizing, and creating in their native tongue. When they learn English in school, they have to learn the sounds, vocabulary, and syntactical system of another language, but they do not have to learn a new set of uses for language as well (Escobedo, 1983). Consequently, when they come to school, they have not only the basic interactional skills needed for social exchange, but they also are conversant with the types of genres school personnel expect students to use to display their cognitive and academic skills.

If all the genres noted here as valued in the school are not available in the home, can institutions within the community provide them? Yes. Retail and service institutions give children the opportunity to interact and watch their parents communicate with individuals who are not intimates. Thus, in the exchange of goods and services, children have to explain their meaning, ask for clarification, and recognize that what they say is not always understood as they intended. Whether in English or in their native tongue, children need extensive practice in having to explain themselves to those who do not share their specific home experiences, assumptions about meaning, and expectations of outcomes. Church activities, especially those focusing around discussion of written texts, provide opportunities for practice of genres similar to those used in school. Participation in voluntary associations, such as sports teams,

Scout groups, and music lessons, give added practice in uses of language similar to those of the school.

A Context for Changes in Classroom Language Uses

A major benefit of teacher's and children's attention to the wide variety of language uses outside the classroom is increased language awareness on the part of all. The range of language uses within classrooms is amazingly small and does not begin to measure up to the range of uses many occupations require. Current research suggests strongly that the greater the extent to which the school can foster metalinguistic awareness (or attention to language *per se* in children), the greater the chance that children will transfer any language-related instruction beyond the immediate instructional setting (Goelman, Oberg & Smith, 1984; Heath, 1985b; Olson, 1984; Wilkinson, Barnsley, Hanna & Swan, 1980). Through such talk about language and attention to how language is used in a wide variety of oral and written contexts, students learn not just literacy skills (e.g., how to alphabetize, recognize letters and clusters, etc.) but the much more important literate behaviors (e.g., comparing the theme of one story to that of another, assessing the style and factual content of written materials) that are critical for success in academic environments (Heath, 1985c).

Information from local communities may be used to alter practices in the school so that they might include explication of, as well as opportunities for, practice of certain critical genres. Comparative information from across language minority communities also helps emphasize the value of multiple, repeated, reinforced practice of different language uses; a brief explanation and two weeks of coverage in class is no match for the hundreds of thousands of times certain children may have practiced such language uses in their preschool experience. Thus, certain language skills cannot be seen as appropriate for one brief portion of the sequence of skills to be covered and thereafter assumed to be acquired as the basis for the development of other skills viewed as higher order. The ideal way to accommodate children across a variety of language minority backgrounds is to give them redundant, reiterative, and interdependent occasions for practice along a wide range of genres of language uses. Of those named here as important in school, none is inherently more elementary than another. All are necessary at all stages of schooling, and all can be incorporated into the curriculum of any grade level or subject area. Teachers must, however, be culturally and linguistically sensitive to the kinds of language uses they are offering students and the cognitive and academic, as well as linguistic, demands they are making of students.

Further research is certainly required in language minority communities before we know the answers to many of our questions regarding sociocultural environments of language development or the varied types of genres possible within each community. However, we now know enough to be assured that both cultural ways of life and the social relationships of language minority communities to the larger society combine to shape children's early language experiences. The extent of attention language minorities give to creating images of the future for children and linking past and present experiences to these images, as well as their tolerance for questions from children, help determine how prepared children are for the cognitive and academic demands of the school.

FOLLOW-UP QUESTIONS AND ACTIVITIES

1. Heath points out on page 106 the typical assumption that all children have to some extent internalized language uses *before* they come to school. Analyze the list of language uses she presents. In what way(s) do the assumptions present a paradox? Think about your own home and community background. Did you have experience with these kinds of language uses before you went to school? Provide some specific examples.

2. Contrast the two models of development discussed by Heath: language learning as cultural learning versus the single developmental model reflected in mainstream schools. What do you think are the historical bases for these models? Do you see any evidence of a shift away from the single developmental model in the schools with which you are familiar? If so, what changes do you see? If not, what do you think is preventing change from occurring?

3. In groups, assign each member the task of designing an activity/lesson for one or more of the following genres of language use:

   a. Label quest
   b. Meaning quest
   c. Recount
   d. Account
   e. Eventcast
   f. Story (in the Heath sense)

4. Relate Cummins's notions of BICS and CALP and common underlying proficiency (CUP) in Chapter 2 to Heath's perspective on literacy development in the home and community. What do the two views have in common? Can you think of any ways in which they diverge?

5. Heath defines ethnography as the long-term study of the daily habits of a particular social group in which the researcher both observes and participates in the lives of those being studied. How do you think you could become "teacher as ethnographer"? Do you think you would have to modify this definition? How could you use Heath's descriptions of language uses and genres to look for their applications in your content area? What methods would you employ?

9

Providing Culturally Sensitive Feedback

Robin Scarcella   *University of California, Irvine*

Editors' Introduction

Have you ever had a cross-cultural encounter that left you feeling a bit uncomfortable— for instance, having your body space violated or realizing that the rules for eye contact in other cultures were very different? These experiences can be both interesting and a bit unnerving, especially if we have frequent contact with particular cultural groups and we do not know very much about them. In classrooms that contain language minority students from a variety of cultural groups, the potential for cross-cultural misunderstandings is great. In this chapter, Robin Scarcella provides valuable information about many important cross-cultural differences between what is called ''mainstream American'' values and customs and those of language minority students. She focuses specifically on providing effective feedback in the classroom to these students, including helpful suggestions for interpreting student feedback, complimenting and criticizing, correcting student errors, requesting clarification, putting students in the spotlight, questioning and answering, and pausing.

As teachers of multicultural classes, we must provide effective feedback to language minority students of diverse cultural backgrounds. This means accurately interpreting our language minority students' reactions to our lessons and understanding our own methods of giving feedback. By maintaining certain expectations about communication, teachers may unwittingly ask language minority students to violate deeply ingrained cultural patterns. For example, mainstream American teachers usually expect students to look them in the eye when answering their questions. If the students fail to maintain eye contact when addressing a teacher, the teacher may become annoyed and view the students as insolent. When their teacher's use and interpretation of feedback is

From Robin Scarcella, Teaching Langauge Minority Students in the Multicultural Classroom, © 1990, pp. 130–145. *Adapted by permission of Prentice Hall, Inc., Englewood Cliffs, New Jersey.*

inconsistent with their own, language minority students may become victims of the miscommunication.

How can information about cross-cultural differences help us provide our students with more effective feedback? Children learn feedback patterns in their homes, but once they reach the age of five or six, their days are spent at schools where their teachers usually do not share their use and interpretation of feedback.[1] Students who are unable to acquire mainstream American feedback behaviors are handicapped in our schools.

This chapter provides teachers with ideas for providing language minority students with feedback that is sensitive to the needs of diverse cultural groups. Although a compendium of feedback with respect to all cultural groups is not given, the cultural patterns discussed here are shared by many and suggest areas in which possible cultural misunderstandings might occur. The following aspects of feedback are considered:

1. Interpreting student feedback: how teachers interpret the feedback students use to let them know they are following and understanding their lessons; what constitutes *paying attention* and *understanding* from the teacher's point of view.
2. Complimenting and criticizing: what constitutes *compliments* and *criticism* from the teachers' and students' perspectives.
3. Correcting student errors: how students value error correction.
4. Requesting clarification: how students make requests for clarification and help; how teachers interpret these requests.
5. Spotlighting: how teachers call attention to an individual student's behavior in front of others; the teacher's use of *singling out*.
6. Questioning and answering: how questions are used by teachers to check student comprehension and how students answer these questions.
7. Pausing: how much time students need to respond to their teacher's questions; how fast the teacher and students interact.

Each of these aspects of feedback is discussed later. However, before turning to this discussion, it is important to consider the serious problems involved in generalizing research about cross-cultural differences to specific students. Cultural groups are not homogeneous. Such factors as age, gender, personality, motivation, and acculturation affect the students' use and interpretation of feedback. For instance, Native Americans come from many tribes with

---

[1] In general, teachers begin instructing students in the use of these norms (raising hands, taking speaking turns, talking when called on, etc.) in the early grades, but in the more advanced grades, teachers usually expect students to know how to give and interpret middle-American forms of feedback appropriately. As students advance in school, they find themselves giving and receiving more complex forms of feedback, such as that given in extended question/answer periods (see Heath, 1986).

distinct languages, values, and rituals of their own. Latinos speak different dialects of Spanish, come from diverse social and economic classes, and follow different cultural norms and traditions. The Asian and Latino students in your classes may be immigrants who recently arrived in the United States, but they may also be sixth- or seventh-generation Americans. All this means that you will need to consider whether your students actually use the feedback patterns discussed. With this reservation in mind, I would like to turn to a discussion of those patterns said to lead to cultural misunderstandings in multicultural classrooms.

CROSS-CULTURAL DIFFERENCES

Interpreting Student Feedback

One possible misunderstanding may result from misinterpreting your students' feedback. How do you interpret the feedback your students give you when talking to them? You may be used to seeing considerable enthusiasm on the part of mainstream American students. Your students' eye gaze, nods, and smiles let you know that they are paying attention and understanding you. But attention and interest are displayed differently across cultures. Choctaw (Native American) students don't display as much excitement as mainstream American students, but that doesn't mean that they are not interested or that they dislike you (Richmond, 1987). Latino students may avoid looking at you when you speak, but their lack of eye contact may indicate respect and is not intended to display dislike, defiance, or disinterest. Head nods may signal that Asian students are politely listening, not necessarily *understanding* what you are saying. The Asian student's smile may simply mean that the student is politely attending to your speech, not that he agrees with you, finds your lessons amusing, or comprehends what you are saying. Many Asian children are taught to mask their emotions. Displays of emotion are not encouraged by many Asian adults; when these displays occur, parents may punish children for not controlling their feelings (Stover, 1962).

Cross-cultural differences in this area can lead to serious misunderstandings. When Mohatt and Erickson (1981) observed a mainstream American teacher instructing Odawa Indian children, they noted that the mainstream American teacher called on those children who seemed most interested in their lessons and seemed likely to know the answers to their questions. Mohatt and Erickson point out that, for mainstream Americans, the most salient cue that a student is following you is that he or she is *looking up at you*. Yet, Odawa Indian children do not use the same nonverbal behavior to signal their interest. They look down when addressed. Eye contact, as practiced in the United States, is not a universal signal that a student is listening. This explains the *silent*

Indian phenomenon so frequently discussed in the literature (see Philips, 1972, 1974, 1983).

Complimenting and Criticizing Students

Just as you may misinterpret the feedback your students give you, your students may misinterpret the feedback you give them. For example, some Japanese students may be confused when they find check marks on their papers. Damen (1987) comments "the Japanese system of marking answers correct or incorrect includes the following: correct–O or X; incorrect–V. Can you imagine how confusing this might be for a Japanese student who receives all check marks from an uninitiated teacher?" (p. 234).

How do you praise your students? Most mainstream American teachers give their students frequent compliments. In fact, many mainstream American children have come to expect happy faces on their papers and frequent compliments. When students do not receive such praise from their teachers, they may feel as though they have done something wrong, that they are incompetent in some way.

Students from some cultures do not value compliments to the same extent as mainstream Americans. For example, Asian students may view frequent verbal praise as insincere (Condon, 1986). One university student from Japan specifically asked me to give him poor grades on his essays and only an occasional high grade. "This way," he said, "I will believe you when you say my essay is good." Some Asian children may be surprised to find happy faces drawn on their papers on a daily basis and may be unaccustomed to stickers and stamps. Praise might even cause some students shame since humility is considered a virtue in many Asian cultures. Iwatake (1978) states: "Asians, with their strong sense of humbleness, feel uncomfortable accepting compliments. They tend to reject compliments sincerely feeling unworthy" (p. 80).

In contrast to some Asian groups, other ethnic groups may expect more praise than is usually given by mainstream American teachers. Some groups of Latinos, for instance, give and expect more positive comments (such as *right, good, yes*) than mainstream Americans and prefer praise to be given in more personal, face-to-face encounters (Scarcella, 1983). This is not surprising since personal attention is a vital ingredient in Latino communication (Damen, 1987).

Some children are accustomed to more body contact than is usually given by mainstream American educators. Mainstream American teachers apparently have less tactile involvement with students than Latino teachers. A young Brazilian teacher who taught mainstream American children in the United States told of her students' surprise when she patted them on their shoulders and backs (Harrison, 1983). Cross-cultural differences in tactile behavior could be difficult for Mediterranean and Latino children who may be more accustomed to embraces and pats than mainstream Americans (Byers & Byers, 1972; Collier, 1973; Dumont, 1972; Mehan, 1973).

In line with this, the body gestures mainstream American teachers use to convey positive feedback may be misunderstood by students or may be perceived as offensive. For instance, some Arabs may perceive touching a student of the opposite sex and winking to be offensive; some East Asians may perceive touching a student on the head and hugging as offensive, and some Latinos may perceive the *okay* sign as taboo, since it means *Screw you!* (Damen, 1987).

The distance from which praise is delivered might affect teacher/student communication in more subtle ways. The observation that Latinos and Middle Easterners appreciate interpersonal communication at closer distances than mainstream Americans do is frequently discussed in the literature. Mainstream Americans talking to one another stand at least one foot further back than some groups of Latinos (Harrison, 1983). Praise delivered in front of others instead of face-to-face in close proximity may seem impersonal to some students and embarrassing to others (refer to discussion of *spotlighting* below).

In sum, language minority students may find mainstream American praise effusive, insufficient, or inappropriate. They may also fail to recognize their mainstream American teacher's efforts to give them positive feedback. As Saville-Troike (1977) puts it "direct eye contact with a student may be positive, but it may be interpreted as aggressive or humiliating; smiling may be positive, but it may be derisive; touching may be positive, but it may be embarrassing or repugnant" (p. 107).

Like positive feedback, there are wide disparities in the use and interpretation of negative feedback. For this reason, teachers should particularly avoid reprimanding students in front of others. In Mexico, for instance, any public action or remark that may be interpreted as a slight to the person's dignity may be regarded as a grave offense (Condon, 1986). Most Saudis, like most Latinos, are easily affected by public criticism and normally do not respond positively. Middle Easterners regard the mainstream American's willingness to openly criticize as immoral; for the Middle Easterner, one should not go on record describing other's faults (Frechette, 1987; O. D. Parker, 1986). Most Asian groups seem to view direct confrontation as rude and inappropriate (Condon, 1986; Iwatake, 1978).

Psychological difficulties undoubtedly affect the perception of criticism. Immigrant students from Afghanistan, Central America, Cambodia, Vietnam, Laos, and Lebanon have suffered trauma from war and political violence. Many have lost close friends or relatives and have themselves been threatened by excessive violence, starvation, and war atrocities. Along with differences in feedback patterns, these students often bring to the classroom their psychological problems. One student writes:

> The tragedy during the war hurts inside when I remember what happened in the past. I try not to think about it, but at night I dream and see my brother who they killed. I dream about him trying to find us. I dream they keep shooting him and shooting him until I wake up. (10th grade Cambodian boy, immigrated at age 12 [reported in Olsen, 1988, p. 22])

Latinos who come to the United States illegally and are separated from family members, lost, or deserted also suffer from emotional turmoil. A Mexican student states, in describing his trip to the United States:

> It was scary to me. We went separate across. I was caught the first time and sent back to my aunt's house. This time she paid a lot of money to a coyote [who smuggles people across the border] to get me across. He put me in a sack in the back of a truck with potatoes and told me to be totally quiet until he came to get me. I was hot and couldn't breathe and so scared. I cried with no sound until he came to get me. I had gotten across. But where was my mother? (9th grade Mexican boy, immigrated at age 7 [reported in Olsen, 1988, p. 26])

Students who are emotionally troubled may be particularly vulnerable to criticism. Since teachers really cannot know the traumas individual students may have experienced, treating them gently in general is a better guideline. Less criticism as a rule is better than more.

Correcting Student Errors

Just as the perception of compliments and criticism varies widely across cultures, so too does the perception of error correction. Many cultures place great value on explicit correction. In the United States, many teachers explicitly correct their students (making such explicit statements as: ''That's an incomplete sentence,'' ''You got the wrong answer,'' and ''Try harder.'' ''You've forgotten the right answer.'') Other cultures may, however, place an even greater emphasis on error correction. For instance, in examining classroom practices by French teachers, Dannequin (1977) observes that pupils do not have the *right* to make mistakes but must instead conform to teachers' standards. One important aspect of Japanese life is learning the proper form. Great value is placed on doing things *right*. According to Thompson (1987a): ''The traditional Japanese regard for authority and formality is in tune with teacher-dominated lessons where much heed is paid to the *correct* answer, learning of grammar rules and item-by-item (rather than contextualized) vocabulary'' (p. 223). A salient feature of Chinese education is obsessive concern with correctness (Maley, 1986). Lewis (1974) observes the stress in Soviet pedagogy on the value of error correction. It is not surprising then that students from these cultures experience frustration when participating in a class in which there is no error correction.

However, not all cultures believe that error correction is important. For instance, Chipeweyan adults assume that good grammatical performance is expected only of older people. It is generally believed that Chipeweyan takes a lifetime to learn because it is so difficult. Similarly, Blount (1977) notes that in Luo and Koya society caregivers are not responsive to the language mistakes made by children. Schieffelin (1983) reports that the major strategy for teaching young Kaluli children to talk involves telling the child what to say to someone in ongoing interactions. The mother provides the model utterance, followed by the imperative, *Say like that.* This approach to language development does not entail any error correction at all.

Requesting Clarification

The ways in which students ask their teachers to clarify their lessons may also lead to misunderstandings. Mainstream American students are often eager to ask questions when they don't understand their teachers. Yet, some Latino students may be unaccustomed to asking their teacher to clarify and feel that it is impolite to take the teacher's time in this way. Many Asian students are also reluctant to request clarification (Sato, 1981). Like some Latino students, they may be afraid that such admissions on their part will seem aggressive and disrespectful. Some Native Americans may make silent requests, looking up from seatwork to ask for help silently. Students who expect more formal, structured classroom environments (such as those in many Asian countries, India, Saudi Arabia, and the Soviet Union) may be surprised that mainstream American teachers expect students to make requests for clarification in the middle of such activities as lectures, story-time, and reading sessions.

Spotlighting

Students from many cultures are unaccustomed to the mainstream American technique of spotlighting, singling out a student and asking this student to perform correctly before others. Directives (such as ''Joe, stand up.'') can put the spotlight of public attention on children in front of an audience. Mohatt and Erickson (1981) note:

> Part of the *spotlighting* effect comes from using the name of an individual student. Another part can come from what Hall (1966) terms a proxemic relationship—interpersonal distance that carries social meaning. If the teacher calls out a directive to a single individual from all the way across the room, the spotlight effect is heightened, giving the directive the force of a command or rebuke rather than a suggestion. (p. 223)

Loudly referring to the names of the students you are not teaching also heightens the negative effect of spotlighting. (For instance, reprimanding a student who is in a math group when you are working with the reading group accentuates the spotlighting effect.) The effect is further heightened when you give a direct command (such as ''Come here.'') instead of an indirect one (such as ''Would you mind coming here?'' or, yet less direct, "I need to talk to you for a minute").

Richmond (1987) found that Choctaws (Native Americans) find being put on the spot in front of peers may directly conflict with home training. She states, ''At home, they [Choctaws] quietly observe the skills they are to learn, practice them by doing as much with an adult there to watch and help, and then demonstrate them when they are reasonably certain of success'' (p. 234).

Similarly, Philips (1972, 1974, 1983) found that Warm Spring Indian children participated more enthusiastically and performed more effectively in classroom activities that minimized the obligation on the part of the students to perform *publicly* as individuals and in settings where the teacher did not control performance of the students and correct their errors.

Like many Native Americans, many Asians do not like spotlighting (Sato, 1981). Condon (1984) writes, ''The Japanese do not care to be put on the spot in public; getting it wrong can be a cause of real shame, especially in front of classmates who are younger or socially inferior.'' (p. 58).

Questioning and Answering

Questions allow teachers to assess their students' comprehension of their lessons and are frequently used by mainstream American teachers. Unfortunately, they present a number of difficulties for our language minority students. The questions you use may be entirely misconstrued by your students. For example, Heath (1982a, 1983b), who examined questioning strategies in African American and white working-class communities, found that the questions mainstream American teachers used at school were misunderstood by their African American students. The most frequent type of question these teachers used was a question to elicit an answer that the teacher already knew, as in ''What is this?'' (said while pointing to a calendar). Questions of this type accounted for nearly half the data. In the homes of African Americans, children were asked questions of a different type. They were generally asked, ''What's that like?'' or ''What's happening?'' Heath (1982a) cites classroom incidents in which a teacher persisted in asking questions about a story the children had just read. When the teacher asked ''Who is it the story is talking about?'' one child replied, ''Ain't nobody can talk about things being about themselves.'' The boy could not understand why the teacher so often asked questions when she already had the answers to these questions. Heath notes that when the teacher asked the children question types with which they were familiar, the children responded and became involved in the lessons because they knew how to answer.

Another type of question that might present a stumbling block for some groups of students is the personal opinion question, (''What do you think of X?''). Mainstream Americans have been given extensive training in stating their own opinions—at bedtime, story-time, in show-and-tell, in question/answer sessions with parents. In many cultures, however, children are taught *not* to give their own opinions. Levine (1982) points out:

> Asked by teachers, *What do you think?* or *What is your opinion?* a Saudi student may simply offer a rote response. This response is not indicative of an inability to articulate an original or creative thought, but rather reflects educational training that discourages independent thinking. Some Saudi students have reported that a teacher who elicits opinions in class or allows a student to challenge ideas is incompetent and therefore unqualified to teach. (pp. 101–102)

Like the Saudi student discussed by Levine, many Asian students may also have difficulty stating their own opinion. These students have not been taught to give personal opinions and may be reluctant to give an opinion different from the teacher's out of fear of receiving a negative evaluation.

A further area of potential misunderstanding concerns the mainstream American teacher's expectation that students will volunteer to answer questions. Mainstream American students usually feel free to answer questions when they know the answers. However, when you ask language minority students questions to check their comprehension, they may or may not volunteer to answer. For example, Asians may not volunteer to answer because volunteering answers displays their knowledge, and they have been taught to be humble. Iwatake (1978) notes, ''The traditional classroom in Asia places the teacher at the front of the room, lecturing. When the teacher asks a question, he usually calls on a student to answer'' (p. 80) (See also Sato, 1981). Asian students may also feel that if they give the wrong answer, it not only humiliates them but also brings shame on their families (Sue, 1983). Cole (1987) reports that Haitians may also be shy, reticent, and reluctant to volunteer answers. In cultures that place great value on spoken interaction (such as Iran, Turkey, and Saudi Arabia), students may be eager to answer teacher questions when they have the English proficiency to do so. If these students take up too much class time, this too can lead to difficulties. Thompson (1987b), for example, states that ''Turks tend to voice their opinions openly and attach little importance to compromises'' (p. 168).

Another serious problem affecting the language minority students' difficulty answering questions concerns the school setting. Language minority students may feel so uncomfortable with an unfamiliar school setting that the very situation may make them reluctant to answer teacher questions. For example, Philips's (1972, 1974, 1983) careful observation of the Warm Spring Indians suggests that Warm Spring Indian children were so uncomfortable with the structure of the classroom that they failed to answer questions, giggled nervously, and remained silent. Boggs (1972) reports that Hawaiian children participate in choral responses and individually volunteer information to teachers when they can sense receptivity but become silent if called on by name. Dumont (1972) contrasts two Cherokee classrooms—one in which children are silent and one in which children talk excitedly and productively about all their learning tasks. In the silent classroom, teacher-dominated recitations fail. In the other classroom, children have choices of when and how to participate, and small group projects not directed by the teacher are encouraged. These observations suggest that children from several minority groups are more likely to perform in situations that are more congruent with their expectations of schooling. Teachers of these students might find it helpful to give longer periods of individual attention to students and to arrange for more group work.

Perhaps the most serious problem related to questions is that mainstream American teachers tend to question students of their own ethnic backgrounds to a greater extent than they question students of other ethnic backgrounds.

Unfortunately, teachers often *pass over* students whose ethnic identity is different from their own. Jackson and Cosca's (1974) report found that mainstream American teachers directed 21 percent more questions to mainstream Americans than to Chicanos. They conclude that, "Chicanos in the Southwest receive substantially less of those types of teacher behavior presently known to be most strongly related to gains in student achievement" (p. 227).

Pausing

Wait time, that is, the amount of time students take before answering teacher questions, seems to constitute another source of potential misunderstanding between the teacher and student. In the United States, questions tend to be answered fairly quickly (Richards, 1980). Teachers often feel uncomfortable with silence and tend to interpret silence as an indicator of the student's inability to answer a question. Mainstream Americans usually associate silence with something negative—tension, hostility, awkwardness, or shyness. Yet, in some cultures, students take considerable time to answer questions. For instance, in many Asian and Native American Indian cultures it is courteous and respectful to pause and weigh one's words before responding to a question or comment. Mohatt and Erickson (1981) point out that Odawa Indians frequently speak slowly, pause often, and respond to teacher questions after reflecting on the question for some time. Among many East Asian students, silent periods of reflection are appropriate responses to teacher questions and "lowered eyes and bowed heads, rather than silence, are more likely to be the nonverbal signals indicating no response is coming" (Condon, 1984, p. 302). On the other hand, some Iranian and Saudi students may appear to *jump* to answer questions, even answering them before the teacher has had a chance to finish. It is not unusual for a Saudi student to rush to a teacher's side to loudly answer a question (Damen, 1987). Damen suggests that Arab loudness means strength. In their culture, responses to questions are given quickly and indicate interest and active involvement, not aggression. In this culture, interruptions are permitted at times. In fact, speakers in this culture often overlap one another when talking, trying to display friendliness and interest.

Thus far, we have examined cultural differences with respect to specific behaviors that may result in potential misunderstandings in the multicultural classroom. Yet, three other factors affect these behaviors: peers, age, and gender. These factors are discussed in the following sections.

Peer Feedback

In most mainstream American classrooms, it is the teacher who provides feedback to students in the classroom. Yet, in classrooms across the world, this is not always the case. In many Korean elementary classrooms, for example, students help one another. The students work in small groups and each student is responsible for his or her own work as well as the work of his or her entire group. In all Mexican elementary schools, children work together on group projects. This cooperative work makes the better students responsible for giving feedback to the weaker students. While adults are primarily responsible for teaching young children in the United States, in other cultures, peers as well as adults are responsible for teaching small children. This is the case in Samoa (Ochs, 1983), in Hawaii with Hawaiian children (Boggs, 1972; Au & Jordan, 1981), in Papua New Guinea with Kaluli children (Schieffelin, 1983), and in Mexico (Laosa, 1984), as well as in many Native American groups (Philips, 1972, 1974, 1983; Weeks, 1983). For these groups, it may be useful to form peer teaching/learning interactions. (See Chapter 18 for a more detailed discussion of peer teaching.) Bear in mind, however, that the feedback immigrant students receive from mainstream American peers is not always supportive. One student reports:

> Before I came to America I had a beautiful dream about this country. At that time, I didn't know that the first word I learned in this country would be a dirty word. American students always picked on us, made fun of us, laughed at our English. They broke our lockers, threw food on us in the cafeteria, said dirty words to us, pushed us on the campus. Many times they shouted at me, *Get out of here, you chink, go back to your country.* Many times they pushed me and yell on me. I've been pushed, I had gum thrown on my hair. I've been hit by stones, I've been shot by air-gun. I've been insulted by all the dirty words in English. All this really made me frustrated and sad. I often asked myself, *Why do they pick on me?* (Christina Tien, Chinese Immigrant Student, Public Testimony, Los Angeles [reported in Olsen, 1988, p. 34])

Another student comments:

> There is lots of teasing me when I don't pronounce right. Whenever I open my mouth, I wonder, I shake and worry, will they laugh? They think if we speak Tagalog that we are saying something bad about them, and sometimes they fight us for speaking our language. I am afraid to even try. And I find myself with fear about speaking Tagalog. (10th grade Filipino boy, immigrated at age 14 [reported in Olsen, 1988, p. 38])

This means that, to provide optimal feedback group work, teachers need to be sensitive to patterns of prejudice and conflict.

Age and Gender

In many cultures feedback patterns vary as a function of age and gender. In hierarchical cultures such as Thai, in which seniority in years is respected, it is critical in classes of mixed ages to make sure "that older learners are not in any way made to lose face (for example, by leaving a long pause after a question which the learner cannot answer, brushing aside pedantic questions as irrelevant, etc.)'' (Smyth, 1987, p. 262). In addition, the casual mixing of genders in the classroom can cause emotional havoc for many cultural groups. Shackle (1987) points out that teachers may find it hard to elicit responses from some female Indian students unless they are in all-female classes. In group work, males from some cultures may prefer receiving feedback from males, and females from females. Also, Smith (1987) advises that female teachers remember that in many Arab countries ''men are not allowed to speak to any women outside their own immediate circle'' (p. 154). This might make it difficult for female instructors to provide some Arab students with constructive criticism.

PRACTICAL STRATEGIES

I asked earlier how information about cross-cultural differences can help teachers provide students of diverse cultural backgrounds with more effective feedback. My purpose here has been to highlight potential areas of cultural misunderstanding rather than specific between-group or within-group differences. I reiterate here the danger of overgeneralization of information concerning cross-cultural differences. Although it is impossible to provide teachers with a definitive list of do's and don'ts (*do give this type of feedback, don't give this type . . .*), some general strategies are helpful in providing feedback to language minority students of all cultural backgrounds. A list follows:

1. Develop cross-cultural tolerance; given the tremendous possibility for cultural misunderstandings in the area of feedback, be tolerant of your students' feedback behaviors and avoid stereotyping.
2. Join forces with your students, community leaders, and others who speak your students' first languages to gather information about the types of feedback your students prefer. Find out about feedback strategies that work for others from successful teachers. Watch native speaker volunteers interact with your students and observe successful feedback behaviors (Richmond, 1987).
3. If appropriate, show students the types of feedback you use and how you interpret student feedback. When people from diverse cultures are aware of areas in which cultural behaviors differ, they are not as likely to misunderstand one another. Explain, for example, your system of marking papers. Also, to the extent that strategies of questioning are different at home than they are at school, teachers need to openly discuss with students the different kinds of questions and answers that they expect to be used in the classroom (Heath 1982a, 1983b). (See Chapter 8 for further suggestions.)
4. Try to adapt your feedback to make some provision for the different feedback patterns of your students. For example, you might use some of the questioning strategies which your students are familiar with.

Heath (1982a) suggests that the mainstream American teachers she observed might use some questions like "What's this like?" and "What's happening here?" with the African American students she studied; if appropriate, you might also want to allow for group work and informal peer feedback.

5. Do not assume students will volunteer to answer your questions. Develop a plan that will allow *all* students opportunities to answer your questions. Students may feel more comfortable answering your questions in face-to-face encounters or small groups.

6. Organize classroom seating arrangements to maximize student opportunities to participate and to minimize discrimination. Many teachers tend to communicate more with those students who share their own ethnic identity and literally *pass over* students who do not share their ethnic identity. For this reason, you need to consciously form a plan that will call for interaction with all students.

7. Be aware of your means of complimenting students. Students from all cultures are likely to appreciate praise that is delivered sincerely and is specific. Compliments such as "I like the way you write your name so clearly" (said to a kindergartner) seem more sincere than general, all-purpose compliments such as "very good."

8. Encourage students to ask questions when they do not understand and make it clear to them that demands for clarification, simplification, and repetition are welcome, expected, and even desired. You might lower your language minority students' anxieties by reminding them that they have not mastered English yet and are not expected to understand everything they hear or read. Modeling appropriate interruption behavior can help some students. You can also tell students that they are welcome to interrupt with such expressions as "What?" and "Excuse me. I'm not sure I understand." (Chapter 15 contains useful strategies for helping language minority students to improve their questioning and answer skills.)

9. Do not assume students will ask you questions when they do not understand something. Also, when you ask students if they understand you, and the entire class nods *yes*, do not assume that the students understand. Frequently check your students' understanding (when appropriate, by questioning them using true-false quizzes, or asking students to participate in a follow-up activity such as group work).

10. Question your students in a nonthreatening manner. When you use questions, you may want to avoid relying upon the verbally demanding open-ended questions "Why?" and "How?" and use the following question types, which are verbally less demanding:

Yes/no questions: "Did John ride his bike to school?"
Choice questions: "Did John ride his bike or skateboard to school?"
What questions (with one word response): "What did John ride home?"

You might want to accept written nonverbal answers, or short answers. Also, when you are speaking individually with students, there is no reason why they should not answer your questions in their native language when their proficiency in English is insufficient to allow communication to take place and you know their first language.[2]

11. Give students plenty of *wait* time. Your language minority students may need more time than native speakers to respond to your questions. (Some teachers like to count to five silently.) It is probably best to discuss differences in wait time with your students and then provide students with plenty of time to answer your questions. All students (including mainstream Americans) might appreciate this procedure.

12. Avoid strategies that embarrass or frustrate students, such as the mainstream American technique of *spotlighting,* putting one student *on the spot.* One way to avoid *spotlighting* is to have your students participate in small group activities; another is to arrange to give students feedback individually in face-to-face situations.

13. Establish good rapport. Good rapport with your students can help them overlook misunderstandings. Be patient in establishing relationships.

14. As Moskowitz (1978) suggests, set ground rules. Do not allow *put downs.* Encourage students to help one another and ask questions when they do not understand your lessons. Do not force students to participate before others; students are entitled to the right to *pass.*

15. Be consistent with your feedback. Wong-Fillmore (1985) suggests that the most successful teachers of language minority students are those who provide consistent feedback and employ systematic turn-allocation at least some of the time. Students will be able to interpret your feedback better if you use it consistently.

CONCLUSION

Many mainstream American strategies used to interpret and to provide feedback in our classes may be ineffective with students in multicultural classrooms.[3] Culturally-sensitive feedback, tailored to your students' individual backgrounds

---

[2] This implies only that you might use your student's first language when speaking individually with him or her. In a multicultural classroom, if you speak Spanish and English, your Korean, Chinese, and Tagalog speakers may feel less valued and important.

[3] Research done in the Kamehameha Early Education Program (KEEP) in Honolulu (Au, 1980; Au & Jordan, 1981; Jordan, 1978) suggests that successful educational programs for culturally diverse students are sensitive to the feedback patterns of the students. These programs accept some of the patterns of the students but not all. For example, children in the KEEP Program are allowed to overlap one another's answers and to receive help from peers rather than the teacher. On the other hand, the teacher in the KEEP Program does not use the *Creolized* forms of feedback used in the children's homes. These programs also attempt to reverse some of the children's feedback patterns so that children reared in a peer-affiliation milieu "become attentive to the adult teacher." (Cazden & Legett, 1981, p. 82)

(taking into account their ages, proficiency levels, goals, etc.) seems most effective. After all, feedback should instill a sense of success in students from all cultural backgrounds.

RECOMMENDED READINGS

Heath, S. B. (1983). *Ways with words.* Cambridge: Cambridge University Press. Classic ethnographic study of children living in two neighboring working-class communities—one white and one African American. On the basis of her research, Heath demonstrates that the style of school language for the African American children conflicts with the style of language used in the children's homes.

Philips, S. (1983). *The Invisible Culture: Communication in Classroom and Community on the Warm Spring Indian Reservation.* White Plains, NY: Longman. Philips describes her research in the Warm Spring Indian community and schools. Because Warm Spring Indian children do not share the verbal styles of their mainstream American teachers, Philips argues that they are at an immediate disadvantage when they enter schools taught by mainstream Americans.

Swan, M., and Smith, B. (Eds.) (1987). *Learner English: A teacher's guide to interference and other problems.* Cambridge: Cambridge University Press. This book provides descriptions of the first languages and, in many cases, communication styles of language minority learners of diverse cultures.

Trueba, H., Guthrie, P., and Au, K. (Eds.) (1981). *Culture and the bilingual classroom: Studies in classroom ethnography.* New York: Newbury House. Includes research papers related to home/school discontinuities that prevent language minority students from achieving success in our schools.

FOLLOW-UP QUESTIONS AND ACTIVITIES

1. Imagine you teach social science to junior high school students. You have just given a lecture. Describe three specific ways you can determine whether your students understood your lecture.

2. At UCLA, Harold Garfinkel asked his students to consciously insert specific pause fillers such as *uhm, er,* and *ya know* into their speech. His students failed miserably. To what extent do you think it is possible to consciously change your own feedback behaviors? Do you think it would help your students acquire mainstream American feedback patterns if you taught explicit rules? Why or why not?

3. How can a teacher with several different cultural groups represented in the class provide effective feedback for all students?

4. At Stanford University, Charles Ferguson conducted an experiment in which he did not provide the types of feedback others expected. For example, if others greeted him, he said nothing. Try not to give feedback to others. For example, avoid giving back channel cues such as *uhum* and *right* and look down when your addressee speaks to you. Then, make observations about what happened. Was this a positive or a negative experience?

5. If you are currently a teacher, try not to correct your students' mistakes publicly for one whole class period. Then, make observations about what happened.

PART III

The Classroom: Instructional Practices and Materials

The selections included here focus on pedagogical strategies and classroom management issues across the content areas. They work together to provide various means for meeting differing proficiency and cognitive levels, taking into account cultural factors and how they might affect the learning process. Strategies are also presented for developing skills in various academic areas of study by integrating content and language learning. It should be kept in mind that, although several chapters might be oriented to particular age groups and purposes, the recommendations need not be limited to those situations only. Creative teachers will see a wide variety of ways in which the ideas can be adapted to other classroom settings. The questions and activities that end each chapter encourage applications to specific teaching situations.

In Chapter 10 Patricia Richard-Amato and Ann Snow suggest ways to give classroom instruction specifically tailored to the developing proficiency levels of the students. Suggestions for materials adaptation and lesson planning are given by Deborah Short in Chapter 11. Ideas for using reading strategies in whole-language classroom situations are presented by Gina Cantoni-Harvey in Chapter 12. Improving academic writing skills is the subject of Chapter 13 by Faye Peitzman and of Chapter 14 by Joy Reid. Carmen Simich-Dudgeon, Lynn McCreedy, and Mary Schleppegrell, in Chapter 15, present ways for conducting verbal reviews to increase students' participation. D. Scott Enright and Mary Lou McCloskey then shift the focus to the physical aspects of the classroom environment itself in Chapter 16, in which they advocate student-centered arrangements. Bernard Mohan, in Chapter 17, encourages us to reassess our tests to make sure they are indeed testing what is intended. In Chapter 18, which ends Part III, Patricia Richard-Amato offers means by which peer teachers can be used to facilitate the learning process.

10

Strategies for Content-Area Teachers

Patricia A. Richard-Amato   *University of Nevada, Reno*

Marguerite Ann Snow   *California State University, Los Angeles*

Editors' Introduction

Content-area teachers of language minority students are likely to find themselves in one of three situations: in mainstream *classes made up of a mixture of native and nonnative speakers of varying levels of proficiency;* sheltered *classes consisting of nonnative speakers only who operate at similar proficiency levels; or* adjunct *classes which are paired with mainstream classrooms and offer additional language assistance to students in relation to the subject being studied. This chapter presents means by which teachers can make the language and content more accessible to language minority students. It offers a synthesis of both cognitive and affective strategies to provide optimal environments for teaching and learning across the content areas and across grade levels. In addition, typical language behaviors found at the various levels of proficiency are discussed to give teachers a better idea of what they can reasonably expect of the students in their classes.*

Teachers assigned to mainstream, sheltered, or adjunct classes are often in need of specific strategies to help them teach the subject matter to their language minority students. Mainstream teachers in particular are likely to find themselves at a disadvantage in that they are frequently asked to teach without the benefit of adequate preservice or in-service training that deals specifically with the instruction of language minority students.

To make matters worse, support systems for language minority students in mainstream classes are often limited or missing. A surprisingly large number of these students may not have received instruction in English as a second language (ESL) at all. Many language minority students have been submerged into mainstream classes with little thought given to their level of proficiency or their readiness for the transition. Other students may have been in ESL classes that focused on the development of basic interpersonal communication skills; however, they may still lack experience with the kinds of cognitive/academic language required to do well in content-area classes.

Some language minority students have been more fortunate, however. They have received the early support in ESL necessary to the development of academic skills. Their content-area teachers have been adequately trained. Their classes have included some combination of the following: (1) mainstream classes for which adequate preparation and transitioning has taken place; (2) sheltered classes in which only non-English-speaking students at similar levels of language development are present; (3) adjunct classes in which a content-area mainstream class is paired with a language class for non-English speakers and/or (4) a language program in their native tongue (see Figure 10.1).

It is possible, some may say ideal, for non-English-speaking students to begin their studies with a beginning-level ESL class and at the same time receive instruction in math, science, and social studies in their own native language, provided the necessary teachers and materials are available. Such instruction (see the native language program component in Figure 10.1) is designed to prevent students from falling behind their native English-speaking peers in those subject areas. Later the students may progress from ESL to sheltered and/or adjunct classes and finally into mainstream classes in which they are completely integrated with native English speakers. At this time, instruction in the native language may be continued so that it can be maintained and so that literacy skills in their native language can be further developed.

Regardless of the classes or combination of classes language minority students may experience, to do well in academics they must at some point receive considerable instruction specifically tailored to their developing levels

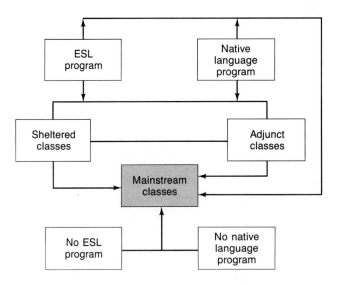

Figure 10.1. *Typical Program Options for Language Minority Students*

of proficiency. The purpose of this chapter is to describe a variety of strategies and techniques that content-area teachers can use to make subject matter accessible to language minority students. We begin by describing characteristics of the typical stages of language development as a context for making appropriate instructional decisions. These stages with their associated behaviors are as follows.[1]

The *low-beginning* student is dependent on gestures, facial expressions, objects, pictures, a good phrase dictionary, and often a translator in an attempt to understand and to be understood. Occasionally, the student comprehends words and phrases. It is not uncommon for students at this level to be submerged (in a sink-or-swim fashion) into a mainstream class.

The *mid-beginning* student begins to comprehend more but only when the speaker provides gestural clues, speaks slowly, and uses concrete referents and repetitions. The student speaks very haltingly if at all. The student shows some recognition of written segments and may even be able to write short utterances.

The *high-beginning to low-intermediate* student comprehends even more but with difficulty. The student at this level speaks in an attempt to meet basic needs but remains hesitant, makes frequent errors in grammar, vocabulary, and pronunciation, and often falls into silence. The student can read very simple text and can write a little but is very restricted in grammatical structure and vocabulary.

The *mid-intermediate* student may experience a dramatic increase in vocabulary recognition. However, idioms often present difficulty. The student often knows what he or she wants to say but gropes for acceptable utterances. Errors in grammar, vocabulary, and pronunciation are frequent, and the student is often misunderstood. The student can read text that is more difficult but still concrete and can write with greater ease than before.

The *high-intermediate to low-advanced* student is beginning to comprehend substantial parts of normal conversation but often requires repetitions, particularly in academic discourse spoken at normal rates. He or she is gaining confidence in speaking ability. At this stage, errors are common but less frequent. The student can read and write text that contains more complex vocabulary and structures than before but experiences difficulty with abstract language.

The *mid-advanced* student comprehends much conversational and academic discourse spoken at normal rates but sometimes requires repetition. Idioms still present difficulty. Speech is more fluent but contains occasional errors.

---

[1] The typical behaviors associated with each level of proficiency are adapted from Richard-Amato (1988, pp. 212–213). Other behavior matrices that teachers might find useful are the ACTFL (American Council on the Teaching of Foreign Languages) and the SOLOM (Student Oral Language Observation Matrix) developed by the California State Department of Education. The latter is limited to comprehension and the informal oral assessment of skills in fluency, vocabulary, pronunciation, and syntactical usage.

Meaning is usually clear, but vocabulary and/or structures are used inappropriately at times. The student reads and writes with less difficulty materials that are commensurate with his or her cognitive development but demonstrates some problems in grasping intended meaning.

The *high-advanced* student comprehends normal conversational and academic discourse with little difficulty. Most idioms are understood. The student speaks fluently in most situations with few errors. Meaning is generally clear, but the student experiences some regression at times. He or she reads and writes both concrete and abstract materials and is able to manipulate the language with relative ease.

COGNITIVE CONSIDERATIONS ACROSS THE PROFICIENCY LEVELS

Lessons in the content areas at early levels of English proficiency need to be concrete. Activities at these levels should involve the students physically whenever possible. For example, in teaching math skills, students might be asked to perform specific actions. (Draw a circle. Draw a line that divides the circle in half. Draw another line that divides the circle into quarters. And so forth.) In geography students might be asked to point to Laos on the map or to list the names of the countries that are part of the African continent. Students need exposure to visuals and realia (i.e., real objects) to aid understanding, and they need effective questioning and task-oriented strategies designed to help them attain higher-order levels of thinking in English as a way to facilitate the learning process.

At later levels of proficiency, ESL students might be asked to follow more complex directions or to demonstrate a simple process. In home economics it might involve preparing an ethnic food. In physical education it might include learning a set of dance steps or playing a game. At another time, students might be asked to perform tasks and answer questions requiring an even greater application and/or synthesis of knowledge. (Create your own map. Write about what you would do if stranded on another planet. Solve a word problem in math by graphically representing the information given.)

As the students begin to make progress, they can gradually meet increasingly greater cognitive demands. Now the tasks, although more challenging, are still fairly concrete. (Complete a chart indicating the differences and similarities between poetry and the short story. Perform an experiment in science by following a set of written directions. Illustrate an isosceles triangle. Draw figures to show how it differs from other kinds of triangles.) At some point, the students might be able set up a science experiment, create word problems in math for others to solve, and write their own short scenarios or poetry in language arts. As students reach increasingly more complex ways of thinking in English, they will eventually be able to visualize science experiments and write up the results given various conditions. They will be able to participate in debates in social studies after considerable planning, organization, and research. And they will be able to write research papers, create stories and dramas, and even form their own hypotheses and test them.

Keep in mind that some students will have had little prior schooling and will be in special need of concrete explanations and examples of what it is they are expected to do. Often perfunctory requests (e.g., ''Answer the questions at the end of the chapter,'' or ''Take notes'') may not be clear to one who has never completed such tasks in any language.

INSTRUCTIONAL STRATEGIES

During the time when the students are learning English, content-area teachers will find certain instructional strategies to be particularly efficacious at various levels. The rest of this chapter is devoted to a discussion of instructional strategies appropriate for content-area teachers who work with language minority students. We have chosen to present the strategies according to two different categorizations. First, we divide the suggested strategies by student proficiency level. Certain techniques are more suitable for beginning to mid-intermediate students, whereas others are more appropriate for high-intermediate to advanced students. Second, we have delineated the strategies by class type—sheltered or mainstream—because homogeneous versus heterogeneous classes present very different sets of conditions for the delivery of content-area instruction. It is intended that the content-area teachers adapt those strategies that best meet the language needs and age levels of the students for whom their courses are intended.

Student Proficiency Level: Beginning to Mid-Intermediate

Strategies for Mainstream Teachers
Provide a warm environment in which help is readily available to the language minority student. One way to do this is to set up a partner system in which native or near-native English-speaking students are paired with language minority students. A similar technique is peer teaching (see Chapter 18), in which a native or near-native English speaker teaches one or more nonnative speakers. Group work, in general, increases the chances that the student will receive the necessary help. In addition, it increases the amount of interaction and comprehensible input received (see the discussion of cooperative learning in Chapter 5).

Record your lectures or talks on tape. Make the tapes available to language minority students who may need to listen to them many times to achieve understanding.

Ask some of your native English-speaking students to simplify the textbook by rewriting portions of the more difficult chapters. The job can be made as easy as possible by giving each native English-speaking or near-native English-speaking student just a few pages to simplify. The students who do the rewriting benefit also in that the task serves as a review for them.

Choose native- or near-native English-speaking students who take effective, comprehensible notes to duplicate them for language minority students. By this means, the language minority students can be provided with study aids.

If possible, use a "satisfactory/unsatisfactory" grade option until the nonnative student is able to compete successfully with native speakers. Students may be ready sooner than expected because many of them will adapt very rapidly. It is important to remember that often the students, particularly those who are older, will already have a high level of academic understanding in the first language (L1) and may even surpass native speakers once they have proficiency in English.

Strategies for Teachers of Mainstream and Sheltered Classes

Collaborate with colleagues to plan the most effective instruction for language minority students. Encourage ESL teachers to observe your classes and examine your course materials so that they can better prepare ESL students for the demands of your content area. It may be possible in certain settings to coordinate assignments. For example, the language teacher might guide the students in comprehending the basic concepts necessary for successful participation in a specified unit of work, while the content area teacher expands on the concepts and relates them to the requirements of the lesson. In addition, strategies and ideas that work well with language minority students can be shared with colleagues to create a team effort and to increase efficiency in lesson planning for language minority students at all levels of proficiency.

Communicate individually with the language minority students as much as time permits. It is important to use the students' names and to pronounce them correctly.

As you deliver your lesson, use a slower speech rate, enunciate clearly, and emphasize key words and phrases through gesture, facial expression, and intonation. This is especially important for students at beginning levels of proficiency. However, avoid distorting your delivery to the point at which it becomes unnatural and condescending.

Use visuals to clarify key concepts. Real objects, pictures, maps, props, illustrations on the chalkboard or transparencies, filmstrips, diagrams, charts, and mapped-out ideas provide multiple clues to meaning. Advance organizers from geography and home economics lessons help students to organize information and recognize important categories (see Figure 10.2 on page 151 and Figure 10.3 on page 152).

Demonstrate and act out when appropriate. For example, to show how water can be distilled, the teacher may want to set up an apparatus to demonstrate

Country	Location	Climate
Argentina	South America	Warm summers Temperate winters
Canada	North America	Warm summers Cold winters
Vietnam	East Asia	Hot summers Temperate winters

Figure 10.2. *A Chart Used to Clarify a Geography Lesson*

the concept. On other occasions, acting out may be necessary to make the meaning clear. If when studying a piece of literature, students need to know what it means to do the two-step, the teacher may indicate a dancing movement taking two steps to the right followed by two steps to the left. To make clear the meaning of the word *plead*, for example, the teacher may place her hands together as if in prayer and look imploringly to indicate a certain amount of desperation.

Use simplifications, expansions of ideas, direct definitions, and comparisons to build in redundancy. The following examples are based on a history lesson:

> *Simplification:* "The government's funds were depleted. It was almost out of money."
>
> *Expansion of ideas:* "The government's funds were depleted. It had spent a lot of money on many things: guns, equipment, help for the poor. It did not have any more money to spend on anything else."
>
> *Direct Definition:* "The government's funds were depleted. This means that the government spent all of its money."

Thus, the key vocabulary "funds were depleted" can be made more comprehensible. It should be noted here that adding new *elements in the discourse* rather than *replacing* difficult items with simpler forms will help the student stretch toward higher levels of language proficiency. It is essential to expose the students to a rich language environment in order to more fully develop their academic skills in the new language. Of course, it is important also not to have too many new elements in the discourse so that the student has nothing familiar to use as a scaffold on which to build. In addition, it is important at first to avoid using complex sentences and a lot of idiomatic expressions. Even pronouns may present problems to beginners. With beginners, use cognates and high frequency vocabulary when possible. Complexities can be added gradually as the student becomes more able to handle them.

Avoid forcing students to speak. Allow them to speak when they are ready—in other words, when they volunteer. The students' right to a silent period

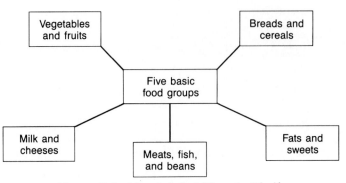

**Figure 10.3. *Mapped Out Ideas to Clarify
A Home Economics Lesson***

needs to be respected, especially when they are being introduced to new concepts.

Reinforce key concepts over and over in a variety of situations and activities. Hearing about the concepts once or twice is not enough. Students need to be exposed to them several times through a wide range of experiences in order for internalization to take place. For example, in home economics if a student is learning the names of vegetables, the teacher might have the student point to various vegetables, pick up specific ones, give them to others to hold, and so on. Later, the teacher might demonstrate how to make a salad with various vegetables, having each student bring one vegetable from home to contribute. As a culminating activity, the teacher might ask students to plan and prepare a vegetarian meal for guests.

In addition, take into account the fact that learning styles and preferences will vary. For example, in a history class, some students may need only a well-delivered description of events to understand their importance. Others may need to experience an acting out of the events to really understand them. Yet others may need full-blown stories with either factual or fictional characters from history for a history lesson to be meaningful.

Establish consistent patterns and routines in the classroom. This technique is especially important for beginning-level students who may not understand oral instructions but who can rely on established routines to provide a familiar context.

Prepare the students for your lessons and reading assignments. Relate what they will be expected to do or learn to their past experiences. Have them share what they already know about the subject. (There is often a tendency to underestimate what language minority students already know about a topic or concept.) Encourage them to look for main ideas by giving them a framework or outline beforehand. Another strategy is to ask them to predict outcomes and then to verify their predictions. Or have them respond to knowledge-based questions and then listen or read to verify their initial responses.

Allow students enough wait time to volunteer answers to questions. Students will need ample time to formulate their responses. Avoid immediately answering the question yourself or calling on someone to respond. If after a sufficient time you still do not receive a response, you might want to rephrase the question and/or answer it yourself. The question/answer process helps students to acquire the appropriate classroom language associated with taking turns.

Make all corrections indirectly by mirroring in correct form what the students have said. For example, suppose a language minority student says, "My book home." The teacher can repeat, "I see. Your book is at home." Remember that ungrammatical forms are to be regarded as normal while the student is progressing toward more complete competence in English. When the student is ready to move to another level, the indirect correction will probably be picked up and internalized after it is heard several times in a variety of situations. In particular, avoid correcting accents. Changes in pronunciation (including accent) will occur naturally through communication over time. The speech may never become "native," especially in adults. However, that should not be cause for concern. The important thing is that the student be able to communicate. Overcorrection of errors both in syntax and pronunciation will create undue anxiety and may serve as a barrier to normal language development.

When evaluating the student's written production, a few suggestions can be made for improvement as long as they are balanced with positive comments. Keep suggestions simple and offer only what you think each student can handle at his or her proficiency level. Written errors can also be corrected indirectly by mirroring what the student has written. Note the following example from Richard-Amato (1989):

> The student has reacted in writing to a story in which a man has committed suicide.
> *Student:* "The story was very scary. I was not sure if the man live or die. My uncle tried that once. I mean commit suicide. Many people try that. I think they are very unhappy."
> *Teacher:* "The story also scared me. I, too, was not sure if the man would live or die until the very end. I hope that in your uncle's situation there was a happier ending."

The teacher's response reveals sensitivity and a genuine interest in the student's ideas. In addition, new structures and vocabulary are presented within a framework with which the student is already familiar. Thus, he or she is encouraged to stretch cognitively to higher levels of meaning and expression. Notice the indirect error correction of the second sentence. (See Chapters 13 and 14 for more suggestions for responding to student writing.)

Try to answer all questions that the students ask but avoid overly detailed explanation. Simple answers that get right to the point will be understood best. If possible, point to objects and pictures, or demonstrate actions to help get the meaning across.

Summarize and review frequently. Concepts can become more firmly established with this additional reinforcement. In addition, a summary or review can provide perspective and context not only for the concepts that have already been learned but for the new ones to come.

Check often to see that what you have said has been understood. Ask questions specifically related to the content. For example, after saying, "In Arizona rainfall is minimal during most of the year," you might check for understanding by asking, "Does it rain much in Arizona?" Asking a question such as this to confirm interpretation is yet another means by which students can be exposed to new words and concepts without losing the meaning of the message. Often a more general "Do you understand?" is followed with "yes" or a nod even though the student may not in fact understand but does not want to appear impolite.

Reassure the students that their own languages are acceptable and important. If several students from the same language group are present, do not insist that they use only English in class. No matter how good the intentions of the teacher, refusing to allow students to speak in their first languages is in essence saying that their languages are not good enough. Of course, students may need to be reminded that first languages should not be used to exclude others from discussion.

Become informed as much as possible about the various cultures represented by your students. Knowing how particular students might react to classroom events and being able to interpret nonverbal symbols could help prevent misunderstanding and confusion. (See Part II, "Cultural Considerations," for more detailed discussion of cultural issues in teaching language minority students.)

Acknowledge and incorporate the students' cultures whenever possible. For instance, differing number systems can be introduced in math, customs and traditions in social science, various medicines in natural science, native dances and games in physical education, songs in music, ethnic calendars in art, haiku in literature, and so on. In addition, holidays can be celebrated, languages can be demonstrated for appreciation, and translations of literature can be shared.

Request that appropriate content-area books be ordered for the library in the students' native languages. These books can be particularly useful to students in comprehending the concepts while the second language is being mastered. They also provide the students with a means for maintaining and developing skills in the native language.

Whenever possible, use tutors who speak the native languages of the students. Such help is especially important to students operating at beginning levels.

Encourage students to use their bilingual dictionaries when necessary or to ask questions when they don't understand important concepts. Help them to guess at meanings first by using the context. Assure them that they do not have to understand every word to comprehend the main ideas.

Increase possibilities for success. Alternating difficult activities with easier ones allows language minority students to experience early successes. For example, in natural science one activity might be to create a diary that Neil Armstrong might have kept on his trip to the moon; the next assignment might be to make a list of the personal items, including food, that he might have taken with him. Of course, the tasks as a whole should gradually become more academically challenging as the students become more proficient.

Student Proficiency Level: High-Intermediate to Advanced

Strategies for Teachers of Mainstream and Sheltered Classes

The language minority student at high-intermediate to high-advanced proficiency levels is clearly more able to tackle the cognitively demanding decontextualized language of the content-area class (refer to the typical behaviors on pages 147–148). However, many of the strategies that have been discussed that are essential when teaching the beginning to mid-intermediate student are equally appropriate for teaching the student with higher proficiency. For example, visual aids are very effective with language minority students across all proficiency levels because pairing an image with the written or spoken word adds multiple cues to meaning. It is also important to continue to add redundancy to content lessons to clarify and reinforce key concepts. However, there is also a variety of strategies and techniques that are particularly effective with students in the high-intermediate to high-advanced proficiency ranges. They are as follows:

Prioritize your instructional objectives. Particularly in sheltered classes, teachers must decide which concepts are most important. Many of the techniques suggested in this chapter may take considerable class time and necessitate decisions about what to keep and what to cut. In the long run, language minority students will benefit more from lessons tailored to their developing proficiency levels, even at the expense of breadth of coverage.

Add as much contextual support as possible to your lesson presentations and reading assignments. Although sheltered classes have the advantage of homogeneous grouping of language minority students, the content is still cognitively demanding and a variety of strategies are useful there as well as in mainstream classes. As mentioned, high-intermediate to high-advanced students can also benefit from increased contextual support through the use of visual aids such as charts, pictures, diagrams and from hands-on experiential activities of the type that work well with beginning to mid-intermediate students.

Introducing students to their textbook with a text preview helps them to discover how to use graphics and other ancillary materials such as study questions, chapter summaries, glossaries, and indexes. Another way to add contextual support is to give students partially completed outlines or lists, which help to structure new and/or difficult content into a more manageable form. Other effective techniques for adding contextual support to cognitively demanding content materials are clustering, mapping, and semantic webbing. (See Chapter 20 for examples of these techniques applied to a literature lesson.)

Provide language minority students opportunities to practice critical thinking skills. Recall from Chapter 2 that Cummins makes a distinction between proficiency in conversational language and proficiency in cognitive academic language. To develop the latter, second language (L2) learners need to be exposed to academic tasks that require analysis, synthesis, and evaluation. It is also important to note that teachers often misjudge the language minority student's cognitive capabilities. When teachers hear pronunciation and grammar errors, they often underestimate what second language learners can handle cognitively and, as a result, deprive them of exposure to cognitively demanding content materials.

Identify the key terms essential to understanding what it is you are attempting to teach. The academic and technical vocabulary range of your language minority students may still be quite limited. They will also encounter nontechnical terms used in a specific technical sense. For example, language minority students might correctly associate the word *left* with ''left hand'' or ''turn left,'' but they might be confused by its political connotation in a social studies text.

An array of strategies can be used to help students master new vocabulary. You and your students can create word banks for selected units/topics and can display them around the room. When introducing new vocabulary, an enjoyable technique is the use of word squares. Provide students with pieces of paper on which are four predrawn squares, or have students draw their own squares. Have students write the new vocabulary item in the first box. Have students write in the second box an example or illustrate the new term with a picture. Have them write in the third box an antonym or something that is not an example. And have them write in the fourth square a definition of the term in their own words.

Semantic mapping is another useful vocabulary-building strategy. In this activity, students brainstorm and categorize new terms according to the terms' shared characteristics. Through this process, they learn what types of information are contained in a definition. Thus, they learn that definitions in English typically contain the term, followed by the general group to which it belongs, followed by its distinguishing attributes or features. For example, ''Caffeine is a stimulant that is found in coffee, tea, and some soft drinks.''

It is also important to teach students to guess meaning from context. Second language learners need to realize that they do not have to know every word to understand the gist. Amusing and instructive activities can be undertaken using sentences containing blanks. Students have to guess the meaning from examining the context by using grammar, punctuation, and meaning cues. An example of such a sentence is, ''_____ is chronic difficulty in getting to sleep or staying asleep.''

Be aware of the linguistic demands of your content area. What immediately comes to mind to most content-area teachers is the specialized vocabulary required of each content area. Although clearly teachers must take care to teach key terms using the strategies we have discussed, it is important for them to realize that each content area requires a distinctive mode of analysis far beyond its specialized terms.

Certain types of language structures, connectors, and means of categorization are prevalent in particular content areas. Scientific English typically includes long noun groups (e.g., government energy conservation project) and impersonal verb structures such as the passive voice to describe processes (e.g., the experiment was conducted, subjects were administered). Moreover, precise use of connecting devices such as *consequently* and *therefore* and nouns of specificity such as *phase* and *component* are frequently used in scientific writing to express logical relationships.

In addition, each content area has its own inherent structure. For example, in social studies, the realtionship between sources, facts, main ideas, generalizations, and concepts is portrayed schematically in Figure 10.4. The language

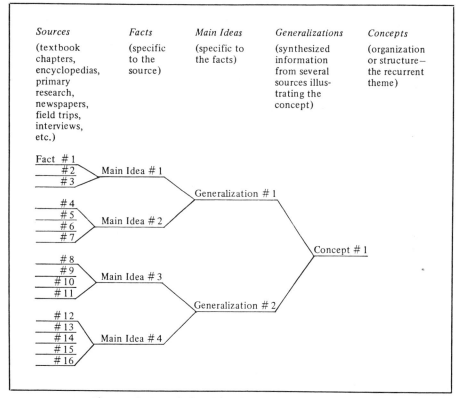

Figure 10.4. *Relationships between Sources, Facts, Main Ideas, Generalizations, and Concepts in Social Studies*

From "Second Language Learning in a Social Studies Classroom" by Phillip C. Gonzales, 1981 (Nov./Dec.), *The Social Studies*, p. 257. Reprinted with permission of the Helen Dwight Reid Educational Foundation. Published by Heldref Publications, 4000 Albemarle St., N.W., Washington, D.C. 20016. Copyright © 1981.

of geography relies heavily on linguistic means for expressing spatial relation-ships; nonverbal data are often found in charts, graphs, and maps and must be converted into prose. The definition and classification modes are common in geography to define members of a class with differentiating characteristics. Although we are not suggesting that you make a comprehensive linguistic analysis of your content area, teachers in multicultural classes must to some degree become sensitive to the language demands of their subject matter in order to effectively teach language development within the content areas.

Design schema-building activities. A variety of strategies can help activate students' background knowledge and thereby provide schema for the new material. Techniques such as reviewing previously covered material, relating concepts to students' own experiences (e.g., the American revolution to the wars in Southeast Asia and Central America), and using brainstorming or clustering activities help to provide a frame of reference for cognitively demanding content materials.

Anticipation guides such as the example that follows used to get students into a reading from natural science about predation can stimulate interest in a topic and help students relate the known to the unknown. (See another example of an anticipation guide for a literature lesson in Chapter 20.) Moreover, they provide teachers with a quick and easy way to assess what students already know about a topic.

> You might not consider human behavior to be in any way like the behavior of a predator hunting prey. But consider these questions: Have you ever tried to catch a frog or a butterfly? If so, you were probably trying to catch it using strategies similar to those of a predator hunting prey. What kinds of movements did you make to capture it? What did it do to get away? Who won in the struggle?
> Read the following statements. Check the ones you think are true.
> a. There are organisms (living things) that spend their entire lives living and feeding on the bodies of others.
> b. An organism's colors can serve as a defense against predators.
> c. Some organisms ''pretend'' to be poisonous to keep from being eaten by predators.
> d. Predators are a nuisance because they ruin the lives of their prey and sometimes cause horrible suffering.[2]

Provide models that students can emulate. Models can be used for a variety of purposes by content-area teachers. Develop study guides for the first chapter in the course textbook to show students how to decide what is important and how to condense the information into smaller units as a study aid.

---

[2] From *Reading in the Content Areas: An Interactive Approach for International Students.* by P. Richard-Amato, 1990, (p. 40). Copyright © by Longman Publishers. Reprinted by permission.

Photocopy a section from an assigned reading in your textbook and, with the whole class, go through the passage discussing what should be highlighted (in yellow, for example) or what should be transferred to study notes. Provide sample lecture notes of one of your presentations. Have students compare the sample with their notes, and discuss suggestions for improving the format (e.g., structure, use of abbreviations). Help students recognize transitions and lecturer emphasis (e.g., "In sum," "What is really critical is . . . "). Select examples of good writing (e.g., a well-developed argument or well-written lab report) from your content textbook, the newspaper, magazines, or from good papers of former students for use in modeling what you expect in an assignment.

Give your students opportunities to write in the content areas. Writing should not be the exclusive domain of the language teacher. The philosophy presented in this book espouses a cross-curricular approach to the teaching of writing. Design a writing assignment with the six steps of the Writing Process in mind (see Figure 10.5). Begin your assignment with prewriting activities in which students discover that they have something to say about the topic before they actually write. After they have written a first draft, have students share their work in groups acting as "peer editors." (See a sample peer editing guide in Chapter 13). Students can then incorporate this feedback along with your assistance. Following this step, have students sharpen their proofreading skills before turning their work in to be evaluated.

Incorporate group work whenever appropriate. As was suggested for the beginning to mid-intermediate levels, language minority students at higher levels also require plenty of opportunities to negotiate for meaning. They need to practice their newly emerging abilities to discuss, in the target language, topics related to specific academic fields. Have students work in groups to make charts, diagrams, murals, or posters with various content themes. They can also prepare TV commercials, skits, and debates, and make up chants, songs, or "raps."[3] Several other ideas for group work can be found in Chapter 5 on cooperative learning and in Chapter 18 on the use of peer teachers.

Teach your students academic information-processing skills. By this, we mean the ability to manipulate course materials by synthesizing multiple sources of information. Studies of the kinds of assignments typically required in college and university classes have revealed that students must demonstrate analytical skills—that is, the ability to reintegrate data from various sources. These sources typically include textbook information, lecture material, personal reflection, or student-gathered data (an experiment, observation, interview, etc). Academic information-processing skills are typically reflected in assignments that contain

---

[3] These group activities were suggested by Alfredo Schifini as enjoyable activities to extract meaning from expository text.

Figure 10.5. *The Writing Process*

From "Teaching Writing as a Process" by Cathy D'Aoust, 1986, (p. 9) in C. B. Olson (Ed.), *Practical Ideas for Teaching Writing as a Process.* Copyright © 1986 by the California State Department of Education. (Available from the Bureau of Publications, California State Department of Education, P. 0. Box 271, Sacramento, CA 95802–0271.) Reprinted by permission.

prompts such as "compare/contrast," "classify," "describe the process," "analyze and take a position," or "provide an interpretation of X." Language minority students, like all students, must be given opportunities to integrate multiple sources in their writing at all levels of schooling.

Coach your students in appropriate learning strategies for mastering content material. Language minority students are often academically inexperienced and lack the necessary repertoire of study skills that native English-speaking students may already have. Give them tips on time management, note-taking organization, and test-taking strategies. Have them develop memory strategies such as the use of mnemonics and techniques for practice and self-testing. Model cognitive strategies to demonstrate how to recognize patterns and structures of the content material. Exposure to metacognitive strategies helps students to internalize the specialized structures and rhetorical organizations of the content area and to grasp the internal language of math, the language of history, and so forth. Finally, teach language minority students effective compensation strategies such as learning to guess intelligently to help them make up for their gaps in language skills and background knowledge.

Plan assignments carefully. In designing assignments, ask yourself the following questions: What background knowledge is assumed? Have I given the students sufficient opportunities to practice the language and critical thinking skills required of the assignment? Have I given them adequate time to work through all aspects of the assignment? Have I anticipated possible problems? Have I provided an opportunity for feedback before the assignment is evaluated for a grade? Have I made my criteria for evaluation clear?

Be on the look out for persistent language problems that may interfere with a student's work. When serious language problems arise, seek assistance from ESL or English teachers. Language minority students may require special individualized attention in specific areas.

RECOMMENDED RESOURCES

In the past few years a number of commercial materials that focus on language development in the content areas have been introduced. They may be of use in sheltered and mainstream classes.

Chamot, A. U. (1987). *America: The early years.* Language development through content. Reading, MA: Addison-Wesley.

Chamot, A. U. (1987). *America: After independence.* Language development through content. Reading, MA: Addison-Wesley.

Chamot, A. U. (1987). *Teacher's guide: America: The early years/America: After independence.* Language development through content. Reading, MA: Addison-Wesley.

Chamot, A. U. (1988). *Mathematics: Book A.* Language development through content. Reading, MA: Addison-Wesley.

Crandall, J., Dale, T. C., Rhodes, N. C., & Spanos, G. (1989). *English skills for algebra.* Englewood Cliffs, NJ: Prentice Hall Regents/Center for Applied Linguistics.

Fathman, A. K., & Quinn, M. E. (1989). *Science for language learners.* Englewood Cliffs, NJ: Prentice Hall Regents/Center for Applied Linguistics.

Johnston, J., & Johnston, M. (1990). *Content points A: Science, mathematics & social studies*. Reading, MA: Addison-Wesley.

Johnston, J., & Johnston, M. (1990). *Content points B: Science,mathematics & social studies*. Reading, MA: Addison-Wesley.

Johnston, J., & Johnston, M. (1990). *Content points C: Science, mathematics & social studies*. Reading, MA: Addison-Wesley.

Lim, P. L., & Smalzer, W. (1990). *Noteworthy: Listening and notetaking skills.* New York: Newbury House.

Richard-Amato, P. (1990). *Reading in the content areas: An interactive approach for international students.*White Plains, NY: Longman.

Terdy, D. (1986). *Content area ESL: Social studies*. Palatine, IL: Linmore Publishing.

The following teacher reference books contain useful resource material for content-area teachers:

Brinton, D. M., Snow, M. A., & Wesche, M. B. (1989). *Content-based second language instruction.* New York: Newbury House.

Oxford, R. L. (1990). *Language learning strategies: What every teacher should know.* New York: Newbury House.

FOLLOW-UP QUESTIONS AND ACTIVITIES

1. Discuss the sorts of problems students might have if they are thrown "sink or swim" into mainstream classrooms without the benefit of ESL, sheltered, or adjunct program components.

2. Let's say you find yourself placed in a school in which many language minority students are present. You are surprised to learn that the school does not have ESL, sheltered, or adjunct components in its curriculum, nor do school personnel think that such programs are important. In fact, you heard a school official say that his ''grandfather came to this country without knowing the language and he did just fine.'' If you are convinced of the need for ESL, sheltered, and/or adjunct components in the curriculum, how would you convince the school official of their necessity?

3. In what ways might you establish consistent patterns and routines (see page 152) in your classes? Compare your ideas with those of a partner.

4. With a partner in a similar teaching situation, decide what some of the specific linguistic demands might be (see page 157) for a particular content

area. How might you make it easier for your language minority students to meet these demands in your classes?

5. Plan a lesson appropriate for a specific teaching situation. Assume that your language minority students are operating at the low-intermediate proficiency level. Try your lesson with a small group of your fellow students. Include a description of the unit of which this lesson is a part. Make a special effort to incorporate into the lesson several of the following suggestions from this chapter:

a. Use slower speech, clear enunciation, emphasis on key words and phrases through gestures, facial expression, and intonation. At the same time take care to remain as *natural* as possible and not sound condescending.
b. Include visuals to clarify key concepts.
c. Demonstrate or act out when appropriate.
d. Use simplification, expansion of ideas, direct definitions, and comparisons when needed (see page 151).
e. Allow group members pretending to be your language minority students to volunteer their contributions without being forced to speak. Give enough wait time for them to respond to questions you might have.
f. Check often to see that what you have said has been understood.

After the lesson tell how you would reinforce key concepts in other lessons and situations and ask for feedback from the group.

11

Adapting Materials and Developing Lesson Plans

Deborah J. Short *Center for Applied Linguistics*

Editors' Introduction

Even teachers who become highly skilled at adapting their oral presentations to make the content of their lessons more comprehensible are often at a loss when it comes to adapting the written texts to which their students are exposed. Because written materials are oriented generally to native speakers of English, second language (L2) learners often find them too difficult semantically and syntactically. Moreover, they may find them culturally biased (see also Chapter 17). In this chapter, Deborah Short offers means for bringing textbooks within reach of language minority students. She recommends ways to build on prior knowledge, to simplify syntax and vocabulary, and to clarify basic organizational patterns without watering down the content.

When teachers are asked to describe the process of adapting materials, they often focus on vocabulary. They suggest replacing words with simpler synonyms or defining terms at the beginning of a reading passage. Some teachers will also point to sentence length and suggest writing shorter statements. At least one teacher in a group will likely voice concern about "watered-down" materials. "When I simplify materials, I lose the substance," that teacher might say. This may indeed occur, but it need not.

Successful materials adaptation goes far beyond simplifying vocabulary and shortening sentences and avoids watering down essential information. Materials adaptation is not rewriting prose at a lower grade level but adapting information to make it accessible to language minority students. Certainly, one of the end goals is to develop students' ability to read standard textbooks, reference materials, and news articles; but many limited English proficient (LEP) students find prose passages very threatening at the start. The visual presentation of information is, therefore, key to adaptation.

From "Adapting Materials for Content-Based Language Instruction" by D. Short, 1989, in the ERIC/CLL Bulletin, 13(1), (pp. 4–8). Adapted by permission.

Pictures, charts, and timelines make materials more "user friendly." A series of pictures or a flowchart can convey a process to a student more rapidly than a paragraph or two filled with transitional adverbs and complex-compound sentences. Through comprehensible chunks of words and phrases, an outline can concisely convey essential information drawn from a passage. Timelines can subtly encourage the higher-order thinking skill of sequencing, whereas charts exercise the skill of comparing and contrasting. Formats such as these highlight specific points and diminish extraneous information.

While adapting or creating, teachers have the opportunity to use authentic materials in an abridged form. News articles may be adapted; post office or banking transactions may be taped and used as listening exercises; authentic literature may be included in the lessons. Teachers, having greater control over the content and being sensitive to the cross-cultural differences among students, can adapt materials to meet the students' level of cultural and linguistic understanding.

It may be useful here to review an original passage and its adaptation, and then look at specific considerations for adapting materials. The original text, *United States History 1600–1987*, distributed by the U.S. Immigration and Naturalization Service to applicants seeking citizenship, was recently adapted for limited English speakers. The following two paragraphs are taken from a chapter in the original text on the first two permanent colonies in North America.

Virginia

The first permanent colony was Jamestown, Virginia (1607). These colonists came from England to try to make money by trading with Europe. They believed they would find gold and silver as the Spanish had found in South America, and then they would be rich. When they got to Jamestown, most of the men tried to find gold. They did not want to do the difficult jobs of building, planting food crops and cutting firewood. One of the colonists, John Smith, saw how dangerous this could be. He took charge and made everyone work to survive. He is remembered for his good practical leadership. Still, less than half of the colonists survived the first few years. Only new settlers and supplies from England made it possible for the colony to survive. The discovery of tobacco as a cash crop to be traded in Europe guaranteed that the colony would do well.

Massachusetts

Many of the colonists came to America to try to find religious freedom. The Catholics had troubles in England and other parts of Europe. The rulers of these countries told their citizens that they must go to a specific church and worship in a certain way. Some people believed differently than their rulers and wanted to have their own churches. The first group to come to America for religious freedom was the **Pilgrims** in 1620. They sailed across the ocean in the *Mayflower* and landed at Plymouth, Massachusetts. Before landing at Plymouth, the Pilgrims agreed on the government they wanted. The agreement was called the **Mayflower Compact.** It had two important principles:

the people would vote about the government and laws; and,

the people would accept whatever the majority chose.[1]

For a beginning or intermediate language learner, these passages are full of pitfalls. For instance, an immigrant to California, who has been in the United States for only a few weeks, may have no knowledge of the location of Massachusetts and Virginia. That same immigrant may not recognize that England is part of Europe, nor that the Pilgrims were not Catholic. The syntactic and semantic structures of the passage may also pose problems: less common verb tenses (e.g., had found, to be traded), temporal and relative clauses, indirect speech, and complex lexical words and phrases (e.g., less than half of, whatever).

Figure 11.1 is an adaptation of the passages developed for high beginning-level students. This layout, which uses a map to show the first two permanent English colonies in North America and highlights the information about each colony in a comparable manner, offers LEP students access to the pertinent details of the passages.[2] The map places the colony names in context. The inclusion of the compass symbol can lead to a class activity on map skills. The information is structured to explain:

when the colonies were formed

who the colonists were

what the colonies were named

why the colonies were formed

an interesting fact about each colony

Information has been conveyed through a pictorial representation (the map) with chunks of information that can be processed more easily than sentences. Teachers can use this adaptation as the basis of a lesson, and build upon the information as appropriate to the proficiency level of their students. Although Thanksgiving was not mentioned in the original text, it was included as an interesting fact about Plymouth Colony so that teachers could expand the cross-cultural awareness of students in discussions about that holiday.

Both language and social studies teachers could use this adaptation in the classroom. Language teachers may ask students to use the information to write sentences comparing the two colonies, or they may encourage predictions about the seasons according to the different latitudes of the colonies. Social studies teachers may expand on this material by having groups of students

---

[1] Immigration and Naturalization Service, U.S. Department of Justice. (1987). *United States History 1600–1987.* (p.6). Washington, DC: Government Printing Office.

[2] Short, D., Seufert-Bosco, M., & Grognet, A. (1991). *Of the People: U.S. History.* Englewood Cliffs, NJ: Prentice Hall Regents/Center for Applied Linguistics.

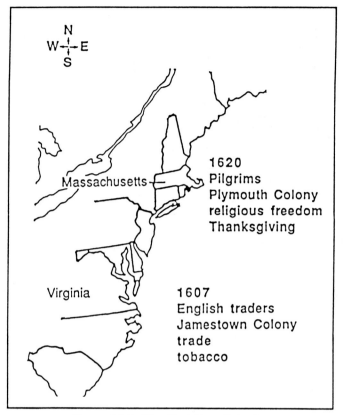

Figure 11.1. *The First Two Colonies*

research one of the colonies in more detail. Because the students will have already been presented with this background information, they have a schema upon which to add and link more facts and impressions.

STEPS IN ADAPTING MATERIALS

Figure 11.1 is one example of adapting an original text passage. There are a number of steps for teachers to follow in adapting materials. Many of these are described in *How To Integrate Language and Content: A Training Manual* (Short, Crandall, & Christian, 1989).

Consider the Students' Proficiency Level

The first step in materials adaptation requires a teacher to consider the proficiency level of the students and then review possible formats for the presentation of information. Does the information to be presented lend itself to a graph, chart, outline, or simplified prose version? Pictures, diagrams, and graphs are suitable as introductory formats because they tend to be labeled with fewer words. Outlines, timelines, charts, and prose versions will offer more of a challenge. Overall, it is best to vary the format of the presentation. Exposing students to different formats will help to cater to different learning styles and to relieve boredom. (See Chapter 10 for the behavior characteristics of each proficiency level.)

Build on Students' Prior Knowledge

The second step involves the teacher's moving from the known to the unknown, and from the concrete to the abstract, while relating materials, as much as possible, to student experiences. For instance, in the example given in Figure 11.1, the map depicting the eastern coast of the United States and the Atlantic ocean is a familiar sight for most students; it immediately places Massachusetts and Virginia in context. To relate materials to personal experiences of the students, teachers can initiate conversation about the colonists' reasons for coming to America—religious freedom and trade—and then lead into a class discussion in which students explain their own reasons for coming to the United States.

Highlight Specific Text

As teachers begin adapting written material, they should try to reduce the amount of text. Main points should be highlighted, and extraneous detail can be excluded. During the course of a lesson, though, teachers may insert details if students express interest in the subject. By using bold typeface, underlining, and italics, teachers can provide visual clues that point to the main idea and the supporting facts.

Control New Vocabulary

When teachers adapt materials, they can control vocabulary. For this process, teachers should follow certain recommendations. Vocabulary can be simplified, but key technical terms must be retained. Students are being prepared for mainstream classes, so they need to learn the academic language that accompanies the content-area subjects. The use of synonyms should be minimized to avoid confusing students who are trying to grasp the essence of the prose. The language in mathematics classes, where synonyms abound in word problems, may be problematic. For example, the operation of subtraction may be referred to in more than ten ways in simple word problems (e.g., subtracted from, decreased by, diminished by, less than). Teachers should wait for the students to master the mathematical concepts before introducing synonymous terms. Finally, new vocabulary should be clearly introduced (and, where possible, explained before a reading—unless the purpose of the activity is for students to discover vocabulary meaning in context) and reinforced within the adaptation and subsequent materials.

Simplify Grammar

At the start, teachers should use simple verb tenses, such as present, present continuous, simple past, and simple future. Commands (imperative verb forms) are appropriate for asking students to perform an experiment or discovery exercise. Teachers should simplify word order in sentences by eliminating clauses and relying on the common subject-verb-object format. They should also write in the active voice and limit the use of pronouns and relative clauses. By repeating the subject noun or breaking the *who* and *which* into separate sentences, teachers write straightforward prose that facilitates student comprehension. Similar care should be taken with negations. Students learn the *verb + not* structure fairly quickly but are often confused by *hardly, no longer,* and *no more.*

Structure Paragraphs Carefully

If teachers plan to adapt material in prose form with paragraphs, they must remember certain points. The topic sentence should appear first. Students can then recognize the main idea of the paragraph and learn to look for supporting information in the following sentences. Also, key features of the text that guide the flow of information should be maintained. Terms such as *first, next,* and *then,* indicate sequence; *but* indicates contrast; *because* can indicate cause and effect. As students develop higher-order cognitive skills, they learn to recognize these markers.

SAMPLE ADAPTATIONS

Following is a passage from a fifth-grade social studies book that has been adapted three ways for different proficiency levels and activities. (For additional activity suggestions with adapted materials, see Brinton, Snow, and Wesche, 1989.)

First is the original version from *The United States Yesterday and Today:*

Agriculture—Farmers in the Middle Atlantic States grow many kinds of crops. In much of the region, the soil is fertile, or rich in the things plants need for growth. There is usually plenty of sunshine and rain. Each state has become famous for certain crops. New York is well known for apples. New Jersey tomatoes and blueberries, Delaware white sweet corn, Pennsylvania mushrooms, and Maryland grains are other well-known crops. Herds of dairy cattle and livestock for meat are also raised in the Middle Atlantic States. The region produces a great deal of food for the millions of people who live there.

Truck Farms—New Jersey is famous for its truck farms, which grow large amounts of many different vegetables for sale. *Truck farms* usually sell their products to businesses in a nearby city. New Jersey truck farms are the best known, but truck farms are found in all the Middle Atlantic States.

Another way truck farmers sell their crops is at *farmers' markets* in cities. Sometimes a farmers' market is outside, on the street or in a city park. A market may be in a railroad station or in the lobby of a skyscraper. At a farmers' market, city people and farmers can meet each other face-to-face.[3]

In the first adaptation, shown in Figure 11.2, teachers focus on map skills. Students learn about the well-known crops for each state and how to read a key. This adaptation is suitable for beginning-level students because it is largely pictorial. It can also lead to a class discussion or a simple writing exercise.

In the second adaptation, shown on page 171, teachers create an outline of the passage. This can be used with lower-intermediate-level students. Teachers may have groups of students use the outline as a basis for writing sentences or paragraphs. They may also use this as a cloze exercise (see page 193) with more advanced students who can read the original passage. By filling in blanks on the outline, students practice study skills as they read the text.

[3] From *The United States Yesterday and Today*. © 1988 Silver, Burdett & Ginn Inc. All rights reserved. Used with permission. (Italicized words indicate vocabulary highlighted in the original.)

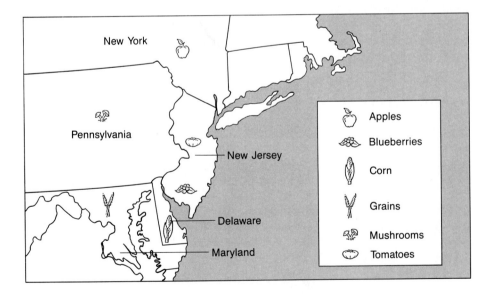

Figure 11.2. *A Graphic Adaptation*

Middle Atlantic States

   I. Agriculture
      A. Many kinds of food crops
      B. State crops
         1. New York—apples
         2. New Jersey—tomatoes, blueberries
         3. Delaware—corn
         4. Pennsylvania—mushrooms
         5. Maryland—grains
      C. Cows for milk and meat
  II. Truck Farms
      A. Many truck farms in New Jersey
      B. Sell vegetables to stores in a city
 III. Farmers' Markets
      A. Farmers sell crops in the city
         1. On a street
         2. In a park
         3. In a train station
         4. In a building
      B. Farmers and city people meet

The third adaptation is a rewritten version of the prose. It may be used in a lesson for intermediate-level students. The students may be asked to respond to comprehension questions or to write their own outline about this paragraph. They may also be asked to create a key for a map of the Middle Atlantic States. A dictation or listening cloze could be based on this passage. These paragraphs provide only an overview, but they could be the basis for more detailed group reports about agriculture in these states.

Agriculture in the Middle Atlantic States

Farmers grow many foods, or **crops,** in the Middle Atlantic States. The soil is good for plants. The plants have enough sunshine and rain to grow. Each state has one or two special crops:

    New York—apples
    New Jersey—tomatoes and blueberries
    Delaware—corn
    Pennsylvania—mushrooms
    Maryland—grains

The farmers also raise cows. They get milk from some cows. They get meat from other cows.

New Jersey has many **truck farms.** The farmers grow a lot of vegetables. They bring the vegetables to the city by truck. They sell the vegetables to stores in the city.

Farmers also sell their crops at **farmers' markets.** Some markets are outside. They can be on streets or in city parks. Other markets are inside. They can be in train stations or in buildings. City people and farmers can meet each other at the markets.

BENEFITS OF MATERIALS ADAPTATIONS

There are many benefits of using adapted materials. The first is teacher control over content. Teachers can adjust both language and format to the proficiency level of their students. A second benefit is teacher control over cultural bias in materials. Teachers can eliminate language that assumes a particular cultural background, control the introduction of new cultural information, and relate content to the students' native culture.

A third benefit is teacher control over skills development. Teachers can provide a wealth of skill-development exercises. Students can practice transferring information using one basic language skill and then another. For example, after reading a graph, or looking at a series of pictures, students can retell the information orally or in writing. In this way, they exercise more than one language skill. Timelines and charts lend themselves to information-gap activities and other listening activities.[4] Study skills are honed when students take notes, draw diagrams, or make outlines, charts, or graphs from prose adaptations.

In addition, by using adapted materials, teachers can help students develop the cognitive academic skills required in mainstream classes. Charts can be used to explain the rhetorical styles of cause and effect, or comparison and contrast. Timelines can be used to encourage students to make predictions or hypotheses. Furthermore, by reducing prose to a skeleton of salient points, teachers require students to analyze information, draw inferences, and reword information. This process tests and encourages development of students' higher-order thinking skills.

Finally, by adapting materials, teachers can readily integrate language and content. They can focus on the particular needs of their own students and use their own curriculum. When language teachers and content teachers collaborate, they plan their instruction to reinforce the information presented in other classes. This careful pairing of language and content better prepares language minority students for academic mainstream classes.

---

[4] In an information-gap activity, a student with some information works with a partner with complementary information to complete a timeline, chart, map, and the like.

RECOMMENDED READINGS

Cantoni-Harvey, G. (1987). *Content-area language instruction: Approaches and strategies*. Reading, MA: Addison-Wesley.

Crandall, J. A., Dale, T., Rhodes, N., & Spanos, G. (1989). *English skills for algebra*. Englewood Cliffs, NJ: Prentice Hall Regents/Center for Applied Linguistics.

Crandall, J. A. (Ed.). (1987). *ESL through content-area instruction*. Englewood Cliffs, NJ: Prentice Hall Regents/ERIC Clearinghouse on Languages and Linguistics. (ERIC Document Reproduction Service No. ED 283387)

Curtain, H. A., & Martinez, L. S. (1990). Elementary School content-based foreign language instruction. In A. M. Padilla, H. H. Fairchild, & C. M. Valadez (Eds.), *Foreign language education: issues and strategies* (pp. 201–202). Newbury Park, CA: Sage.

Jacob, E., & Mattson, B. (1987). *Cooperative learning with limited-English-proficient students. Q & A*. Washington, DC: ERIC/CLL-Center for Language Education and Research. (ERIC Document Reproduction Service No. ED 287314)

Krashen S., & Terrell, T. (1983). *The natural approach*. San Francisco: Pergamon/Alemany Press.

Mohan, B. (1986). *Language and content*. Reading, MA: Addison-Wesley.

Northcutt, L., & Watson, D. (1986). *S.E.T.: Sheltered English teaching handbook*. Carlsbad, CA: Northcutt, Watson, Gonzales.

Willetts, K. (Ed.). (1986) *Integrating language and content instruction*. Los Angeles: Center for Language Education and Research, UCLA. [CLEAR Educational Report # 5] (ERIC Document Reproduction Service No. ED 278262)

Willetts, K. & Crandall, J. A. (1986). Content-based language instruction. *ERIC/CLL News Bulletin, 9 (2)*. Washington, DC: ERIC Clearinghouse on Languages and Linguistics.

FOLLOW-UP QUESTIONS AND ACTIVITIES

1. Locate a portion of text intended for native speakers of English in a specific content area. Using several of Short's recommendations, adapt it to meet the needs of intermediate L2 students. Refer to page 147 for language behaviors typical of intermediate levels before beginning this task.

2. What manipulatives, maps, charts, or other visual aids might you use to supplement your adapted text? Create two or three.

3. Prepare a lesson using the materials you prepared in Activities 1 and 2. Be specific about the age and proficiency levels of the students with whom you might use it. Present your lesson to a small group and ask for their feedback. To what extent was it successful? What would you revise?

4. Can you think of practices to avoid when adapting materials for language minority students? Explain.

12

Facilitating the Reading Process

GINA CANTONI-HARVEY   *Northern Arizona University*

EDITORS' INTRODUCTION

The work of Kenneth Goodman (1982), Frank Smith (1975, 1978), and many others has brought us a more holistic approach to the reading process. No longer do we feel compelled to focus on isolated skills to be drilled, sometimes by painful means—for example, endless workbooks and worksheets. Instead, we can focus on the reader—the reader's individual needs, valuing systems, existing knowledge and culturally determined schemata, all in relation to the content. In this chapter, Gina Cantoni-Harvey presents several ways in which we may readjust our sights without placing decoding skills (written symbols, sound-symbol correspondences, etc.) in jeopardy. One of these methods, the language experience approach (LEA), gives written form to the oral language that the students already possess. In addition, the whole language *classroom is explored as it pertains to current theory. In this classroom, students read mainly for enjoyment and information. The teacher acts as a facilitator, guiding students to become increasingly independent readers in their new language. Although the recommendations presented are oriented to children, they can be applied across the content areas to a variety of age and proficiency levels—beginning through advanced. As you read, think about ways in which they can be adapted to your own teaching situation.*

A reader applies processes that lead to comprehension of the language input obtained from graphic symbols. Since reading is a language-based activity, it is difficult to understand a text written in a language one does not know well. The difficulties caused by a student's limited English proficiency are often compounded by other problems, including inadequate decoding skills.

The processing of written material occurs at the word and sentence level as well as at the higher level of paragraphs and larger units of discourse. The reader assigns meaning to the words on the page, stores these concepts in working memory, and integrates them into abstract models by combining them with the mental schemata constructed previously. These new models are continuously revised and expanded as a result of the ongoing processing of additional material (Perfetti, 1985). The linguistic knowledge involved in these processes includes the semantic, syntactic, and phonological system that is shared by oral and written language. However, it is important to remember that listening and reading are not the same.

A reader does not receive the same kind of input as a listener; a reader can process the information as slowly or as quickly as needed and is free to scan ahead or to review a difficult passage. Punctuation marks provide a reasonable approximation of intonation patterns, and blank spaces between words allow the reader to segment the text with a degree of precision that might be difficult or impossible for a listener. However, a reader cannot address questions to the writer or force the writer to change the subject. The content of a written text is controlled by the author, and the reader must either adjust to it or give up. When people participate in a conversation, they tend to discuss personal topics and mutually interesting experiences. On the other hand, a reader is not necessarily familiar with the content discussed by a writer and might seriously misunderstand it. When reading a novel, a student might make incorrect inferences about the motives and intentions of its characters unless he or she is acquainted with the cultural context in which the author has placed them. Because of limited knowledge of the world, a child may find the events discussed in a story quite startling and the writer's conclusion very arbitrary.

Many children find the transition from oral contexts to the more abstract ones of written communication quite difficult, since they must not only master a new coding system but learn to construct meaning without the benefit of the additional cues that are available during face-to-face interactions. Many older students continue to find reading difficult despite their teachers' sustained efforts; although their problems may be due to a variety of interrelated factors, inadequate decoding skills often intensify them.

According to Perfetti (1985), decoding instruction can be helpful to students who are reluctant to read because they cannot recognize many of the words they see. Sustained practice in inferencing, summarizing, predicting, and other higher-order processes does not eliminate the need for proper attention to the lower-level abilities necessary for processing written information quickly and accurately.

Unfortunately, the materials and procedures used for teaching lower-level reading skills are often dull and childish, and may, therefore, further alienate those learners who are already convinced of their own inadequacy. This danger can be alleviated by incorporating decoding practice into story reading (Beck, 1981); when students become engrossed in the content of a story, the teacher will find it easier to hold their attention while explaining how they can unlock the meaning of an important word.

Decoding skills can often be taught successfully, even to the most reluctant readers, by allowing them to use computers and selecting software that has been proven effective for this purpose. This approach has an additional advantage: It combines the motivational features of computer games with the recordkeeping and feedback efficiency of computer-assigned instruction (Perfetti, 1985). Several suggestions for using computers during reading instruction can be found in Wilkinson (1983) and Frederiksen et al. (1983).

THE BEGINNING LEVELS OF READING INSTRUCTION

During the initial stages of reading instruction, the learners must interact with written input appropriate for their level of development and language proficiency. A native speaker of English becomes ready to read by engaging in a variety of meaningful experiences and discussing them orally; oral language activities are even more important in the case of second language learners, since they promote proficiency as well as reading readiness.

LEP students can acquire a large amount of English vocabulary by participating in classroom routines and listening to the teacher and to peers. In addition, they can increase their knowledge of many useful words by engaging in total physical response (TPR) activities (Asher, 1982).[1] The early stages of this approach promote listening comprehension, which leads to oral proficiency.

Total physical response activities can also be used during reading instruction. When children are able to identify the objects mentioned by the teacher, they can be taught to recognize the written words that represent them. At first the teacher should attach flashcards to the objects named and draw the pupil's attention to them when they obey the commands. Later, the teacher can remove some of the cards and ask the children to place them on the appropriate items. These activities can help children acquire a sight vocabulary, but they should not be used as substitutes for decoding instruction. However, the ability to recognize written words at a glance can be quite useful, especially when they are not spelled regularly.

One of the most effective strategies for preparing children to read consists of reading to them. LEP students as well as native speakers of English should have many opportunities to hear the teacher read their favorite stories aloud. After listening, they will want to discuss their feelings and reactions and express them in a picture or a piece of writing.

While reading to the children, the teacher might record the story on a cassette and place it in the listening center, where they can hear it again as often as they wish. They should be allowed to borrow the text and look at the pictures or read along aloud or silently.

---

[1] Total physical response activities involve the student in physical responses to commands in the target language. For example, during a lesson on geographical locations, the teacher might say, "Point to the equator on the map." The student demonstrates comprehension by complying with the request.

The Language Experience Approach

Every child needs to experience reading as a rewarding and successful process. However, it may be difficult to assemble an adequate supply of literature for the wide range of abilities found in every classroom, especially if some of the learners are not fully proficient in English. Nevertheless, a teacher can accumulate a considerable amount of reading material relevant to the students' backgrounds and suitable for their level of English proficiency by using the language experience approach (LEA).[2] The rationale for using language experience texts is explained in Van Allen's famous lines (Van Allen & Halvoren, 1961):

What I can think about I can talk about.
What I can say I can write.
What I can write I can read.
I can read what I write
and what other people write for me to read.

Although his approach was not intended for second language learners, it is eminently suitable for them; no mass-produced texts can ever reflect individuals' experiences, interests, and language as accurately as the stories they create. See Figure 12.1 for a first-grader's story about his motorcycle.

When a language experience story is completed, it can be copied in large clear letters onto a chart for permanent display. It should also be typed (if possible, on a primary typewriter) and reproduced so that each child can have an individual copy. Thus the story becomes a reading text for the authors and for their classmates, and an appropriate context for introducing or reviewing the word-attack and comprehension skills they need in order to reconstruct its meaning.

A sample experience story produced in a primary classroom follows:

The Boy and the Cow
This is a cow.
The cow is big and white.
The cow gives us milk.
The boy likes the cow.

by Danny Lee

Most children are very interested in reading and rereading their own stories and those produced by their friends; however, they may not be able to do so (although they have no problems with the content) if they have not yet learned

---

[2] The language experience approach requires that students draw from their oral language repertoire to describe events or produce reactions to experiences. The teacher writes down their utterances for them so they can see what the words look like in written form. The utterances may come from just one individual or from a small group. Students may then be asked to copy what they have produced and perhaps illustrate to clarify and enhance the meaning.

Figure 12.1. *A Language Experience Story Produced by a First-Grader*

how to process written information. The teacher who elicited and recorded Danny's story found that he had memorized it but could not read it; when she changed the order of the last three sentences, he continued to recite the original text.

Activities like the following might help pupils who are just beginning to read to recapture the meaning of their own stories after they no longer remember them exactly. The teacher's selection of the strategies most appropriate for utilizing such a story should be guided by knowledge of the children's needs and abilities. The pupils who are able to read it easily should be excused from these activities and given more appropriate assignments.

Activity I

A. Purpose:
   1. To help the children understand the story
   2. To help the children identify individual words presented orally
B. Materials needed:
   The chart of "The Boy and the Cow"
C. Procedure:
   1. Display the chart.
   2. Read it aloud.

3. Discuss the content, asking questions such as these:

> What does the cow give us?
> Where do we get milk?
> Why do you think the boy likes the cow?
> Are all cows white?
> Are cows as big as goats? as big as elephants?

4. Ask individuals to come to the chart and point to a word as you utter it out of context.

Activity II

A. Purpose:
   1. To help the children recognize entire sentences presented orally
   2. To help children recognize individual words out of context
B. Materials needed:
   1. The chart
   2. Flashcards of each word included in the story
C. Procedure:
   1. Read the story aloud.
   2. Ask individuals to come to the chart and point to a sentence as you utter it out of sequence.
   3. Ask individuals to come to your desk, pick up any flashcard, and match it with the same word in any sentence.

Activity III

A. Purpose:
   To help children develop the ability to read a familiar text silently
B. Materials needed:
   Individual copies of the story
C. Procedure:
   1. Distribute copies of the story to the children.
   2. Ask them to read it silently.
   3. Tell them that they can help each other recognize words they might not remember.
   4. Circulate among the students and provide additional assistance.

Activity IV

A. Purpose:
   To provide practice in matching initial sounds with corresponding letters
B. Materials needed:
   1. Old magazines
   2. A pair of scissors for each child
   3. A bulletin board
   4. Masking tape

    5. Several rolls of tape
    6. Flashcards of the words "boy," "milk," and "likes"
C. Procedure:
    1. Divide the bulletin board into three vertical sections with strips of masking tape.
    2. Tape each flashcard onto one of the three sections.
    3. Divide the children into groups of three or four.
    4. Ask the children to think of words that begin with the same sounds as "boy," "milk," and "likes" and discuss them with their partners.
    5. Distribute a magazine and a pair of scissors to each group.
    6. Ask the children to proceed as follows:
        a. Each child should find one or more pictures of objects represented by words that begin with the same sounds as "boy," "milk," and "like," and cut them out.
        b. Each child should tape his or her pictures onto the bulletin board in the section identified by the proper flashcards.
        c. After completing this task, each group may remain by the bulletin board and discuss the pictures contributed by others.
    7. If some children have chosen pictures that do not belong in the display or have placed them in the wrong section, help them individually to rectify their mistakes.
    8. Discuss the completed display with the children, inviting each one to name pictures and identify the initial sound and letter of the words that represent them.

Activity V

A. Purpose:
    1. To help the children recognize words out of context
    2. To help the children recognize entire sentences
B. Materials needed:
    1. Flashcards of each word in the story
    2. Sentence strips of each sentence in the story
C. Procedure:
    1. Remove the chart.
    2. Show the flashcards one at a time in random order. Ask the class, and then individuals, to call out the word written on each flashcard.
    3. Display the sentence strips one at a time in random order. Ask the class or individuals to read them aloud.
    4. Tape the strips to the bulletin board in random order, and leave them on display.

Activity VI

A. Purpose:
    1. To reinforce the children's ability to read sentences
    2. To help the children recognize isolated words and find them in a sentence
B. Materials needed:
    1. The sentence strips displayed on the bulletin board
    2. Flashcards of the words in the story
C. Procedure:
    1. Ask individuals to read the strips aloud.
    2. Hold up individual flashcards and ask individuals to read them aloud and point to a sentence that contains them.
    3. Remove the sentence strips from the bulletin board.

Activity VII

A. Purpose:
   To help the children recognize known words in recombined contexts
B. Materials needed:
   1. Sentence strips of the following sentences:

> The cow likes the boy.
>
> The boy is big.
>
> The cow is white.
>
> The boy likes the big cow.
>
> This is a boy.

   2. Masking tape
C. Procedure:
   1. Tape the sentence strips onto the bulletin board.
   2. Ask individuals to read one of the sentences aloud.
   3. Remove the strips.

Activity VIII

A. Purpose:
   To help the children understand and construct new sentences by recombining
   familiar words
B. Materials needed:
   1. The following sentence strips of incomplete sentences:

> The cow is _____ .
>
> The cow gives _____ .
>
> The boy likes _____ .

   2. Flashcards of various words suitable for completing each sentence
   3. A pocket chart
C. Procedure:
   1. Arrange the strips in the pocket chart and display it.
   2. Ask individuals to complete a sentence by using any suitable flashcards.
   3. Ask other individuals to read the resulting sentences aloud.

Activity IX

A. Purpose:
   To help the children use context cues
B. Materials needed:
   Individual copies of the following worksheet:

A. The Boy and the Cow	B. cow
This _____ a cow.	the
The _____ is big and white.	is
The cow _____ us milk.	gives
The boy likes _____ cow.	and

C. Procedure:
  1. Distribute the worksheet.
  2. Ask the students to draw a line from each word listed under B. to the proper blank.
  3. Display the chart of "The Boy and the Cow."
  4. Ask the children to check whether their completed worksheets match the chart.

Activity X

A. Purpose:
  To help the children read new sentences resulting from substitutions of the original words with new ones
B. Materials needed:
  1. The original sentence strips
  2. Flashcards of these words:

goat	wool	brown
sheep	eggs	small
hen	apples	tall
tree	peaches	green
shade	black	

C. Procedure:
  1. Arrange the sentence strips in a pocket chart.
  2. Construct new sentences by covering some of the words with appropriate flashcards.
  3. Display the chart.
  4. Ask the class and then individuals to read the new sentences aloud.
  5. Remove the chart.

Activity XI

A. Purpose:
  To provide the children with a selection of items for their word banks
B. Materials needed:
  1. A copy of the following handout for each child:

black	goat	tree	wool	likes	the
brown	sheep	shade	eggs	gives	this
small	hen		apples		is
tall	cow		peaches		us
green					
white					

  2. A pair of scissors for each child
C. Procedure:
  1. Distribute the handouts.
  2. Ask the children to cut out any of the words they want to place in their individual word banks.

During language experience activities, word-attack strategies are not taught in a preestablished order; many teachers, therefore, prefer a more traditional approach and use LEA for enrichment. When language experiences constitute the entire reading program, teachers must make sure that the authors do not merely memorize their own stories but are actually able to read them, and that other children can read them, too. When children engage in sustained and extensive LEA practice, teachers will soon find in their stories many examples of every sound-symbol correspondence they need to teach; by discussing them with the learners, teachers will enable children to decode many of the words they encounter when they read books.

The Whole Language Approach

In a whole language classroom, the children engage in reading for enjoyment and for the purpose of locating information, rather than in order to earn a good grade. Teachers are available to give them the help they may need at a particular time, but the guidance teachers provide makes children increasingly independent in seeking their own solutions and monitoring their own performance. The learners have a considerable amount of freedom in selecting the books they want to read and the way in which they use the information they obtain. Although they are seldom required to do so, they are usually eager to communicate what they have experienced and learned from reading to their friends and to their teachers, in writing as well as orally.

Workbooks and graded readers are not used in the whole language classroom; therefore, some teachers worry about the danger of neglecting decoding instructions. However, those children who have the opportunity to read extensively acquire many of the necessary information-processing skills without explicit instruction; during individual conferences, teachers can help each pupil overcome the particular problems they have not been able to resolve independently, as the following anecdote illustrates.

Little Ratna was reading a story about an ant named Marina. It included the following passage (Herman, 1983):

> One day as she was sweeping her patio, she discovered an old coin. She thought about what she would be able to buy. ''Perhaps I could buy a blue dress . . . but I don't have enough money.'' (p. 2)

When she saw the word *patio,* Ratna did not recognize it, stopped reading, and asked for help. The teacher advised her to read a little further and then come back if she still needed assistance. After a while Ratna returned; she had found the word *discovered,* which was also unfamiliar to her.

The teacher had several possible alternatives for dealing with this situation. She could tell Ratna what the words were, or help her apply her word-attack skills to each one; she could encourage her to use context clues or urge her to continue reading the story without worrying about the vocabulary she could not recognize. The teacher's choice was determined not only by her knowledge of Ratna's strengths and weaknesses but also, as is usually the case in the classroom, by external factors such as the amount of time she could spend working with her.

If she had been in a hurry, she would have selected the first alternative; Ratna might have added the two words to her sight vocabulary and later discovered the sound-symbol correspondences they represent. However, the teacher had organized her day so that she could give individual attention to each of the children engaged in silent reading. She knew that Ratna tended to use phonics extensively and did not enjoy reading unless she could decode every word. The teacher, therefore, decided to strengthen her ability to use context cues.

To put Ratna at ease, she asked her why she had chosen that particular book and how she liked what she had read so far, and invited her to tell what the story was about. Ratna replied that it was about a pretty ant who lived in a pretty house. "What happened to her?" asked the teacher. And Ratna answered that Marina was going to go shopping but did not have enough money to buy a dress.

"I wonder what Marina is going to buy," said the teacher. "She doesn't have enough money to buy a dress."

The child nodded.

"How much does a dress cost?" asked the teacher.

Ratna was silent for a while, and then said, "Maybe ten dollars. Maybe more. I don't know."

"How much money does Marina have?" asked the teacher.

The child shrugged.

"Do you think she has any at all?"

Ratna nodded. "Maybe a quarter. Maybe only a nickel," she said.

"Well, she can still buy something if she has a quarter, or maybe a dime or a nickel."

Ratna nodded.

"Where did she get that nickel, or dime, or quarter?" asked the teacher.

"She found it on the floor," said the child.

The teacher knew then that Ratna had formulated a correct hypothesis about the meaning of the words she could not recognize but needed to be reassured about its validity. When she asked, "How do you know that?" Ratna pointed to the picture above the text; it showed Marina in the act of sweeping flagstones.

"What was she doing?" asked the teacher.

"Sweeping the floor," said Ratna.

"Do you think she was inside the house or outdoors?"

Looking at the picture, the child said, "Outdoors."

"Right," said the teacher. "I see a big planter of geraniums, and I think that Marina is sweeping the floor of her patio." She wrote the word *patio* on a small flash card, handed it to Marina, and asked, "Is the word *patio* in your story?"

The child looked at the text and nodded.

"Now you can read the first line aloud to me," said the teacher, and Ratna did, stopping after the word *she* and looking up expectantly.

"What did you say happened when she was sweeping the patio?" asked the teacher.

"She found an old coin."

"That's right. But the story uses a different word instead of *found,* a word that does not begin with the letter *f.* Can you think of a different way of saying that she found an old coin?"

Ratna thought this over. "She saw one."

"That would be another way of saying it," commented the teacher. "One day as she was sweeping the patio, she saw an old coin. Does the book use the word *saw?*"

Ratna shook her head.

"How do you know?" asked the teacher.

"They are not the same," answered the child.

"Right," said the teacher. "*Saw* begins with *s* and the word in the book begins with a *d.* *Saw* is a short word, and the other one is long. I'll help you figure it out."

The teacher masked the prefix and the suffix of *discovered* with two pieces of paper and asked Ratna if she recognized the middle portion of the word. The child said "cover." Then the teacher uncovered the suffix, and Ratna said "covered." Then the teacher removed the other piece of paper, and the child uttered the word correctly.

Knowing that the ability to pronounce a word does not imply understanding of its meaning, the teacher helped Ratna relate it to previous experiences. She said, "Yesterday we talked about who discovered America. When Columbus came to this part of the world, it was new for him, and so we say that Columbus discovered America. But there were people already living in this country; they had found or discovered it many, many years before Columbus. Do you remember that?"

Ratna nodded.

"In your story," continued the teacher, "Marina discovered an old coin and was surprised because she did not know it was there. You knew what was happening in the story even before I helped you with the words *patio* and *discovered.* Now you can go ahead and read, and if you find more words that you do not know, don't worry. Read a couple of pages, and then come back and tell me what happened to Marina. I am really curious to know what she decided to buy. When you tell the story to your friends, you can say that she saw or found an old coin, or that she discovered it; they'll understand what happened.''

Oral and Silent Reading

Language minority children tend to function much better in a whole language context than in ''round robin'' reading circles in which they are expected to read aloud. Most reading circles consist of pupils who read at the same level; they are, therefore, prevented from interacting with their more advanced classmates and learning from them. Minority children tend to be assigned to low-ability groups because of their limited English proficiency; as a result, they often develop or reinforce negative expectations about themselves.

During a ''round robin'' session, the pupils are given individual copies of the same text; each one in turn reads a section aloud while the others follow along silently. Instead of receiving input from an effective model who can read fluently and dynamically, each listener must sit still while his partners stumble through their lines. In many cases, the pupils are not allowed to preview the text silently in preparation for reading aloud. Reading extemporaneously in front of an audience, however small, can be difficult and very threatening; therefore, children who worry about their ability to perform adequately often try to locate the lines they will have to read aloud and rehearse them surreptitiously. While they concentrate on them, they miss the cues provided by the preceding passages as well as the teacher's discussion of the words and concepts they contain.

The difference between oral and silent reading has important implications for the selection of classroom practices and the most effective allocation of instructional time. Oral reading can be a valuable tool for diagnosing reading problems and discovering each learner's preferred learning strategies; after listening to a child, the teacher can determine which activities will be most appropriate for him or her. However, the information contained in a text cannot be processed rapidly and efficiently when one reads aloud, since it is necessary to attend to every word, regardless of its importance; on the other hand, during silent reading one can and should ignore those items that do not contribute new meaning.

When they read aloud, even the most proficient students, who can grasp the meaning of an entire phrase or sentence at a glance, must adjust their reading rate to the time-consuming process of articulation. An excessive emphasis on oral reading does not foster students' ability to vary the speed of their reading according to the difficulty of the material and the amount of information they must identify and remember. Consequently, the amount of time allocated to silent reading should be significantly greater than that allocated to oral reading. Those learners who enjoy reading aloud need not be discouraged from engaging in this activity, but the teacher might suggest that they preview the material silently, since they will be able to deliver it more effectively after they have become familiar with its content.

Oral reading plays a limited but legitimate role during reading instruction. A class may perform a choral reading during a school function; a group may present a dialogue to the class; an individual may read a beautiful poem to a friend. By engaging in these activities, the students can increase their ability to speak clearly and effectively; they will gain new insights into the meaning and aesthetic quality of a text, and so will their listeners. The purposes of these activities and the skills they reinforce are important but quite distinct from those of reading.

To become efficient and independent learners, the students need extensive practice in silent reading. Teachers can promote their progress by providing guidance and feedback; before the reading, teachers may give a brief overview of the content and help the students formulate a purpose for the task. As a follow-up, teachers can check the children's factual and inferential comprehension and help them plan how they will use the information they have obtained.

Teaching Initial Literacy to Older Learners

Students should be assigned to the grade level most appropriate for their age and maturity, even if they do not speak or read English. Therefore, special arrangements must be made for those learners who need initial reading instruction but do not belong in a primary school. Unfortunately, an upper elementary and secondary classroom is a far from ideal setting for the acquisition of a second language and initial literacy. The abstract and cognitively demanding tasks performed in these grades provide very little comprehensible input to someone who is not proficient in the language of instruction.

LEP students who are already literate in their own language and have a solid academic background may be able to function in a regular classroom if they receive some help from the teacher. They should be mainstreamed in courses such as art, music, and physical education, and enrolled in the English as a second language (ESL) program where they can acquire the language skills they need to succeed in other classes.

A much more difficult situation exists for older students who have had little or no schooling and are illiterate in their first language (L1). If possible, they should enroll in a bilingual program in which they can receive ESL instruction and study other subjects in their native language. When this alternative is not feasible, they must at first be assigned to classes that place minimal demands on language proficiency, and receive individualized instruction or tutoring in ESL.

If several students need initial English and literacy instruction, and speak the same first language, they can be enrolled in a special class taught by a teacher who is proficient in their language. The instructor can use the learners' first language and their previous experience to develop their English skills by using the problem-posing approach developed by Freire (1970).

During a problem-posing session, the teacher brings to class one or more pictures of a situation or event familiar to the students. Using their own language, the learners do not simply describe the pictures but discuss their content in terms of their own concerns. The instructor listens, responds reflectively, and directs the conversation unobtrusively, making sure that everyone has a chance to participate. If, for example, the pictures represent some of the foods and beverages usually served in the school cafeteria, learners can tell the class whether they like or dislike them. One student may declare that he hates milk, which is good only for babies; another might wonder why the cooks never serve the kind of meals she used to eat in her native country.

The teacher then summarizes the discussion in the students' native language and recapitulates it in very simple English, making extensive use of gestures and other visual cues. The teacher also asks the students to think about possible solutions to their problems and present their suggestions to the class during the next session.

At the beginning of the next lesson, the teacher distributes and reads aloud a summary of the previous discussion written in their first language, and a simpler one written in English. The teacher explains the English words and asks the students to copy them into their notebooks. Using their own language, the students then discuss the advantages and disadvantages of the various solutions that have occurred to them. The instructor facilitates the conversation without indicating a preference for a particular suggestion or recommending other alternatives. The teacher summarizes their conclusions in both languages, as during the previous session, and prepares written summaries for the next meeting. Gradually, the students become less dependent on their native language and begin to use some English during their discussions. They can also utilize the vocabulary they have entered into their notebooks to write messages to each other and to other friends who are not in the class. The instructor can begin to reduce the extent to which he or she uses the students' native language as soon as most of the learners understand the gist of what is said or written in English. At this point the instructor will respond in English even if a student has used his or her first language.

If the school cannot locate an instructor who speaks the students' language, or if the learners come from different linguistic backgrounds, the students must be placed in the hands of a skillful teacher trained in ESL methodology. In such cases, it will not be possible to draw upon their experiences until they have acquired some basic communicative skills in English. Therefore, the teacher can use some total physical response activities to familiarize the learners with the vocabulary of their immediate surroundings (Asher, 1982). TPR activities can be used for several weeks, progressing from simple commands such as "Open the window" to more complex ones such as "Touch your shoes," "Bring me a big red balloon," "Point to the picture of a cat sleeping on a chair," "Give the eraser to the girl in the blue sweater." The students will gradually begin to give commands to each other and should be encouraged to read and copy various words representing the objects they have handled. In addition, they can produce and read individual and collaborative language experience stories.

Many additional suggestions can be found in the textbooks and manuals used in adult and vocational education. These materials approach the teaching of literacy from a pragmatic point of view, because the students need and want to learn how to read signs, advertisements, and announcements, write letters, fill out forms, and so on. The learners can be mainstreamed when they have achieved a level of oral and written proficiency sufficient for communicative purposes. Because of their inadequate schooling, they will still find it difficult to meet grade-level requirements, but they should be able to participate in many activities with some individual assistance.

THE MORE ADVANCED LEVELS OF READING INSTRUCTION

As they become more mature, the students are expected to read an increasing amount of difficult material, and to utilize written texts for specific purposes. They must not only perceive and remember the facts and opinions stated by a writer but also apply various cognitive processes to this body of knowledge. They must analyze it, make inferences, draw conclusions, and formulate valid generalizations. For example, after reading the history of several communities, a student should be able to state why their founders established them in their specific sites and what factors tend to attract settlers to particular kinds of locations.

Mature students read critically; they verify the accuracy of the information obtained from a text and assess the soundness of the author's conclusions. They must integrate what they have learned from reading with the knowledge they have obtained from other experiences. Instead of accepting the claims of politicians and advertisers at face value, they will check them against documented evidence and make informed decisions about how to vote and what to buy.

Mature readers derive satisfaction from reading; they read for pleasure as well as for information. The teacher can help students discover the intrinsic rewards of reading by allowing them to choose freely from a variety of books and magazines (Fader, Duggins, Finn & McNeil, 1976). In selecting materials for a class library, the teacher must take into account the learners' individual reading abilities and select a variety of materials written at different levels of difficulty. However, the teacher must keep in mind that the appropriateness of a particular text for a particular audience cannot be determined by applying readability formulas such as Fry's (1968).

Since readability formulas are based on word length and sentence complexity (as the experts who developed them have pointed out), they cannot take into account the conceptual difficulty of the content or the density of the language in which it is expressed. Some texts contain short sentences and monosyllabic words, yet require careful reading because of their very conciseness; others are intrinsically difficult because they deal with abstract and highly specialized concepts. These additional factors, which require a more subjective evaluation of the appropriateness of a text, cannot be ignored by a teacher who wants to challenge students without frustrating them.

Moreover, a minority student may find a text difficult, even one written in simple language, because it is based on unfamiliar culturally determined assumptions. In such cases, the learner should discuss the material with the teacher and ask the teacher to explain the passages he finds obscure or disconcerting.

Instructional Strategies

Comprehension is the outcome of cognitive processes in which the reader interacts with a text. The higher-order skills involved in this process can be learned and practiced most effectively in a language in which a person is already proficient; consequently, bilingual instruction can help the students become more effective readers even if they are not yet fluent in English.

Since the ability to process information resides in the reader and not in the text, the cognitive processes that lead to more advanced comprehension can be taught and reinforced orally. When the students discuss what they have read or are about to read, the written texts are used as reference; they can be consulted for checking the accuracy of one's recall of specific facts or for locating the passages that must be read slowly and carefully and those that can be skimmed or ignored. Poor readers can contribute to the discussion by presenting some relevant information obtained through listening, observation, and firsthand experiences. They can analyze a news broadcast, predict the outcome of an incident they have witnessed, formulate hypotheses about the variables involved in a science experiment, or evaluate the effectiveness of a new strategy introduced by the football coach.

Students who are unable to read a text should have the opportunity to listen to its content from a recording and discuss it orally with the teacher and with their friends. This strategy is especially appropriate for those students who have high cognitive ability but are not proficient or literate in English. However, they cannot succeed academically unless they overcome these problems; listening is not a substitute for reading. The support of audio recordings should be gradually removed as the learners become able to participate in the reading and writing activities appropriate for their age.

Directing Reading Tasks

The students can become more efficient in locating, processing, and utilizing written information when they establish a purpose for reading and develop appropriate strategies for extracting meaning selectively. To help them acquire these abilities, the teacher can begin by directing some of their reading tasks and encouraging them to follow similar procedures when they read independently. (See also Chapter 19, Directed Reading Thinking Activity, page 293.)

In preparation for a reading assignment, the teacher should arouse the students' curiosity about the information they are about to receive and help them bridge the gap between what they already know and what they are about to learn. After they have read the text, the students should discuss it with each other and with the teacher. These interactions provide the teacher with valuable insights about the accuracy and depth of the learners' comprehension; they also provide the students with an opportunity to gain a deeper understanding of the new concepts they have learned.

Reinforcing Word-Attack Skills

Efficient readers use appropriate strategies in dealing with unfamiliar words and therefore become increasingly independent in gathering the information they need and in acquiring new vocabulary. The professional literature contains many useful suggestions for helping the learners develop effective word-attack skills.

When students encounter an unfamiliar word, they should finish reading the sentence, or even the entire paragraph, to determine whether the word is essential to its comprehension. Many adverbs and adjectives are superfluous and can be ignored. For example, the meaning of *Scott's magnanimous behavior earned him the admiration of his friends and the respect of his enemies* is quite clear even if one does not know the word *magnanimous*. After they finish the sentence, readers know that Scott's behavior was considered admirable; therefore, *magnanimous* must have a positive meaning and must be a descriptive word applicable to humans, such as *brave, generous,* or *clever*. They can tentatively accept this hypothesis as correct and continue reading. During a second, slower reading they can check its accuracy by applying appropriate word-attack strategies.

When students need to identify a word they do not recognize, they should proceed in the following manner.

Step 1. Finish reading the sentence. Return to the unfamiliar word, and identify the sound represented by the first letter or group of letters. Read the sentence again; when you reach the unfamiliar item, produce the beginning sound. It might bring to mind a word that makes sense. Check whether it is the same as the one on the page. If none of the words that occur to you match the one on the page, go to Step 2.

Step 2. Try to recognize a portion of the word, and pronounce it. Pronounce it again, adding the sounds represented by the letters that precede and follow it. Determine whether you have uttered a word that makes sense in the context of the sentence; if it does not, go to Step 3.

Step 3. Ask for help or consult a dictionary.

These strategies make use of sound-symbol correspondences, but readers must also rely on context and on their previous knowledge in order to determine whether a word makes sense; it is not very useful to pronounce a word correctly unless one knows what it means.

Instead of stopping in the middle of a sentence to consult a dictionary or figure out words, efficient readers feel confident about their ability to make sense of a passage even if some of the details are still unclear. The students can be encouraged to deal with a certain amount of ambiguity by reading easy material in which some of the information has been deleted. When teachers use a cloze exercise for this purpose, they must not ask the learners to fill in the missing items, for to do so would encourage them to pay attention to every word.[3] They should instead prepare one or two questions about the overall meaning of the text, give them to the students, and instruct them to find the answers by reading the passage as quickly as possible, ignoring the blanks. An example is given below:

THE STORY OF GIANG DUNG

Read the following paragraph from *Master Frog in the Brocaded Slipper*, without trying to fill the blanks, then answer the following questions:

1. What happened to Giang Dung's husband?
2. What did people expect Giang Dung's child to do?

Giang Dung was a plain girl, so plain in fact that all the townspeople marveled when her parents finally found her a husband. Then they nodded their heads knowingly _____ whispered to one another that the _____ man must have been after her _____ money. She had plenty of it, _____ was true, and Giang Dung was _____ only child. The day of the _____ came and passed, and the people _____ interesting things to gossip about _____ a few months later when Giang's _____ husband died.

"It's fortunate that _____ is expecting a child," one person _____ , and the rest agreed. "At least _____ will have someone to look after her _____ her old age. It's certain she'll never find anyone else to marry her."[4]

---

[3] The cloze procedure involves deleting every nth (for example, every seventh) word from a passage. Students supply the missing words based on semantic and syntactic considerations.

[4] Adapted from Vuong (1982), pp. 65–66.

When they have become aware of the considerable amount of information they can gain in spite of reduced cues, the learners can accelerate the rate at which they read other material. In order to increase their efficiency, the teacher can reserve special times for rapid reading practice, and ask the students to record their reading rates and make a conscious effort to improve them. At other times, however, they should adjust their speed to the level of difficulty of the text they read and to the purpose for which they read it.

Reading Literature

The English curriculum places considerable emphasis on the understanding and appreciation of literature, but a student who is not fully proficient in English may find the language of various literary genres quite difficult (see also Chapter 20).

The problems are often caused by a difference between the author's assumptions and those of the reader. Moreover, a writer often withholds information deliberately; for example, by saying ''Rosemary blushed'' instead of stating that she was embarrassed or angry, he invites the readers to interpret the changes in her face as if they had seen it with their own eyes. Instead of playing a passive role, they become observers and participants; however, in order to make accurate inferences, they must be aware of the unstated and culturally determined conventions that had been violated when Rosemary blushed.

A skillful teacher can make the study of literature a meaningful and enjoyable experience for all students by selecting appropriate texts, clarifying what they mean, and promoting an awareness and appreciation of their quality.

Some teachers use short stories to introduce the narrative genre because of their brevity, but the very conciseness of these texts requires a considerable amount of inferencing on the part of the readers. Other teachers prefer to use novels; however, if the details and subplots are intricate and complex, the students may be confused unless they consistently outline and review the material.

Poetry compresses many layers of meaning into a concise format and is, therefore, difficult to understand. To appreciate a poem, one must be able to associate the words used by the poet with the images he intends to evoke. Students who have not yet established these associations during their previous experiences may become discouraged by the amount of effort necessary to develop them and derive no pleasure from reading poetry. They may become more motivated if the teacher chooses short texts such as haiku or narrative ones such as ballads.

The learners can gain deeper insights into the quality of a poem by listening to someone who reads it effectively than they would by merely reading it themselves. The teacher should read some selections aloud and play professional recordings of others. Similar considerations apply to the teaching of drama. Before asking students to read a play, the teacher should try to arrange for them to watch it in a theater or on television. After attending a live or recorded performance, they will be better prepared to read and discuss the script. In addition, they might be encouraged to perform a selection they have particularly enjoyed.

The study of ethnic literature can enhance the cross-cultural awareness of all students. The teacher can discuss various books and magazines that portray the lives and experiences of minorities, and encourage the learners to choose additional ones for independent reading. Unfortunately, some of this literature may reinforce negative stereotypes even if the author is sympathetic to the characters described. The students who belong to the group represented in such a work may be embarrassed and defensive, and their sense of identity and self-esteem might be damaged.

Before introducing a story that portrays life in the ghetto, the barrio, Chinatown, or other ethnic communities, the teacher needs to preview it carefully. Some of these works reflect a biased point of view, while others may include scenes that might be highly disturbing to young learners. In such cases the damage that might be caused by these materials outweighs their potential benefits, and the teacher should look for more suitable alternatives. However, the teacher cannot shelter the students from every work that portrays racial problems, and should not attempt to. Such material is always available from public and school libraries and frequently shown on movie and television screens; the students will be better prepared to deal with its content if they have the opportunity to discuss similar works in their classroom.

Many suggestions for teaching ethnic literature in the elementary and secondary grades are available from professional books and journals; for example Banks (1977) recommends the works of Hunter (1969), Graham (1958, 1965, 1969), and Bonham (1965) as suitable for familiarizing the students with the experiences of African American people. Other books, such as *The Jazz Man* (Weik, 1967), might cause young readers to develop highly negative stereotypes about African American families unless the teacher points out that some of the characters are the victims of discrimination. By using well-planned questioning and discussion techniques, the teacher can help the readers develop empathy and concern for all the people who suffer from racial injustice.

To understand the attitudes and behaviors prevalent in a particular ethnic group, the students should become familiar with the literature produced by individuals who were raised in it and who can accurately represent its hopes and aspirations. Since the number of works produced by minority writers is steadily increasing, the teachers can find many selections suitable for the interests and maturity of their classes.

The study of literature plays an important role in the overall development of reading proficiency and positive attitudes toward reading. A skillful teacher who makes this progress more rapid and enjoyable fosters the growth and development of mature, self-directed readers and will continue to influence them long after they have left his or her classroom.

RECOMMENDED READINGS

Carrell, P. L., & Eisterhold, J. C. (1983). Schema theory and ESL reading pedagogy. *TESOL Quarterly, 17*(4), 553–572.

Fader, D., with Duggins, J., Finn, T., & McNeil, E. (1976). *The new hooked on books.* New York: Berkeley.

Feeley, J. T. (1983). Help for the reading teacher: Dealing with the limited English proficient (LEP) child in the elementary classroom. *Reading Teacher, 35*(7), 650–655.

Goodman, K., Goodman, Y., & Flores, B. (1979). *Reading in the bilingual classroom: Literacy and biliteracy.* Rosslyn, VA: NCBE.

Henry, G. H. (1978). *Teaching reading as concept development: Emphasis on affective thinking.* Newark, DE: International Reading Association.

Herber, H. L. (1978). *Teaching reading in the content areas* (2nd ed.). Englewood Cliffs, NJ: Prentice Hall.

Hill, R. W. (1979). *Secondary school reading: Process, program, procedure.* Boston: Allyn & Bacon.

King, D., & Watson, D. (1983). Reading as meaning construction. In B. Busching & J. Schwarts (Eds.), *Integrating the language arts in the elementary school.* Urbana, IL: National Council of Teachers of English.

Lapp, D., & Flood, J. (1978). *Teaching reading to every child.* New York: Macmillan.

Manning, M. M., & Manning, G. L. (1979). *Reading instruction in the middle school.* Washington, DC: National Education Association.

Mason, G. E., Blanchar, J. S., & Daniel, D. B. (1983). *Computer applications in reading* (2nd ed.). Newark, DE: International Reading Association.

Neville, M. H., & Pugh, A. K. (1982). *Towards independent reading.* London: Heinemann.

Orasanu, J. (Ed.). (1985). *Reading comprehension: From research to practice.* Hillsdale, NJ: Erlbaum.

Readence, J. E., Bean, T. W., & Baldwin, R. S. (1981). *Content area reading: An integrated approach.* Dubuque, IA: Kendall/Hunt.

Renault, L. (1981). Theoretically based secondary language reading strategies. In C. W. Twyford, W. Diehl, & K. Feathers (Eds.), *Monographs in language and reading studies: Reading English as a second language: Moving from theory.* Bloomington, IN: Indiana University, School of Education.

Rigg, P. (1981). Beginning to read in English the LEA way. In C. W. Twyford, W. Diehl, & K. Feathers (Eds.), *Monographs in language and reading studies: Reading English as a second language: Moving from theory.* Bloomington, IN: Indiana University, School of Education.

Rumelhart, D. E. (1981). Schemata: The building blocks of cognition. In J.T. Guthrie (Ed.), *Comprehension and teaching: Research reviews.* Newark, DE: International Reading Association.

Shepherd, D. L. (1982). *Comprehensive high school reading methods* (3rd ed.). Columbus, OH: Merrill.

Thomas, E. L., & Robinson, H. A. (1982). *Improving reading in every class* (3rd ed.). Boston: Allyn & Bacon.

Thonis, E. W. (1981). Reading instruction for language minority students. In *Schooling and language minority students: A theoretical framework.* Los Angeles: Evaluation, Dissemination and Assessment Center, California State University, California State Department of Education.

Vacca, R. T. (1981). *Content area reading.* Boston: Little, Brown.

FOLLOW-UP QUESTIONS AND ACTIVITIES

1. According to Cantoni-Harvey, what are the advantages of the language experience approach? Can you think of additional advantages? What about possible problems? How might they be overcome?

2. How would you go about adapting the language experience approach for a specific content area and age level? Could a version of it be used with a whole class or small groups to accomplish such diverse tasks as creating a chart, writing a short soap opera, summarizing the main points of a reading? Develop several alternative ideas, and share them with a small group for their feedback.

3. How does a whole language approach differ from other approaches to reading? How is unfamiliar vocabulary handled in this approach? How about decoding skills?

4. For what reasons does the author eschew "round robin" reading sessions? Does her reasoning have credence in your opinion? Explain. Under what conditions might students' reading aloud be a positive experience?

5. The author mentions the importance of bridging "the gap between what students already know and what they are about to learn" (page 192). What might be the advantages of such a practice? Locate a reading that you would be likely to use in your own classroom. List the questions you might ask or other strategies you might use to explore existing knowledge. You might want to create an "anticipation guide" (see pages 157–158).

6. Using the same reading you selected in Activity 5, plan postlesson activities to review, synthesize, and extend the content of the reading. Consider questions you might ask during discussion. Plan activities that include whole-class, small-group, and individual work.

7. How would you treat sexist reading material such as the excerpt from the fairy tale on page 193? What about material containing violence or cultural stereotyping?

13

Coaching the Developing Second Language Writer

Faye Peitzman   *University of California, Los Angeles*

Editors' Introduction

All too often, language minority students enter content classes inexperienced in academic writing tasks. Such writing tasks need to be experienced not only in language courses especially designed for that purpose but in all classes across the content areas. In science, for example, the students may describe the steps of an experiment that they have just conducted. In social studies, they may write a paper supporting their point of view on some issue of concern. In music, they may compare jazz and hard rock. Whatever the task, the content classroom can be transformed occasionally into a workshop environment such as the one described in this chapter by Faye Peitzman. This environment is consonant with an approach to the teaching of writing which emphasizes composition as a process and a tool for communication and learning.

OF ENABLING ENVIRONMENTS

Orchestrator, model, coach—these are some of the roles enabling teachers play when teaching students to write. As orchestrators, the teachers convert the classroom to a low-anxiety, task-oriented writing workshop. In this workshop setting, they guide students through the processes of prewriting, drafting, sharing, commenting, revising, publishing. They first help students to understand the general writing task and then to make it their own. They lead students to understand that *their* intentions for a piece of writing are all important. They build trust and self-confidence by guiding students to help each other with early drafts in peer groups or with partners. Teachers comment themselves on drafts that students will revise, but they put grades on only the final, best version that the student is capable of writing. They give sufficient time both in and out of class for the searching, drafting, and rethinking that are essential for meaningful writing.

From "The Enabling and Responsive Teacher: Coaching the ESL Writer" by F. Peitzman, 1989, in From Literacy to Literature: Reading and Writing for the Language-Minority Student *(pp. 114–127). Copyright © 1989 by the Regents of the University of California. Adapted by permission.*

To model the writing process, enabling teachers brainstorm with the class, put their own cluster on the board, write in their own journal every day, bring in drafts of stories or reports that they are working on, write to students in their journals and on drafts of their papers. They also read and distribute many samples of student writing—both by nonnative and native English speakers.

Finally, as coaches, these teachers believe in pushing student writers to their limit—one giant step further than where they were before; offer praise along the way; make very specific suggestions for changes that empower students to revise successfully; and emphasize that hard work and trying again are the norm for any person who writes.

MISGUIDED ASSUMPTIONS ABOUT WRITERS' NEEDS

Research tells us that when students have the benefit of this enabling environment, they will take the risks that help them to grow as writers. This research does not distinguish between the first (L1) and second (L2) language speaker-learner. The enabling teachers for language minority students, however, understand that this optimum environment is an essential one if their students are to achieve biliteracy. They haven't been trapped in the net of misguided assumptions that ensnare so many of their well-meaning colleagues. The *erroneous scenario* runs like this:

Errors in student writing abound.

Impulses to take responsibility/ownership away from students by playing proofreader/editor increase.

Gradually the entire notion of a writing workshop becomes sabotaged: Peer writing groups disappear because of a faulty belief that students can't help one another.

Because students make so many errors and often ramble, the teacher focuses on correctness and structure with too little emphasis on content.

No extended writing assignments are given because the teacher believes students need to get individual sentences right before they go on to paragraphs, perfect paragraphs before they go on to the essay.

The scenario ends with Writing Sample 1. The student writes a paper in one sitting. The teacher, rather than responding to meaning and purpose, corrects every error of grammar and syntax and edits for conciseness.

Responding to Writers: The Problem

Student Writing Sample 1: My Immigration

My name is Thai, Hon. I'm from Vietnam. I came here since 1979 because I couldn't live with the communists. The United States of America is a greatest country and it is a free country.

I came here with my parents and my cousins and my brother was in the United States. He has been living here since 1975. My brother goes to work and he sponsored my parents, and my cousin to the United States. I went to the United States by airplane, and I have been in Hong Kong. Hong Kong is a nice place and has lovely landscap. When I arrived here, I felt very good, and my brother took me to go to the school but I was afraid because they asked me and I didn't understand and later I understood what they said, I was not afraid anymore and I have many American friends and I though this country saves my life, and my family life, because the United States has not communists making the war.

I've got used to it. Many American are very nice and kindly. I liked to live in America and I would like to stay here. But if my country have no more communist, I will come back, and stay there.

The following is an unhelpful response to this paper.

you should write your first name first

My name is Thai, (Hon) I'm from Vietnam. I came

in

here ~~since~~ 1979, because I couldn't live with ~~the~~

in my country

communist~~s~~. The United States of America is a great~~est~~, *and free*

country. ~~and it is a free country.~~

I came here with my parents and my cousins. ~~and~~

M   *at the time.*

~~my~~ brother was in the United States, He has been

living here since 1975. My brother ~~goes to~~ works, ~~and~~

H

~~h~~e sponsored my parents, and my cousin to the

United States. I went to the United States by airplane.

First,   *went to*   *and lovely*

~~and~~ I ~~have been in~~ Hong Kong. Hong Kong is a nice,

place. ~~and has lovely landscap.~~ When I arrived here, I

happy(?)   *M*

felt very ~~good,~~ ~~and~~ ~~my~~ brother took me to go to ~~the~~

              people   *questions*

school. ~~but~~ I was afraid because (they) asked me, and I

      them. L   *when I could*   *people*

didn't understand, ~~and~~ ~~later,~~ I understood what (they)

were saying

(said), I was not afraid anymore. ~~and~~ I have many

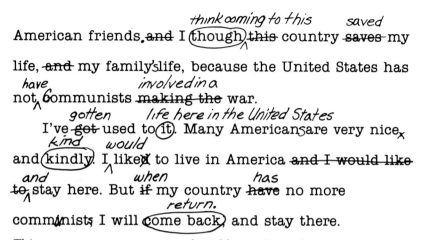

This response presents several problems. First, the teacher's corrections have cut off all further learning possibilities from this paper. In revising and editing the paper for Hon, the teacher has done the work. In not asking Hon to build on the strong feelings exhibited, the teacher ignores what is potentially a powerful piece of writing. The paper is treated like a series of sentences to be edited rather than as a heartfelt communication. Errors have been corrected, regardless of whether Hon can take in the linguistic structure in each case. With most errors marked and no sense of how the teacher arrived at the corrections, Hon might well feel discouraged about his writing despite the B+.

While there is no best of all possible comments, a more helpful response might look like this:

Dear Hon,

I was moved by your writing. Your words made me feel how much you appreciate America and how much you must miss Vietnam.

I think you might improve your essay if you tell us in your next draft about the things you especially miss. That will help us get a better understanding of why you want to return to your country if you can.

Here are some more specific suggestions:

1. The second paragraph might be clearer if you put it in chronological order. What happened first? The part about Hong Kong distracted me. Is it important for you to talk about Hong Kong in this paragraph?

2. Can you take the many ideas in the last sentence in paragraph 2 and divide them into two or three different sentences?

3. You will return to Vietnam and stay there. Why? Can you add a few more sentences to let your reader understand?

Good luck on your revision. I look forward to reading it.

If teachers are to build on the promise of language minority students, then they need to embrace the following key premises about language learning and teaching:

Students' intentions are more important than correctness—and should be acknowledged first.

Language acquisition takes time—not all errors will disappear in one semester or year.

Students grow as writers as they draft and redraft—as they tackle and solve revision problems.

COMMENTING GUIDELINES

The guidelines that follow, a combination of techniques based in theory, work equally well with the written comment and the one-to-one conference.

Suggestions for Teacher-Coach	*Rationale*
Skim the entire paper before writing comments.	This way teachers have a much clearer sense of what students are trying to say/do in writing.
Address the student by name.	The personal connection is invaluable.
Pinpoint a major strength and weakness of the paper.	Students need an umbrella overview of their major successes and problems in the papers they write.
List questions/suggestions for change; note sentences and paragraphs that are particularly effective or important.	Students are often able to answer questions rooted in their own text. They also benefit greatly from rereading the best parts of their papers.
Phrase comments tentatively ("perhaps," "do you think"), where appropriate.	This is, after all, the student's paper—not the teacher's.
Let students work on solving the problems of development, organization, style.	Students do not benefit much when the teacher does both problem finding and solving.
Correct only those errors the student is likely to understand.	Students are overwhelmed when teachers correct every infelicity of grammar, usage, and mechanics.
Before the student leaves class, ask: What do you plan to concentrate on in your next draft?	Teachers need to make sure written comments or oral conferences have given students sufficient direction.

TECHNIQUES AND OTHER STUDENT SAMPLES

These guidelines can be used by teachers from elementary through university levels with both beginning and advanced writers. The following pages give examples of student writing and teacher response. The first section includes samples of student drafts in grades 2 and 7. Students will revise once more before submitting their papers for a grade. The second section, using an advanced ESL paper, illustrates how teachers can help students to work with peers to improve their writing.

Section 1: Teacher as Partner/Guide

Commenting on Drafts

Context
A secondary ESL class "adopted" a grade-2 bilingual class. Students wrote and illustrated letters to the second graders, sent them Chinese New Year's candy, made a cassette of one of their favorite lessons, and silk-screened a T-shirt for a second-grade teacher.

Writing Task
You have read through the letters the high school students have sent. Select a pen pal and then write a three-paragraph letter to the chosen pal. In paragraph one, express your gratitude. In paragraph two, let your pen pal know something about you. In paragraph three, ask your pen pal questions you really want her or him to answer.

March 21, 1986

Dear Miguel Alvares,

   Thank you for all the stuff that you send us. The Candy was good. Thank you for everything you gave us.   You know I work very hard to pass to 3rd grade. I am 7 ears old. When I grow up I am goging be a secretery.
   Where do you live? Is your school far away? Is all your famili in the u.s.

Friend

Diana

Diana,

I'm sure Miguel will be thrilled to receive your letter and find out about you. Maybe he'd like to know even more. In your second paragraph, can you tell Miguel more about how you work hard at school? I think your questions for him are great!

—FP

For this paper, a teacher has a range of possible suggestions for improvement to draw on. The first paragraph is a bit vague. What "stuff"? What kind of candy was it? How did it taste? The third paragraph also might be improved. What does Diana mean by "where do you live?" Does she really want an address? This second-grade bilingual student, however, did a pretty good job of fulfilling the assignment. The three paragraphs are clear—even though one of them didn't make it to a new line. (Note how the student did skip spaces within the line, however.) This student needs a push—attend to one content item—not a shove that will make her doubt her ability to write a good letter.

Context and Writing Task

After much discussion and prewriting activity, seventh- and eighth-grade students in an English transitional class are directed thus: Select your own topic. Write two versions—one to an adult and one to a five- or six-year-old child.

Playing With Matches

It is bad playing with matches. You must not play with matches because you might burn your home and you won't have a place to live in. You can hurt your and maybe even your friends or your brother and sister. You can in trouble with your mother or father if you burn a hole in the sofa or in the carpet. So don't play with matches.

by Chieu

Playing with Matches

It is very dangerous playing with matches. I have many reasons why it is dangerous. First, it might catch fire and burn down a house. A house is very expensive, so if you cause a fire you might have a lot of trouble and your family will have to pay. Secondly, you might burn yourself by accident. You could get hurt really bad and might even died. Thirdly, you might hurt other people or even a member of your family so don't play with dangerous matches.

by Chieu

Chieu,

   I like the way you change your style of writing in each piece. The paragraph to the adults gives a sense of being more formal, more deliberately organized. My only question: Do you think adults need to be warned against playing with matches? How do adults usually cause house fires or get burned? Or perhaps adults need to know more about teaching their children not to play with matches. Try revising this section.

Great first attempt!

                              —FP

Readers who are familiar with seventh- and eighth-grade classes will realize that these paragraphs are quite good. The student did try to adjust style and tone for the intended audiences: the scolding fitting for the young child, the organized exposition appropriate for the logical adult. This success with style and tone is more important to highlight than the missing words. The student will easily fill in the blanks as soon as he reads the piece aloud.

Section 2: Peers as Partners and Group Guides
The writing coach is usually just one person in a class of thirty students, five times a day. In the interests of self-preservation and feasibility, such coaches must find ways to enable students to help other students with their writing. Peer partners—two students helping each other—seem to work best for lower-level or younger students. Peer groups, usually four students per group, work well with intermediate and advanced writers. Although some teachers are doubtful that their writers are sufficiently proficient to help another student, it is clear that when the focus is on content rather than mechanics, students can be important early readers of each other's work.

Context and Writing Task
Students in a college-level ESL writing class spend two weeks reading investigative reports by professional writers and slightly more advanced students. They read the reports closely and discuss research techniques needed to interview, observe, analyze. They brainstorm possible questions they personally want answered.

   With the interview as your primary source, define a research question and shed some light on it for yourself and your readers. The personal ''I'' is appropriate here. Four typed pages.

Student Response
Second Draft

Right Culture for Second Generation?
As an immigrant who faced the difficulties of accepting a new culture, I was curious about how second generation Korean-Americans were educated and guided at home concerning their original culture. Since it seemed that they were absorbed into the presently dominating environment, the American culture, I had to expect most of them to be unfamiliar with their original background, the Korean culture. But, how do the second generations balance the two totally different cultures? To obtain an answer, I needed to find out about their backgrounds and their personal opinions or attitudes towards this issue.

My first interviewee, Sun, as I will call her, majoring in English at UCLA, showed her interest in my assignment and responded with care. But during the interview, I realized that she was so Americanized that I almost mistook her as American. According to her, she considered herself as an American because she was a born citizen and was raised in America with its unique cultural ways. To me, she seemed to be unreasonable about her idea of identifying herself with birth and raised place. But after I realized her situation, I found her answer very frank. She explained her answer, ''When I was nine, I recognized myself being different in appearance from other kids in town. Since our family was the only non-American, my parents didn't guide me in Korean way so that I wouldn't feel isolated, I realized.'' When I asked how she regards this matter now, she said, ''I like to keep myself as I am now not because I dislike Koreans or anything related to it, but simply because I am so involved in my present environment and society that I can not be what I am not.''

As opposed to Sun, my second interviewee, Young, seemed to know more about her original background. She studies economics at UCLA and is able to speak Korean even though English is her first language. Since her parents, especially her father, were so strict that she had to converse with in Korean at home. Her father even sent her to Korea two summers and her mother taught her Korean cuisine. She expressed herself appreciating Korean culture and said, ''When I was young, I wondered why I had to go to Korean Language school every Saturday. But now, I realize how much it helped me to learn ideas about my country and people. Since I lived far from downtown where most Koreans lived, going to school also helped me to make Korean friends who were in the same situation as I was, being second generation.''

My two interviewees were so different from each other—one being Americanized and the other being typical Korean-American. From this point, I started examining their situational differences and similarities. They were similar in their economic standard of living and family structure. But I discovered that the parental influence was one of the important factors that causes the different opinions of second generations. In these two cases, I realized that parent's role determines the involvement and participation of their children in their own cultural affairs. According to Sun, her parents were concerned about obstacles which would cause her being unable to adjust to the American society because of too much involvement with Koreans. On the other hand, Young's parents wanted her to handle both cultures and showed her a specific direction. Here another question arises; how do they feel about the parent's role and do they appreciate the parent's view concerning the mixing of culture? As I expected, the answers from my interviewees were towards the appreciation over their parents' views, but of course in different aspects. Sun agreed with her parents because she achieved their goal and hers which was to be accepted in American culture. On the contrary, Young appreciates her parents for helping her out to recognize original culture.

It is difficult to determine which set of parents have the more desirable way of raising their children involving their own cultural affairs. Therefore, it can't be assumed that Sun's parents were not aware of their culture because they were concerned the environment which she will live long. On the other hand, Young's parents helped her out to balance the two cultures to some degree. But, the degree of success is not absolute so that the second generations should realize their own way of obtaining originality.

The author's peers initially read their first drafts aloud to one another, in groups of four, offered some comments on the spot, and then composed a written response to help group members with draft two. They were guided by these general procedures described under the ''Peer Group Guide'' and ''Peer Commenting Guide'' that follow.

Peer Group Guide

Each person in your group should have a photocopy of his or her paper for you. Follow the paper as the author reads aloud. The following procedures should help you help one another.

> The author reads the paper aloud.
>
> One or more members of the group repeat the gist of the paper.
>
> The author tells the group members particular areas of the text he or she would like members to focus on. The author may pose specific questions to the rest of the group.
>
> The group members tell the author what they liked in the piece.
>
> The group members let the author know what questions they have, what areas might be developed further, what paragraphs or sentences are unclear.
>
> The author tells the group what his or her goals will be for the revised draft.

They also have a list of key questions specific to the writing task to help them help one another.

Peer Commenting Guide

Remember that your main job is to offer a personal response to the pieces of writing you have before you. While writers benefit from having their attention directed to areas that are undeveloped or unclear, they also benefit from knowing what they did well. Try to balance your comments so the writer has a good idea of both strengths and weaknesses.

Some specific issues you might want to note in the investigative paper are:

Is the investigative problem clear?

Has the writer engaged in primary research as we defined it in class?

Is there a good balance of direct quotation and paraphrase? (The writer does not have to use direct quotations if they would not help the paper.)

Is the order of presenting findings logical?

Does the writer provide transitions between paragraphs?

If the writer explicitly tells the reader something about his or her own background/beliefs, does this information help the paper? Should he or she do more or less of this in the report?

Think of your comment as a letter. Write most of your comments on a separate sheet of paper, addressed to the author. On the author's paper, place numbers in the margin when you want to refer to specific lines and paragraphs.

It should be noted that students are helping their peers primarily with issues of content and organization. They are asked to be real readers, not editors—and in this task, they can succeed quite well.

Growth in Student Writing

At times, the final products are not clearly better than earlier drafts but show signs of a mind at work problem solving. Perhaps because of the difficulty level of the revision tasks, the student does not have time both to revise conceptually and to reconstruct the whole text for a reader. This is still a sign of purposeful revision and is indeed a sign of growth. Teachers need to acknowledge this growth—both to themselves and to their students.

Finally, teachers need to assess in what ways their students grow as writers over a more extended period during the academic year. Ideally, teachers will sit down with each student and review the portfolio of writings that the student has kept. When that is not possible, or in addition to that mutual review, students may be asked to evaluate themselves. At the end of the year, students may be asked to review their portfolios and answer such questions as the following:

List your papers in a rank order—from favorite to least favorite. Describe in some detail why you like certain ones better than others. Are you making these decisions because of the overall writing quality or because of the content?

Do you see any improvement in your writing from September to June? Are there things you are better at now?

Do you think that the third drafts are better than the first and second? If so, in what ways? If not, which draft level do you prefer and why? (Be specific here.)

What kinds of things did you learn from your peer groups? Did group suggestions often prompt you to revise?

Which of my comments were most helpful to you? Which weren't very helpful?

Students usually are quite able to explain their choices of favorite writings, and from their comments teachers may learn just how important it is to give students leeway with choosing writing tasks. They may also learn that students have engaged in kinds of writing that they have never tackled before. And thus, if paper five, a persuasive piece, is not as strong as paper two, an investigative report, the writer may not have regressed after all. Indeed, if we as writing coaches try too hard to ensure improvement from one paper to the next, we may diminish the chances of students' pushing toward major long-term growth as writers. However, by using the techniques described in this chapter, content-area teachers can create enabling environments, thereby assisting language minority students over time to become effective writers in English.

FOLLOW-UP QUESTIONS AND ACTIVITIES

1. Vygotsky (1978) spoke of the two levels involved in cognitive operations: the actual level of functioning and the potential level, which can be achieved under the guidance of the teacher or more advanced peer. The distance between the two is what he refers to as the zone of proximal development (see also Chapter 18). Explain how Peitzman's recommendations might make it possible for the students to function more fully within their zones of proximal development.

2. Which of the ideas presented in this chapter did you find most applicable to your own teaching situation? As a writing coach, what other ideas can you come up with that would be not only applicable but consonant with the views expressed here?

3. Plan a writing workshop with the members of your class. Choose a short, managable writing assignment for each to complete. Class members may work in pairs, alternating the teacher/student and peer reader/student roles. Larger groups may be formed for other kinds of collaborative activities involving the same piece of writing. At the end of the workshop, discuss with your class the advantages and possible disadvantages of such an approach to writing.

4. Describe two or three writing assignments that may be typical in a particular content area, be it at the elementary, secondary, or college/university levels. Show how each might be handled in a workshop environment.

14

Helping Students Write
for an Academic Audience

JOY M. REID *University of Wyoming*

EDITORS' INTRODUCTION

*Although this chapter is oriented to college and university English as a second
language (ESL) teachers, its insights are applicable to other levels at which second
language (L2) students need to be introduced to the kinds of academic writing
skills required for success. Particularly important are the insights the chapter
offers into culturally determined stylistic differences and the misunderstandings
that can result in their use. While it also is important that students experience
writing as a process, one of this chapter's recommendations is that second
language (L2) students be exposed to authentic academic writing in specific
content areas in order that they be made aware of the schema, purpose, and
rhetorical/syntactic conventions employed. In short, it stresses that teachers' overall expectations be made very explicit in writing assignments given to developing
second language writers across the content areas.*

The problem of poor unsuccessful communication is not fundamentally a question of language proficiency, although frustrated university professors may—
for want of a more precise way of articulating their frustrations—lay the blame
for unsuccessful written communication on what is most immediately obvious:
"I can't understand what this student is doing; I think he needs work in
grammar." For an ESL student with very limited English proficiency, this
assessment may be true, but most students admitted to higher education programs must first meet rigorous standards of language proficiency. Even with
adequate language skills, these students will still have some errors in written
work, but those errors are generally little more than extraneous noise that
academic readers get through, not a major cause of inadequate communication.

*From "English as a Second Language Composition in Higher Education: The Expectations of the
Academic Audience" by J. Reid, 1989, in D. Johnson and D. Roen (Eds.)* Richness in Writing:
Empowering ESL Students *(pp. 221–234). Copyright* © 1989 by Longman Publishers. Adapted
by permission.

In other words, professors will overlook second language (L2) errors or consider them less important if the writing fulfills their expectations in terms of content and general form (Carlson & Bridgeman, 1983; Carlson, Bridgeman, Camp & Waanders, 1985; Lindstrom, 1981; Vann, Meyer & Lorenz, 1984).

More often, the problem of communicating successfully originates from the ESL student's limited or skewed perception of what is expected. Typically, in the United States nonnative English speakers from other cultures operate with a somewhat different set of cultural assumptions; they are therefore likely to resort to coping skills that have worked in their native languages and cultures but that are inappropriate for the expectations of the U.S. academic audience. Examples: the freshman composition essay that is highly philosophical and generalized instead of being highly specific and personalized as the professor expected; the political science paper that has elaborate language and irrelevant materials that do not address the point; the research paper that has been copied from one or two sources. When an academic audience evaluates these assignments, misunderstandings abound: The professor decides that the student does not understand the content because the writer cannot successfully respond to a (seemingly) transparent task; the student, who does understand the content and expected a more positive evaluation is mystified, frustrated, and insecure. In this case, the student clearly is penalized because he or she is not familiar with the culturally accepted conventions of academic prose.

If students choose to adjust their writing to meet the expectations of their academic audience, they need to understand two consequences. First, a similar readjustment will be necessary when they resume writing in their native languages. Just as their styles and presentations of written material change to fulfill the expectations of the U.S. audience, they will have to reexamine their planning and producing strategies when they write academic papers in their native languages. There is the (perhaps apocryphal) story about the Korean student who received honors on his U.S. doctoral dissertation after having struggled for many years to achieve the necessary mindset to produce acceptable English academic prose. When he returned to Korea and sought to publish a research article based on his dissertation, the article was panned; the editors of the Korean journal said that the article was poorly written and "not good Korean."

Second, students need to know that adjusting writing styles is not easy. Teachers might tell their students of Jean Zukowski/Faust's attempts to learn to write Turkish prose while she was teaching English in Turkey.[1] Her tutor kept returning Zukowski/Faust's essays asking her to revise them because, although the grammar was error free, the writing was not Turkish, it was "cold, like a fish." During the same time, while marking her Turkish students' papers, Zukowski/Faust "discovered contrastive rhetoric" as she found herself writing

---

[1] My thanks to Jean Zukowski/Faust (Northern Arizona University) for permission to use her story.

comments such as "Get to the point" and "Why say this when it's not relevant?" Students who hear these stories should not, of course, despair. Rather, the stories underscore the importance of teachers' explaining to their students what is not English and what is. And the students should understand that making adjustments in their writing will probably be hard work that will involve raising their awareness about prose styles and practicing appropriate forms and structures.

USING CONTRASTIVE RHETORIC

One way to begin raising students' awareness of U.S. academic prose is a frank discussion among teachers and students about rhetorical differences between English academic prose and the rhetoric—the presentation of written material—in the students' native languages (cf. Connor & Kaplan, 1987; Doushaq, 1986; Hinds, 1983; Kaplan, 1983; Matalene, 1985). A discussion about contrastive rhetoric, in which the teacher describes characteristics of languages and asks for feedback from students who speak that language, is a good stimulus for structuring discussions about coping strategies. Skeletal summaries of such discussions might begin as follows:

1. Although I don't speak Arabic, students in classes like this one and research I have read have indicated that Arabic is a traditional, poetic language, that the skill of writing is considered extremely difficult, a skill that only the gifted possess, and that the presentation of written material in Arabic relies on philosophical (abstract) statements—the audience "reads between the lines," drawing conclusions and extending the information. However, U.S. academic prose requires competent (simple, not beautiful) writing that consists of paragraphs containing a single main idea supported by facts, examples, or description. U.S. students learn to "prove it or cut it!"

2. Although I don't speak French (Spanish, etc.), for writers of Romance languages like French or Spanish, elaboration, using the language beautifully, is essential to the successful presentation of written material. If you look at a résumé prepared by a Spanish speaker, for example, you will see that the document is many, many pages of extended prose. However, U.S. academic English, especially scientific and technical writing, requires a kind of stripped down prose. Even in elementary school, U.S. students are taught: "Tell 'em what you're gonna tell 'em, tell 'em, and tell 'em what you told 'em."

3. Although I don't speak Japanese (Chinese, Korean, etc.), there are actually two different levels of writing by which writers present written material in these languages. In other words, writing for a youthful audience relies on simple sentences, direct and directive information, and use of

specific detail. If the audience is mature, however, written material is presented more subtly, and readers are expected to draw their own conclusions. In U.S. academic prose, however, the audience expects written material to be direct and specific. The use of detail is prized as clear evidence that the writer's ideas are valid.

4. Although I do not speak Thai, a paragraph of academic material in Thai usually begins with an anecdote, has some specific detail, and occasionally finishes with a statement of overall intent in the last sentence. In U.S. academic English, the general paragraph is reversed: the overall idea is stated first; then specific detail is given to explain, clarify, and support that main idea.

USING AUTHENTIC WRITING TASKS

Once the students trust their teachers, the rest is relatively straightforward. First, students should study authentic, commonly assigned writing tasks such as the critique, the short answer or essay test, and the research paper to determine the purpose(s) of each assignment and the expectations of the academic audience. Teachers must act as informants, as builders of schema, for their students (Carrell, 1986; Chimombo, 1987; Johns, 1987). Initially, they must gather academic assignments from across the curriculum, assess the purposes and expectations, and present them to the class. The students should study these authentic, cross-curricular writing tasks: (a) learning to identify the purpose of each, (b) investigating the specific demands of each, and (c) analyzing the rhetorical conventions expected by the academic audience. In the examples that follow, key words and phrases that are central to the task are italicized. Each could serve as a springboard for discussion; if student writing samples that successfully fulfilled each assignment were also available for study, students could gain additional confidence in their abilities to address each task.

Writing Assignments

Economics short answer test (undergraduate):

Define 4 of the following terms in 1 or 2 sentences:
A. Fixed input
B. Pure profit
C. Elasticity of supply
D. Variable cost
E. Marginal product

Freshman composition placement examination (1 hour critique):

Read the following passage. In an organized and detailed essay, summarize its main ideas. Then explain why you agree or disagree with what the ariticle says. Support your agreement/disagreement with specific examples from your experience or outside reading.

Biology test for undergraduate majors (1 hour):

You are the only doctor in a small, rural town. People of all ages begin coming into your clinic with the following symptoms:

Headache
Fever of 102° F.
Aches in joints
Swelling in the abdomen

The people in the village are not familiar with the germ theory of disease, and they are very frightened. Write an explanation of the disease process for these people.

Second, the students should have ample opportunity to identify and practice procedures that will assist them in collecting and evaluating materials for writing assignments. Again, the teacher must act as the informant by providing oral communication activities that will allow students to practice acceptable ways of gathering information for their academic writing tasks. For example, what questions would a professor consider legitimate about an assignment, and how and when can students ask those questions? Possible examples for discussion or role playing include the following.

About a writing assignment (to the professor):

NOT "I don't understand what you want."
BUT "This is the first paper/review/report I have written at a U.S. university. May I make an appointment to talk with you during your office hours?"

In the library (to the librarian):

NOT "I have to write a paper, and it's due tomorrow. What should I do?"
NOT "Find these books for me."
BUT "I've found three books about the topic of cellular cofferdams, but I can't find *this* one. Could you please help me?"

Teachers might also help their students learn how to consult with other students, including native English speakers who are working on the same assignments. The most significant barrier for nonnative English speakers is summoning the courage to initiate communication with classmates. Teachers can prepare students for such encounters by supplying appropriate conventions and oral language, with role playing, or with "What's wrong with this dialogue?" discussions.

NOT "Tell me what the teacher said."

BUT "Hi. I'm [NAME] in your [x] class. Do you have the assignment for tomorrow's class?"

NOT "What means this?"

BUT "Do you understand what the professor said about [x]?"

Finally, students need to learn about ways to use their experiences as they analyze and execute writing assignments; that is, they should discover how to use their cultural backgrounds to advantage in approaching academic writing tasks. Possible scenarios for discussion are:

1. For a freshman composition assignment about dating or dormitory life, students could compare/contrast what they have observed in the U.S. (with clear qualifications about their limited experiences) with what they know occurs in their countries. Interviews with native speakers in their classes could add to the U.S. experiences, and specific detail about their home country experiences will certainly be of interest to their U.S. audience.

2. For a writing task pertaining, for example, to irrigation techniques, students should use the information they have learned in that irrigation class (and, if the assignment requires, read articles outside of class to increase their information base); in addition, they can relate the discussion (analysis/report) to the problems and/or solutions of similar situations in their countries. Again, the home country information will be of interest to the audience, and the students will be applying what they are learning—the essence of relevance in international education.

USING RHETORICAL AND SYNTACTIC CONVENTIONS

Next, teachers should present another group of strategies, this time rhetorical and syntactic (cf. Brodkey, 1983; Hall, Hawkey, Kenny & Storer, 1986; Jenkins & Hinds, 1987; Martin, 1983; Smith & Reid, 1983). For example, students must learn basic and alternative formats that are expected in academic assignments; possibilities include:

1. The basic format of the summary with its necessary balance and objectivity (cf. Johns, 1987).

2. The formats for English composition: the five-paragraph expository theme, the argumentative essay, and the response to written material (cf. Reid, 1988).
3. The basic organization of the experimental research paper (introduction, literature review, methods and material, data, results, and conclusion) and alternative organizational forms of nonexperimental research papers (cf. Swales, 1987).

In addition to these rhetorical strategies, students should also begin to look closely at syntactic forms that are commonly used in U.S. academic prose. Some questions and exercises to stimulate awareness and discussion are:

1. Underline the verbs in this abstract. How many are passive voice? Why is passive voice used so extensively?
2. Are there personal pronouns in this journal article? Why or why not?
3. Look at the introduction to these three articles. What verb tense(s) is/are used in each introduction? Is there a pattern?

To give students necessary practice in rhetorical and syntactic strategies, teachers can design initial assignments that parallel the elements of academic assignments but that are easier to produce. For example, using relatively simple reading material—a short controversial article that is not culture-bound or field-specific—for all students to critique will allow students to concentrate on communicating with the audience. The assignment that follows is representative of such tasks; because all the students begin with the same information and the same directions, they do not have to develop additional information to construct their responses. Instead, they can focus, either individually or in group work, on the strategies and writing techniques that will result in acceptable critiques.

Assignment

Directions: A recent magazine article discussed a new trend among young adults in the United States, their tendency to return to their parents' home to live after graduating from university. The following is a brief excerpt from the article:

> Until now, American parents have exhorted their young to . . . go to college, go to work—in short, to get out. But inflation, recession, and rising divorce rates are now persuading young people to . . . move home.

Below are two letters which responded to the article. Read the letters. Then choose the letter you *disagree* with. Write an essay that states your reasons for disagreement, and support those reasons with specific details from your reading or personal experience.

Dear Sir:

Children who return home to live with their parents after they graduate from the university are acting in a way that is seriously detrimental to their personal growth and development. Even when live-at-home young adults are contributing money and labor to the household, the fact is that parents provide psychological protection; consequently, the child will not take as many risks, make as many errors, or become as independent. All of these are essential components of learning about life and about oneself.

Furthermore, parents who allow children to return home after they are adults may be using their own loneliness to divert attention from their own problems. Therefore, living at home after graduating from college or getting a job is a process of returning to childhood that ultimately is bad for both parent and child.

Sincerely

Dr. Paul King
Chicago, IL

Dear Sir:

During the past generation in America, the family has deteriorated; children left home at the earliest possible age and became independent in every way. Now they are returning to that sacred institution. The giving, the sharing, the love and the loyalty of that foundation of society have not been lost after all! Both parents and children are finally realizing their mutual need: the parents to care for the children, and, later, the children to care for their parents.

In fact, often the returning child is a helpful adult who can provide companionship and sometimes additional financial support for the parents. Moreover, the selfishness of the 1970s may now fade; family ties will most certainly be made stronger. More importantly, family solidarity may eventually be reflected in the rest of American society. After all, in order to get along with the rest of the world, you have to start someplace—getting along with your parent may be the starting point.

Anne Hughes
Denver, CO

Similar practice in writing a research paper also requires the teacher to be an informant. To ease the information overload and give the students a chance to concentrate on form rather than content, the teacher can provide the students with common data, then demonstrate techniques of integration and referencing, and have students practice those techniques, perhaps in pairs or small groups. Horowitz (1986) offers the following exercises on the reintegration of material, the ''encoding of data into academic English'':

1. Students are presented with a number of very similar short essays written in such a way that although they are all based on the same data, they are in fact responses to different questions. The students' task is either to match each answer to the correct question or to select the most appropriate answer to one question. The main value of such an exercise would come in the discussion or why one answer was thought to be more appropriate than another. This would focus attention directly on different ways the same data can be arranged and the reasons for arranging them in different ways.

2. A variation of the above makes use of short student essays, all written from the same data in response to the same issue. Students are required to use all the data provided, so the resulting essays vary mainly in how the data are integrated. Students then read their classmates' responses and discuss the strong and the weak points of each essay. To ensure that attention is paid to information structuring rather than to grammar, teachers might want to provide sentence-level corrections before the essays are examined in the class.

3. Since reorganizing data is at least partly a matter of changing the order in which they are presented, students can be given a numbered list of facts and a question. Their task is to choose the order in which to present the facts in response to the question. Here again, because there is no correct answer, the value of the exercise would be in the discussion of why a given order of presentation was chosen. (pp. 458–489)

Finally, to gain experience in using the rhetorical strategies appropriate for technical writing, students might work individually on a detailed assignment that is content-based (Celce-Murcia, 1987) such as the one that follows (Kroll, 1987).

Assignment

Directions: Think of two contrasting terms related to your major field of study. Write a three-part essay based on explaining what one term means in contrast/comparison to the other closely related or quite opposite terms. Your audience might be students new in the field who don't know very much about your subject. Or the audience might be professional peers for whom you are presenting a prelude to a larger discussion. Your essay structure should resemble the following:

Part 1. Introduce the topic briefly and identify the key terms you want to discuss.
Part 2. Focus on explanation of the following sort: "X is not like Y in that. . . . A student must bear in mind that X is really Z and Y is really Q. . . ." Your aim is to contrast the focus term with another term that is easily confused or is not truly related.
Part 3. Concentrate on explaining how your focus can be seen as somehow connected to the contrasting term. You might begin your paragraph with a statement such as, "On the other hand, X and Y have certain . . . in common." Some suggested terms:

> Chemistry: organic chemistry vs. inorganic chemistry
> Biology: botany vs. zoology
> Economics: microeconomics vs. macroeconomics
> Engineering: electronics vs. electrical engineering
> Philosophy: metaphysics vs. empiricism
> Computer Science: hardware vs. software

EVALUATION

Finally, teachers must be prepared to evaluate student writing in light of the anticipated audience. More than simply marking errors and commenting on content, teachers must play the role of the academic readers their students will encounter. To do this, they must thoroughly understand what is expected in a variety of academic assignments; just as important, they must be able to identify unacceptable or inappropriate prose from the perspective of the academic reader. Both global and discrete questions about form need to be asked.

1. Is the student following an expected and acceptable format?
2. If not, where does he or she deviate? For what reasons?
3. Is the deviation successful? That is, what is the resulting impact on the academic reader?
4. If the deviation is not acceptable to the academic audience, exactly what should the student do to repair the break in communication?

In terms of syntax errors, prioritizing is even more important. Because errors are almost always going to occur in the writing of developing second language students, they must know which of their errors are critical to successful communication and which are not. Recent survey research concerning error gravity—that is, which L2 errors interfere with communication and/or irritate the U.S. academic reader—indicates that it is possible to prioritize syntax errors (cf. Green & Hecht, 1985; Khalil, 1985; Kroll, 1982; Lindstrom, 1981). In particular, Vann, Meyer, and Lorenz's (1984) survey of academic readers across the curriculum reveals that

> respondents tended to be more accepting of those errors commonly made by native speakers of English (e.g., spelling, comma splices, or pronoun agreement) as well as those errors in English which linguists often term the most "idiosyncratic" (e.g., articles and prepositions). On the other hand, respondents judged as least acceptable those errors which, for the most part, are global and/or are relatively rare violations for native speakers (e.g., word order, *it* deletion, tense, relative clause errors, and word choice). (p. 432)

Following the teacher's identification and prioritizing of student writing problems, the next logical step for the teacher is to communicate that knowledge of appropriate responses and acceptable prose to the students, to explain the problems, and to suggest changes that will result in more successful communication. Besides discussion, one excellent way of having the students discover differences in the quality of completed writing tasks is to train *them* to become the academic audience and to have them evaluate writing samples. Perhaps the easiest and quickest form of evaluation training is to teach students to score papers holistically. There are several ways to organize such a training session:

1. The TOEFL Test of Written English has a fully developed scoring guide and benchmark papers. These benchmarks are student samples of the thirty-minute writing task at each of the scoring ranges, 1 to 6. Students can see and articulate the differences between a 1 and 6 paper easily; training at the 3 to 4 level takes a little more time.[2]
2. Students can design their own scoring guides. By reading through sample student papers (probably written by students not in the present class), the students can, with assistance from their teachers, develop criteria for a scoring guide. This process takes more time than the other two, but the benefits in terms of awareness and understanding of expectations are great.

CONCLUSION

In short, teachers of nonnative English speakers must be pragmatists. They must discover what will be expected in the academic contexts their students will encounter, and they must provide their students with the writing skills and the cultural information that will allow the students to perform successfully. They should guide their students explicitly, not just in the prewriting, writing, and revising protocols that have proven worthwhile strategies for native English speakers but also in the prewriting processes of discovering the purposes of academic writing assignments (i.e., the intentions of the instructor assigning the tasks), and of developing strategies to meet the expectations of the academic audience in terms of content, of form, and of language. Demystifying the writing process and its resulting product can offer a variety of opportunities to put these new schema to work: The students will consequently become better able to identify, collect, and articulate acceptable written material. For nonnative

---

[2] The TOEFL Writing Examination Evaluation Guide, as well as sample benchmark papers, are available upon request from the TOEFL Program, Educational Testing Service, Princeton, New Jersey 08541.

English speakers, this cross-cultural and cross-curricular knowledge will enable them to understand what the professor wants and feel secure about being able to fulfill those expectations.

FOLLOW-UP QUESTIONS AND ACTIVITIES

1. Locate copies of typical, authentic writings accomplished by students in a particular content area. You may need to use teachers in your field as sources. For example, in language arts typical writings might include a book report, a critical paper, a narrative, and so forth. Explain how you might present each for analysis to your language minority students. When and under what circumstances might you present each? What specific questions might you ask to facilitate discussion?

2. What are some writing assignments (include specific topics) you might give in your teaching situation to encourage students to draw on their knowledge of their own cultures? Make a list. Share it with a small group of fellow students to receive their input.

3. Refer to Chapter 13 in which a composition workshop format is described. How might you use a similar format in preparing your language minority students for the academic writing expectations associated with a particular content area?

4. Make up three writing assignments for students in your teaching situation. With a small group, evaluate these prompts in terms of clarity, feasibility, authenticity, and expectations. Revise the prompts as necessary.

5. Devise grading criteria for written assignments in your content area. Keeping in mind the research on error gravity cited by Reid, how would you prioritize the various components of an essay (e.g., organization, content, grammar, and so forth)? How might your priorities differ for various age groups?

15

Conducting Verbal Reviews

Carmen Simich-Dudgeon *Office of Bilingual Education
and Minority Languages Affairs,
U.S. Department of Education*

Lynn McCreedy *The Center for Applied Linguistics*

Mary Schleppegrell *Peace Corps*

EDITORS' INTRODUCTION

A common characteristic of American classrooms is extensive use of verbal review, which is defined by the authors as the phase of a lesson when students are asked questions to determine whether or not they have learned what has been taught. The authors' recommendations for orchestrating effective verbal reviews are based on research aimed at identifying features associated with successful student/teacher interactions. Linguistic, cognitive, and interactive features of verbal reviews are discussed and examples are given to aid teachers in maximizing students' participation. The authors conclude, among other things, that language minority students succeed best in classrooms where there are clearly established routines, where expectations are known, and where teacher-directed activities are balanced with group and individual work. Examples from science and math classes are provided. However, the strategies are applicable to other content areas as well.

This chapter deals with strategies for integrating limited English proficient (LEP) students more fully into the ongoing verbal interaction in the classroom. It highlights issues related to the verbal participation of these students and provides suggestions for encouraging them and helping them improve their oral skills.[1]

---

[1] The ideas here are the result of a research collaboration between the Center for Applied Linguistics (CAL) and two elementary schools in Fairfax County, Virginia, funded by the Center for Language Education and Research (CLEAR). The goal of the research project was to identify the features of successful student/teacher interactions in order to apply that knowledge to help the LEP student. Seven third- and sixth-grade teachers collaborated with researchers by inviting them into their classrooms to observe verbal interaction during science and math activities. Students identified by their teachers as "effective communicators" or "unsuccessful communicators" were interviewed and videotaped to determine why some students succeed in verbal classroom interaction while others do not.

From Helping Limited English Proficient Children Communicate in the Classroom: A Handbook for Teachers *by C. Simich-Dudgeon, L. McCreedy, and M. Schleppegrell, Winter 1988/89. National Clearinghouse for Bilingual Education, Program Information Guide Series, No. 9. Adapted with permission.*

The language skills of the LEP student can be developed through techniques that make the social and instructional features of classroom language clearer. The student best succeeds in a classroom where a routine is established and clear to every student, so the rules for appropriate conduct are explicit and each student knows what is expected. LEP students also do best when they are expected to contribute but do not have to constantly compete for the teacher's attention. The most successful environment for such students is one where there is a balance between teacher-directed activities and individual and small-group work and where lessons are organized in a predictable fashion so that students know what to anticipate and how to focus their attention. Predictable consistency encourages these students to focus on the communication of information rather than on procedure or form.

Sometimes teachers assume that when LEP students are mainstreamed and appear to be fluent in English, they do not have communication difficulties and that any problems they have in school reflect cognitive or academic, rather than communication problems. Research shows, however, that it takes longer to achieve competence with academic language than with casual conversational language. For this reason, explicit teaching of academic vocabulary as well as explicit teaching about what constitutes an effective academic question and response is very important for the student.

Many teachers worry that making accommodations for LEP students means slowing down or watering down the content of their programs, with negative consequences for their native English-speaking students. What we found, however, is that those classroom interactive practices that are helpful to LEP students are helpful to all students.

This chapter focuses primarily on the use of language by students and teachers during the classroom activity we call *verbal review*. Verbal review is that time during the lesson when the teacher stops to ask questions about material previously taught. It is a time for students to find out what is important and to express new concepts in clear language.

We found that verbal reviews follow certain general patterns of organization. In the "typically good" verbal review, the teacher does the following:

1. Gets the students' attention, and *redirects* it *from* the previous lesson activity (experimentation, teacher presentation, seatwork) to the upcoming verbal review.
2. "*Frames*" the verbal review, reminding students of the topic of the instructional unit, and also how this lesson or activity fits in with it.
3. Begins with *factual recall* and *factual description* questions about the activity.
4. Expands the discussion with questions that require students to
   —*compare* the behavior or characteristics of things being studied, and/or
   —*apply or generalize* from the facts, and/or
   —*explain* the math processes or scientific principles behind the facts.
5. Closes the discussion with a *summary*.

Verbal review has the potential to help students develop important skills in verbal academic language competence, such as describing, explaining, exemplifying, comparing, and relating real events to abstract principles. All too often, however, the opportunity is missed because students are not encouraged to go beyond one- or two-word responses. Teachers should try to refrain from doing all the work in verbal review discussions by following these guidelines:

Avoid fill-in-the-blank questions in favor of questions requiring descriptions or comparisons. Rather than "The fourth planet from the sun is what?", ask "Who can compare the positions of the Earth and Mars in the solar system?" Both questions check essentially the same factual learning, but the latter also gives the student the opportunity to develop communicative competence. If such questions have been given as part of a seatwork or homework assignment, or have been gone over in small-group or partner discussions, LEP students are given a fairer chance of succeeding in answering them.

Give students more time than usual to think through challenging questions. Comparisons, generalizations, and explanations are difficult to formulate well, and research has shown that if teachers wait three seconds for a response (instead of the usual one-second wait), they get more responses and better responses.

WHAT'S GOING ON HERE?

Being on task requires different behavior in different situations, including active involvement in a science experiment, attentive listening during teacher presentations, or oral participation during verbal reviews. Some students, especially students from different cultural and linguistic backgrounds, may be willing and able to be on task, but do not understand the particular demands of each situation. Students need to know when to pay attention and how to participate. The teacher can help by providing clear signals about the goals and rules for interaction in different lesson activities.

What Teachers Can Do

Mark transitions between activities very clearly. Identify the activity by name, and explain how it will be accomplished. For example,

T: Now, first we're going to review your homework answers, and then I'm going to ask you some questions about it. Then we'll start on today's lesson.

To do well, students have to know "What's going on here and what is my responsibility?" To help them answer these questions, discuss with them the different types of questions you asked and the times during the lesson that lead to different purposes for your questions. For example, during instructional activities, questions are most often used to involve students in a discovery approach to learning, and they are not held responsible for providing the "right" response but instead are encouraged to provide opinions and make guesses while they learn new concepts and skills. On the other hand, during verbal review or quiz time, questions are asked to determine if students have learned what has been taught, and they are held responsible for their answers. Understanding these differences may help students be more active participants.

Throughout the lesson activities, signposts should be used to guide students to successful completion of the tasks.

Closing activities explicitly is as important as marking the opening. Use a summary of what has transpired to help students clarify what you have done and what they should have learned.

WHY ASK QUESTIONS?

Teachers ask questions to find out what students know. But questions and answers also fulfill another function in the classroom. They help students to clarify concepts and deepen their understanding of lesson content by listening and volunteering responses.

What Teachers Can Do

Be aware of the instructional function of questions and answers to make sure that the concepts you are teaching are verbalized clearly. This gives students another chance to learn through the interaction.

Be aware that your question, although addressed to and answered by an individual, is useful for the whole class. As one sixth-grade student said, "Teachers ask questions mainly to teach the class so if somebody in the class *does* know, it will help the other people in the class who don't know. It's not actually for individuals—more like for the whole class." Repeat and rephrase student responses so they are heard and understood by all students. LEP students say that even though they might not raise their hands and actively participate in the discussion, they learn a lot from questions and answers.

Ask questions often during the lesson. Use questions and answers to summarize what has been learned at each step. For example,

> Why do you think I asked you to do this?
> What was the purpose of this?
> Can you tell us what that means?

Allow many students to participate. When more students participate, a "good answer" is developed collaboratively, and topics are discussed more fully. This increases the instructional potential of verbal review.

Allow the students plenty of opportunities to speak—by listening to them you can learn more about what they understand and where they need further instruction. Use questions to give students an opportunity to describe what they have learned, gain confidence in themselves, and come to conclusions. Questions and answers are a time for thinking and talking together.

Use follow-up questions to allow a student to revise an incorrect answer rather than going immediately to another student. One sixth-grade "unsuccessful" responder told us that "when you don't know and someone else is called on who does, you don't learn because you're not listening." This indicates that a successful response should be built from the unsuccessful attempt if the instructional value of verbal reviews is to be promoted.

HOW DO TEACHERS KNOW THAT STUDENTS KNOW?

Students who do not frequently participate in question-and-answer exchanges (often language minority students or the less confident students) are unable to "show their smarts." Teachers cannot involve all students equally due to time and other limitations on participation. We know that those students who are outspoken and raise their hands frequently participate more than others. Teachers should develop verbal review activities that increase minority students' participation, increase the instructional value of oral reviews, and democratize oral reviews by minimizing student differences in verbal performance and maximizing the focus on content knowledge.

What Teachers Can Do

Conduct your oral reviews in small groups as well as large. Change the composition of the small groups so that students who rarely participate are sometimes grouped together and at other times grouped with more active students.

Tell students in advance what questions you will review with them, and give them time to organize and plan their answers in small groups. This gives them a chance to discuss related topics and issues and increases their verbal participation.

Increase the instructional value of verbal reviews by extending the discussion beyond the one-word answer. Ask students to give reasons for their views and provide evidence for their answers. Encourage other students to ask questions and contribute to answers.

Plan your verbal review in two stages: First ask questions about content knowledge and the information that has been taught to clarify the topic. Then "recycle" the review, and extend your questioning to expand the topic and give students the opportunity to relate what they have learned to broader questions and to predict the next step in learning.

Use plenty of visual aids. Write on the chalkboard and demonstrate whenever possible. This helps LEP students as well as those who learn best through a visual modality.

NOW, WHERE WERE WE?

The successful verbal review is *cohesive,* with teacher and student contributions fitting together clearly and new topics linked to the ongoing discussion. Students do cooperate in this, but it is the teacher who is primarily responsible for managing a cohesive verbal review. One important way experienced teachers do this is by providing frequent signposts that keep the class informed of where they have been and where they are going.

What Teachers Can Do

In planning the verbal review, identify places where signposts will be needed. These include every place where the discussion changes direction.

> At the beginning: *"Before we go over the homework, let's review what we have to do when we add or subtract fractions. Let's look at this problem."*
>
> When you give or ask for an example: *"Okay, everybody, ah, let's think a little bit about the word 'float.'* When you go fishing, what makes that fishing line stay up?"
>
> When you return to the main point after talking about a subpoint: *"Now, we're going to look at our objective, to find out the next step in our sequence after multiplying. What is it, Terry?"*
>
> When you resume the verbal review after the class has worked an example, and/or a set of problems: *"All right. We matched the term 'prediction' with its definition, 'telling what you think will happen.'* Now, what did you have for 'buoyancy'?"
>
> When you shift from talking about specific examples to talking about general principles: *"So, we've seen that you used foil boats, you used clay boats, you used a paper bag with air, and without air. What is it about these things that makes them float?"*

Focus students' attention on your signposts by using focus-of-attention words and phrases such as *okay, all right, now, so,* and *well,* spoken with some emphasis (slightly louder and either slower or faster than you had been talking). The foregoing examples all include focus-of-attention markers.

THE RIGHT WORDS

Students need to learn the right words to use in answering teachers' questions. Vocabulary should be presented and practiced so that as students learn concepts, they also learn the words they need to express those concepts. This is especially important for the LEP student who may not know common words that other children know, or their range of meaning and use.

What Teachers Can Do

Identify new and important vocabulary related to each new lesson. Write these words on the chalkboard or display them on a wall chart in the classroom.

Help students understand the meanings of words by using them in meaningful contexts. Here's an example of how a teacher effectively provides a definition for a word in the workbook.

T: The first question says: "Name the *properties* used to describe the powders." We didn't call them properties, but *what words did we use to describe the powders?* Eric?
E: Color, shape, smell (teacher writes these on the board)
T: These things are the *properties* of the powders. . . .

Guide your students in using the correct terms. By using the correct words, students will better remember the concepts you are teaching.

S: . . . because the soap makes the water heavy?
T: Is heavy a good word to use for that? When something flattens that way, what kind of power do we say it has?
S: Adhesive force?
T: Good.

Don't restrict yourself to simple words when talking with LEP students. Allow your language to be rich (see also pages 151–152). But use synonyms often, so that the student who doesn't recognize one word may recognize another word for the same thing.

T: What did you *find out* about powder number six? Leah?
T: What did you *discover* about powder number nine? Terry?

SAYING IT THE RIGHT WAY

Although teachers say that they listen for the meaning the student is expressing, it is clear that if a student does not express a concept in the way the teacher expects, the teacher may not understand the child. It is important to separate form from content; an answer might be correct but said "wrong."

What Teachers Can Do

Listen for the meaning or intent of the answer the student is giving. Sometimes teachers are so focused on listening for a particular word or phrase that they do not acknowledge correct answers when they are given in a form that the teacher doesn't expect. Try to be open to each answer and consider what the student is contributing to the discussion, even if the answer takes the discussion in a different direction than you had intended.

When you recognize that a student is having difficulty expressing a correct answer coherently, acknowledge the basic correctness of the response. Then rephrase the response and/or redirect the question to another student.

T: What is the most important thing to remember?
S: Put the zero, . . . you times . . .
T: [To the whole class] I know what she means and you know what she means—who can say it another way?

Allow the student enough time to give an answer. As one teacher told us, "Sometimes when you allow the student time to explain his or her thinking, you can unscramble the confusion and get an effective response."

Don't be distracted by nonstandard grammar or other features of a student's dialect when listening for content. One sixth-grade student told us ". . . you say it in the wrong way but you be right, and she don't quite understand what you are saying." Dialect should not be a factor in your evaluation of student responses in content areas. Just as with grammatical errors by LEP students, these responses should be accepted for their correct *content*. As you work with students with nonstandard dialects, you will come to understand their intentions and meanings when they are expressed in nonstandard forms.

Students have different styles of organizing their answers. We expect responses to be *topic-centered,* and most are. Another organizational style that you may encounter is the *topic-associating* style, which makes use of parallelism, analogy, and other associations between seemingly unrelated things. When you expect a topic-centered response but get a topic-associating response, it may seem muddled or even incoherent. In such cases, further probing for connectedness among the points the student wants to make should clarify whether the student is "packaging" pertinent and valid information differently, or is just plain "off-base." As one teacher put it, "You know, it's a whole lot easier to get *them* to make the connections clear if you assume that the connections are there in the first place."

TALKING ABOUT NUMBERS

Because the typical math problem has only one correct answer, question-answer exchanges during math tend to be very short and allow the students little opportunity for talk. We know, however, that talk during math instruction can help students to understand concepts and procedures and to develop the language skills they need to communicate and extend mathematical ideas.

What Teachers Can Do

Ask questions that will encourage talk during math instruction. Even though there is only one correct answer, many questions can lead the student to coming to that answer.

Why did you choose that operation?

What key words in the problem might help you?

How will you do the work?

Can you estimate an answer? Does your estimate sound sensible?

How will you know? Where can you look? What do you need to know?

Can you check your answer? How?

Ask students to explain the process they have gone through when they get a wrong answer. Often, merely explaining the difficulty they are having will help them see where they have gone wrong. The act of expressing their thoughts aloud in words helps students clarify and organize their thoughts.

Ask students to talk as they work at the chalkboard, describing what they are doing. Or have them work together in pairs, explaining the processes they go through to solve math problems.

Ask one student to tell another student who is at the chalkboard exactly what to write and what the next step is. This helps them verbalize mathematical processes. Students often enjoy catching each other giving incomplete instructions.

Remove yourself from the role of saying whether each answer is correct or not. A technique we have seen used successfully to accomplish this follows.

T: Number seven, Jeff?

J: Thirty-eight.

T: Anyone else get that?

Ask students to compose original word problems applying the math concepts they have learned.

As in other subject areas, use synonyms to expand your students' vocabulary and to aid the LEP child in comprehending what you are saying. For example:

T: So you say we can reduce the fraction four eighths, because two can *go into* four and eight. Four and eight are *divisible* by two. Four and eight can be *divided by* two.

DEVELOPING SCIENTISTS

Hands-on activities in science can provide a springboard for a well-structured verbal review. When a verbal review directly follows the experimental activity, the experienced teacher will often begin with factual recall and factual description questions about what the students have just been doing. Then, questioning can be expanded to issues of comparison, the explanation of the causes of what the students observed, or the principles being illustrated by the experiment. The expansion of the verbal review into questions of *comparisons* and *causes* is an important means of linking the hands-on activities to the students' science concepts. Our purpose here is to help teachers to develop an awareness of effective ways to discuss comparisons and causes, as well as some pitfalls to avoid.

What Teachers Can Do

About Comparisons

Many two-way comparisons stem from the design of the experimental activity (e.g., things that sink versus things that float, or liquids exhibiting cohesion versus liquids exhibiting adhesion). But even when there are more than two things to be compared, you can begin on a two-way level for clarity and simplicity.

"Now which of the mystery powders contain starch and which do not?"

Confusion can be caused by inexplicit comparisons. Consider this example, in which the discussion has just compared the densities of, first, metal and wood, and then, wood and water.

T: Okay, so metal, as Lee said, would sink, but wood has a *lower* density, so what would happen to it?

S: It would float.

Does wood float because it has a lower density than metal or because it has a lower density than water? In both questions and responses, the *than* part of the comparison is important.

About Causes

Asking questions about causes often involves shifting the level of abstraction from the *concrete* experimental situation to the *abstract* principles connected with it, or vice versa. Certain clause introducers mark these shifts from what occurred (X) to what caused it (Y):

X, *so* Y; *if* X, *then* Y; *when* X, Y; X *because* Y.

LEP students need to be aware that questions that include these words are important because they often concern the *point* of the activity.

"*So,* the ship that's floating is really displacing the water, isn't it?"

"Would it have floated *if* you had not put the air in?"

"Soapy water flattens out, and won't mount up, as plain water does. *Because* we said water has what kind of power?"

Why questions are a typical way to ask about causes. If a student's response is not at that level of abstraction, guide him or her with a follow-up. Here, for example, the student responds to the "why" question with a *description* of an experimental procedure, rather than the *explanation* of the cause behind what was observed.

T: Why did the powder turn purple?
S: Because I added iodine.
T: Okay, and what did this *prove?*

Help students develop the vocabulary needed for communication about the abstract and concrete levels of science experiments.

> Concrete questions/responses include words such as *see, touch, notice, behave* (e.g., "What did you *see/touch/hear/smell/notice* when you . . . ?").
>
> *Abstract* questions/responses include words such as *principle, example, property, explain, generalize* (e.g., Can you *explain/generalize* about the *principle/property* behind what you saw?).

Some words are used to describe both levels, among them: *discover, happen, make, cause.* This is because occurrences and causes can be thought of on both a physical, concrete level and an abstract level of principles, as illustrated by the "why" questions example above. Note also that concrete verbs such as *see* and *show* are frequently used on the abstract level as synonyms for *understand* and *prove,* respectively. When either-level words are used in a question (or response), make sure there are other indicators of which level is intended.

Avoid questions that are vague as to level of abstractness (e.g., "What happened?"). Instead, ask "What happened when you added soapy water to the plain water?" for a concrete description, or "What happened to the surface tension of the water drop when you added soapy water to it?" for a more abstract explanation.

CAN THEY APPLY IT?

By the kinds of questions teachers ask, they can help students not only to show that they have really learned it but also to extend and strengthen their understanding. Even while students are in the process of learning the basic facts and skills of a subject, teachers can reinforce students' learning of these basics by asking them questions that require them to see connections among facts and to apply factual knowledge to their understanding of their larger world. Unlike factual questions, these higher-order cognitive questions require the student to craft his or her own response, rather than coming up with the exact word or phrase that the teacher (or text) had in mind. Higher-order cognitive questions are thus demanding from both a cognitive and linguistic standpoint; the student must not only do some higher-level thinking, he or she must express that thinking using language that has not been "prepackaged." This does not mean, however, that only the most apt students are ready for higher-order cognitive questions. Research has shown that *all* students can develop skills with these more challenging questions when given the opportunity to do so.

What Teachers Can Do

LEP students often face particularly difficult linguistic demands when responding to higher-order cognitive questions. Techniques that may help include the following:

> Base your higher-order cognitive questions on homework or seatwork, so that students can have more time to think about and compose their responses.
>
> Give students practice in asking each other for summaries and explanations by having them conduct review discussions in pairs. This reciprocal teaching technique gives them more opportunities to formulate more difficult responses in a less pressured setting. Formulating questions for one another also trains students to anticipate the kinds of questions teachers might ask, an invaluable study habit.

Teachers are often understandably reluctant to put students who are usually unsuccessful responders—native and nonnative English speakers alike—on the spot by asking them higher-order cognitive questions. Comments by the teachers who cooperated with our study indicated that the way the teacher *follows up* in such cases may be the important thing.

> Encourage the less efficient responder with more questions.
>
> ''If I ask a person such as N. [an unsuccessful responder] a question that may be difficult for her to answer, then I accept her answer and add a comment to clarify.''

DO THEY *KNOW* WHAT A GOOD ANSWER IS?

Students identified by their teachers as effective responders knew more about the content characteristics of successful answers than those students identified as unsuccessful. The successful students were very aware of procedural and interactive features of the good response; for example, not shouting out, waiting your turn, not fooling around. But the unsuccesssful students were less able to verbalize what it takes to give an answer that is correct and shows knowledge.

What Teachers Can Do

Make explicit your expectations for a good verbal response. Some of the features of a good response identified in this study follow.

Using the appropriate words (relevant vocabulary)

Including details and description; being specific

Giving a complete, well-organized answer

Giving an on-topic, thoughtful answer, not just guessing; showing you know what you're talking about

Giving the correct answer

Choose particular features from this list and focus on a different feature each day, asking the students to be attentive to whether answers have the feature. Write the feature on the chalkboard to remind all the students and to provide extra support to the LEP students.

Give students practice in making effective responses. Ask them to work in small groups, asking each other questions about what they have learned. Give them a checklist to rate each other on how well each answer meets the criteria you have established (which might include features from the list as well as other features you think are important for answers in your classroom). They can help each other to expand their answers to provide more information.

When a student gives an effective response, indicate to the other students why that response was good. For example,

T: Which would weigh more, a block of metal or a block of wood the same size? Matt?

M: The metal, 'cause the wood floats.

T: Good, you told us your evidence for your answer.

LET ME ASK THAT ANOTHER WAY

Now and then, even the most experienced and skilled teacher can be found looking out over a classroom full of blank or puzzled faces, after having posed what she or he believed to be an easy and straightforward question. There can be several reasons for this, including the following:

The question may have included vague reference.

The question may have included unfamiliar key terms.

The question may not have been framed adequately.

The class may be having trouble following the teacher's plan for the discussion as a whole.

What Teachers Can Do *When* This Happens

The difficulty is, of course, that when these problems occur, you must attend to them immediately, without being able to stop to analyze the probable cause. This is further complicated by the fact that when you are standing in front of the class teaching (in this case, leading a verbal review), you normally pay more attention to *what* you are saying than to *how* you are saying it. The safest course is to assume that all the foregoing four factors might be the root cause of the confusion. Fortunately, all four factors can be dealt with efficiently by rewording the question, keeping these pointers in mind.

First, *tell the class why you are asking* the question, or give some *background information,* or otherwise link the question specifically to what the students can be expected to know *and* be thinking about.

To avoid vagueness and comprehension problems in the reworded question, pay specific attention to your use of the following:

Pronouns (*it, that, you,* etc.) and nonspecific noun phrases (*the thing, something,* etc.), as well as verbs and adverbs with very general meanings, such as the verbs *have, do,* or *be,* and the adverbs *then* and *there.* The exact meanings of these words are determined situationally, so it becomes even more important to clearly frame questions containing these words.

Technical labels and descriptions of key concepts. If in doubt as to whether the question was phrased above the students' heads, replace these terms in the reworded question.

What Teachers Can Do *Before* This Happens

To lessen the likelihood of whole-class befuddlement during verbal reviews:

Frame the verbal review as a whole, telling the class the general topic up for discussion as well as providing some information about its scope and organization.

Plan for the use of topic bridges to make your organization clear and easier for the class to follow.

Make a list of synonymous terms, phrases, and descriptions of key concepts used in texts and other instructional materials. For concepts that seem particularly difficult to explain, having these alternates on a three-by-five-inch card may be useful when rewording a question. The list making itself could be a good auxiliary instructional activity, with students working in pairs or small groups to compare lists and to justify them.

RESPONDING TO RESPONSES

Verbal reviews are more than sequences of questions and answers. Following the student's response comes the teacher's *evaluation* of that response. Whatever a teacher says or does following a student's answer is usually interpreted by students as an evaluation of that answer. Evaluations play an instructional role in the verbal review because they allow the teacher to say what counts and what should be set aside in a student's answer. Students find out what is correct and what the teacher sees as important both in terms of content and in terms of how the content is expressed. Students know that teachers have different styles of evaluating—some teachers almost never reject an answer, preferring instead to focus on the right answer and expand on that, whereas others are quite animated about both praise and correction. Teachers indicate acceptance by positive statements ("Excellent!" "Terrific") or more matter-of-fact acceptance ("Right" "Okay" "Yes"), or by repeating the answer or simply nodding and moving on to the next question. Answers are rarely rejected outright, but the teacher's negative evaluation is usually nonetheless apparent ("Does anyone have a different answer for that?"). Knowing the role of evaluation can help teachers maximize its value during verbal review.

What Teachers Can Do

Recognize that evaluation may not always be appropriate. Evaluation can become so automatic that everything students say is evaluated, including opinions, questions, and comments. Evaluation tells students whether their understanding of lesson material is valid and is thus appropriate when lesson material is being reviewed.

Evaluate appropriately:

> Don't praise a simple calculation or factual recall answer with "Excellent!" or "Great!" Giving praise *highlights* both the responder and the response, so praising an answer solely to encourage the student who volunteers it may embarrass (or even insult) the responder and may confuse students about the important points of the discussion.

> Don't leave conflicting answers unresolved, and don't leave clearly wrong answers unevaluated. When two (or more) different calculations are put forth, make sure students know which answer is correct; be very cautious about assuming that the correct answer is obvious. In such cases, follow-up usually also entails making sure the class knows how the correct answer was arrived at. One effective way we have seen these problems resolved is for the teacher to work the problem at the board, with the class (in unison) directing the teacher as to the steps to take to correctly solve the problem. If (math) errors are resolved by the whole class as a matter of routine, the erring student is not put on the spot, nor is he or she corrected by the brightest students' answers.

If you turn the evaluation over to students ("What did you think of that answer, Mary?"), make sure it is done generally enough that your most apt responders aren't the only ones doing the evaluating. You can ensure quality control by the fact that you can evaluate their evaluations.

WRAPPING IT UP

How the teacher ends a verbal review discussion can either enhance or detract from its educational value. Although an unsummarized verbal review may have served its *evaluative* purpose, by giving the teacher some notion of how well the lesson material has been learned, it will certainly be less *instructional* than a verbal review with a good summary.

What Teachers Can Do

The summary should relate the foregoing discussion to the knowledge base that the students are in the process of acquiring. This usually means relating the discussion to the purposes and structure of the curriculum unit or the overall subject. The scope and detail of the summary will, therefore, vary according to the place the lesson material being reviewed has in the curriculum unit. In any case, a good summary will do the following:

Provide the students with some labels for organizing their knowledge base into manageable chunks, as in this example:

> "Okay. Good thinking. Good work. You had some great ideas on how to make these things float, and what makes them float, and that's what this is all about. Okay. I want you to put all of these things back."

Involve students actively in organizing their knowledge base, as in these examples:

> "Okay, now, we need to summarize what we've learned today. But first, who can tell me what a summary is?"
>
> "Okay, now that you've finished your assignment, what did you think as far as your objective was concerned?"
>
> "What did you *learn* from this unit on the behavior of mealworms?"

Provide teachers and students with an opportunity to *co-construct* students' developing knowledge base, as in this example, in which the teacher provides the broader labels but asks students to provide the important details:

> "Our first objective was to practice the multiply-add sequence. And your second one was to multiply a two-digit number by a one-digit number, with trading. What are some of the things that you have to know in order to do that successfully? Who can sort of wrap it up for me? Kisha?"

ASK A SIMPLE QUESTION

Democratizing class participation is a difficult balancing act indeed! It may be helpful to bear in mind that during the course of a class discussion or verbal review, questions can be posed at varying levels of linguistic sophistication and cognitive demand, offering opportunities for participation to students of varying proficiency levels. Although all students should be given practice in responding to higher-order cognitive questions, factual recall questions do predominate in verbal reviews. Factual recall questions, while relatively undemanding from a cognitive standpoint, can vary considerably in their linguistic difficulty. The following suggestions are intended for teachers of recently mainstreamed students who have learned the basics of English but are not yet fluent.

What Teachers Can Do

Fitting questions to the students' level of English proficiency involves two considerations: the linguistic difficulty level of the question and the linguistic difficulty level of the (appropriate) response. *Choice questions,* which ask the student to pick the correct answer from alternates given in the question, should be the easiest, since the question contains the answer:

> "So, do the heavy things float, or do the heavy things not float?"
>
> "Which is more like a gas: desks in a classroom or leaves blowing?"

However, choice questions that are long and/or structurally complex, or contain unfamiliar words can be linguistically taxing for the nonnative English-speaking student:

> "Which is more like a liquid: a sidewalk with lots of people walking on it, or a crowded elevator?" [The LEP student might confuse *elevator* with *escalator.*]
>
> "If you could weigh a block of water and weigh a block of wood that are the same size, which would weigh more?" [The *If/then* complicates.]

The next easiest type of question is the more usual *factual recall question,* in which the student is required to respond with a calculation, name, date, or other very short factual response. Linguistically, these responses are simple (and often also easy), but the linguistic difficulty level of the *question* may be a source of comprehension problems for LEP students, as can inadequate signposts indicating the direction of the discussion. In such cases, rephrase the question (perhaps as a choice question).

Support comprehension by repeating students' answers while modifying for correction and elaboration as needed. This not only reinforces correct answers; it also helps students to extend their concepts and meanings through listening to your elaboration.

WHAT ABOUT GRAMMAR?

Teachers agree that they don't evaluate LEP students' responses according to their English proficiency but rather according to whether or not their answers are correct. But teachers are also aware that lack of proficiency in English can be seen by others as a lack of intelligence, and they want to know what they can do to help improve their LEP students' oral proficiency.

What Teachers Can Do

Focus on the *content* of what the child says, and respond to the *meaning,* while modeling the correct form (see also page 153). An effective strategy is to repeat what the student said, supplying the correct grammatical form. For example:

S: Did the kids went outside already?
T: Did the kids go outside already? Yes, they did.

S: Some them high.
T: Yes, some of them are high.

Write student responses on the chalkboard. This is another technique that allows you to recast the response into appropriate and grammatical forms without giving overt correction. Writing the responses has the additional advantages of reinforcing the information and providing a correct model of the grammatical form. For example:

T: Okay, what did this prove? Juan?
S: If it purple, it's with starch.
T: [writes on board] What did this prove? If it turned purple, it had starch in it. If it didn't turn purple, there was no starch in it.

Be realistic about the impact you can have on the LEP student's grammar development. English is acquired slowly through interaction and practice, not by memorizing rules. Correcting speech errors only draws attention to the inadequacies of the LEP student, and is not likely to help improve his or her grammar. The best medium for working on grammar mistakes is writing. During oral reviews, use the student's written work to comment on grammar and focus on *what* the student is saying, not *how* he or she says it.

WHAT IS ACTIVE PARTICIPATION?

Usually when teachers talk about active participation, they refer to social behaviors such as hand-raising or waiting to be called on. The successful—and active—participant also shows good content knowledge by giving full and correct answers, using the right words, and being clear. The goal of many teachers is to foster this sort of active participation in all students. We advocate some caution in this for the following reasons:

It is ethnocentric to assume that children from all cultures share these conventions for participation; they don't.

Attentive students are developing their listening/thinking skills even though they may not respond correctly or may not offer responses.

If participation is seen only in terms of *responding*, being able to formulate intelligent questions may not receive appropriate emphasis.

To learn to respond appropriately, LEP students must become familiar with the academic functions of questions in the American classroom. This familiarity can be developed through listening, as well as practice in active participation.

What Teachers Can Do

Those students who do not actively participate in the sense we have outlined may be following different cultural conventions for classroom participation. Learn more about classroom participation in the cultures from which your LEP students come. Some cultures do not value the student who volunteers answers or speaks out. Social studies lessons can be a good time to have students role-play or describe how lessons are conducted in the countries they come from. This can give you—and the whole class—insights into what other cultures consider appropriate classroom behavior.

Remember that LEP students can understand before they are able to speak. Their seemingly passive behavior may mask their active role in attending to and learning from the interaction that is taking place. Listening and reflecting thoughtfully are also active processes.

Teach and reteach the characteristics of good responses in terms of how you expect information to be organized and presented, as well as in terms of the social behaviors you associate with active participation.

Teachers use a variety of question types during verbal reviews. Students must recognize the function of each question type and the appropriate form of the response. These include factual recall questions, which elicit definitions or repetitions, and higher-order cognitive questions, which elicit predictions, substantiations, opinions, and explanations. Provide your students with opportunities to practice answering questions of different types. For example, you might talk about *predicting*, and show them a variety of forms that might be used to ask them to predict, such as:

What do you think will happen if . . . ?
Can you predict what will happen when you add iodine to powder no. 23?

Students should be thought of as more than *responders*. They should be given opportunities to formulate and initiate questions that they find important.

Encouraging students to be *questioners* allows them to develop a broader range of functional language skills.

Ask students to work together in small groups to develop questions and answers about topics you have taught. Allow them to share these with other groups or the whole class.

FOLLOW-UP ACTIVITIES AND QUESTIONS

1. How important do you think it is to balance teacher-directed activities with group and individual work? What are the advantages and possible drawbacks of each? Describe a lesson in a specific content area in which there is a balance among the three.

2. Create the dialogue for a short verbal review about a specific topic. Use the pattern of the typically good verbal review found on page 223. Share your dialogue with a partner and ask for feedback. You may want to revise it on the basis of the suggestions you receive.

3. What if you have a student who contributes almost nothing to the interaction? What strategies might you use to encourage that student's participation?

4. The authors use the word *democratize* when referring to the conducting of verbal reviews. What do they mean? Can you think of ways other than those mentioned in this chapter that can democratize classroom participation?

16

The Physical Environment

D. Scott Enright   *Georgia State University*

Mary Lou McCloskey   *Florida Atlantic University*

Editors' Introduction

In a traditional classroom environment, the teacher's desk generally is at the front of the classroom with a chalkboard providing the backdrop. The students' desks face the front and are arranged in rows. Materials are carefully stored out of sight until needed for specific lessons. This kind of setting is most typically associated with teacher-centered classrooms. The teacher acts as the giver of knowledge; the students are the more or less passive recipients. In contrast, the environment recommended by D. Scott Enright and Mary Lou McCloskey in this chapter is integrated and student-centered. It is integrated in that it provides settings for many types of tasks often requiring student interaction and collaboration and in that these settings are conducive to both language and content development; it is student-centered in that students and the teacher are considered partners. This implied relationship is somewhat akin to that described by Freire (1970) in reference to libertarian education. In this case, however, the authors give the teacher the role of the senior partner who plans classroom environments that are functional, flexible, enticing, and student-owned. Although the examples given are oriented mainly to elementary settings, many can be adapted to any other age levels for which they may be appropriate.

The classroom environment should be set up to facilitate many types of activities and many kinds of student interaction and collaboration. It should provide easy access to materials that can be used to accomplish a great variety of tasks, and it should communicate the appropriate uses of the various areas and materials to students. Here are some suggestions for accomplishing these aims.

PLANNING A FUNCTIONAL CLASSROOM

In beginning to plan a more functional classroom, you may find that a map will help you visualize possible changes. Try cutting out scale furniture pieces so that you can try out different classroom arrangements before lugging the actual pieces around! Note that in both sample classrooms (Figures 16.1 and 16.2) various activity areas have been established, where various sets of activities requiring similar materials and furniture have their own special place. For example, both classrooms have activity areas for reading groups, for whole-class meetings, discussions, or teacher presentations, for viewing media presentations or drama, for puppets, for movement, for storytelling, for writing, and so on. Examine the possibilities and decide which of these you might like to add to your classroom. Then work with your model to include them. Remember, many unexpected places in the room and even around the room can be used for activity areas. A closet can be a perfect place to use a filmstrip viewer; the hall is good for paired tutoring or painting a life-size mural; a protected spot on the blacktop is a great place to play games. Also be open to using all possible spaces within the activity areas you plan. For example, learning-center activities could be displayed on a wall or on the side of a file cabinet; a model of the solar system could be mounted on the ceiling.

Once you have decided which activity areas you want to include in your physical environment, plan ways to embed the purposes and rules of the activities for an area into the physical plan. The structure of your environment and its component parts must make their intended functions clear to all of your students, including beginning second language (L2) learners. Moreover, part of providing a warm, supportive environment is providing a safe environment. Not only should a classroom environment be physically safe but students should also be safe from conflicts and criticism that come from their not understanding what is expected of them.

Because many second language students don't understand your oral language or English print well enough to be told the rules or to read them, the classroom setup itself can be used to clarify its uses. Various areas can be labeled in pictures and words with activities that occur there. Lots of devices are available for communicating the rules of a particular center. The ever-popular art center could have a hat rack with as many painters' caps as the number of students that are allowed to use the center at one time. A student would know just by looking at the hat rack whether there were room for one more. A reading center could also have a sign saying "Quiet, please" and a rebus symbol (perhaps a picture of the "speak no evil" monkey) to indicate that talking was not allowed there.

The storage and display of materials can also be used to communicate their use. Most materials in the classroom should be stored openly and near where they are to be used. For example, supplies of paper, pencils, pens, and binding materials should be placed in the writing area; headphones should be

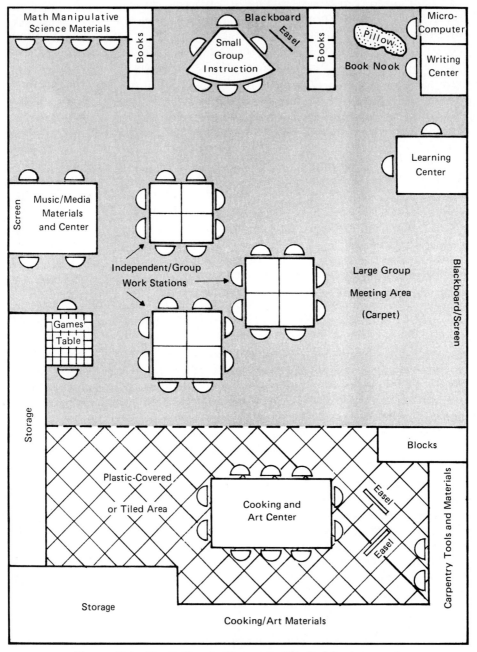

Figure 16.1. *Mr. Nations's Classroom Physical Environment*

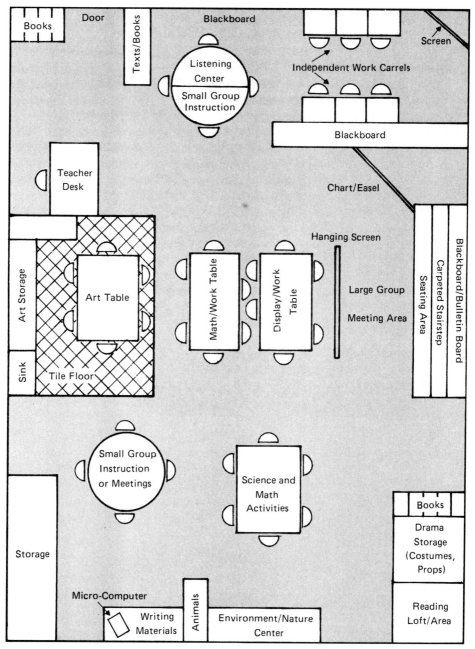

Figure 16.2. *Mrs. Gomez's Classroom Physical Environment*

anchored to the listening-center table. Materials should be color-coded or labeled with pictures for easy access and putting away. For example, a pegboard could have outlines of different articles, showing where they are to be placed when not in use. Pictures of articles that are kept in a cupboard or drawer or on a shelf could be painted or could be cut out from a magazine or catalog, laminated, and taped on or near the storage place. Written labels, in combination with the pictures, could provide opportunities for practicing reading vocabulary.

A tiled area (or a sheet of heavy plastic taped to the floor) could communicate, ''Here's where it's okay to do activities that might get messy.'' In a classroom meeting area, a taped circle or a drawn-in pattern on the rug could say, ''Here's where we have class meetings or circle time.'' A list of rules with accompanying pictures, as illustrated in Figure 16.3, could communicate

Figure 16.3. *Rebus Rules for Listening Time*

what happens during ''listening times.'' These rules could be put on a wall or some other clearly visible surface.

The physical environment of the classroom can also be used to help students understand and follow the rules you have developed. For example, at first, arts and crafts materials can be introduced to your students in small-group activities during which they are taught how to use the art area independently; how to follow instructions for specific activities; how to use materials; how to place materials where they belong; and how to clean up and put away materials. After a while, students can work independently at the center, and newly arrived students can be trained by veterans. A similar procedure can be used to teach students the proper use of equipment in a listening center.

Early in the year, students can be taught how to use the record player and tape recorder and can be issued ''operator's licenses'' when they demonstrate understanding of the appropriate procedures. Then, as long as one licensed operator is included, groups of students can be assigned to use the listening center independently while other classroom events are taking place.

Once you have embedded the purposes and procedures of your activities into the physical environment, and as your students (including your second language students) become accustomed to that environment, you can begin to extend students' use of speech and print. As the year goes on, the rebus signs and pictures explaining the procedures for the various materials and activity areas can be accompanied or replaced by written procedures. The schedule for the day (see Figure 16.4) can also be posted on the chalkboard rather than explained to the students, and class members can be responsible for figuring out what they are to do next, with designated native English speaking and advanced second language students serving as coordinators to help beginning second language students and new students. Similarly, books from the Book Nook can be checked out for class or home use by a student librarian, and pairs of student gardeners and zoologists can follow the posted procedures to care for the class plants and animals. Children can make a class guest book, and designated hosts can be responsible for welcoming visitors to the classroom, showing them around and answering their questions, and asking them to sign the guest book. Of course, a class job chart listing all of these job titles would be posted (see Figure 16.5) and children's name cards would be frequently changed on the chart so that everyone would have a chance to do different jobs and to read the chart many times in the process!

The following list summarizes the steps we have just described.

How To Make Your Classroom Functional

1. Make a map of your classroom and plan activity areas for different sets of activities with similar needs (including materials, furniture, and space).
   a. Use many different places (a closet, the hall, the steps) as activity areas.
   b. Use many different spaces within activity areas (walls, the side of a file cabinet) to accomplish your activities' purposes.

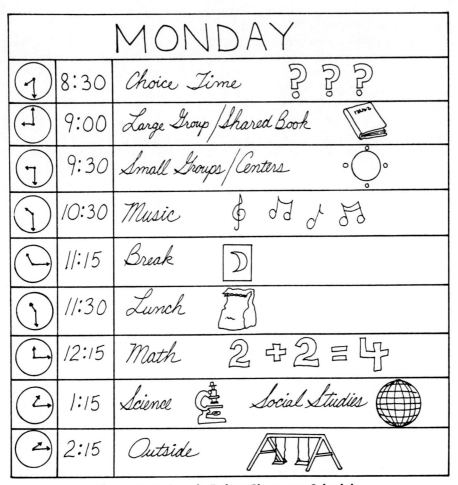

Figure 16.4. *Sample Rebus Classroom Schedule*

2. Embed purposes and rules of activities into their areas.
   a. Label activity areas.
   b. Provide signs or signals for rules within the activity areas.
   c. Label materials, and store them in or near the places where they are to be used.
3. Introduce activity areas one at a time, explicitly teaching the rules for each area.
4. Find ways to combine the classroom functions and procedures with speech and print.

Clean Tables	*Maria and Avia*
Attendance	*Pablo and Carlos*
Library	*Luis and Ku*
Feed Fish	*Rosita and Sophy*
Sweep	*Cuong and Tran*

Figure 16.5. *Sample Rebus Job Chart*

PLANNING A FLEXIBLE CLASSROOM

In the creation of activity areas for your classroom, keep in mind the requirements of each activity, including the amount of verbal interaction (which will affect the noise level); movement; space; and traffic in and out of the activity (if any). Noisy, busy activities such as drama or blocks should be located as far away as possible from quiet activities such as those that occur in the reading, writing, independent study, and listening areas. These quiet areas can be separated to some degree with a bookcase, screen, or other barrier to minimize noise and distraction, and should be located away from the door to keep movement near the area at a minimum.

Furniture that can serve a variety of purposes and that can be easily arranged is helpful in this environment. If you can, choose light tables and/or movable desks rather than attached desk chairs or other heavy or unwieldy items for your room, and choose stackable chairs that can be put aside to provide space for an active movement event or large-group activity where students will be seated in a carpeted area. For example, a set of carpeted stair steps can provide a very successful multipurpose activity area. Students can be seated there for media presentations, because it permits such good vision of the event for everyone. It can be used for class performances and for teacher or visitor demonstrations. If it suits the purposes of the dramatists, the stairs can be used as the stage, with the audience seated on the floor. When the area is not in use for full-class meetings, it can be used for small-group games, for small-group dramatic play or rehearsals, or for individual students who want to read.

Like stair steps, much of the furniture in the classroom can be used by more than one person at the same time, thereby permitting the collaboration that is so necessary for language development. Tables can replace desks to add flexibility, and desks can be shoved together to create group workspaces for the same purpose. Classrooms can have the flexibility to facilitate the activities of a more traditional classroom without being organized exclusively for the use of those activities.

In a similar manner, the materials chosen for the classroom must also be flexible and multipurpose whenever possible, and the classroom rules and expectations should encourage their use in new ways and in many different activities and activity areas. For example, art materials should be given their own prominent area in the classroom, owing to their diversity of potential uses: In addition to being used to create works of art, they can be used to illustrate stories or poems or to create puppet shows (language arts); to make dioramas (social studies); and to make rocket and jet models (science and math). Similarly, display areas lend themselves to multidisciplinary integrated use. A display of fossils and arrowheads can be used for social studies (Native American ways of life); for science (types of rocks and formation of fossils); for language arts (imaginary stories or reports about the physical articles); and for math (counting, weighing, and measuring the articles and graphing results).

Finally, reading and writing materials should be available all around the room for use in conjunction with your multipurpose materials and your general activity areas. A library area and a writing area where quiet prevails are *musts*, but beyond that, writing materials and relevant books should be distributed whenever and wherever they might contribute to students' content and language learning. Puppet-making books and play scripts, for example, could be placed at the art center, along with writing materials for creating original puppet shows. A display of students' rock collections could be accompanied by geology books and books on rock identification, with worksheets for students to write in their guesses as to the types of rocks being displayed. Or small weighing scales could be placed alongside the rocks, and directions and worksheets could be provided for weighing and comparing the various kinds of rocks. One teacher we know even turned his windows (and his children's daydreaming!) into opportunities for language and literacy development by placing books about clouds under the window accompanied by a list of ''sky-gazing'' suggestions and a large display sheet for recording observations. The point is that the more accessible writing and reading materials are, the more likely it is that children will integrate these materials into their ongoing language- and content-learning activities.

The following list summarizes the steps we have suggested for adapting your classroom environment.

How To Make Your Classroom Flexible

1. In your creation of activity areas, keep in mind the following concerns:
   a. Noise level of activities (verbal interaction).
   b. Movement required in the activities (nonverbal interaction).
   c. Space requirements of activities.
   d. Traffic in and out of activity areas.
2. Use furniture that can be easily rearranged (e.g., light tables and stackable chairs). Beg, borrow, and scrounge!
3. Choose furniture that can serve a variety of purposes (e.g., tables and movable desks rather than attached desk chairs).
4. Choose multipurpose materials and encourage their use in new ways and in many activities and activity areas.
5. Provide reading and writing materials all around the room, to be used in conjunction with other materials.

PLANNING AN ENTICING CLASSROOM

As the classrooms in both Figures 16.1 and 16.2 illustrate, many of the materials that are to be used are displayed and stored openly in order to suggest their use. If language learning truly involves meaningful communication and reflection, often about concrete and mutual referents, then it is crucial that you have all kinds of different enticing objects for display and use in your classroom, and ones that appeal to all the senses. All kinds of "stuff" relating to a unit of study can be placed on a theme/realia table. One week there may be a rock collection and photographs of geological formations on the theme table, while another week an ant farm, a picnic basket, and a weather chart may be displayed there. Similarly, in a language/music/media theme center, students might find musical instruments, filmstrips, and language games related to a unit on Central Africa. You don't have to limit yourself to materials that are typically associated with school (e.g., books, paper, pencils). You can feel free to add many nontraditional materials (e.g., natural objects, trash, road signs). Not only do objects give a focus for language, they also focus attention primarily on themselves and on the task rather than on the learners, so that second language students, who feel less self-consciousness and less concerned about making a mistake, are more free to respond. You can also use objects that are familiar to students in order to introduce unfamiliar concepts and language and ways to use language, thereby bridging the known and the unknown.

You can also use the walls of your classroom to entice students into using the various kinds of discourse. Walls can be covered with posters and displays of children's work; directions for learning centers; signs; and drawings. As just one example, you might introduce an upcoming unit by erecting a "wall

Figure 16.6. *An Activity in an Enticing Classroom*
Enticing objects that appeal to all the senses are essential in the classroom. These children have made their own 3-D glasses and are looking at objects in their classroom in a new way.

center" consisting of items such as animal pictures from *Ranger Rick* or *National Geographic World,* with a question under each picture. Answers could be hidden under a flap so that students could check after they'd guessed, or could be revealed at the end of the week. In like manner, there might be a place on a wall of your classroom for the "math problem of the week," or the "riddle of the day," or a stretch of wall or bulletin board formally marked as a place for students to put up writings, art work, memos, and announcements and interesting memorabilia that they want to share with the class.

Your environment and your daily routines hold much potential for enticing literacy activities as well. "Discovery cards" and "curiosity cards" can be tacked up in your activity areas and integrated into your current curriculum theme. For example, during the Superheroes unit, you could place a card at the library center asking students "Can you find information about the following real-life heroes in our library? President Lincoln, Reverend King, Madame Curie? Your favorite hero?" You could also place a card at the art center suggesting: "Make the vehicle or map the routes used by one of these heroic explorers: Marco Polo, Amelia Earhart, Ferdinand Magellan, Neil Armstrong."

A class thermometer or that ever-beckoning window can serve as the focus for daily observations and weather reports, recorded on a chart and shared at the end of the day or end of the week. School bulletins, lunch menus, and so on can be displayed on a designated bulletin board, and a class "reporter" can read or summarize them for the rest of the class; students themselves can write or copy notes to parents about class or school activities.

You need not have a graduate degree in interior design to create an attractive, inviting classroom that encourages communication and L2 and literacy development. You can use parents, aides, friends, or other teachers with design skills and resources as valuable classroom consultants. To ease the task of year-round room decorations, you can develop a color scheme for the classroom and use backgrounds that needn't be changed with every display. Remember that students will stop "seeing" displays and activity cards after they've been up for a while unless you refer to them or use them in instruction. Design displays with curriculum goals in mind, refer to them often, and change them periodically. Change displays of student work frequently to allow exciting new creations to take their place.

In summary, to make your classroom an enticing place for students, make sure you have a lot of interesting things to talk about, to read about, and to write about in your classroom, and then anchor those things within thematic units, classroom rules, and activities that efficiently direct the ways in which they are talked, read, and written about! This one strategy will directly assist your second language students with their acquisition of both language and content.

The following list summarizes the preceding key steps.

How To Make Your Classroom Enticing

1. Use materials that students can touch, taste, smell, see, and listen to, and read, write, think about, and talk about!
2. Use materials that students can use independently.
3. Use a variety of materials, those which are typically associated with school (e.g., books, paper, pencils) and those which are not (e.g., natural objects, trash, road signs).
4. Use materials that are familiar to the students in order to introduce them to those which are unfamiliar.
5. Organize materials and displays around class themes or units of study and include materials produced by the students themselves.
6. Find ways to add activity areas to your units and to add literacy activities to the daily routine and the overall classroom environment.
7. Store materials openly.
8. Display materials attractively.
9. Change materials and displays regularly and refer to them often.

PLANNING A STUDENT-OWNED CLASSROOM

It is not necessary to sacrifice control in a classroom in order to promote student initiative. Rather, a valuable, indeed essential, part of your exercise of control as the senior partner in your students' education is to involve them in all aspects of daily classroom life, from curriculum planning to tutoring to cleaning up. One way of using the physical environment to do this is to delegate to students various leadership roles and classroom responsibilities, such as attendance keeping; lunch count; room maintenance; supervision of lining up; tutoring; putting up displays; interviewing and escorting visitors; and setting up activities. Anything that students can do that will promote their language learning, growth in self-esteem, and autonomy, they should do. Your task is to prepare them to succeed at these tasks.

As you carefully teach, demonstrate, and model classroom rules, you should also do the same with classroom tasks and procedures. Learning aids can be developed to make these tasks more efficient. A sample procedure for keeping attendance and lunch records can serve as an example: Write each student's name on a clip-type clothespin, and clip the pins around the edge of a large can. Then, as students enter the room in the morning, they can unclip the clothespins and drop their names into labeled cans (milk only, soup lunch, full lunch, etc.). Students keeping attendance can glance at the clothespins not put in the can and know who is absent. They can count the clothespins in each can for the lunch report. At the end of each day, the attendance keeper can pin all the clothespins around the edge of the can again. Alternatively, students can mark their attendance or lunch count on a chart as they walk in the door in the morning, or they can take turns reading and "taking roll" orally.

Students should also be involved whenever possible in classroom planning and in the arrangement of the physical environment. We've already discussed the need for including children in curriculum development; other examples of this strategy in practice might include using students' likes and dislikes to assign small groups for a project or having children make a classroom map to scale in order to figure out where to put the puppet stage that they are building. Also in keeping with this principle, you can see to it that students' work (not just the best students' work, but every student's best work) is prominently and attractively displayed in your classroom. For example, you could laminate a large mat for the work of each student in the class and label it with the student's name. Each week the students could then select their favorite works to display on the mat. As mentioned earlier, you could also provide a permanent free space for children to post and display materials of their own selection. A large cardboard or papier-mâché mailbox for classroom correspondence encourages students to use writing for their own purposes throughout the school year and also gives you an opportunity to provide meaningful responses to their writing. Similarly, a class suggestion box gives students a voice in the business of the classroom, if you read the suggestions openly and try to respond to them (our favorite, from an intermediate-second language first-grader, is "holkum wey downt gayt a brak fron rooken?" Translation: "How come we don't get a break from working?"). It is also important to place student activities and displays at their eye level rather than at an adult's eye level. This makes it clear that the room and its contents are for the students to use. Besides creating rich opportunities for students to use speech and print and giving them ownership in the classroom, these activities will all promote students' pride in their own creations and will develop their self-evaluative abilities.

Another strategy for giving students increased ownership is to get them to supply items of their own for the classroom: for example, pictures, stories, objects brought from home, or objects collected on a field trip or found on the school grounds. Many of the displays can be student-created, in the same way that the curriculum is often student-inspired and that many of the activities in communicative classrooms depend on students' creative and active participation. An interesting insect that was captured by two or three children at recess could easily become the vehicle for science, math, reading, and ESL instruction before being eventually replaced at the nature center by some other

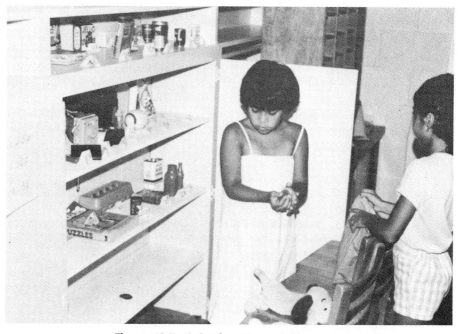

Figure 16.7. _A Student-Owned Classroom_

In this flexible and student-owned classroom, objects students bring in from home can be used for a "store" center, first with teacher structure and supervision and later as a free-time activity.

fascinating item! Or a wonderful book brought from home may be read to the children, only to become a class favorite to be shared and reshared for several days to come!

The following list summarizes the preceding steps.

How To Make Your Classroom Student-Owned

1. Give students leadership roles and classroom responsibilities.
2. Involve students in planning and arranging the classroom.
3. Display every student's best work, and change displays often.
4. Give students control over classroom spaces and resources (e.g., bulletin boards, a mailbox).
5. Use materials and ideas brought in by students to create classroom curriculum, displays, conversation, and texts. Also use students' creations (e.g., a composition, artwork) to create curriculum.

CONCLUSION

In this chapter, we have described the physical environment in classrooms. If any single generalization can be made in contrasting the physical environments of the traditional classroom and the integrated classroom, it is that the former is organized primarily on the basis of adults' interests, goals, and needs, whereas in the latter, the interests, goals, and needs of students are the primary impetus for organization. We believe that if you can turn your classroom social and physical environments ''inside out,'' then you will be assisting the education of all your students.

RECOMMENDED READING

Cohen, E. G. (1986). *Designing groupwork: Strategies for the heterogeneous classroom.* New York: Columbia University, Teachers College Press. Clear explanation of the rationale for cooperative groupwork, ways to plan groupwork and to prepare students for the activities, specific suggestions for bilingual classrooms, and many groupwork activities and cooperative training exercises.

Garvey, C. (1977). *Play.* Cambridge, MA: Harvard University Press. Discussion of the history, importance, nature, and development of children's play.

Loughlin, C. E., & Suina, J. H. (1982). *The learning environment: An instructional strategy.* New York: Columbia University, Teachers College Press. Complete text on a conceptual view of environment, organization of space and learning materials, and using the learning environment for special purposes including promoting literacy and supporting children with special needs.

Savignon, S. J. (1983). *Communicative competence: Theory and classroom practice.* Reading, MA: Addison-Wesley. Chapter 4 offers a thoughtful discussion on the selection and use of materials.

Silberman, C. E. (Ed.). (1973). *The open classroom reader.* New York: Random House. Part Three, Chapter Two, "How to Manage Time and Space," includes many suggestions for designing and using the physical environment. The entire book is filled with interesting ideas and practical techniques for the student-centered classroom.

ADDITIONAL RESOURCES

Hannah, G. G. (1982). *Classroom spaces and places.* Belmont, CA: Pitman Learning.

Lay-Dopyera, M., & Dopyera, J. (1987). *Becoming a teacher of young children* (3rd ed.). New York: Random House.

Wendelin, K. H., & Greenlaw, M. J. (1984). *Storybook classrooms: Using children's literature in the learning center.* Atlanta, GA: Humanics.

Zeigler, N., Larson, B., & Byers, J. (1983). *Let the kids do it!* (Books 1 and 2). Belmont, CA: David S. Lake Publishers.

FOLLOW-UP QUESTIONS AND ACTIVITIES

1. What strategies to encourage group work might you use in planning the physical environment for a specific activity or lesson?

2. Which ideas from this chapter do you find particularly appealing? Can they be adapted to other age levels? Give two or more examples.

3. Think of a major unit that you might develop in a specific content area. What materials might you enticingly display to suggest their use?

4. Although it may be easier to imagine how centers might work at the elementary levels, they can also be very appropriate at secondary levels and above. Can you think of specific ways they can be incorporated into classrooms for older students?

5. How might you respond to a teacher who laments, "But I can't create a classroom like that. We only have traditional desks. . . . We don't have special materials, and we don't have money to purchase them." Suggest several ways these problems might be overcome.

6. Plan your "dream" classroom environment for a specific situation. Draw up a basic plan (see Figures 16.1 and 16.2). Discuss your plans with a small group to receive their feedback. You may want to modify your plans after consulting with your group.

17

What Are We Really Testing?

BERNARD A. MOHAN   *University of British Columbia*

EDITORS' INTRODUCTION

When assessing students' knowledge in language classes or in any content area, be it social studies or home economics, the question that is the title of this chapter needs to be carefully considered. We may not, indeed, be testing what we think we are. Although a major portion of each test we give may be appropriate, it is possible that a significant number of test items are evaluating something entirely different from what we intended. The resulting problems can be especially detrimental to language minority students. They may find themselves the recipients of lower grades than deserved, or even more devastating, they may find themselves misplaced academically. In this chapter, Bernard A. Mohan discusses the problem of content validity in relation to a variety of factors. He looks at the extent to which language and content tests overlap and may be confused. He examines the ways in which language tests may be culturally biased or may in fact be tests of cultural knowledge in disguise. He distinguishes between semantic inference and factual inference and explains the implications of each for the process of evaluation.

Testing and evaluation are areas where it is important to distinguish between language knowledge and content knowledge. Everyone is familiar with the distinction between language tests and content tests. Language tests include tests of grammar and tests of reading comprehension, while content tests include achievement tests in areas like biology or economics. It should be apparent that each type of test should test only what it claims to. It should not include, intentionally or otherwise, areas outside its purview. Language tests should test language, and content tests should test content. But what seems apparent is not so easy to accomplish in practice: Language is intertwined with content.

There is obviously a language factor in content tests, because it is not possible to understand content questions without an understanding of the

From *"Where Language and Content Should not be Confused"* by B. Mohan, 1982, in B. Mohan, Language and Content *(pp. 122–135). Copyright © 1982 by Addison-Wesley. Adapted by permission.*

language they are written in. Suppose you had to take an economics test written in a language unfamiliar to you. It goes without saying that the test would be an invalid test of your knowledge of economics because of the language factor. When students take an achievement test in a language other than their native language, there is a possibility that the language factor will affect the validity of the test.

Is there a content factor in language tests? Do language tests assume non-linguistic knowledge that second language (L2) learners lack? One type of nonlinguistic knowledge is knowledge of the culture of the second language. To what extent are language tests hidden tests of cultural knowledge? To what extent are language tests culturally biased? We will examine the question of cultural bias in reading comprehension tests.

CULTURAL BIAS IN READING COMPREHENSION TESTS

Cultural differences can lead to differences in interpreting questions in a reading comprehension test. This is true for many second language learners when they lack knowledge of the host culture. In test situations such differences of interpretation become serious difficulties. Some test items in reading comprehension tests require both language knowledge and cultural knowledge. For instance, various standardized tests contain such items and thereby discriminate against English as a second language (ESL) students. Consider three such problems that reading comprehension tests can pose:

1. Is there cultural bias in reading comprehension tests, and if so, does it matter that there is bias? Would a bias tend to discriminate against certain students?
2. How can teachers and students, the consumers of the tests, identify bias if it exists?
3. Is cultural bias in reading comprehension tests inevitable in principle, or are there systematic ways in which it can be avoided or at least minimized?

To examine these three issues, question items from tests can be analyzed by means of a linguistic approach rather than the more usual statistical one.

Is There Cultural Bias in Reading Comprehension Tests?

Many people believe that no bias exists in these tests. Robert L. Ebel (1977), a specialist in educational measurement and a past president of the American Educational Research Association, writes:

Standardized tests of educational achievement have also been attacked for their alleged bias against cultural minorities. . . . How could evidence of bias in a test of educational achievement be produced? To get it one would need a set of biased tests and a set of unbiased tests of the same achievement. Then if a person or group made consistently lower or higher scores on the biased than on the unbiased tests we would have evidence of bias. But note the problem. If they are tests of the same achievement they must be composed of items meeting the same task specifications and hence drawn from the same item pool. Yet if one set is biased and the other is unbiased, there must be some systematic difference between them. To show bias we must show the tests to be the same and yet to be different. This is obviously a logical impossibility. For this reason demonstration of bias in a properly validated achievement test is impossible, and if bias cannot be demonstrated, there is no good reason to believe that it exists. (p. 39)

On the other hand, if bias *does* exist, perhaps Ebel has not tried hard enough to find methods of demonstrating it, and perhaps some of the standard approaches to the analysis of tests are inadequate for this task.

Let us examine items from widely used tests of reading comprehension: the Stanford Diagnostic Reading Test, the Canadian Test of Basic Skills (a revision of the Iowa Test of Basic Skills for Canadian use), the Gates McGinitie Reading Test, the Nelson-Denny Reading Test, and the Gapadol Reading Comprehension Test. These items have been chosen to show a range of cultural knowledge and have been altered for reasons of brevity. In each case the form of the test and the item number are given so that the original can be identified.

In these test items a student will have to rely on specific sociocultural knowledge to get the right answer. In turn, cultural knowledge covers various aspects of a specific human society, including its history, geography (e.g., animals, plants, climate), literature, art, social institutions (e.g., law, government), family life, housing, nutrition, customs, cultural attitudes, and values.

1. *Patriotic objects:* There are red and white stripes and white stars in our flag. Our flag contains one _____ for every state.
   a. stripe   b. star   (S.D.R.T. Form X. Level 1. #3)

2. *Food:* In the story the French regarded potatoes like most Canadians regard:
   a. spinach   b. tomatoes   c. horsemeat   d. margarine
   (Note: in the story, the French dislike potatoes.)   (C.T.B.S. Form 1. #89)

3. *Customs:* In this poem, what does April Fool! mean?
   a. The person who said it was fooling.
   b. It was not April at all.   (C.C.T.B.S. Form 1. #98)

4. *Games:* Sam won at marbles because he could _____ straighter than Bill.
   a. show   b. shoot   c. draw   d. run   (G. McG.D. Form 3M. #1)

5. *History:* In the first colonies in America, making clothing took time. The women first had to spin the yarn. Clothes for the colonial family were usually made in _____ .
   a. factories   b. homes   c. luxury   d. China (G. McG.D. Form 3M. #14)

6. *Geography:* The Yankee peddler traded as far west as the Mississippi and as far south as Louisiana. He operated _____ .
   a. over most of the country
   b. as far south as Louisiana (N.D. Form D. #10)

7. *Folklore:* Pam went to the party with a tall pointed hat, long black cape and a broom. She was dressed as a _____ .
   a. witch   b. ghost   c. cowgirl   d. pumpkin
   (G. McG.C. Form 1. #4)

8. *Housing:* Bill ran out on his front porch to watch the firetruck. He lives in _____ .
   a. a big apartment   b. a city house   c. a trailer
   (C.T.B.S. Form 4. Level 9. #1)

9. *Culture-bound metaphors:* What does applying soft soap mean in paragraph 6?
   a. looking clean in public
   b. flattering people (C.T.B.S. Form 1. #131)

10. *Stories familiar to particular cultural groups:* The person was holding tight to the handle of an open _____ , dangling by one hand like a doll tied to the string of a balloon. . . .
    (Cloze text example)
    (Note: the answer is "umbrella")

Test items 1 to 10 require a knowledge of (successively): the symbolism of the United States flag; Canadian food preferences; April first customs; how the game of marbles is played; early American history; American geography; the garb of the typical witch; the layout of different types of North American homes; an English idiom; and the story of Mary Poppins. It is clear that special cultural knowledge is required. Therefore, contrary to Ebel's claim, cultural bias does exist in reading comprehension texts.

Though cultural bias clearly exists, is the presence of bias an important matter? Certainly at least three of the tests from which items (1 to 10) are drawn are widely used: the Stanford Diagnostic Reading Test, the Gates-McGinitie, and the Canadian Test of Basic Skills. Moreover, the frequency and distribution of biased items in these widely used tests is important. The percentage of biased items in a test can be counted. My investigation (Mohan, 1979) of the Canadian Test of Basic Skills, Form 1 (grades 3 to 8) indicates that 7 percent of the items are biased. This is by no means negligible in its likely effect on the scores of culturally different students. Moreover, the biased items are unevenly distributed, so that in the fifth grade section of the test the percentage of biased items is 15 percent. Other tests show such clustering too. Thus the Gates-McGinitie Primary C Form 1 test contains 10 percent biased items, and in the Stanford Diagnostic Reading Test Form X Level 1, the percentage rises to 16 percent. These percentages are high enough to have a marked effect on scores. In addition, these figures are somewhat conservative and almost certainly underestimate the amount of bias. Items that are borderline cases have not been counted. And as a member of the host culture, I am likely to overlook some of the less obvious cases of bias.

The decisions that can be made about individual students on the basis of biased reading comprehension tests are not trivial. Reading comprehension scores are often used to assign students to reading groups of different levels of competence. Here a biased result is likely to lead to incorrect diagnosis of difficulties in reading and inappropriate teaching. More serious is the situation in some schools where reading comprehension scores are the means for placing students in streams of different general academic ability (i.e., a low score puts students in a slow class, possibly for the rest of their school career). When a reading comprehension score is used as an index of academic ability, a biased score and the decision following from it can have all the force of a self-fulfilling prophecy.

Even if it is accepted that bias exists in quantity and that it may affect important decisions, some might argue that bias is not a matter worthy of serious attention. One argument is that students should be tested on cultural knowledge, since they will not be able to function properly in North American society if they do not learn about North American culture. Although it is certainly appropriate to test for cultural knowledge, such testing should not be confounded with reading comprehension. Cultural knowledge should be tested separately, specifically, and systematically, as some modern language teachers do.

Some teachers do not believe that cultural knowledge should be tested separately. They assert that special cultural knowledge should be a necessary part of reading comprehension tests. This argument has been advanced by competent and thoughtful ESL teachers and is based on the claims that special cultural knowledge will inevitably occur in reading materials that students will have to deal with and that a reading test should faithfully reflect the reading tasks and materials facing the student.

While there are a number of objections to be made here (e.g., how much special cultural knowledge is actually required by a math textbook?), the crux of the problem is that this view concentrates on the students' performance but ignores the evaluation being made of that performance. Suppose two students give the wrong answer to a reading comprehension item. One student is native born, the other is a recent immigrant. The former may be weak in reading comprehension, the latter may be missing some cultural knowledge. The task they both face is the same, but the interpretation of what they do should be different. The immigrant is not necessarily weak in reading comprehension despite the incorrect answer choice. Where evaluation is incorrect, remediation will also be incorrect.

How Can the Consumers of Tests Identify Bias?

One procedure that can be used to identify biased items is to ask the following two questions:

Question A
Does the item test only language knowledge or does it test knowledge of the world too?

Question B
Does the item test:
(a) knowledge of the world that is available to all cultures, or
(b) knowledge of the world that is readily available only to particular cultural groups

It might seem that knowledge of the world concerning witches and Halloween is needed to answer the following item:

11. The playmates wore costumes to Sandra's Halloween party. Nellie _____ a tall, black, pointed hat.
    a. walked   b. wore   c. cared   d. hurt   e. looked
                                                (G. McG.D. Form 3M. #7)

Yet on closer inspection, it becomes clear that the item can be answered on the basis of language knowledge since *wore* (answer b) is the only one that fills the slot to make a semantically acceptable sentence. It is ungrammatical to say that she walked, cared, or looked a hat and it is nonsensical to say that she hurt one.

12. Sam and Bill played the whole day. In the evening they felt _____ .
    a. rested   b. small   c. tired   *(S.D.R.T. Form X. Level 1. #17)*

Item 12 tests knowledge of the world. This, not language knowledge, is the basis for seeing a connection between playing all day and feeling tired. However, since it is reasonable to assume that every cultural group would see such a connection, the item does not depend on a piece of special cultural information. It does not test knowledge of the world available only to particular cultural groups.

    Thus by asking our two key questions (Questions A and B) we can see that items 11 and 12 are not considered to be culturally biased, although at first they might have appeared to be. On the other hand, items 1 to 10 on pages 260–261 are considered culturally biased, for in each case special cultural information is required, and that information is readily available only to particular cultural groups.

    How can teachers identify bias and what actions can they take? They can investigate the items in the reading comprehension test currently used in their school and in any other available reading test that might be used in its place. The procedure for doing so has been outlined. Group discussion of the items, either with other teachers or with ESL students, works well. The lone reader often passes over difficulties that a group will detect and may also make cultural assumptions that ESL students would not. Furthermore, the procedure is justifiable as a learning activity, since it requires careful reading and interpretation. If the current reading comprehension test turns out to be more biased than an available alternative, then a case can be made for switching to the alternative test. Secondly, once biased items have been noted, teachers can check to see that the bias is taken into account in the interpretation of test scores and in the decisions about students based on the interpretation.

Is Cultural Bias in Reading Comprehension Tests Inevitable?

What has been demonstrated so far is that some test items confound language knowledge and cultural experience. In effect these items are not simply testing the ability to read the comprehension passage; they are testing for other information as well. As such, they are poor tests of reading comprehension. The maker of standardized tests has certain procedures of statistical item analysis that are intended to ensure that items meet standards of validity and reliability, yet these do not seem to have been successful in eliminating culturally biased items in the tests examined. One reason for this is that the initial scrutiny of items for suitability (or content validity) is very crude and allows the biased items in. This content validity check needs to be refined. The remedy offered here (see Questions A and B) is to relate the analysis of items to semantic theory in order to show that such analysis can be based on semantic principles. This is helpful for clarifying both cultural bias and the general validity of reading comprehension items.

COMPREHENSION AND SEMANTIC THEORY

An important part of competence in reading comprehension is the ability to draw inferences from written text. Research in reading must therefore investigate the nature of inference. Semantic theory is centrally concerned with the nature of inference (or implication or consequence) in language; it offers a principled basis for saying whether one sentence can be inferred from another. If the role of inference in reading comprehension test items is made clear, the connection between the analysis of these items and semantic theory can be shown.

The following item is a clear example of the inference/implication/consequence relation:

13. Three girls put frosting on the cakes that had cooled. We learned a new word for frosting. At the bakery it was called icing.
    Q: What were the three girls doing?
    A: (i) cooling the cakes
        (ii) putting icing on the cakes
        (iii) making frosting for the cakes   *(C.T.B.S. Form 1. #9)*

Is it possible to infer the right answer (ii) from the passage? The passage implies that answer ii is "true," for it asks the reader to decide whether *three girls put frosting on the cakes that had cooled* implies *the girls were putting icing on the cakes,* where *icing* can be substituted for *frosting.* One way to check the appropriateness of this implication is whether *therefore* or *consequently* can be inserted between these two sentences but not between the passage sentence and the other possible answers. And the passage gives no grounds for choosing the other answers.

The concept of inference has an important bearing on the analysis of cultural bias. It has already been noted that the cultural bias problem in reading comprehension tests arises because both language knowledge and cultural knowledge are required in these tests. Clearly it would be helpful to distinguish between language knowledge and cultural knowledge in a principled way. The question about icing and frosting (13) tests language knowledge, and the one about how witches dress (7) tests cultural knowledge. Both require the recognition of an inference. The inference in the former is based on language knowledge, and the inference in the latter is based on cultural knowledge.

SEMANTIC INFERENCE AND FACTUAL INFERENCE

Linguistic semantics distinguishes carefully between the relation of item 14a to item 14b and the relation of item 15a to item 15b:

14. a. He is a bachelor.
    b. He is an unmarried man.
15. a. He is Pierre Trudeau.
    b. He is a former Canadian Prime Minister.

Item 14 is a case of semantic inference. We know that (b) follows from (a) because of our knowledge of the English language. If we were challenged to prove it, we could draw on linguistic analysis and the grammar and dictionary of English. It is this kind of knowledge that is central in tests of language knowledge and skill. Item 15 is a case of factual inference. We know that (b) follows from (a) because of our knowledge of the world. To prove it we would go to yearbooks of Canadian facts and ultimately to the encyclopedia. This is the kind of knowledge that is central in achievement tests.

INFERENCE IN TESTING

Figure 17.1 shows different types of tests and different bases for inference. All of these tests require the student to read, but they differ in their aims.

Bases for Inference in Tests

Test Type	Aim of Test	Main Type of Inference	Additional Requirement	Bias Against Second Language Learner
A. Reading comprehension tests	knowledge of language	semantic inference	general knowledge of the world	cultural knowledge assumed
B. Achievement tests	knowledge of a subject area	factual inference	reading comprehension	high reading level assumed
C. Culture tests	knowledge of a culture	factual inference	reading comprehension	high reading level assumed

Figure 17.1. *Bases for Inference in Tests*

Reading comprehension tests aim to test knowledge of language through reading. They require semantic inference. They also assume general common-sense knowledge of the world. When they assume special cultural knowledge, they are biased against second language learners. *Achievement tests* aim to test knowledge of a subject area and require factual inference. They also assume reading comprehension. If they assume a high level of reading comprehension they are biased against second language learners. *Culture tests* aim at knowledge of the culture and require factual inference.

One type of content test is a test of cultural knowledge. H. N. Seelye (1974) describes "cultural assimilators," which are items designed to test specifically for cultural knowledge:

16. As a young American tourist in Tours, France, you have been invited to dinner at the home of a French business associate of your father. You know that under such circumstances it is considered polite to bring a bouquet of flowers to the hostess. Accordingly, you arrive at the door of the apartment with a handsome bouquet of white chrysanthemums. As your hostess greets you, you offer the bouquet to her. You notice a look of surprise and distaste cross her countenance before she masters herself and accepts your offering graciously.

    All evening you are haunted by the feeling that you have done something wrong. You would like to apologize—but you are at a loss to know what for.

    What could explain your hostess's reaction?
    i. A bouquet of chrysanthemums is considered an apology for a serious blunder in French culture.
    ii. A bouquet of chrysanthemums is considered a proposal of marriage in French culture.
    iii. Chrysanthemums are considered the flower of death in French culture.
    iv. The hostess was allergic to chrysanthemums. (p. 108)

The correct answer is (iii). Armed with this item of French cultural knowledge, we can draw the factual inference that a French hostess presented with such a bouquet would be unpleasantly surprised. Such direct tests of cultural knowledge can play a valuable role in L2 education.

Of course, content tests testing cultural knowledge are unusual. The most frequent type of test of content knowledge is in the achievement test (B in Figure 17.1), where specialized knowledge of a subject area is at issue as in tests of biology, chemistry, geography, economics, psychology, and so on. The following geography example is typical of the kind of item that appears in examinations for prospective graduate students.

17. The fact that Tacoma, Washington, has a growing season of 245 days, while Atlanta, Georgia, has a growing season of 224 days can best be explained by the
   i. latitude of Tacoma as compared with the latitude of Atlanta.
   ii. longitude of Tacoma as compared with the longitude of Atlanta.
   iii. marine climate of Tacoma.
   iv. humid subtropical climate of Atlanta.

To get the right answer (iii), a complicated sequence of factual reasoning is needed, taking into account both the geographical position of Atlanta and Tacoma and the influence of different climatic types on the growing season, as well as rejecting the distracting information about longitude and latitude. All of this calls for specialized geographic knowledge, which is quite legitimate, for the item is aimed at discriminating between those students who have an adequate knowledge of geography and an ability to reason geographically and those students who do not.

The difference between a reading comprehension item and an achievement test item as in this geography example, like the difference between knowledge of language and knowledge of the world, is so obvious that it hardly seems to merit discussion. Yet even here problems arise when language knowledge and content knowledge are intertwined, as they often are. The geography question assumes that the test-taker can manage a certain level of reading comprehension successfully, because the student has to read the item and understand that what is demanded is not an explanation of the growing season in Atlanta but an explanation of the longer growing season in Tacoma. Many achievement tests assume a threshold level of reading comprehension. A second language learner who is a capable mathematician may perform poorly on word problems in mathematics tests because of the language barrier. In cases like these it becomes clear how knowledge of language is a necessary condition for demonstrating content knowledge.

Reading comprehension tests can be biased if the content factor looms too large: that is, if they demand special cultural knowledge or if they require special subject knowledge. This is where analysis is needed of the intertwining of language and content. In tests of language knowledge and use, items often assume knowledge of content information. If an individual lacks this content knowledge, the item becomes a test of content knowledge, not of language knowledge. If standard procedures of test analysis cannot detect this, then linguistic analysis is needed.

A comparable problem can arise with achievement tests if they demand too high a level of reading comprehension of the student. Just as there is a problem with language tests when the content factor is too high, so there is a problem with content tests when the language factor is too high.

SUMMARY AND CONCLUSION

Items such as 1 to 10 are not appropriate reading comprehension questions for ESL students because they require special cultural knowledge that is available only to particular cultural groups. Such special knowledge should not be incorporated into reading tests. Reading tests should essentially test the ability to use knowledge of the language and reading skills to get meaning from the printed page. It is the task of achievement tests (of biology, social studies, and so on) to test for nonlinguistic knowledge. It is legitimate to draw on nonlinguistic knowledge in a reading comprehension test only where it plays a neutral, supporting role and is common to all students properly assigned to take the test. It should be standard policy to eliminate specific cultural items from tests when those students taking the test include culturally different groups. In fact, eliminating material irrelevant to the aims of the test would be likely to improve the test for all groups. If the item tests knowledge of the world available only to particular cultural groups, it should be discarded.

Greater awareness is needed of the content factor in language tests and of the language factor in content tests. If either of these is too high, it will cause problems. Problems are particularly likely to occur when tests developed for students of one language and culture are taken by students of a different language and a different culture.

The intertwining of language and content can be a positive advantage in many aspects of education. But in testing and evaluation it is a source of disadvantage for the second language learner. To reduce this disadvantage, we need to distinguish between semantic inference and factual inference. Here the teacher has an important role to play as an advocate for the students' best interests.

RECOMMENDED READINGS

Anastasi, A. (1976). *Psychological testing* (3rd ed.). New York: Collier-Macmillan. Contains a discussion of the use of culture-fair tests.

Condon, J., & Yousef, F. (1975). *An introduction to intercultural communication.* Indianapolis, IN: Bobbs-Merrill. Reviews a variety of issues in intercultural communication.

Flaughter, R. (1978). The many definitions of test bias. *American Psychologist 33* (7), 671–679. A discussion of the ways in which tests might be biased.

Gunnarson, B. (1978). A look at content similarities between intelligence, achievement, personality and language tests. In J. Oller and K. Perkins (Eds.), *Language education: Testing the tests.* Rowley, MA: Newbury House. Looks at the similarities in various different types of standardized educational tests by taking a close look at test items and seeing what they require the examinees to do.

Mohan, B.A. (1979). Cultural bias in reading comprehension tests. *On TESOL, 79,* 171–177. This publication, *On TESOL '79,* also contains a number of other articles on bias in testing.

Oller, J. (1979). *Language tests at school.* London: Longman. An overview of language testing which looks at the overlap between the constructs of language proficiency, intelligence, and academic ability.

Pearn, M. (1978). *Employment testing and the goal of equal opportunity: the American experience.* London: The Runnymede Trust. Reviews American work on the question of test bias and discrimination in employment selection and relates it to the British context. An aspect of the Runnymede Trust's work on the collection and dissemination of information and the promotion of public education on immigration and race relations.

Seelye, H. (1974). *Teaching culture: Strategies for foreign language educators.* Skokie, IL: National Textbook Company. A practical guide, with useful activities for classroom discussion, which offers specific insights into how cultures may differ.

FOLLOW-UP QUESTIONS AND ACTIVITIES

1. What recommendations might you give a school district that bases important decisions concerning student placement on the scores of a single standardized test? What about recommendations to the teacher who determines final grades by relying mainly on a teacher-made final exam? In each case, are there other important factors you would mention that were not dealt with in this chapter?

2. Find a test of achievement (either standardized or teacher-made) that has been used in a specific content area. After examining the items carefully, discuss how the following may or may not play a role in judging its content validity.

   a. Linguistic knowledge (Does it contain items that test a mastery of the language instead of content?)

   b. Cultural knowledge (To what extent does it depend on specific knowledge of the culture?)

3. Write a ten-item, multiple-choice test on some aspect of a specific content area. Try to keep a dependence on linguistic and culture knowledge as minimal as possible within each item. Share your test with at least one other person in your class. Ask that person to comment on your test's content validity.

4. Are there classroom activities other than testing in which cultural bias might play a role in outcomes? Discuss with members of your class.

18

Peer Teachers:
The Neglected Resource

PATRICIA A. RICHARD-AMATO
University of Nevada, Reno

> *And gladly would I learn and gladly teache.*
>
> Chaucer

EDITORS' INTRODUCTION

Establishing a classroom in which peer teacher assistants are used to help the teacher facilitate the learning process for others is yet another means for letting go of traditional authority and getting teachers off center stage. Potential peer teachers, although in plentiful supply in most schools, remain a largely neglected resource. Although to some the training and use of peer teachers might appear a radical idea, to others it is a very natural way to provide meaningful learning experiences for language minority students in supportive classroom environments. For those teachers interested in pursuing the use of peer teachers, this chapter outlines guidelines for training peer teachers and suggests a variety of peer teaching configurations.

In response to a discussion about people abandoning their pets in the country, a high school student in one of my classes designed for problem writers produced the following:

> I Feel Sorry for the Animels Bo there is nothing I can do. I thing if more people found out what thay Are doing to the Animels when thay let them go out in the country if More people Knew About Dumb frends leag [the Dumb Friends' League] I doent think that kind of thing would hapen as much But there still is some people who get there Jolleys out of leaving An Animel or Killing them.

> *Paul*
> *January, 1974*

Although this student is a native-English speaker, his errors, both random and systematic, would probably earn him the label "limited English proficient" (LEP) in today's content-area classrooms. After working with a trained peer teacher in the classroom for approximately three hours a week for ten weeks, this same student independently wrote the following:

> If I could vacation any where I wanted, I think Maryland would be the place or some place like that.
>
> I see pictures of medows and nice green fields with trees and strens in books, but never in real life. It seems real peaceful and quiet and I think I would like to be there. If I get there and I find all of that stuff was just in books, I would go to South Dakota.

> *Paul*
> *March, 1974*

Even though this student still has a way to go in improving his writing, it is easy to see that his sentence structure is now more sophisticated and that the number of errors is greatly reduced. Other compositions subsequent to this one also indicated rather remarkable improvement.

Paul was not the only one to progress so quickly; many others showed similar improvements in writing after working with peer teachers for extended periods. The peer teachers, in addition to helping students overcome basic writing problems, assisted in brainstorming topics of interest, provided guidance when necessary in the gathering of information, helped to shape an overall plan, and enabled the students with whom they worked to discover personal strengths and weaknesses with language. Thus peer teachers helped students *stretch* to more complicated syntax, concepts, and ways of thinking. Similarly, peer teachers can aid in many skill areas across the curriculum—for example, solving elementary as well as fairly complex problems in math, setting up experiments for basic scientific inquiry, understanding intricate human problems posed in social studies, and so forth.

It is perhaps in working with language minority students, however, that the full advantages of peer teachers as a resource can be realized. Not only can they assist students and challenge them cognitively in specific content areas, but they can make it possible for these learners to frequently negotiate for meaning in the target language; to receive enough comprehensible input to make acquisition likely; to build up confidence in themselves and their abilities to communicate, both orally and in writing; to receive encouragement, motivation, and challenge; and to be exposed to native or native-like speech and writing on a regular basis in order that second language development not be arrested.

Perhaps one reason that peer teachers hold so much promise as a resource for language and content-area teachers alike is that peer teachers can help to create what Vygotsky (1978) refers to as the zone of proximal development. The zone refers to the "distance between the actual developmental level as determined by independent problem solving and the level of potential development as determined through problem solving under adult guidance or in collaboration with more capable peers'' (p. 86). The failure of many teachers to recognize advanced peers as an important source of knowledge and skills to be shared with others greatly reduces possibilities for learning development in the content areas. If what Vygotsky proposes has validity—that learning development is indeed a social phenomenon—then it makes sense to provide situations in which it is most likely to occur. Unfortunately, students who are limited in any way, be it due to lack of prior experience and knowledge or low levels of proficiency in English, often find themselves thrown into highly mechanized programs in which they are exercised and drilled in an attempt to remediate when what they really need are more opportunities to interact with the teacher or with more advanced learners in specific areas of study.

THE ROLE OF THE TEACHER

The use of peer teachers in no way lessens the role of the teacher. On the contrary, the role of the teacher is still prime but different. The teacher no longer needs to carry the burden of always having to be the expert and supreme source of knowledge. Instead, the teacher functions as a *facilitator and guide,* one who challenges and supports others and brings out the best in everyone. But, of course, the teacher is still the one who is ultimately responsible for what happens or fails to happen in the classroom. The teacher's success depends on the extent to which he or she has been able to execute an effective program and build an atmosphere of mutual respect and shared responsibility.

THE ROLE OF THE PEER TEACHER

The role of the peer teacher falls somewhere on a continuum between a *full teacher role* and a *minimal teacher role.* The differences between programs lie mainly in how the *role* of the peer teacher is perceived. Toward the full teacher end of the continuum are the programs in which the peer teacher is a more integral part of the classroom environment itself rather than an adjunct. It is likely that the teaching will take place during class hours and that, after extensive training, the individual will take on a role more akin to that of the teacher. In programs falling at this end, the peer teacher is more apt to be involved in classroom organization, lesson planning, facilitating, and even in evaluation and materials preparation, albeit under the guidance of the teacher.

Toward the minimal teacher end of the continuum, the peer teacher fills a somewhat more limited role, perhaps as an adjunct to the classroom, helping students after school, or volunteering during other free time. This person is usually seen as an assistant carrying out the teacher's plans rather than being an essential part of the planning and implementation process. Of the two, the minimal teacher role (often known as the peer tutor role) appears to be far more common and, particularly during the first half of the 1970s, was the focus of a flurry of research activity.[1]

RELATED RESEARCH

Although it is not the purpose of this chapter to describe in depth all the research supporting the use of peer teaching, a few of the more significant findings are included here with their references. Those readers desiring a complete, detailed account of the studies should go directly to the sources. In making a decision about which studies to mention, I wanted to include only those that were, in my opinion, systematic and well designed. If the research was experimental in nature (and most of it is to date), than it had to have been done under controlled conditions to ensure that a reasonable attempt was made to control as many variables as possible (e.g., differing abilities of participants or the initial level of proficiency in the relevant content area).

These studies revealed that benefits were found both for the students being assisted and for the peers doing the assisting. The results are as follows:

Benefits for the Students Being Assisted

1. Reading was significantly improved by peer assistance (Cloward, 1967; Erickson & Cromack, 1972; Harris, 1971; Klosterman, 1970; Poole, 1971).
2. Teacher-assigned grades improved in math for students receiving peer assistance (Horan, DeGirolomo, Hill & Shute, 1974; Mevarech, 1985).
3. Self-concept scores were improved as a result of peer assistance (Poole, 1971; Scruggs & Osguthorpe, 1986).
4. Significantly greater learning occurred in students who were assisted than those receiving whole-class classroom instruction for an equal time period (Bausell, Moody & Walzl, 1972; Klosterman, 1970; Russell & Ford, 1983).
5. Increased verbal skills resulted from peer assistance (Shaver & Nuhn, 1971).
6. English as a second language (ESL) students increased their vocabulary comprehension as a result of peer assistance (Johnson, 1983).

Benefits for the Peers Doing the Assisting

1. Peer assistants experienced an improvement in reading skills (Poole, 1971).
2. Performance in math improved as a result of being a peer assistant (Poole, 1971; Rust, 1970).

---

[1] It should be noted that the term *peer tutor* is often used interchangeably with *peer teacher* in the literature. One needs to look carefully at individual programs to determine where on the continuum each falls.

3. Peer assistants showed increases in self-concept after working with students (Robertson, 1971).

Although this summary is by no means exhaustive, it is noteworthy that some of the benefits to the peers who were receiving assistance were also experienced by the students who were giving assistance.

Additional research that may be of special interest are the studies that examined specific aspects of peer assistant/student combinations (Bierman & Furman, 1981; Cicirelli, 1972; Foster, 1972; Sapiens, 1982 [in Gaies, 1985]; Szynal-Brown & Morgan, 1983; Topping & Whiteley, 1988). These studies looked at such factors as the gender, age, socioeconomic status, behavioral style, and ethnicity of the participants. A few studies explored the optimal number of students per peer assistant (Klosterman, 1970; Shaver & Nuhn, 1968), the frequency and length of the sessions during which peer assistance occurred (Cloward, 1967), and the amount of training peer assistants received *a priori* (Niedermeyer, 1970).

However, not enough research has been done in these areas at various levels and in differing situations to warrant generalization. In addition, the complexities of peer assistant/student relationships present many variables that are extremely difficult (if not impossible) to control, considering the constraints of experimental design when applied to human behavior. Thus, we may find the movement toward descriptive studies a welcome addition to the research agenda, bringing with it another dimension to our knowledge of peer teaching. By making greater use of interviews, questionnaires, and other qualitative devices, we may greatly increase our chances to discover more and more about the attitudes, motivation, relationships, and other factors associated with peer assistant situations (see especially Goodlad and Hirst, 1989, Chapter 5). Perhaps, too, we can find out more about interactional functions and patterns and their effects on learning through greater use of naturalistic observation.

PROGRAM ALTERNATIVES

If one is convinced that peer teaching or a version of it is a viable classroom management strategy and worthy of incorporation into a particular course of study, there are many program alternatives from which to choose that deal with such factors as duration, timing, credit, and grouping configurations. Consider the following menu of choices:

1. *Short term versus long term.* The content-area teacher may want to have the same peer teachers assigned to the same students for the short term (perhaps a week or maybe even only one class period) or for the long term (let's say a quarter or a full semester). The decision will depend on what is being taught, the learner, and the situation. For example,

if one is working on a skill such as writing, long-term groupings generally work better. If one is following up on a single teacher presentation with a further simplification of concepts for those who need it or with one-to-one assistance on a single task, short-term grouping may be all that is necessary.

2. *During class time versus after or before school.* Having the peer teaching occur during class time appears, based on my own experience, to have the following advantages: the teacher can more directly serve as a guide if needed, can be more certain that necessary resources and materials are available, and can make sure that the students needing help are indeed receiving it. More important, peer teachers will have had the benefit of being present for the introduction of topics of study, the concepts involved, and explanations of course assignments. However, there are situations in which after or before school programs are highly effective. If such programs are well organized and if the teacher, peer teachers, and students needing the help are committed to devoting the extra time necessary, these programs, too, can accomplish their goals, whatever they might be.

3. *Credit versus volunteer.* If possible, the peer teacher should receive credit toward graduation or the completion of a program for working with students. It has been my experience that peer teachers rewarded in this way take the job more seriously and are usually more dependable than those receiving no such credit. However, this is not always the case. Volunteers given no extrinsic rewards can also be very conscientious, depending on the extent of their commitment.

4. *Pairs versus larger groups.* If enough peer teachers are available and if the numbers of students needing assistance are fairly small, pairs might be feasible. Otherwise, the peer teacher may need to work with anywhere from two to four students (I personally do not recommend more than four). However, even with larger groups, the work can still be individual (one-on-one) when needed. If carefully orchestrated (i.e., all students requiring help are challenged and involved with various tasks simultaneously with minimal wait time), the peer teaching with larger groups can be highly productive.

5. *Same age versus cross age.* In same-age programs, both the student(s) and the peer teacher are of approximately the same age; in cross-age programs they are not. Usually in cross-age programs, the peer teacher is the older of the two. This age difference may have advantages in that younger students often try to emulate those older than themselves, and their sense of self-esteem is frequently heightened by the increased attention they receive. The older ones often view themselves as responsible caretakers of younger persons placed in their charge.

6. *Same sex versus opposite sex.* The student(s) receiving assistance and the peer teacher may both be of the same sex or of the opposite sex.

The selection made here may make a difference especially for refugees and immigrants who often work better in same-sex groupings.

7. *Native speaker versus nonnative speaker.* Often it is advantageous for non-native speakers to have a native-speaking or near-native-speaking peer teacher in order to provide them with an optimal linguistic model. If this is not possible, a nonnative-speaking peer teacher can still provide the necessary interaction and can be an excellent source of knowledge in a given content area. In any content-area course, it is also very possible and in many cases more common to have native speakers working with each other in the peer teacher/student relationship.

8. *Intraschool versus interschool.* Peer teaching programs can be contained within a given school from which both the peer teacher and the student come (intraschool), or they can involve two or more schools (interschool). Interschool programs offer advantages in cross-age programs or in programs that require the peer teacher to be a native speaker or a near-native speaker. In these cases it may be necessary to recruit peer teachers from other schools if older peer teachers or native-speaker/near-native speaker peer teachers are not readily available.

9. *Intraclass versus interclass.* Peer teaching programs can be contained within a given class from which both the peer teacher and the student come (intraclass), or they can involve two or more classes (interclass). The latter may be advantageous especially if the students needing assistance are nonnative speakers and native speakers or near-native speakers are not available within the class environment itself. Peer teachers may also be recruited from other classes if older peer teachers are desired.

The choices made will depend entirely on each situation, the content area involved, the characteristics of the students needing peer assistance, teacher and learner preferences, and the extent to which principals, other teachers, and the community are committed to the program's success, to name a few of the many factors.

USING PEER TEACHERS IN THE CONTENT AREAS

If we are convinced that peer teacher use may indeed bring about positive results, then it is quite possible that classrooms across the content areas could become better environments for learning. Moreover, it is probable that by this means all students, native and nonnative alike, could receive the necessary assistance, encouragement, attention, appropriate instruction, and time needed to improve performance in a variety of skills, from composition to computer use.

The teacher might then have more time to spend on structuring and facilitating whole-class activities, diagnosing the needs of the students, training peer teachers, exploring new methods and strategies, working with students who may have special needs, giving additional guidance to those peer teachers needing it, and coordinating more closely with faculty and staff to provide a supportive total school environment.

Ideas about how peer teaching can be used in the content areas follow. Before their implementation, selections need to be made from the menu of alternatives in the foregoing section. The choices should be based on their appropriateness for the situation in which each will be used.

Short-Term Suggestions

During short-term peer teaching experiences, whole-class presentations introducing specific topics can be given in any content area—for example, the planets, their characteristics, and their physical relationship to one another in science; the experiences of earlier immigrants to the United States in social studies; solving problems with fractions in math; painting with water color in art; and so forth. Such presentations need to be appropriate to the age levels at which they will be taught, and the tasks involved need to be congruous with the cognitive levels of the students who are expected to perform them. In addition, they need to be within reach of language minority students who may be enrolled in the class (see the strategies recommended in Chapter 10). Follow-ups utilizing peer teachers may include individual activities for some and small-group activities for others. Some students will be able to explore additional areas of study related to the topic or apply the concepts and related skills to other situations, either independently or with guidance; others may need peer teacher assistance to more fully understand the concepts and expectations associated with the presentation itself. Those students in the latter category may work in a one-to-one situation with a peer teacher or in a small group led by a peer teacher. In either case, additional explanations, visuals, charts, and other aids may be useful.

Long-Term Suggestions

During long-term peer teaching experiences, students work with the same peer teachers for several weeks or even several months. Such long-term experiences are particularly advantageous when students are attempting to improve in specific skill areas (e.g., writing, reading, and computing). The peer teachers can thus become involved in the goals and plans of each student and can become more aware of the student's strengths and weaknesses in each skill area. Moreover, because the duration of the teaching is long term, they have a better opportunity to bond with the students to whom they have been assigned in a relationship from which all can benefit. Staying with the student long enough to see growth over time and being able to facilitate that growth are important factors. Long-term activities assisted by peer teachers can include a variety of projects for groups and individuals that can be interspersed with whole-class participation. The projects may integrate several skill areas depending on what each student needs at any given moment. One student may need help with map reading in social studies, another may need to practice word problems in math, yet another may need to produce an essay in language arts. Whatever the project, the peer teacher is needed to guide the student through the process to its successful completion.

THE SELECTION AND TRAINING OF PEER TEACHERS[2]

Although modifications can be made for lesser roles played by the peer teacher, let us assume for the purpose of discussion, that the peer teacher role will fall toward the full teacher end of the continuum—that the peer teachers will be integral parts of the classroom environments with which they are involved and that they will help to plan, facilitate, and evaluate under the guidance of the teacher. They first need to feel that the role they are being asked to fill is important and worthy of respect. A lot of positive feedback along the way from the teacher will encourage them to perform at their very best. Because much will be expected of them, the peer teachers should meet certain qualifications: They must have attained levels in the specific skill areas above those at which they will be teaching, enjoy aiding others, have a lot of patience, be supportive, be dependable, and be willing to work hard. (It may be helpful to ask other teachers for recommendations.)

Concerning the training of peer teachers, remember that if the peer teachers are very young, they will probably not benefit much from formal training sessions except at the simplest level and will probably require considerable supervision from the teacher throughout the peer teaching process. However, for peer teachers coming from the upper grades (fifth or sixth) or from secondary and adult levels, formal training workshops may be highly advantageous in the following areas:

1. Development of cultural sensitivity (see Part II, Cultural Considerations).
2. Knowledge of the instructional procedures the teacher chooses to use (see Chapter 10).
3. Familiarity with the methods, activities, techniques, and materials with which they will be working (role-play might help here—they can gain practice by trying out particular strategies on each other in hypothetical situations).

---

[2] This section is adapted from Richard-Amato (1988), pp. 190–192.

4. Pertinent background information on the students with whom they will be working—cultural information, individual needs, common problems, and so on.
5. Strategies for creating friendly, supportive relationships.

Following is a collection of strategies for helping others that could be discussed at a training workshop:

Strategies for Helping Others

1. Become familiar with the correct pronunciation of the student's name and use the name frequently.
2. Have an easy smile.
3. Be friendly. Get to know the student.
4. Be a good listener. Encourage the student to talk. Ask questions to find out more about what the student is saying.
5. Show recognition of and enthusiasm for the student's accomplishments no matter how small. Praise genuinely. Make it as specific as possible. Try to build intrinsic motivation by getting the student to reflect on what he or she has done. Questions such as ''How does it make you feel to have _____ ?'' or "You must be very proud of _____ " encourage the student to be self-motivating.
6. Be accepting of the person's right to his or her own opinions and beliefs. Avoid put-downs.
7. When asking questions, give the student enough time to respond. Be patient.
8. Give the student sufficient time to work at his or her own pace without feeling hurried.
9. Instead of responding with a flat ''No, that's wrong,'' say something more encouraging such as ''You're giving it a good try. But maybe we should look at it in a little different way. . . .''
10. If the student does not understand a concept after several attempts, go to something that you know the student can do with success. Later when you return to the more difficult task, it may come more easily. At this time, you might want to try some different approaches or contexts.
11. Check for understanding before going on to something else.
12. Frequent, quick reviews are highly effective.
13. If the student is obviously troubled or upset, give him or her a chance to talk to you about it. The task at hand can wait.
14. Use language that the student can understand. Repeat frequently. Use pictures and/or act out concepts whenever necessary.
15. Keep your directions clear, short, and simple.

16. Be honest with the student. If you don't know the answer to a question you have been asked, be willing to admit it. Often you and the student can pursue together information about an area of mutual interest.
17. Remember that the teacher is there to help you when you need it. Do not hesitate to ask for assistance when there is something you can't handle.

In addition to training workshops, the peer teachers need opportunities to meet with one another to share ideas and concerns. Moreover, they need to meet with the teacher regularly to make flexible lesson plans and to talk about possible problems and the ways they might be approached. Figure 18.1 shows an evaluation checklist to ensure frequent communication between the teacher and peer teacher concerning the progress of the students.

Evaluation Checklist

Name of peer teacher _Elena_   Date _3-12_

Name of the student being assisted _Stefan_

1. What did the student accomplish this week?
   He learned to more clearly distinguish the life cycles of the mammals described in the reading assignment.
2. Were there any problems?
   Yes. He had trouble understanding the text in general. I helped him map out the ideas graphically as you suggested last week.
3. What activities will you work on next week?
   He seems ready to do another draft of his report on mammals. I want to discuss with him the changes he would like to make. Then I'll give him time to work on it. After reading the new draft, I'll see what I can help him with. We'll then move on to reptiles. This time I want to see if he can map out the ideas on his own.
4. Can the teacher help you in any way?
   Reptiles interest him a lot (we've already talked about them a little). Do you have other reading materials on reptiles? It might help to start with something easier

Comments:
   He seems to have a little more confidence in his own interpretation of the text. He is not so hesitant to tell me what he thinks.

Figure 18.1. *An Evaluation Checklist*

ROOM ARRANGEMENTS

As far as room arrangements are concerned, there are two plans that have worked well for me to incorporate peer teaching (see Figures 18.2 and 18.3). In Figure 18.2, a *private work station* has been set up for each peer teacher where the students to whom he or she has been assigned go for assistance. While working on their own, these students remain at the tables in the center of the room. This particular configuration works well when the tasks are mainly one-to-one, requiring a certain degree of privacy. Figure 18.3, on the other hand, illustrates the *flexible cluster work station* where the students assigned to a particular peer teacher sit together, with the peer teacher at the apex. This

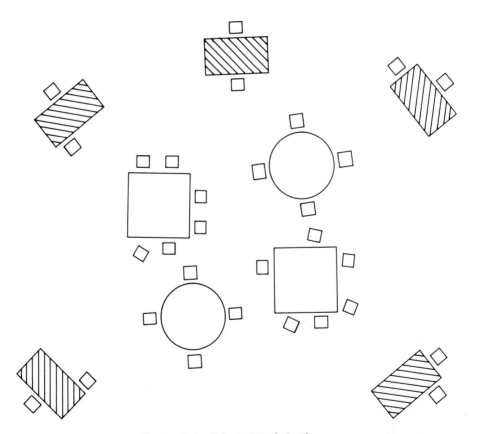

Figure 18.2. *Private Work Stations*
Comfortable chairs are found at each table. The tables with diagonal lines running through them are work stations for the peer teachers. The teacher, too, might have a work station. Note that for whole-class activities, the students can all be at the tables in the middle.

Figure 18.3. *Flexible Cluster Work Stations*
Movable desks cluster around the tables which serve as work stations for peer
teachers. A similar station may be set up for the teacher. Note that for whole-class
activities, the tables can be moved to the periphery of the room, and the movable desks
can be moved to the center to form a circle or any other configuration needed.

arrangement is ideal when group instruction or a group project is undertaken.
However, the cluster is flexible enough so that by rearranging the desks, the
peer teacher can still work somewhat privately with one or more members
of the group.

In addition to the work stations mentioned, other areas can be clearly
defined for special purposes. For example, an elementary classroom might
include one corner for story reading, another for free play, yet another for working on spontaneous art projects related to some unit of study. In a secondary
classroom, there might be a book corner for comfortable, private reading, a
writing station with a typewriter for student use, a hands-on display area, and
so on. See Chapter 16 for additional ideas.

CONCLUSION

Effective use of peer teachers is one way to create a highly participatory,
dynamic classroom environment in which students are challenged to achieve
goals and realize their full potential. By taking advantage of peer teachers as

a resource, content-area teachers can increase their chances to meet the needs of their students while at the same time enhancing their own abilities to make education a satisfying experience for all involved.

FOLLOW-UP QUESTIONS AND ACTIVITIES

1. Can you think of benefits of using peer teachers other than the ones mentioned in this chapter? Discuss with your class.

2. In the past there has sometimes been a growing sense of professionalism among teachers that was patronizing toward the idea of mere children taking on teaching roles. Describe this sense of professionalism and how it may have come about. Is there any justification for it in your view?

3. In what ways might young children (K to 3) serve as peer teachers? How do you think their peer teacher roles would differ from those of older children? Of teenagers? Of adults? Explain the differences age in general might have on peer teacher training, concepts and skills taught, and program implementation.

4. Plan a program using peer teachers for a specific class you would be likely to teach. In your description include the ways in which you might use the peer teachers (see possible selections from the menu on pages 275 to 277), the kinds of units of work in which you might use them, and the room arrangement(s) that might be most appropriate. Develop strategies for peer teacher training and program implementation. Share your ideas with a small group for their feedback.

PART IV

Readings in Specific Content Areas

Being exposed to direct applications of strategies in specific content areas gives teachers in training a multitude of ideas for future implementation. Witnessing the ways in which vital issues are dealt with by experienced teachers provides new insights and perspectives into their own classroom situations. Included here are suggestions for teachers in specific subjects across the curriculum, at a variety of levels. Some descriptions stress language and/or cognitive factors. Others stress cultural considerations. Many even suggest means for making cultural awareness part of the content itself. Although several chapters are oriented to specific age levels, many of their ideas can, with some modification, be used at other levels.

Unlike the first three parts of this book in which the chapters are intended for any interested teacher regardless of subject-area background, the chapters here are intended mainly for teachers in the field to which each pertains. The section is also intended for elementary teachers who typically teach in several content areas. Whether the reader is a teacher in a training program or simply reading for professional development or personal growth, it is hoped that the relevant chapters will form starting points for further reading in specific content areas and that references (where they are available) will lead to other sources. It is suggested that teachers in training be grouped according to their specific teaching situations so that applications can be explored and ideas shared.

Melissa King, Barbara Fagan, Terry Bratt, and Rod Baer (Chapter 19) offer a variety of instructional means by which the concepts of social studies may be more easily grasped by language minority students. Ways to introduce literature and make it meaningful are discussed by Linda Sasser in Chapter 20. James Rupp presents ideas for creating exciting science classroom environments for language and content

learning in Chapter 21, and Theresa Dale and Gilberto Cuevas
provide techniques for language-sensitive math instruction in
Chapter 22. Multicultural aspects become an integral part of the
content in art (Chapter 23 by Jo Schuman), in physical education
(Chapter 24 by Marianne Torbert and Lynne Schneider), and in
music (Chapter 25 by Jack Dobbs). And last, Joan Friedenberg
outlines practical ideas for developing programs in business education in Chapter 26.

19

Social Studies Instruction

MELISSA KING, BARBARA FAGAN TERRY BRATT, AND ROD BAER
Arlington County, Virginia, Public Schools

EDITORS' INTRODUCTION

Because immigrant and refugee students often find themselves caught up in a political process, they are usually strongly motivated to find out more about social studies and its related issues. Have others before them had similar problems on first coming to this country? What expectations did the new culture have of them? Were they able to meet the challenges? These and other important questions help to give life to what otherwise might be considered a dull but necessary subject. In addition to suggestions for making social studies more meaningful, this chapter explains how the concepts involved can be brought within the grasp of second language (L2) students in both sheltered and mainstream classes through a variety of instructional strategies such as semantic webbing and Directed Reading Thinking Activities (DRTA). Although oriented to secondary teachers, many of the chapter's recommendations can be adapted to elementary social studies instruction.

New information presented in social studies lessons is often a catalyst for further academic and language learning. The motivation for language learning arises naturally as students become involved in understanding concepts of history, geography, culture, and so on. At the same time, social studies knowledge strengthens and enriches an increased awareness of self, the community, and the environment. A lesson on westward movement in the United States in the 1880s, for example, may activate students' interest in migration patterns throughout U.S. history. This knowledge may also lead them to discover more about recent immigrants and where they have settled, and eventually to explore how they themselves fit into these patterns of movement as newcomers to the United States.

From King/Fagan/Bratt/Baer, ''ESL & Social Studies Instruction,'' in ESL Through Content-Area Instruction: Mathematics, Science, Social Studies, JoAnn Crandall, ed., © 1987, pp. 94–99, 105–114, 116–120. Adapted by permission of Prentice Hall, Inc., Englewood Cliffs, NJ.

THE ROLE OF BACKGROUND KNOWLEDGE

Social studies plays an important role in the acculturation process of limited English proficient (LEP) students. When they first come to the United States, they are expected to participate in classroom settings and to operate within a society that they do not fully understand. Because they may not be aware of American rules and behavioral expectations, language minority students are at a disadvantage. LEP students bring with them their cultural framework for social interaction, as well as subconscious assumptions about acceptable behavior and belief systems. Culture is the context within which people think, exist, feel, and relate to others (Brown, 1980), representing a blueprint for personal and social existence. People unconsciously learn what to notice, what not to notice, how to divide time and space, how to relate to other people, how to handle responsibility, and, to some extent, whether experience is seen as whole or fragmented. Because their values may be dramatically different from North American values, foreign students may encounter confusion and conflict trying to adjust to life in the United States. A social studies class can give LEP students an introduction to the American experience, helping them to understand American values and relationships with the outside world.

LEP students, naturally, are as unaware of their assumptions as anyone; each culture has its own reality (Hall, 1976). These students can never participate fully in American society unless they understand the American reality.

A social studies class should be concerned with more than historical facts, geography, and terminology. It can promote the development of critical concepts of American history, thereby helping culturally different students to understand their new country and its origins. In a social studies class, students can learn about the spirit of independence and the sense of individualism that characterizes American behavior. They can study U.S. laws and institutions that are, in fact, a reflection of American people. They can identify with the colonists' struggles for freedom and appreciate the significance of the Bill of Rights as a protection of this freedom. Students can discover how the U.S. government functions and what is expected of responsible citizens. Indeed, the social studies class can be a support system for LEP students who are trying to adjust to a new culture. In expanding their knowledge, the students envision a more realistic picture of the new culture and how they might operate within it. A more positive attitude and concept of self in turn enhances language proficiency (Oller, Baca & Vigil, 1978).

CURRICULUM DEVELOPMENT
AND PROGRAM DESIGN

If students are to be prepared to cope with the academic mainstream, they must acquire not only the language skills but also the critical thinking and study skills required in content-area classes. The locally designed curricula of most school districts correlate with adopted texts. Generally, schools set grade-level objectives by subject area that students must master as they progress through the system. School districts with large LEP populations have experienced difficulties in efforts to tailor content-area instruction to meet the needs of second language students. The following problems have become evident:

LEP students may not have had social studies instruction in their native countries.

Social studies concepts may not have been adequately developed in classes LEP students have attended previously.

The content of American social studies instruction may differ greatly from that of other countries (there may be gaps in students' knowledge).

LEP students may lack the English-language skills needed to participate on grade level in social studies classes.

Social studies materials are often too difficult for LEP students (texts assume a specific reading level for each grade).

LEP students are unfamiliar with social studies vocabulary and have trouble keeping pace with native English-speaking students who have a broad vocabulary base in social studies.

The cumulative nature of social studies often creates situations in which LEP students fail to grasp concepts or ideas because they have missed previous instruction.

Curriculum Development

Curriculum development is a major concern of proponents of social studies instruction. Administrators and teachers need to find ways to create meaningful learning situations that build on previously acquired knowledge and are realistic for the culturally different and LEP student. Through meaningful learning, new material becomes an integral part of existing cognitive structures (Ausebel, 1963). F. Smith (1975) contends that a learning situation can be meaningful only if the learner can relate the new learning task to prior knowledge and if the task itself is related to an existing knowledge structure. For the teacher of social studies, this idea is extremely important. For the teacher of social studies classes with LEP students who come from a wide variety of backgrounds, developing this idea becomes an awesome challenge. Is there a viable solution? One of the most effective approaches seems to be one that makes few assumptions about students' prior knowledge of social studies. Teachers should start with the most basic concepts and gradually develop related ideas into broader units of study, especially in sheltered classes (see page 145).

Rather than adapting a fifth-grade textbook for fifth-grade LEP students, the teacher may want to develop a series of lessons that incorporate important concepts from grades 1 through 4 or 5. Students who have not yet grasped concepts introduced at an earlier level may experience difficulty with the fifth-grade social studies curriculum. To ensure more depth of understanding, particularly as it relates to historical developments and social studies concepts, teachers may need to adopt an approach that is comprehensive and cumulative in nature. This does not imply a "watered-down" approach (see also Chapter 11) but stresses the need for the learner to be given an opportunity to acquire new knowledge in a meaningful and relevant fashion, rather than in a piecemeal approach.

Many of the significant events and historical developments covered in social studies lessons can be related to fundamental concepts that may apply to a variety of situations and settings. Before beginning a unit on the American Civil War, for example, the teacher should discuss the idea that differences can eventually lead to conflict. Students may well understand this concept from their own personal experiences. This understanding can be extended into an exploration of their awareness of social, political, and economic differences among groups of people and nationalities. The teacher can then focus on specific facts related to differences between the North and South in the ante-bellum period, which eventually led to the Civil War. A basic concept can thus become the starting point for a social studies unit. An appreciation of such fundamental concepts and their role throughout history is an essential component of social studies instruction. Students who memorize facts and figures, but fail to comprehend the important concepts, will not really master the content of social studies. In addition, by relating the current unit of study to the students' own background knowledge, the teacher promotes understanding and stimulates enthusiasm for the topic. ESL students, for example, may not be keenly interested in the Confederacy in the 1860s, but they will probably be anxious to discuss their own personal problems with being "different." The teacher capitalizes on these experiences by tying them into the social studies concept and the events leading up to the Civil War.

EFFECTIVE TEACHING STRATEGIES

Specific teaching strategies have proven to be highly effective in reaching LEP students. Some of these strategies are discussed in the following section, with practical suggestions for incorporating these strategies into social studies lessons. They are intended to show how teachers can adapt some conventional instructional activities to take "language advantage" of social studies lessons. The strategies illustrate how teachers can readily use social studies content to enhance language development. It is evident that content-area subject matter provides a rich body of knowledge through which creative instructional activities may emerge.

Use of Manipulatives and Multimedia Materials

Many of the concepts presented in social studies lessons are abstract ideas that may be particularly difficult for nonnative students. Pictures provide students with visual experiences that transcend language barriers. For example, describing a scene from an old western mining town in the 1850s is simply not the same as showing a photograph or picture of the scene. When language proficiency is a problem, verbal or written descriptions are inadequate and need to be supplemented with pictorial representations. The visual image makes an immediate impression on the viewer and does not rely solely on an oral or written explanation that may elude LEP students. Without such visual experiences, teachers cannot know whether they have reached all students with important ideas and information.

Real objects or historical artifacts that reinforce social studies concepts provide students with tactile as well as visual experiences. Concrete objects bring ideas to life and make learning exciting and fun. A discussion of the common tools and household objects of the early eighteenth century, for example, does not have the same impact as a display and demonstration of these objects and how they were used. Such a display and demonstration is a memorable experience that students can relate to new vocabulary and concepts.

A wide variety of media materials for social studies is available in most public school libraries. Large-sized study prints and picture sets keyed to specific themes are useful for relating information and stimulating thinking in the classroom. Filmstrips are easily adapted for use with LEP students because the teacher can take advantage of the visual experience while altering the actual text to accommodate for different levels of English proficiency. Numerous 16mm films for social studies are also available but must be chosen with care because the language is often beyond what LEP students can comprehend. Ideas presented in films depicting historical events or processes may make reading and writing assignments associated with these ideas less difficult to process (Sinatra & Stahl-Gemake, 1983). In addition, periodicals such as *National Geographic* serve as excellent supplementary resources for social studies lessons. Vivid photographs and current themes make such resources a perfect complement to other instructional materials.

Language Experiences

Shared experiences initiate the desire for communication. In the traditional language experience approach (see also Chapter 12), the teacher encourages spontaneous language from students that eventually becomes the foundation for a written story (Lee & Allen, 1963). Because LEP students may have limited abilities in spontaneous oral English, the teacher may want to adapt this approach, particularly in sheltered classes. In an adapted language experience lesson, the teacher becomes a participant in an activity with the students. In advance, the teacher targets specific vocabulary, structures, and concepts to incorporate into the lesson and during the active experience elicits this language from students. Throughout the experience both spontaneous and guided language are evident, and literacy skills are encouraged with the use of flashcards and sentence strips for language produced. A story created by the class with the teacher's help is a natural follow-up.

Social studies lessons lend themselves well to this approach. In a unit on democratic government, for example, the teacher may want to stage an election of class officers to illustrate voting procedures and the concept of representative democracy. During and after the election, the class can discuss the process and the teacher can help them put their ideas into writing. The experience itself makes an impact on the students, helps clarify meaning, and assists in long-term memory. Research on the kinesthetic memory system indicates that when the body is actively involved in the learning process, ideas and concepts are integrated rapidly. Learning by doing is highly effective (Wayman, 1985).

The following hypothetical example is included to illustrate how a social studies teacher can turn to experiences to clarify the meaning of new concepts.

In a sheltered social studies class studying the role of the Constitutional Convention in writing the U.S. Constitution, the concept of reaching compromises to make decisions may be an entirely new idea. The social studies teacher needs to determine whether the students can recall aspects from their own experiences that might be similar, such as the various lawmaking bodies of their countries. If the students do not clearly understand this topic, then the teacher must create an experience that the students can draw from later. For example, the students could role-play various scenes from colonial times, when power was concentrated in the hands of a few. They could represent different interest groups, each arguing to have certain laws passed. With the teacher as facilitator, the students will come to understand that they must compromise or give up certain wants if any progress is to be achieved. Once the students have understood the concept of compromise, the teacher can proceed with the lesson on the Constitution and how its laws were created.

Managing Multilevel Classes

Most classroom teachers have experienced the difficulty of working with multilevel classes. The range of abilities can be as great as four or five reading grade levels. Teachers feel that many subjects must be taught in small groups in order to meet individual needs. However, the wide range of English proficiency levels does not completely preclude total-group instruction. Because many social studies lessons may be in the form of directed teaching and discussion, they provide excellent opportunities for involving the whole class. Students at lower proficiency levels benefit from the exposure to the language provided by the more advanced students during oral language activities and discussions. Students at advanced levels benefit from the increased amount of reinforcement of vocabulary and concepts that is provided for lower-level students.

Creative drama, role-playing, hands-on experiences, field trips, and music and art projects are some of the many activities that can be implemented in the multilevel social studies classroom. These activities challenge and enrich all students, regardless of language proficiency in English. Because of differing language and ability levels, students may not come away from a lesson or activity with exactly the same gains in knowledge, but they all will have benefited from the experiences.

Directed Reading Thinking Activity

The Directed Reading Thinking Activity (DRTA) is a highly effective strategy that can be applied in social studies lessons for LEP students. The three main steps of a DRTA are to predict, to read, and to prove. These steps motivate students to apply higher-level thinking skills. By brainstorming with the class before reading about a specific topic, the teacher finds out how much the students already know about that topic. This strategy is especially useful with second language students because of the variety and range to be found in their background knowledge and experiences. By encouraging students to predict what might be in the reading, the teacher asks students to call on prior knowledge that might be useful in this assignment. Students are immediately involved in the topic through oral discussion and are anxious to make appropriate ''guesses'' about what will be in the reading. As they read, students may have to revise their predictions, and they are challenged to make corrections in their own assumptions, weighing and evaluating what they know with what they read. In so doing, old information is assimilated into new information, and cognitive growth occurs. The teacher guides students through this activity and follows up on the reading with questions to check comprehension of subject matter. By this means, the teacher can find out how much the students actually understood and how well they can respond to probes of the subject matter.

The DRTA might be used for a sheltered lesson on immigration to the United States in the early twentieth century. Before assigning a reading, the teacher may discuss ESL students' own experiences with immigration. The class might then discuss all the photographs or pictures presented with the reading. They should compare and contrast their personal experiences with what is depicted. Then they might read through the passage in a step-by-step manner with the teacher, stopping at appropriate places to make predictions about what might follow. Finally, the teacher will help the students to discover how accurate their predictions were and to summarize what they have read.

Semantic Webbing

Outlining and note-taking are advanced study skills that require students to summarize important ideas in specific formats. LEP students often have trouble developing outlines and taking notes because they feel they must comprehend the entire message (given orally or in writing) before they can extract the main ideas and important details and arrange them in an appropriate form. Semantic

webbing is an extremely helpful way to teach students how to perceive relationships and integrate information and concepts within the context of a main
idea or topic (Freedman & Reynolds, 1980). The graphic representation afforded
students by semantic webbing bridges the gap between concrete images and
more abstract ideas. The core of a web is a key question or term that establishes
the purpose of the reading or topic for discussion. Following an oral discussion or a reading, students construct web strands and web supports by putting
key words or phrases in boxes or in some other visual arrangement. The boxes
can then be connected to illustrate relationships or subheadings under the main
idea(s). Such a visual scheme highlights important ideas and categories, greatly
aiding overall comprehension.

An example of semantic webbing is shown in Figure 19.1. In this diagram,
students list events and key words about the Revolution in a web format.
This web can be extended to include new information and additional details.
Students can order events chronologically to show sequence, or draw diagrams
to show cause-and-effect relationships. The web serves as a graphic model that
stimulates students to expand on their own ideas in formulating concepts. For
learners who have difficulty perceiving relationships between main ideas and
details, the spatial arrangement helps crystallize the concepts.

SQ4R

The SQ4R method (Robinson, 1962) is an effective means for teaching students
how to outline new information presented in a specific chapter in a social
studies text. It is highly recommended that students develop skills in using
this method early in the year, because it encourages them to organize and
summarize new information systematically and independently. Its value for
LEP students is that it teaches them a specific and routine method for breaking
down difficult reading material. The steps for SQ4R are the survey, questions,
and reading, reciting, recording, and reviewing.

Survey
Students skim the chapter for an overview of topics and material. They read
subtopics, look at visuals and graphs, and read highlighted vocabulary.

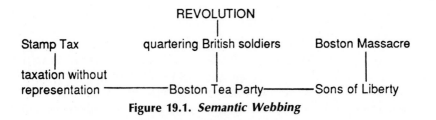

Figure 19.1. *Semantic Webbing*

Questions

Students fold notebook paper in half (vertically). On the left side, they list any questions that come to mind about the first subheading in the chapter, thereby establishing a purpose for reading. For example:

Spain's Empire Grows [subheading]

> Where was Spain's empire?
> What lands were in the empire?
> How did the empire grow?
> When did this happen?

Reading

Students read the text under this subheading to learn about the new topic and to answer the questions they had.

Reciting

Students try to answer as many of their own questions as possible from information gained from the reading. These responses should be oral in order to reinforce the new information.

Recording

Students write down answers to their questions, making the transfer from oral to written language.

Reviewing

Students immediately review what they have written. Then they are ready to move on to the next subheading and repeat the SQ4R process.

By continuing through the chapter with this method, the students will have created their own study sheet containing pertinent information about the chapter. The folded question sheets they have developed can be used by the teacher to test students on new material, providing a means of evaluative feedback.

SQ4R motivates students to deal with new information independently and efficiently while strengthening their note-taking skills. For LEP students in mainstream classes, this is one approach to difficult social studies texts that present heavy loads of new concepts and vocabulary.

Paraphrasing and Summarizing

Limited English proficiency will undoubtedly hamper students when they take notes in class, answer essay questions, and write reports. Moreover, reproducing lessons learned by rote or material produced by copying (methods many students used in their native schools) is unacceptable in most American classrooms. Therefore, paraphrasing and summarizing are essential skills for LEP students. Too often, teachers assume students will develop these skills independently, when, in fact, these skills must be taught and reinforced through repeated practice.

One activity that shows students how ideas can be restated is called ''Who said this?'' After teaching a unit on the causes of the American Revolution, the teacher gives students a list of statements and asks them to identify the speaker of each one as either King George or Thomas Jefferson. Sample sentences could be, *I refuse to pay taxes if I can't elect my own leader* or *I insist that the colonists pay a higher tax on tea.* After students have labeled the statements by speaker, they can list the reasons for their answers. Students should be told that they are actually paraphrasing what they have read. As a follow-up activity, students can write three sentences that summarize the causes of the American Revolution. LEP students at a more advanced level could be asked to write a chapter summary by first skimming each paragraph for the main idea and jotting it down. They might then restate the idea in their own words and use these restatements for a chapter summary.

Writing in the Content Areas

Social studies lends itself well to the development of writing skills. Recognizing that there are different levels of response in writing, teachers can incorporate various expository writing activities into social studies lessons. By following the writing process of brainstorming for ideas (see Chapter 10), organizing, prewriting, proofreading, and rewriting, teachers help students learn how to express themselves on paper. The richness of social studies vocabulary and concepts provides a great deal of content for generative writing. In applying this vocabulary in writing exercises, students also receive reinforcement of grammar and reading skills. Controversial topics that may arise in social studies discussions often stimulate the expression of ideas and personal opinions and can challenge students to write more effectively and persuasively.

Study Skills

Social studies classes afford excellent opportunities for developing students' study skills. Following directions, reading maps and charts, outlining, note taking, using textbooks, preparing oral and written reports, interpreting cartoons, and using library references are among the skills that can be reinforced in content-area lessons. While learning new subject matter, students can apply specific study skills for specific purposes. In so doing, they are not only learning new material; they are also strengthening skills that are essential for academic success. Social studies content provides a meaningful context for the application of such study skills.

MODEL LESSON

This section outlines a model lesson for the secondary level. This model lesson is meant to illustrate how a variety of teaching strategies can be combined to create unique experiences that stimulate students' interest and promote the learning process. Teachers are encouraged to experiment with ideas and approaches as they develop their own lessons around social studies themes, for there is no one single best way to teach content-area subjects to language minority students. The most successful lessons are the ones that incorporate a variety of strategies and activities into carefully planned learning experiences.

Model Lesson—Secondary Level

Objective
To provide students with an understanding of why Spain decided to explore the New World, and to learn about the explorations of Columbus, Magellan, Balboa, and other Spanish explorers.

Grade level
Secondary sheltered or mainstream social studies class

Materials
Large wall map, flashcards, yarn

Target vocabulary
voyage	colony	navigation
empire	explore	claim

Procedure

MOTIVATION. Using a large wall map, the teacher and students review trade routes used by Italian states and other European countries in the 1400s for trading with India and China. Students brainstorm as to why Spain would want to find an alternate route. Teacher should accept all responses such as: *Spain wants to get rich. Spain wants to be famous. Spain wants to be powerful.* (In this case, the teacher may want to ask the students to turn the statements into the past tense.) Students will practice and develop linguistic skills by agreeing or disagreeing with the reasons given. This activity may be done in small groups to maximize individual students' oral participation.

This part of the lesson is essential because it stimulates students to become involved in the new ideas. It also allows the teacher to find out how much background information the students have related to this topic.

INFORMATION. The teacher uses the students' predictions and ideas from the motivation section as a basis for presenting new information about Spanish exploration. The teacher may want to present each new explorer with flashcards that give explorer's name, dates of discoveries, and the area explored. Students will need to refer to a wall map to trace the paths of exploration and may find it helpful to use different colored yarn pieces to show where explorers traveled. Students can tell *who* explored, *where* they went, *when* they went, and *why* they explored.

After the new material is presented orally and visually, the teacher has students skim the headings and subheadings of a reading, such as a chapter in a textbook that covers this unit. This is the "survey" part of the SQ4R method. This technique may be used so that students can create a study sheet related to the new information. After the students have completed this sheet, the teacher should review each subheading in the reading to check for basic comprehension. Students may be asked to state the main idea of the reading and to locate specific sentences that support their answers. New vocabulary pertaining to the exploration unit is emphasized throughout the lesson, and students are encouraged to use context clues whenever possible to understand anything unfamiliar.

The teacher may want to show a filmstrip or movie about the Spanish explorers to reinforce new concepts.

Practice

The students now need to review new vocabulary and concepts that they have learned in the chapter. This is an appropriate time for some type of evaluation: Both short answers and essay questions would show an understanding of the new material. For example, students can write a paragraph describing Columbus's voyages, construct a chart listing dates, explorers, and routes the explorers used, or describe why Spain decided to explore westward.

ENRICHMENT AND EXTENSION. Students need to have a chance to choose an activity that will enable them to enrich their understanding of Spanish explorers. They are building on new information they have recently learned, and they now need to apply it to a new situation. Some possible activities to foster this extension of their learning are:

Students conduct research in the library on a Spanish explorer to find out the route traveled, problems encountered, discoveries, and so on. This information can be filled in on a chart or completed on a poster.

Students role-play Spanish explorers in a panel discussion. The teacher acts as moderator and poses leading questions such as *Tell us, Mr. Columbus, what problems did you encounter on your voyages?* All students will benefit from participating and listening to the responses.

Students can pretend they are explorers who want to find new land. They must describe where they want to sail, how they would raise funds, what they hope to find, and so on. This can be a writing activity or an oral discussion.

FOLLOW-UP QUESTIONS AND ACTIVITIES

1. Discovering students' prior knowledge is emphasized as a means for transitioning into a particular unit of work in social studies. If you were to teach the following units, what questions might you ask to draw out your students' prior knowledge in each area?

   a. the American Revolution
   b. the Exploration of Space
   c. the Freeing of the Slaves
   d. the Flower Children of the 1960s
   e. the Structure of the United States Government

2. What is a "watered-down" approach? What might its results be in social studies? How can such an approach be avoided in the selection and presentation of materials, topics, and concepts?

3. The use of real objects or historical artifacts to reinforce and clarify abstract concepts is recommended in this chapter. Choose three of the units listed in Activity 1 above and describe what objects, artifacts, or other realia you might include in your lessons.

4. Role-play is mentioned but not described in any detail by the authors. Do you think it might be a viable activity for gaining a broader knowledge base in social studies? Consider the following possibility, for example. The teacher has chosen two volunteer students to play the roles of Ronald Reagan and Eleanor Roosevelt, respectively. They are to be participants in a debate on how best to handle the drug problem in the United States. What advantages might there be in such an activity for the LEP student? Can you come up with other role-play ideas that would be appropriate for your teaching situation? If so, share them with a small group to get their reactions.

5. Using the model lesson on pages 297–299 as your guide, develop a lesson of your own for a specific classroom situation. Incorporate into your lesson some version of semantic webbing (see pages 293–294). Share your lesson with a small group and ask for feedback. You may want to revise the lesson on the basis of the new ideas you receive.

20

Teaching Literature
to Language Minority Students

Linda Sasser *Alhambra, California, School District*

> *Reading literature, writing and speaking are the real basics. Reading widely helps students with skills. Usage, mechanics, vocabulary, and syntax are best learned in context.*
>
> *(California Literature Institute Participants, 1985, p. 3)*

EDITORS' INTRODUCTION

To those working within the constraints of a district-determined curriculum as well as to others, Linda Sasser suggests strategies to bring literature alive and make it a memorable experience for language minority students. By taking students at various age and proficiency levels through the lesson format Sasser recommends, teachers can give them greater access to written language. Further-more, through the interactive process described, the teachers can arouse interest, supply necessary missing schema, and help students relate to prior knowledge, minimize ambiguity, and comprehend and extend what the literature has to say. The author recommends that text be presented in "comprehensible and manage-able" chunks and that it be interwoven with music, drama, art, film, and other visuals to enhance its meaning. Sandberg's Abe Lincoln Grows up, *Gardiner's* Stone Fox, *Twain's* The Adventures of Tom Sawyer, *and Houston's* Farewell to Manzanar *are among the pieces of literature used in the illustrations presented.*

In this decade, curriculum reform movements, teachers of mainstream disciplines, and educational philosophers like Frank Smith and Donald Murray have redefined the basics. Many teachers have welcomed this shift toward the integration of language skills, the creation of meaning-centered classrooms, and the view that literature should be accessible to all, not just the college-bound. As a consequence, waning are the boring skill-by-skill approaches to

---

Used by permission of Linda Sasser.

reading and writing; disappearing too are homogeneous classrooms where students are isolated by ethnicity and/or ability. Influenced by economics and immigrant populations and supported by persistent interest in equality of educational access and opportunity, rapidly changing demographic patterns have resulted in great classroom diversity. Both the elementary language arts classroom and the college-preparatory English classroom may include students who speak any of the world's languages as a first language (L1), students who are fluent in one or more languages, students who speak dialectal varieties of English, students with limited English proficiency, and students whose reading levels range from above to below grade level. Drawing from the knowledge and strategies of experienced language arts teachers, this chapter focuses on the needs of the Limited English Proficient (LEP) student in the language arts and English classroom. Given developmental needs related to language proficiency and age, what kinds of texts are appropriate for these students? How does the classroom environment facilitate acquisition of both concepts and language? Which teaching strategies for literature assist in language comprehension and production? And finally, how can the needs of the LEP student be included in lesson preparation? Teaching literature in today's classrooms presents several challenges—a challenge to choose appropriate literature, a challenge to prepare lessons that will permit access to the key themes, a challenge to make the works comprehensible to all—and yet offers great rewards—to the student, to the teacher, and ultimately to us all.

APPROPRIATE TEXTS

In preparing to teach in a heterogeneous classroom containing students with limited English proficiency, one obvious place to begin is with a review of the curriculum. Since most school districts have curriculum guides and mandatory or recommended texts, teachers must prepare to work within these confines. A review of our texts helps anticipate and identify possible hurdles or stumbling blocks such as cultural unfamiliarity, difficult vocabulary, complex themes and characters, and/or academic or archaic syntax. Many works present difficulties even for the native speaker of English; for instance, as a college freshman I recall making lists of unfamiliar Russian names to distinguish between characters in *Crime and Punishment*, yet the social context of the novel was comprehensible to me. Many texts formerly included in the college English program are now found in high school syllabi. Imagine, however, what obstacles such works would present to a bright, hard-working refugee with interrupted schooling. Addressed in isolation, these hurdles can be surmounted, but if a work contains many impediments to comprehension, both teacher and students may find it defeating unless the barriers have been anticipated and strategies devised to overcome them. For instance, if a text like *Tom Sawyer* or *Great Expectations* is rooted in nineteenth-century historical or sociocultural contexts and contains American or British regional speech, teachers should reflect on how to make the language comprehensible to language minority students from recent Central American or Indo-Chinese backgrounds. Similarly, despite literary merit and award-winning status, adolescent novels like *Roll of Thunder, Hear My Cry,* or *A Wrinkle in Time* present many complex issues to resolve before they are presented to a class containing LEP students. Yet there are ways to resolve these issues.

Schema theory (James, 1987) proposes that good readers comprehend new or unfamiliar elements in texts by drawing on past experiences of many sorts. These experiences can originate in real life or in works absorbed in previous encounters with literature. By comparing data from the most recent text with preexisting knowledge, an unfamiliar work becomes easier to understand. For instance, the theme of Gallico's novella, *The Snow Goose* is familiar to those who have read Perrault's tale of "Beauty and the Beast." Applying these principles to literature choices for LEP students suggests that works with themes comparable to those in students' lives might be more appropriate initial choices than works far removed in time and space.

Students of all ages respond with enthusiasm to poetry and folktales from multiethnic sources and enjoy comparative mythology. Myths and folktales are commonly available in high-quality works of children's literature such as the classic *D'Aulaires' Book of Greek Myths:* Vibrant illustrations of such stories assist in making them highly comprehensible. In recent years there has been a proliferation of African, Native American, Latin American, and Asian folktales and myths in editions for young people. My experience has shown that these work well at all levels. High school LEP students have also responded positively to selected short stories by Langston Hughes, Paul Gallico, Gabriel Garcia Marquez, William Saroyan, and Robert Cormier, excerpts from Maxine Hong Kingston, Amy Tan, and Richard Rodriguez, as well as the novellas of John Steinbeck and Ernest Hemingway. For all ages, English comprehension is facilitated if a teacher's choice of literature is a planned sequence that begins with the more familiar and accessible structures of folktale and myth and uses these as a bridge to more complex works of literature. For example, teachers might consider framing an introduction to the mythology of Greece with the myths of the world's origin centering around the Mayan god Hurakan or the Chinese god Pan-Ku. Such an introduction assists students in activating the concept of myth using familiar names and tales as well as utilizing this structure to support the unfamiliar and highly complex cosmology of the ancient Greeks.

Following a reflection on the choice of literature, teachers can select specific methods and instructional activities such as those included in this chapter to activate student schemas and isolate the features that are important for comprehension and appreciation of the work. In some instances, teachers may elect to teach only portions or chapters of a work or interweave text, film, and other visual aids to clarify and enhance meaning. By slowing the pace slightly, portioning the work into manageable chunks, and increasing the depth of lessons, almost any work can be made comprehensible if student ages, interests, and background have been factored into determining which works of literature will be taught. Shakespeare's *Romeo and Juliet* has been successfully taught to LEP students by teachers who preteach critical vocabulary and use the Zefferelli film to introduce selected original scenes, which students read. The film greatly assists in making sixteenth-century language comprehensible to twentieth-century students.

Recall from Chapter 2 that students comprehend slightly in advance of what they are able to independently produce and that academic language proficiency takes longer to develop than language used for social purposes. Thus, the message for the language arts or literature teacher is this: In the heterogeneous classroom, comprehension will vary among individual students. After independently reading the same text, students above grade level understand on a different level than those below, and student production in speech and writing has an even greater range. To mitigate these discrepancies, the successful teacher will actively employ the classroom environment and a variety of teaching strategies to enhance comprehension and response.

THE CLASSROOM ENVIRONMENT

The classroom environment plays a critical role in comprehension and production. If students are overwhelmed by the enormity of a task (''I'll never be able to understand all this''), pressured by time (''She says we have to read 200 pages this weekend''), and oriented to product (''If I don't get at least a C on this test, I'm going to fail''), they are unlikely to do well. The teacher is responsible for establishing and maintaining an instructional environment where literature is presented in comprehensible and manageable segments; where lessons are paced to focus on comprehension and not on *getting through* the syllabus; where the language skills of reading, writing, and speaking are integrated; and where errors are viewed as natural by-products of attempts to use language. In such an atmosphere, LEP students can and do flourish.

Limited English proficient students can successfully comprehend difficult works of literature if they have the support of their peers—both native English speakers and others who may speak the same first language. Research on cooperative learning (Kagan, 1988; Slavin, 1983) indicates that group work in an interactive classroom environment where teachers guide students to discuss the readings not only reduces anxiety but increases comprehension and production. If students have no understanding or empathy for one another, how can they be expected to have it for literary characters? If LEP students do not explore their responses through discussion and classroom interaction, how can they be expected to produce cogent essays in response to literature? Furthermore, in a class of mixed language proficiency, what one student doesn't understand, another student will: In cooperative teams, as students dialogue with one another, the weak student receives comprehensible input from her or his peers and the strong student is reinforced by the tutoring role (see also Chapters 5 and 18).

Because an interactive orientation stresses comprehension, when LEP students work with and respond to a text, they are constantly being exposed to and working with vocabulary, mechanics, and syntax, and they are simultaneously acquiring all of these. In a literature-based program, after highly interactive reading and response to a particular work, teachers find text-specific syntactic patterns and vocabulary items cropping up repeatedly in the later conversation and written work of language minority students. Note, for example, how a Vietnamese student has incorporated (probably subconsiously) structures he acquired from Saroyan:

> One day back there in the good old days when I was nine and the world was full of every imaginable kind of magnificence and life was still a delightful and mysterious dream. . . . (W. Saroyan, *The Summer of the Beautiful White Horse*)

> Way back in the good old time when I was ten and the world was full of wonderful fantasy, I enjoyed throwing water balloons at such pretty girls. (Vietnamese tenth-grade boy)

TOOLS FOR TEACHING LITERATURE

In the widely reprinted work, *Literature as Exploration*, Rosenblatt (1976), offers guidance for all teachers of literature. These words apply equally well to first or second language speakers and students of all ages:

> No one else can read a literary work for us. The benefits of literature can emerge only from creative activity on the part of the reader himself. He responds to the little black marks on the page, or to the sounds of the words in his ear, and he "makes something of them." The verbal symbols allow him to draw on his past experiences with what the words point to in life and literature. The text presents these words in a new and unique patten. Out of these he is enabled actually to mold a new experience, the literary work. (p. 278)

Any literary work comes into existence only through the interaction between the reader and text: Until a dialectic occurs, the text consists only of those "little black marks," for it is the process of reading that inbues those printed symbols with meaning. It is both insufficient and insignificant for students merely to read a passage, respond to their teacher's oral questioning, and submit to a multiple-choice or short-answer test on the reading—if this is the only level of engagement with a text, the experience is trivialized and routinized. If students miss the power and beauty of literature, it is certain they have also failed to realize their own power and potential.

Drama and film, classical and popular music, poetry and art activities can all be used to unlock the major themes of a work. When students respond to the sounds of instruments or voices used in a dialogue or dramatic interpretation, they are being provided with access to comprehension that supplements or

emotions	actions	sounds	physical pains/conditions

miserable	suffering	ailment	colicky
groaning	aggravated	snort	anxious
moaned	trembled	gasped	mortified
meow	hum	titter	whispers
nudges	winks	giggles	foolish
aches	sore	expectorate	murmur
scrawled	scuffle		

Figure 20.1. *Matrix Used to Sort Vocabulary from* **The Adventures of Tom Sawyer** *(S. L. Clemens, 1986, New York: Penguin)*

complements the text. A tape of Robert Frost reading ''Birches'' or Dylan Thomas reading ''A Child's Christmas in Wales'' imbues poetry with a sense of the poet's life beneath the lines. Music can also enrich the literature experience. Why not present Gluck's ''Dance of the Blessed Spirits'' with its haunting, spiraling flute solos as a way into the myth of Orpheus and a reading of Rilke's poem ''Orpheus, Eurydice and Hermes,'' or compare rock musician Chris DeBurgh's ''Don't Pay the Ferryman'' with selected cantos from Dante's *Divine Comedy?* Such conjunctions powerfully demonstrate the enduring power of myth in today's art. Why not use the powerful Dorothea Lange photos of the 1930s and Woody Guthrie tapes as an adjunct to reading *Grapes of Wrath* or support *The Diary of Anne Frank* with film or video? By listening to music or studying a print or film and linking shade, tone, rhythm, texture, line, and mood to emotion, further pathways to meaning emerge.

Students can also be engaged with meaning through construction of graphic or advance organizers such as clusters, semantic maps, storyboards, matrices, semantic webs, T-graphs, and Venn diagrams.[1] Long used in advertising, mathematics, and science, graphic organizers are powerful tools in the language classroom and can be used by students of all ages and abilities. Figures 20.1 to 20.4

---

[1] Secondary teachers may wish to consult Collie and Slater's *Literature in the Language Classroom* (1987); useful for elementary and secondary teachers is Johnson and Louis's *Literacy through Literature* (1987).

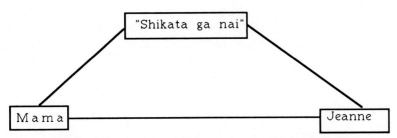

Figure 20.2. *Semantic Web Used to Assist Students in Defining Attitudes and Relationships between Elements in Chapter 2, Farewell to Manzanar (J. W. Houston, 1975, New York: Bantam)*

QUOTATION	MY REACTION
It seemed Abe made the books tell him more than they told other people. All the other farm boys had gone to school and read *The Kentucky Preceptor*, but Abe picked out questions from it, such as, "who has the most right to complain, the Indian or the Negro." Yet what he tasted of books in school was only a beginning, only made him hungry and thirsty, shook him with a wanting and a wanting of more and more of what was hidden between the covers of books. As he read through *Aesop's Fables* a second and third time, he had a feeling there were fables all around him, that everything he touched and handled, everything he saw and learned had a fable wrapped in it somewhere.	

Figure 20.3. *T-Graph Used to Analyze Text from C. Sandburg, Abe Lincoln Grows Up (1928, New York: Harcourt, Brace and Company, Inc.)*

Figure 20.4. *Venn Diagram Used to Compare Little Willie and Stone Fox from J. R. Gardiner,* Stone Fox *(1980, NY: Harper and Row)*

illustrate the use of a matrix, semantic web, T-graph, and a Venn diagram in the teaching of several different works of literature.

Before and during reading, as students locate and list the requested information on these different types of graphic organizers, they are engaged in an analytical response to the text. The act of filling in requires critical thinking skills as students sort, categorize, list, analyze, and evaluate their own reactions and the content of literary passages. Furthermore, the physical form of an organizer imposes structure on many discrete bits of data, locks down abstract ideas in a concrete, visual manner, and allows students to move back and forth at their own pace between the text and their response to it. As students read, discuss, and share ideas and responses with their peers, construct organizers, and respond to literature in quick-writes or journal entries, they are engaged in activities that infuse the text with intellectual and emotional meanings and prepare them for formal written responses.[2] No one of these creative activities should be used in exclusion of the others—rather, all together they comprise the teacher's repertoire.

---

[2] A journal entry can be a thoughtful, reflective piece of writing or a quick-write. The latter is used to discover what the student already knows. Rapidly and without planning or referring to what has already been read or written, the student writes in words, phrases, or sentences for a specified length of time. In a quick-write the student should not be concerned about spelling, grammar, or punctuation for the purpose is to capture meaning.

PREPARING LESSONS

Once the literature has been selected and the teacher has been supplied with strategies and methods, lesson planning begins. The format for literature lessons shown in Figure 20.5 was developed by the California Literature Institute Participants (1985). In this format, every literature lesson is framed as a sequence of *into, through,* and *beyond.* The categories are easy to remember, fit well with the reading and writing processes, and allow for great adaptability.

Into is the phase that occurs before reading begins. Particularly for LEP students, *Into* is a period used to awaken interest and tap prior knowledge, as well as provide the necessary background knowledge of the work. During *Into* the teacher draws upon many resources (e.g., speakers, community, maps, music, art, drama, and realia) to prepare and interest students in reading. Anticipation guides used before reading allow students to identify and think through their positions in relation to complex abstract concepts like truth, responsibility, love, war, or honor. In Figure 20.6, a sample anticipation guide is provided. Used prior to reading Thoreau's ''Civil Disobedience,'' the anticipation guide helps students identify and consider their own opinions before encountering those of the writer.

The students understand themselves
and what it means to be human.

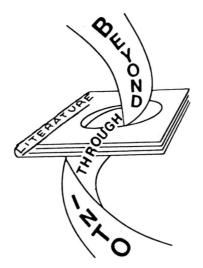

The students bring to the literature
their own knowledge and personal experience.

Figure 20.5. *Into, Through, Beyond*
(adapted from California Literature
Institute Participants, 1985, p. 80)

Instructions: Consider the following statements and decide whether you agree or disagree.

	Agree	Disagree
1. That government is best which governs least.	Δ	Δ
2. Laws do not make people behave well - only people themselves can do that.	Δ	Δ
3. Rebellion or revolution is the people's right of action when a government is inefficient.	Δ	Δ
4. There is little good in the behavior of groups of people.	Δ	Δ
5. Every person has a duty to correct a wrong or injustice.	Δ	Δ
6. If I believe a tax is wrong, I would refuse to pay it.	Δ	Δ
7. Each individual person is more important than the state.	Δ	Δ

Figure 20.6. *A Sample Anticipation Guide*

The teacher may also preface a reading by providing an overview or a simple plot summary to help students anticipate plot structure and characterization. During *Into,* students are urged to use prediction strategies based on a title or plot overview: They can formulate these orally or in quick-writes in a journal entry. Journal entries are particularly valuable because they permit free exploration of a topic without the stress of evaluation; a series of entries allows students to build toward more elaborate formulations.[3] The *Into* period can also be used to introduce critical concepts and vocabulary items to prepare students for later encounters in context. For instance, before reading Poe's ''The Cask of Amontillado,'' activities can be used to establish the concept of irony. Since irony is a subtle form of sarcasm (an art form familiar to many students and teachers), role-play set in the context of a boy greeting a rival for his girlfriend's attention can underscore the meaning of the narrator's irony at encountering Fortunato: ''I was so pleased to see him that I thought I should never have done wringing his hand.'' With LEP students such activities are often pivotal to later comprehension, and it is not unusual for the prereading phase to consume more time than the actual reading of the work.

During the *Through* phase, students are assigned to read the work. For LEP students it is helpful to follow up independent, silent reading by reading aloud from the work. When the teacher reads a selection aloud, supported by the power and texture of the voice, students follow along silently, the inflection, pronunciation, rhythm and stress of a fluid reading greatly assisting in comprehension. During *Through,* neither independent reading nor read-to is a passive activity but an interactive one. To comprehend and appreciate a

---

[3] Fulwiler's *The Journal Book* (1987) is a rich source of ideas for journal or reading log uses.

work, students need to be able to follow an event sequence, recognize fore-shadowing, distinguish flashback, visualize the setting, analyze character and motive, experience the mood, comprehend the theme, and note the use of irony and symbols. Language minority students will need activities to aid them in these tasks. The teacher may select passages for in-depth discussion and analysis, helping to draw attention to what is significant in the work. In an interchange of ideas, individual students compare their personal reactions with one another and the teacher; thus they learn that one work can give rise to multiple reactions. This is particularly important for students schooled in other traditions: Trained to see only one way to respond, they may be visibly uncomfortable with ambiguity and a teacher who insists, ''There is no one right answer.'' Through discussion students also learn that defensible reactions require analysis, a sorting out of the irrelevant from the fundamental aspects of the work.

This level of analysis is particularly difficult for the LEP student, for much of the meaning in literature is based on the assumption that the reader understands and shares in the inferences. It is through inference that readers come to an interpretation broader than the one actually written down. To assist LEP students in grasping inferences and implications, it is useful to provide concrete specific activities, as enumerated earlier in this chapter. Even very young readers can use a semantic web to successfully analyze the inferred relationships between the protagonists in ''Jack and the Beanstalk'' or study structure by creating a plot profile for *Charlotte's Web*. Figure 20.7 is an example of a plot profile that students can use to chart their reactions to events in ''Little Red Riding Hood.'' By connecting the points, they create a visual representation of rising and falling action, climax, and denouement.

Reading logs can be used for open-ended response to a work or to more structured assignments to help students identify and trace the elements of literature.[4] For example, students can be asked to select a word or phrase and explain why it is a favorite, or to tell how someone they know is like a character in the text, or to relate a theme or concept to their own experience. Art activities also deepen appreciation and demonstrate comprehension. Individuals or small groups can create collages and story maps or illustrations for characters or chapters. Similarly, music of a period (Civil War songs paired with *The Red Badge of Courage* or popular music of the twenties with *The Great Gatsby*) heightens comprehension for all. Students may use their knowledge of a text to convert scenes into dialogues, to write letters to or between characters, or to describe some elements in essay form. In doing so, they are working with abstract concepts derived from the literature and using all the skills required for comprehension.

---

[4] Teachers interested in dialogue reading logs should consult Nancie Atwell's *In the Middle* (1987).

Events
1. Little Red Riding Hood gets the basket from her mother.
2. Little Red Riding Hood meets the wolf in the forest.
3. The wolf goes to Grandmother's house.
4. The wolf eats Granny.
5. Little Red Riding Hood knocks on Granny's door.
6. Little Red Riding Hood talks with the wolf in Granny's nightie.
7. The wolf leaps at Little Red Riding Hood.
8. A passing woodcutter saves the day.

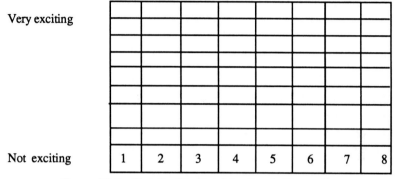

Figure 20.7. *Plot Profile Used to Graph Events for "Little Red Riding Hood"*

Beyond activities extend the appreciation of the work. During *Beyond*, students traditionally write to clarify their thinking and deepen understanding. Well-constructed written prompts serve as composing guides for language minority students. An example from Nemerouf and Williams (1986) follows:

> In "The Fifty-first Dragon," Heywood Broun humorously tells how a cowardly young student knight was turned into a temporarily successful dragon slayer. This was a process that required several steps. You too can be a "dragon" killer. Write an essay in which you identify a modern "dragon," a current fear or social problem, and develop a step-by-step plan to eradicate it. Your plan may be presented in a straightforward manner, or like Broun, you may write it in a humorously ironic style. (p. 59)

This prompt helps students recall the plot of the short story, identifies the process that furthered the plot, asks the writers to relate it to an issue that concerns them, and finally to resolve their concern. This writing assignment allows great latitude in approach—important for the novice writer's emerging voice. Prompts to explicate a reading should be similarly constructed, allowing students to explain an author's idea or purpose, derive its significance, and draw upon their own background in response to that purpose and significance.[5] To become successful writers, LEP students need many models, participation in read-around groups,[6] comments on the content of their writing, peer revision opportunities, and comprehensible feedback on their attempts to use language.

Other useful *Beyond* activities include comparing a text with its film representation (''You've read *Wuthering Heights*—in what ways is the film's portrayal of Heathcliff true to Brontë's novel?'') or preparing a dramatization based on a scene or ideas from the work. The powerful ideas of Kenneth Koch (1970, 1973) and K. Farrell (Koch & Farrell, 1981) can assist students in writing their own poems in response to one they have experienced. Figure 20.8 demonstrates a teaching idea from Koch. LEP students worked with Pound's ''The River Merchant's Wife: A Letter'' and subsequently wrote their own poems. ''Friendship'' was composed by a seventeen-year-old immigrant from Taiwan.

Many teachers have experimented with a newspaper or magazine format in which groups of students approach the work and its context to demonstrate a comprehensive synthesis of theme, style, and period. Such an approach to Munro Leaf's *Ferdinand* or Melville's *Moby Dick* might include wanted posters, letters to the editor pro and con the animal rights issues involved, explanations of the social contexts of bullfighting and whaling, descriptions of implements, and so forth. Personal writing derived from themes in the work and letters to authors posing questions students would like answered are also appealing activities for *Beyond*. In all of this, the teacher is limited only by his or her imagination.

CONCLUSION

The approach advocated here bears little resemblance to the English classrooms of my youth. Napping or daydreaming as teachers talked, we waited for the comprehension questions signaling the end of lectures. Sometimes we participated, reading round-robin and counting down the paragraphs to locate ours, marking it with a finger lest we lose our turn (see also Chapter 12). Had I been a student in the kind of interactive environment described here, perhaps I would have better recall of all that I so diligently and so solitarily read . . . yet the activities sketched here are not incompatible with a literature-based curriculum. Rosenblatt (1976) has said that out of interaction the reader molds

---

[5] For multiple examples of such prompts, see Gadda, Peitzman, and Walsh (1988).

[6] A read-around uses small groups of students as readers/commentators for a set of drafted compositions. The structure of the activity assists all students in developing an internal rubric for what constitutes a ''good'' or ''poor'' paper and allows the teacher to focus student attention on rhetorical structures and devices. For more detailed information, readers should consult Gossard (1986), pp. 132–135.

Friendship

When we were six
We met in Lin Family Village.
The mud painted our faces,
The chickens ran after us,
The birds sang with us.

When we were ten,
We had talked with sun and moon.
The boat and maple in company laughed with us.
Our friendship was like sisters—
Everyone thought we were twins.

When we were fourteen,
We held each other's hands,
Walked on the road to school.
We shared a lunch everyday
And there were two little girls under the umbrella.
That's you and me.

One single leaf fell into the lake.
It recalled to my mind the maple.
It made me vague and hazy:
That was a happy memory.
But today, where are they?
Where are the happy times?
Let me climb the wing of wind
Say to you
I miss you.

Julia Yu

**Figure 20.8. *A Poem Composed by a Seventeen-Year-Old
Immigrant Student From Taiwan***

a new experience—meaning grows out of the stimulation of the senses and the intellect. And Frye (1964) long ago told us that literature belongs to the world we construct—we envision the whole, lay foundations, raise our understanding work by work, frame it with words, and become active builders of that world. There can be no single, proper preconceived way to react to a work: We come to literature's enduring and human problems with myriad experiences and perspectives. Since our ancestors first gathered around the fire to hear a storyteller, we have asked ourselves and the gods, ''how'' and ''why,'' repeating these questions generation after generation. Unlike mathematical equations, the problems of literature cannot be solved, for they have a human face, a human spirit. As we teach literature to students with limited English proficiency, we need to focus on an infinite variety of students, experiences, languages, works, methods, and responses. It is in these ways we find our challenges and rewards.

RECOMMENDED READINGS

Atwell, N. (1987). *In the middle: Reading and writing with adolescents.* Portsmouth, NH: Heinemann, Boynton/Cook.

California Literature Institute Participants (1985). *Literature for all students: A sourcebook for teachers.* Los Angeles: UCLA Center for Academic Interinstitutional Programs.

Collie, J., & Slater, S. (1987). *Literature in the language classroom: A resource book of ideas and activities.* Cambridge: Cambridge University Press.

Frye, N. (1964). *The educated imagination.* Bloomington: Indiana University Press.

Fulwiler, T. (Ed.). (1987). *The journal book.* Portsmouth, NH: Heinemann, Boynton/Cook.

Gadda, G., Peitzman, F., & Walsh, W. (1988). *Teaching analytical writing.* Los Angeles: UCLA Center for Academic Interinstitutional Programs.

James, M. O. (1987). ESL reading pedagogy: Implications of schema-theoretical research. In J. Devine, P. L. Carell, and D. E. Eskey (Eds.), *Research in reading in English as a second language* (pp. 175–188). Washington, DC: TESOL.

Johnson, T. D., & Louis, D. R. (1987). *Literacy through literature.* Portsmouth, NH: Heinemann.

Kagan, S. (1988). *Cooperative learning resources for teachers.* Laguna Nigel: Resources for Teachers.

Koch, K. (1970). *Wishes, lies, and dreams: Teaching children to write poetry.* New York: Perennial/Harper & Row.

Koch, K. (1973). *Rose, where did you get that red?* New York: Vintage.

Koch, K. & Farrell, K. (1981). *Sleeping on the wing: An anthology of poetry with essays on reading and writing.* New York: Vintage.

Nemerouf, A., & Williams, R. J. (1986). *Masters of words, makers of meaning: Designs for teaching writing.* Los Angeles: UCLA Center for Academic Interinstitutional Programs.

Rosenblatt, L. M. (1976). *Literature as exploration.* New York: Noble and Noble.

Slavin, R. (1983). *Cooperative learning.* White Plains, NY: Longman.

FOLLOW-UP QUESTIONS AND ACTIVITIES

1. Sasser refers to her own experiences with literature lessons by saying, "Napping or daydreaming as teachers talked, we waited for the comprehension questions signaling the end of lectures." Have you ever reacted in a similar way to literature lessons in classes you have taken? If so, describe the lessons and tell why you reacted as you did. How did your experiences affect your enjoyment of literature?

2. Choose a literary piece that you might use in your own teaching situation. Suggest how it could be broken down into manageable segments. What might you do to make these segments as comprehensible as possible for LEP students?

3. Select a second piece of literature appropriate to your teaching situation. Describe the *Into, Through,* and *Beyond* strategies you would incorporate. Discuss your ideas with a small group for their input.

4. If you were to compare cultures through the use of literature (see the discussion of comparative mythology in this chapter), what selections would you make? Make a list and describe the cultures and characteristics you would compare in each case. Share your lists with the class.

21

Discovery Science and Language Development

JAMES H. RUPP *California State University, San Bernardino*

EDITORS' INTRODUCTION

In this chapter James Rupp shares with us a few blueprints for establishing science classrooms that are also rich language learning environments. He introduces us to science activities that engage students at all age levels in dialogues to encourage inquiry and discovery. Cooperative learning, thematic units, and learning centers form the foundation for the discussion. Theoretical underpinnings as well as numerous specific examples are given to flesh out the basic ideas. He uses the egg-drop experiment to demonstrate how a lesson intended for one age level can be adapted to another. Hands-on involvement of students at all stages in the learning process is stressed, and students are even included in the planning of lessons.

Students come to school with their own view of what the world is like. They enter the school environment as eager and willing participants in the learning process. Science inquiry begins with students' natural curiosity about the world and how it works. As they become involved in active learning about their world, their view of it continues to change and develop. The teacher's task is to facilitate this growth and development by providing opportunities for active involvement through what is known as discovery science. According to Carin and Sund (1985):

> Scientists are curious about their world and continually improve their investigative skills. If children are to understand science and become capable, active problem solvers, they must also have years of active experience in investigating their worlds. Children must learn, by doing and then reflecting, how to investigate and discover scientific concepts, theories, and processes. Inquiry science teaching sets up a classroom environment to stimulate this active interaction. Discovery, the culmination of inquiry processes, should not be left to chance. (p. 15)

In *all* grades the focus should be on inquiry and discovery and should include the following processes which are at the heart of science instruction: observing, using space/time relationships, using numbers, measuring, classifying, communicating, predicting, inferring, interpreting results, formulating hypotheses, controlling variables, defining operations, and experimenting. These processes are developmental: Those at the beginning of the list should be stressed in the lower grades, followed by the others in the upper grades.

From Cummins's work (see Chapter 2), we know that studying science through abstract, context-reduced language is not the place to begin with language minority students. Discovery science actively involves students in hands-on activities. It provides the kinds of language opportunities in which students are willing to take risks in exploring real experiences using purposeful language. The students' language is focused on what they are doing and on what is being said in a meaningful context.

DIALOGUING

Language development for language minority students, as well as native speakers, can be encouraged in a variety of ways. As science teachers, we must seek strategies to help facilitate this process. One of the most productive is dialoguing. I do not mean the kind of dialoging associated with the audiolingual method of memorizing second language (L2) dialogues and then doing substitution drills. I mean dialoguing in real situations for very real purposes. The use of dialogue in language acquisition is based in part on the theoretical frameworks of Vygotsky (1962) and Freire (1970). Teachers and students must deal with two important contexts. "One is the context of authentic dialogue between learners and educators as equally knowing subjects . . . the second is the real, concrete context of facts, the social reality in which men exist" (Freire, 1970, p. 14).

In the classroom, dialogue can take on a number of different forms. For example, Richard-Amato (1989) discussed four types of "reaction dialogues" in the development of oral and literacy skills:

1. teacher-presented stimulus/student reaction
2. student-presented stimulus/student and teacher reaction
3. student product/teacher reaction
4. student product/student reaction

Hands-on discovery science provides many opportunities for producing these four types of interactions. Such dialoguing can occur in the oral/aural modalities as well as in the reading/writing modalities. In fact, as students work together cooperatively in problem-solving situations, this type of dialogue is essential. Teachers initiate dialogue when they help students to explore hypotheses and solutions in their research. In the process of helping students develop the technical reporting used by scientists, teachers and students can continually dialogue through their writing, responding to one another as they write. For example, keeping a journal in which students write about their science activities is an opportunity for teachers to respond to student writing in a low-risk situation.

One question often raised by science teachers as well as other content-area teachers and/or mainstream classroom teachers is the use of the native language in instruction. We know from Cummins (1981) that language use within the school setting changes as students progress in their schooling. Thus, in the early grades students learn greetings and other daily language that become automatic speech, heavily embedded within the context of the situation. By the time they reach high school, students must make sense of academic textbooks dealing with abstract scientific concepts such as black holes or Newtonian physics. What often happens is that English as a second language (ESL) students fall further behind when the language they encounter becomes more decontextualized and cognitively demanding. Cummins (1981) states:

> It takes much longer for language minority students to approach commonly accepted age/grade norms in context-reduced aspects of English proficiency (five to seven years on the average) than it does in context-embedded aspects (approximately two years on the average). (p.16)

The use of the native language in the discussion of scientific concepts is both effective and efficient. If our first goal is concept development, followed by learning English labels for concepts, then the use of native languages should not be discouraged. In fact, the bilingual Spanish-English science/math program Finding Out/Descrubrimento (DeAvila & Duncan, 1984) has been used effectively in many elementary schools. This program consists of hands-on science activities arranged on activity cards in both languages, which can be used in a variety of instructional approaches and program types. The lessons are particularly adaptable for student-based centers and cooperative groups, both of which are described later. Some of the areas of discovery covered in the series include measurement (including weights), air movement, magnets, and electricity.[1]

STRATEGIES AND APPROACHES

Enright and McCloskey (1985) emphasize the need for content-area teachers to develop communicative classrooms that are organized for collaboration, purpose, student interest, previous experience, holism, support, and variety. Discovery science classrooms can become communicative settings that facilitate language growth in a number of meaningful ways. They can provide large amounts of meaningful, relevant, and purposeful language input. Interactive

---

[1] A detailed description of DeAvila & Duncan's program, including examples, can be found in Kessler and Quinn (1987).

language is not only encouraged, it is essential. For example, most scientific investigation entails data collection and reporting, which can be done through a variety of means. Such language-rich environments can include vocabulary charts, diagrams, various kinds of graphs, timetables, schedules, and pictures, as well as the more formal genres of scientific language such as science fair exhibits and written reports. This variety enables all students to access language from cognitively undemanding and context-embedded lessons to more cognitively demanding and context-reduced academic tasks.

Within a communicative environment several strategies and approaches can be incorporated to further facilitate language development. The first of these is an adaption of cooperative learning (see also Chapter 5). For students from some cultures, working in small groups is one of the most appropriate approaches to follow. Students from cultures in which individual effort is rewarded can also benefit from small-group work by developing social skills that are encouraged by others.

Cooperative learning is one way of organizing small-group activities in science so that all members of the group have a chance to participate. In one version of cooperative learning, each member can receive one of the following assigned functions: reporter, chairperson, recorder, organizer, maintenance engineer, and checker. By giving every member a task, each one has a responsibility and is involved in the group. It is important that all students participate from the very beginning. Some may not feel comfortable being a chairperson, and others may not have developed enough facility in English yet for such a task, but there are other tasks they can do. In addition, having an assigned role gives each member ownership of the group's project. The groups are heterogeneous, so that there is linguistic modeling going on at all times by sources other than the teacher. The students teach one another and learn from one another, not just about science concepts and language but about social interaction and group behavior as well.

The following is an example of an activity that works well with cooperative groups. As described here, it is aimed at the elementary grades 3 to 6, but it can also be modified for use with older students.

The Egg-Drop Experiment

Purpose:
To design and make a protective package to prevent an egg from breaking when dropped from a wall.

Materials/Supplies:
> one raw egg
> plastic straws (the same number for each group)[2]

---

[2] The number used will depend on the drop site. For example, about fifteen straws should be enough for a six-foot drop.

straight pins
masking tape
scissors

Procedures:

1. Brainstorming: Discuss how packages protect their contents in shipping, and the different types of packaging used. Examine samples of various kinds of packaging materials. Discuss the purpose of the activity and visit the drop site.
2. Group work: After being assigned to their cooperative groups, the students will plan and construct their packages.
3. Drop site: One member of each group will drop the group's egg, in exactly the same way as the other group representatives. The recorders should take notes of the results.
4. Results: After the testing is finished, the class should work together to discuss the results and record the data of all the groups.
5. Reporting results: This can be done in one or more ways. The following are a few suggestions:
   a. A report presented by each group to the entire class
   b. A report done by the entire class working together
   c. An article for the class, school, district, or local newspaper
   d. An item in a weekly newsletter to parents
   e. A video of the experience
   f. A journal entry
   g. A letter to pen pal
   h. A report to the school principal, district curriculum director, superintendent, or school board member
   i. A poster for a hallway or other public display.

Language and Cognitive Processes:

observing
using space relationships
using numbers
measuring
predicting
inferring
interpreting results
formulating hypotheses
controlling variables
defining operations

Navarrete and Rivera (1983) developed a science-center-based curriculum for the Title I Migrant Enrichment Center (Albuquerque Public Schools) that incorporated similar science processes using dialogue to explore and investigate the students' world. Summaries of two sample lessons follow:

Lesson I: Rock Study

Purpose:
To examine rocks inside and out

Materials/Supplies:

    paper bags or boxes
    rocks
    hammer

Procedures:

1. Put a small stone in a bag or a box.
2. Hit it with a hammer.
3. Describe what happened. Here are some ideas:
    a. Compare the inside with the outside.
    b. What kind of crystals did you see?
    c. How did it break?
    d. Draw and describe what happened.

Language and Cognitive Processes:

    observing
    recording data
    measuring
    inferring
    formulating hypotheses
    defining operations

Lesson II: Magnetic Mystery

Purpose:
To demonstrate how magnetic properties of magnets are concentrated in two poles

Materials/Supplies:

    steel pins or nails
    magnets
    compass (optional)

Procedures:

1. Take two pins.
2. Magnetize only one pin. (Remember to stroke it on the magnet in one direction.)
3. Test your pin to be sure it is a magnet. It should lift or at least move the other pin.
4. Mix the two pins (they can touch), but don't let them rub against each other.

5. Now, using only the two pins, find out which one is the magnet.
6. Draw conclusions and explain the results.

Optional Activity for Reinforcement of Concepts:

1. Select either pin; let's call it pin A.
2. Touch its point to the end of the other pin B and lift.
3. Whether A or B is the magnet, B will be lifted.
4. Gradually move pin A toward the center of pin B.
5. When the center is reached, either A will attract B or it won't.
6. If A attracts B, A is the magnet.
7. If A doesn't attract B, B is the magnet.
8. Describe and draw what happened.

Language and Cognitive Processes:

observing
describing
changing variables
predicting
inferring
formulating hypotheses
defining operations

The preceding examples of activities integrating science and language can be accomplished in cooperative groups. In discussions of the results it is very important to include both successes and failures. Scientists learn from mistakes and unsuccessful tries. Students will come to understand that they can take risks and that trying is valued. The product (a package) is not as important as the process (designing and constructing).

Another effective strategy for organizing the classroom to give students opportunities to work with one another is to use science learning centers. The three activities described before can easily be adapted as learning centers. When using cooperative learning, the class is divided into groups and all the groups work on the same activity during the same period. Science learning centers can be set up in several ways, either for individual or small-group work. Some teachers create centers for the various content areas and have them placed around the periphery of the classroom. After students finish assigned seat-work or other tasks, they have the opportunity to work at a center of their choice. Others set up the centers, and all the students work at them at specific times in the school day with the students assigned to the various centers on a rotating basis. Many hands-on science activities such as those described can easily be adapted for centers.

Another way to organize centers effectively is to focus on various themes. Like the other activities discussed thus far, the development of language and science concepts can be integrated productively through thematic units. One example of thematic teaching is the Integrated Language Teaching Model, proposed by Enright and McCloskey (1988). At the core of this model are the following five goals for second language learners: joy, community, access, literacy, and power. These goals are applicable not only within the settings of ESL and sheltered classrooms but also in mainstream science classrooms. It is important for all students, and ESL students in particular, to belong to a learning community using real, authentic, and purposeful language.

Several steps are followed in carrying out a thematic unit.[3] The first step is having the students choose a theme based on their interests (dinosaurs or outer space, for example) as the focus of study for a period of time (one day to several weeks). Sometimes the theme comes spontaneously when a particular topic that generates a lot of interest and curiosity comes up.

The next stage is planning for the theme, which begins by using the class "corporate" brain to brainstorm ideas. One strategy to use here is webbing. The theme is written in the middle of the chalkboard, and as the students generate ideas about the theme, the ideas are arranged around the theme. It is important at this stage not to make value judgments about ideas but to include them all. It is also possible to cluster similar ideas together later, forming web-like structures around the theme at the center (see Figure 21.1). Another strategy is to brainstorm two basic questions about the theme: What do we know? What do we want to learn? (See Table 21.1.) These questions can be written on large sheets of butcher paper and displayed in the classroom. The chart can be changed as questions are answered or new ones generated. If there is adequate space in the classroom, the sheets of paper can become a record of what the students have studied.

It is important for the teacher to determine the objectives of the unit with the help of the students. During this step, more brainstorming can be done by the teacher and the class or by the planning committee representing the class. Once decisions are made, the goals can be displayed in the room.

After the goals are set, the next step is to decide which learning activities and materials to use. Teachers usually have materials and resources available or know where to find them. However, it is important that the students be included in this stage also. For example, some students can go to the library to help the librarian find materials for the class reading corner. Some may write to community members, inviting them to participate. Some students can help the teacher to select materials from his or her professional resources. The planning stages can be as creative and rich as the thematic unit itself.

Once the planning is finished, the students and teacher participate in the unit activities. It is important that during the unit and at the conclusion of

---

[3] *Learning and Loving It* by Gamberg, Kwak, Hutchings, and Altheim (1988) is an excellent resource for learning about setting up thematic units.

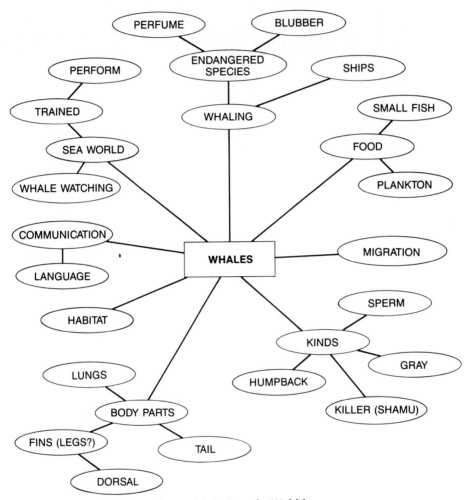

Figure 21.1. *Sample Webbing*

the unit time be set aside for evaluation, not only of what students have learned but of the thematic unit itself. This is another activity in which the students will want to participate fully. They may have insights into what worked and what did not work, which activities were appropriate and which ones were not. This input will help the teacher to revise the unit for future use.

A short description of the science centers used with third- to fifth-graders at Lowell Elementary School in Albuquerque, New Mexico follows the chart on the next page. While studying about the human body, students expressed interest in learning more about the heart. This led to a two-week theme about the heart that included the six centers described.

TABLE 21.1. SAMPLE BRAINSTORMING CHART

What Do We Know?	What Do We Want to Learn?
1. Whales are mammals.	1. What do they eat?
2. They are the largest animals.	2. Why are they hunted?
3. They live in oceans.	3. Where do they live?
4. There are different kinds: humpback, gray, killer.	4. Why do they migrate?
5. They are endangered.	5. Why is a killer whale called a killer whale?
6. They migrate every year.	6. How do they talk?
7. They sometimes beach themselves.	7. Why do they live in the sea?
8. They sing.	8. Are they carnivores?
9. They eat little fish.	9. How big are they when born? When fully grown?
10. They breathe through an airhole.	10. How are whales trained?
11. They can do tricks.	11. How do they know where to go when they migrate?
12. They are sometimes dangerous.	12. How long can they stay under water?
13. They like cold water.	

1. *Listening Center:* The students read a book while listening to it being read aloud on a tape. The book included several illustrations and descriptions of ways to take a pulse and using pulse points. After reading and listening to the tape, the students were asked to find a friend's pulse as described in the book and then record the results.
2. *Pulse Rate Center:* Using stethoscopes, the students recorded their friends's heartbeat in three situations: after standing, after hopping, and after jogging. They then recorded and compared the results.
3. *Model Center:* Using a large plastic model of the human trunk, the students worked together to identify the heart and its main parts, taking the model apart and putting it back together.
4. *Pumping Heart Center:* At the sink, the students cupped their hands together in a basin of water and squeezed them together to find out how the heart pumped blood.
5. *Circulation Center, Part A:* The students read a short passage about how blood circulates. Then they colored a diagram illustrating the process.
6. *Circulation Center, Part B:* The students followed the blood's path through the body by walking through a large chart of the circulatory system that had been placed on the floor. It included a large heart, veins, and arteries.

It was exciting to watch how involved the students were in the activities and the amount of language they used in their subsequent dialoguing. They discussed their work and the tasks they had to do. They negotiated meaning to understand their work. They had to get information and share it with one another. They often asked the adults in the room for clarification or other help. Probably the most exciting dialogue occurred outside our classroom. The students were so thrilled about what they were doing that they shared it with their other classmates, often teaching their peers or bringing them to the science centers to show what they were doing.

Even though these activities were originally intended for younger students, older ones can enjoy them as well in a low-anxiety environment. In some cases, older students have lost their self-confidence and feel they cannot succeed. They need to be part of the learning community again by becoming actively involved in their own learning.

One of the challenges facing a teacher with second language learners is that their cognitive development may be more advanced than their language development. To help meet this challenge, an environment should be established within the science classroom that invites language development through exploration of scientific concepts. Multiple resources can be made available so that the assigned textbook becomes one of many sources of information, rather than the focal point of all learning. For example, in a biology lab, charts and graphs as well as other records of student work either completed or in progress can be displayed. Forms for collecting data can be located near the animals and plants to invite student response. A wide variety of materials and resources for completing projects can be made available to students.[4]

Many activities such as those described earlier can be adapted to give older students a greater challenge. The egg drop experiment, for example, can be used at several age levels. A version for older students follows:

The Egg Drop Experiment

Purpose:
To design and make a protective package to prevent an egg from breaking when dropped from the roof of a one-story building.

Materials/Supplies:
> one raw egg
> packaging material
> adhesive

Procedures:
1. Brainstorming: Discuss how packages protect contents when shipping, and the different types of packaging used. Collect, examine, and discuss various kinds of packaging materials. Discuss the purpose and procedures of the experiment.

---

[4] An excellent resource is *Whole Language Strategies for Secondary Students* by Gilles, Bixby, Crowley, Crenshaw, Henrichs, Reynolds and Pyle (1988).

2. Group work: After being assigned to their cooperative group, the students will gather materials, plan, and construct several packages. They will design an experiment to test and select a prototype and then build a container to test.
3. Drop site: One member of each group will drop the group's egg, in exactly the same way as the other group representatives do. The recorders take note of the results.
4. Results: After the testing is finished, each group will design a technique to present their experiment to the other groups. After deciding how to do this, they will create their presentation and share it with the others.

Language and Cognitive Processes:

measuring
predicting
analyzing data
hypothesis testing
controlling variables
experimenting
sharing information
researching

CONCLUSION

There are a number of reasons why hands-on discovery science can enhance language development of students in general and ESL students in particular. It is a productive way to build a community of learners who are actively involved in the learning process. By starting with concepts that students already know about and by building on their natural curiosity about their world, anxiety is lowered and students will be willing to take risks in order to communicate and use language in purposeful ways. This approach ensures that all students experience and use language in a variety of ways, from the concrete, contextualized language used in taking part in an experiment to the more abstract, decontextualized write-up of the results. In short, the science classroom provides an ideal learning environment for the mastery of content and development of language skills.

RECOMMENDED RESOURCES

There are many books for teachers and students interested in discovery science. The following are particular favorites:

Allen, H. (1979). *Elementary science activities for every month of the year.* West Nyack, NY: Parker. Contains activities for each month of the school year based on featured processes for each month: observation in October and hypothesis testing in February, for example.

Blocksma, M., & Blocksma, D. (1983). *Easy-to-make spaceships that really fly.* Englewood Cliffs, NJ: Prentice Hall. After learning how to make a basic "zinger" with paper plates, students can design and fly their own spaceships.

Falk, J. (Project Director). (1988). *More science activities.* New York: Galison Books. This resource from the Smithsonian Institution has many activities for students using materials found around home.

Herbert, D. (1980). *Mr. Wizard's supermarket science.* New York: Random House. This book is full of activities and experiments using ingredients available in anyone's kitchen. It is surprising to see how many things can be done with vinegar, baking soda, and water.

Poppe, C. A., & VanMatre, N. A. (1985). *Science learning centers for the primary grades.* West Nyack, NY: The Center for Applied Research in Education. A good resource for teachers who want to use centers but aren't sure how to begin. It contains units on the five senses, the human body, space, plants, and dinosaurs.

Zubrowski, B. (1981). *Drinking straw construction.* Boston: Little, Brown. This book contains many projects for students to complete using plastic straws such as building models of houses and testing their strength.

Several student magazines can be used effectively:

National Geographic World

Ranger Rick

Your Big Backyard

Odyssey

3-2-1-Contact

Science Weekly

Zoo Books

NatureScope

Project Wild has excellent training and teaching materials about wildlife, conservation, and ecology. Information can be obtained from any state Fish and Wildlife Agency, or the Western Association of Fish and Wildlife Agencies can be contacted.

AIMS (Activities Integrating Math and Science) has many wonderful activities for science. There is also an excellent newsletter. For more information write to:

AIMS Educational Foundation
P.O. Box 7766
Fresno, CA 93747

Yet another resource is the National Science Teachers Association (NSTA). Their address is:

NSTA
1742 Connecticut Ave. NW
Washington, DC 20009

FOLLOW-UP QUESTIONS AND ACTIVITIES

1. How can science classrooms be particularly conducive to language development according to Rupp? Briefly describe several ideas of your own for promoting such development through the medium of science.

2. Rupp refers to the four types of reaction dialogues identified by Richard-Amato (1989). In what way might these fit in with Freire's (1970) notion that teachers and students should be partners in the learning process? Explain. Can you think of one or two specific activities that might serve as examples of each type for your own classroom situation?

3. How might you include your students in unit and activity evaluation? Why does Rupp feel that it is important to discuss during evaluations both successful and failed attempts to complete experiments? Are there additional reasons for having such discussions?

4. Describe learning centers you might set up in your classroom for a specified unit. Include in your description a summary of the unit, the group for which it is intended, how the specific objectives will be determined, the procedures you will follow, and the expected outcomes. To what extent will you involve your students in the planning process? Share your ideas with a small group for their feedback.

22

Integrating Mathematics and Language Learning

THERESA CORASANITI DALE   *Baltimore City Public Schools*

GILBERTO J. CUEVAS   *University of Miami*

EDITORS' INTRODUCTION

The importance of language in mathematics instruction is often downplayed in the belief that mathematics is somehow independent of language proficiency. In this chapter Theresa Dale and Gilberto Cuevas convincingly demonstrate that this belief is a myth. In their discussion, they address three major areas: the nature of the language used in mathematics, the role language plays in the mathematics context, and instructional strategies and activities that promote both mathematics and language skills.

Picture a seventh- or eighth-grade classroom in which about half the students are nonnative English speakers with varying degrees of English proficiency. The teacher is about to present a mathematics lesson dealing with the properties of equality. She begins by writing the following on the blackboard:

$$(6 + 5) + 4 \ \square \ 6 + (5 + 4)$$

She points to the number sentence on each side of the empty square and asks the class: "Are they equal?" An English-proficient student answers: "Yes, they are." The discussion continues:

TEACHER: *(pointing to a limited English proficient [LEP] student)* How do you know?
LEP STUDENT: They equal.
TEACHER: Yes, we know. But, tell me, why are they equal?
LEP STUDENT: It is equal.

From Dale/Cuevas, *"Integrating Language and Mathematics Learning,"* in *ESL THROUGH CONTENT-AREA INSTRUCTION; Mathematics, Science, Social Studies*, JoAnn Crandall, ed., 1987, pp. 9–54. Adapted by permission of Prentice Hall, Inc., Englewood Cliffs, NJ.

TEACHER: Okay. They are equal because both number sentences have the same sum. Now, what symbol can we write in the empty square?

NATIVE ENGLISH-SPEAKING STUDENT: Equal sign!

TEACHER: Right! Very good! *(now pointng to an LEP student)* Please write the equal sign inside the square.

LEP STUDENT: *(Obviously not quite sure of what it is she is supposed to do, she goes to the board and writes the answer to each number sentence.)*

TEACHER: Good! Tell me what symbol do we write in the *square* to say that this side *(pointing)* is *equal* to this side?

LEP STUDENT: *(Appears embarrassed, lowers her head and does not answer.)*

After class, the teacher wonders how to reach LEP students like the one in this scene. She knows these students are intelligent and eager to learn, but she feels frustrated because she cannot get them to express the mathematical knowledge she thinks they know. Her concern is compounded when she tries to devise ways to teach LEP students whose knowledge of mathematics is also weak.

This is just one illustration of the fact that teaching involves frequent communication between teacher and students. When the dialogue is conducted in a language unfamiliar to the students, difficulties are likely to arise. Morris (1975) describes the nature of the problem:

> The problems of teaching in a second language are accentuated when mathematics is the context of the dialog. This is due essentially to the abstract nature of mathematics and the difficulties which arise in absorbing abstract concepts. Also, the language used has to be precise, consistent, and unambiguous, if mathematical ideas are to be explored and described effectively. And for dialog to become possible, the child must be equipped with a basic repertoire of linguistic concepts and structures. (p. 52)

Morris's statement underscores the importance of teaching the "special" language skills required for mathematics learning. Mastering "mathematics language" skills is essential for all students, but it is particularly crucial for students learning mathematics in their second language. This chapter discusses the integration of mathematics and language skills. The following topics will be addressed:

The nature of the language used in mathematics, including some of the features that may be problematic for LEP students.

A brief overview of the role language plays in the context of teaching and learning mathematics, with special emphasis on learning mathematics through a second language.

Suggestions for practical instructional strategies and activities for promoting mathematics and English language skills development with LEP students in the mathematics classroom.

THE LANGUAGE OF MATHEMATICS

What is meant by the language of mathematics? How is it different from the language used for everyday communication tasks? The English language represents a universe of language skills, and certain areas of language are used for specific purposes. Natural language, the language used in everyday communication, is one of the components, or subsets, of this universe. The language used to discuss computer technology and that used for scientific topics are two other subsets. Linguistically, these subsets of language are referred to as *registers*.

The language register for mathematics is composed of meanings appropriate to the communication of mathematical ideas together with the terms or vocabulary used in expressing these ideas and the structures or sentences in which these terms appear (Halliday, 1975). Like other registers or styles of English, the mathematics register includes unique vocabulary, syntax (sentence structure), semantic properties (truth conditions), and discourse (text) features.

Vocabulary

Mathematics vocabulary includes words that are specific to mathematics, such as *divisor, denominator, quotient,* and *coefficient.* These words are new to most students. However, the mathematics register also includes natural language, everyday vocabulary that takes on a different meaning in mathematics. These words, such as *equal, rational, irrational, column,* and *table,* must be relearned, this time in a mathematics context, since they have a different meaning in mathematics.

In addition to isolated vocabulary items, the mathematics register uses its special vocabulary to create complex strings of words or phrases. In these phrases, often two or more mathematical concepts combine to form a new concept, compounding the task of comprehending the words. The phrases, *least common multiple, negative exponent,* and even an apparently simple phrase such as *a quarter of the apples,* are good examples showing the complexity of mathematical terms.

A subtler and much more difficult aspect of mathematics vocabulary involves the many ways in which the same mathematics operation can be signaled. As students progress through the hierarchy of mathematics skills, manipulation of this vocabulary becomes crucial for understanding the teacher's explanations in class and for solving word problems. Crandall, Dale, Rhodes, and Spanos (1985) have identified groups of lexical items in beginning algebra that indicate certain operations. For example, students must know that addition can be signaled by any of these words:

add	and
plus	sum
combine	increased by

Similarly, subtraction can be signaled by these words:

subtract from   minus
decreased by   differ
less   less than
take away *(a less sophisticated term
 commonly used by children)*

It is important to remember that when talking about the vocabulary of the mathematics language register (or any register), the meanings of the terms are related to the context in which they are used. Hence, it is not enough for students to learn lists of words. They must learn what they mean in a particular mathematical expression. For example, students are taught early in their mathematics education that the word *by* signals multiplication as in the expression *3 multiplied by 10*. However, they later encounter algebraic expressions such as *a number increased by 10* and discover (sometimes the hard way!) that *by* in this case is part of an expression that signals addition. In fact, prepositions in general and the relationships they indicate are critical lexical items in the mathematics register that can cause a great deal of confusion. Another example is *divided by* as opposed to *divided into* (Crandall, Dale, Rhodes & Spanos, 1985, p. 11).

In addition to words and phrases particular to the mathematics register, some examples of which have been given, there is also the set of mathematical symbols used in expressing mathematical concepts and processes. These items are automatically associated with the symbolic language of mathematics. As symbols that stand for a particular meaning in mathematics, they can be thought of as mathematics vocabulary. The symbols used for operations (adding, dividing, etc.) are the most commonly known. As students move through the mathematics curriculum, the number of symbols used increases, and their meanings become more conceptually dense. Students must learn to relate symbols such as $>$, $<$, and parentheses and brackets to mathematics concepts or processes (usually themselves couched in mathematics language) and then translate these into everyday language in order to express the mathematical ideas embedded in the symbols.

It is important to remember when discussing mathematical symbols that some symbols play different roles in different countries. In a number of countries, for example, a comma is used to separate whole numbers from decimal parts—the function of the decimal point in the United States, while the decimal point is used as the comma is in the United States—to separate hundreds from thousands, hundred thousands from millions, and so on.

Syntax

The mathematics language register includes, as all registers do, special syntactic structures and special styles of presentation. Knight and Hargis (1977) point out that since mathematics is a study of relationships, comparative structures are an essential and recurring part of mathematics language. They are difficult structures for many students to master. The following are some examples:

greater than/less than	as in	all numbers greater than 4
n times as much	as in	Hilda earns six times as much as I do. Hilda earns \$40,000. How much do I earn?
as . . . as	as in	Wendy is as old as Miguel.
-er than	as in	Miguel is three years older than Frank. Frank is 25. How old is Wendy?

Munro (1979) cites a number of other frequently used structures in mathematics that are also potentially confusing. They include the following structures with examples taken from Crandall, Dale, Rhodes, and Spanos (1985):

numbers used as nouns (rather than adjectives)	as in	Twenty is five times a certain number. What is the number?
prepositions	as in	eight divided *by* four and eight *into* four
	as in	two multiplied *by* itself two times (multiplication) and x exceeds two *by* seven
passive voice	as in	ten *(is) divided by* two.
or,	as in	x *is defined* to be equal to zero.
or,	as in	When 15 *is added* to a number, the result is 21. Find the number.

One of the principal characteristics of the syntax used in a mathematical expression is the lack of one-to-one correspondence between mathematical symbols and the words they represent. For example, if the expression *eight divided by* 2 is translated word-for-word in the order in which it is written, the resulting mathematical expression $8\sqrt{2}$ would be incorrect. The correct expression is $2\sqrt{8}$. Similarly, to correctly translate the expression, *the square of the quotient of a and b,* students must know that the first part of the expression, *the square of,* is translated last and that the phrase starting with *quotient* requires the use of parentheses to signal the squaring of the entire quotient. The correct mathematical expression in this case is $(a/b)^2$.

This lack of one-to-one correspondence poses considerable difficulty for students, particularly LEP students, who tend to read and write mathematical sentences (presented either in symbols or in words or both) in the same manner in which they read and write standard orthography (Kessler, Quinn & Hayes, 1985). Understanding that there is no one-to-one correspondence between mathematics symbols and their English translations becomes crucial for students who are attempting to make progress through the hierarchy of mathematical concepts. In their work with LEP high school and college students in basic algebra classes, Crandall, Dale, Rhodes, and Spanos (1985) have documented recurring errors in translations of the language of word problems into solution equations. They found that students tend to duplicate the surface syntax of the problem statements in their algebraic restatements. For example, students often incorrectly translated the sentence, *The number a is five less than the number b* as $a = 5 - b$, when the correct translation should be: $a = b - 5$.

Another major characteristic of the syntax of the language of mathematics is its frequent use of logical connectors. Dawe's (1983) study of LEP students showed that the correct use of logical connectors was the one factor that differentiated those students who could reason mathematically in English from those who could not. The results were consistent for both LEP and native English speakers.

Logical connectors are one linguistic device mathematics texts use to develop and link abstract ideas and concepts. Some of these connectors include *if . . . then, if and only if, because, that is, for example, such that, but, consequently,* and *either . . . or.* As Kessler, Quinn, and Hayes (1985) point out:

> Logical connectors are words or phrases which carry out the function of marking a logical relationship between two or more basic linguistic structures. Primarily, logical connectors serve a semantic, cohesive function indicating the nature of the relationship between parts of a text. (p. 14)

When students read mathematics texts, they must be able to recognize logical connectors and the situations in which they appear. They must know which situation is signaled—similarity, contradiction, cause and effect or reason and result, chronological or logical sequence (Celce-Murcia & Larsen-Freeman, 1983). On the level of syntax, they have to know where logical connectors appear in a sentence (at the beginning, middle, or end of a clause), and they must be aware that some connectors can appear in only one position, while others can appear in two or all three positions, and that change in position can signal a change in meaning.

Examples abound in algebra texts of logical connectors used in definitions and to characterize properties—concepts that students must understand and apply in order to solve algebraic problems. These connectors most often appear in complex statements using both words and symbols, as in the following examples from Dolciani & Wooton (1970, p. 77).

> In a beginning algebra text, the *Axiom of Opposites* is stated as:
> For every real number a there is a unique real number $-a$, such that $a + (-a) = 0$ and $(-a) + a = 0$.
> The text then offers the following elaboration of the axiom:
>
> 1. If a is a positive number, then $-a$ is a negative number; if a is a negative number, then $-a$ is a positive number; if a is 0, then $-a$ is 0.
> 2. The opposite of $-a$ is a; that is, $- (-a) = a$.

It is not hard to imagine native English-speaking students having difficulty piecing together the logical statements in this section of text. Clearly, LEP students might have even more difficulty with it.

This complex example is taken from a level of mathematics that most students generally do not face until they are at least in junior high school. It is important to note that LEP students' ability to manipulate logical connectors appears to be tied into a developmental sequence. It is very possible that younger LEP students categorically have more problems with logical connectors than older students (Piaget, 1926; Tritch, 1984, as quoted in Kessler, Quinn, & Hayes, 1985). Younger students often seem mystified by the use of logical connectors such as *if* in relatively simple word problems. Some students may, for example, have considerable difficulty solving the following problem stated using a hypothetical situation signaled by *if:*

> If Frank can type one page in 20 minutes, how much time will it take him to type two pages?

However, the same students may be able to solve the problem when it is stated using a declarative sentence, as in:

> Frank types one page in 20 minutes. How much time does it take him to type two pages?

Semantics

The preceding discusssion shows that correctly manipulating the special vocabulary and phrases and the word order found in mathematics language is intricately tied to students' ability to infer the correct mathematical meaning from the language. Making inferences in mathematics language often depends on the language user's knowledge of how reference is indicated. In algebra, for example, the correct solution of a word problem often hinges on the ability to identify key words and to determine the other words in the problem to which the key words are linked (i.e., knowing how to determine the referents of key words). Problems involving *the number, a number,* and the like require such inferencing. For example:

> Five times a number is two more than ten times the number.
>   To solve this problem, students must realize that *a number* and *the number* refer to the same quantity.
>   The sum of two numbers is 77. If the first number is 10 times the other, find the number.

In this problem, students must know that they are dealing with two numbers. Furthermore, they must know that the way reference is used in the problem links each number with information about it, so that *the first number* and the information given about it refer to one of those numbers; and *the other* refers to the second of the two numbers, *the number* whose value the problem asks the student to find. Finally, students must know that the translation from the words of the problem into the symbolic representation of the solution equation will be based on only one variable and that each of the two numbers will be expressed in terms of that one variable. Given all this, the correct translation and solution of this problem would be:

Phrase	*Symbolic Translation*
first number	$10x$
second number	x
sum	77

Therefore, on the basis of information from the problem:

$$11x = 77 \text{ and}$$
$$x = 7$$

A common mistake is for students to write solution equations with two *different* variables. Not surprisingly, because they see no relationship between the two equations, they cannot solve the problem.

These examples point out another reference feature of the language of mathematics, specifically to the language of algebra: the referents of variables. Identifying variables' referents is essential to correctly translating the words of a problem into the symbols of its solution equation and vice versa. Variables stand for the *number* of persons or things, *not* the persons or things themselves. The following classic word problem illustrates this point:

> There are five times as many students as professors in the mathematics department. Write an equation that represents this statement.

Many students typically write the incorrect equation $5s = p$, which follows the literal word order of the natural language sentence and uses s to represent "students" and p to represent "professors." The correct equation is $5p = s$, which can be determined only if students know that the variable s (or any other variable they choose to use) must represent the *number* of students and that the variable p must represent the *number* of professors. This kind of "reversal error" has been the subject of investigation by a number of researchers interested in the language of mathematics, including Clement (1981) and Mestre, Gerace, & Lockhead (1982). Firsching (1982) points out that recurring reversal errors could result from students' previous repeated exposure in beginning-level mathematics to word problems that feature a one-to-one correspondence between words and symbol. Experienced with such word problems, they incorrectly expect that all problems can be solved in the same manner.

Discourse Features

On a level above vocabulary and syntax, known in linguistics as the *discourse* level, mathematics language also has distinctive characteristics. Loosely defined, mathematics discourse refers to the "chunks" of language—sentences or groups of sentences or paragraphs—that function together as *textual units, each* with a specific meaning and purpose in mathematics. The definition of the communicative property of addition or the explanation of this property in a mathematics textbook are examples of mathematics discourse or "texts." Any word problem is an example of a specialized type of mathematics discourse or text.

All the lexical, syntactic, and semantic features of mathematics language discussed earlier can be considered discourse features of a mathematics text. But instead of looking at isolated features from the "bottom up," discourse views how all the distinctive features of a mathematics text work from the "top down" to form a cohesive, coherent unit that communicates a particular mathematics meaning. This meaning is expressed not as a result of the simple sum of all its lexical, syntactic, and semantic features but rather as something above and beyond these features. To understand a unit of mathematical discourse, students must not only be proficient in mathematics language; they must also have a background in mathematics in order to construct the context needed to process cognitively complex information. At the discourse level, the integration of language and mathematics skills is essential for total comprehension.

Mathematics discourse, especially written discourse, presents considerable difficulties for many students, native English speakers as well as LEP students. Unlike natural language, mathematics texts lack redundancy or paraphrase. Bye (1975) has enumerated a number of additional characteristics of mathematical discourse found in the language of mathematics textbooks. According to his analysis, written mathematics texts:

> Are conceptually packed.
> Have high density.
> Require up-and-down as well as left-to-right eye movements.
> Require a reading rate adjustment because they must be read more slowly than natural language texts.
> Require multiple readings.
> Use numerous symbolic devices such as charts and graphs.
> Contain a great deal of technical language with precise meaning. (p. 3)

These language features, when combined with the mathematics content of the written text, require the student to apply mathematics concepts, procedures, and applications they have already learned. (Students with a weak mathematics background as well as poor language skills are doubly handicapped here.) The student must also recognize *which* previously learned mathematics concepts, procedures, or applications must be applied to the text at hand. In addition, the student must have had enough experience with mathematics texts to know when everyday background knowledge should be applied to the reading comprehension process and when it must be suspended. Finally, the student must be familiar with (have had experience with) the processes involved in mathematical thinking.

Mathematical word problems provide some of the more cogent examples of mathematics discourse features at work, along with illustrations of the difficulties these features present to LEP students, who are for the most part unfamiliar with mathematics discourse in English (and sometimes in any language).

Kessler, Quinn, and Hayes (1985) offer the example of the following word problem, which many of their second-grade LEP students could not solve correctly:

> Sue has 32 cards. She gave Jim 15 cards. How many cards does Sue have?

The authors report that many students responded with 15 rather than 17. They theorize that these students may not have been familiar with the representative function of word problems, by which they would have perceived that having 32 cards and giving 15 of them away represents or sets up a mathematics situation, not the beginning of a narrative or story.

It could be argued that the language of this problem is unclear and ambiguous. Sophisticated problem solvers have learned how to deal with such ambiguity because they know that the function of the language of word problems is to direct them toward a mathematical solution. They suspend the natural tendency to demand details that they might normally require for reading narrative texts. Consider the following problem, for example:

> Food expenses take 26 percent of the average family's income. A family makes $700 a month. How much is spent on food?

Students who can solve this problem generally are not bothered by the fact that the problem does not specify directly the amount that is being asked for, that is, what is the amount per month? the amount per year? Since one time reference occurs in the problem—*a month*—students who know how word problems work infer that they must find the amount spent per month. Students who are not proficient in the language of word problems probably would demand a paraphrase or repetition of the time reference to clarify the problem question. It is clear that LEP students, often literal readers at the early stages of their English development, would have grave difficulties with word problem texts such as this one.

It appears that good problem solvers are the students who can discover the discourse properties of word problems that provide them with both a real-world context and a mathematics context in which to approach the problem. Further, Kessler, Quinn, and Hayes (1985) point out that proficient problem solvers "make use of language for thinking purposes in a real world context" (p. 18). Students need to acquire the skills to integrate complex linguistic and mathematical processes in order to be good problem solvers.

LEARNING MATHEMATICS
THROUGH A SECOND LANGUAGE

In school, students must use language, written and spoken, to express their thoughts and to demonstrate their understanding and mastery of academic tasks. Simply put, language is the vehicle of learning and instruction. As

Cummins (1981) has theorized, the language used for academic tasks is quite different from the language used for basic communication. (See Chapter 2 for further discussion.)

Cummins argues that Cognitive Academic Language Proficiency (CALP) is cross-lingual, that is, students can acquire CALP, part of what he calls ''a common underlying proficiency,'' via any language as long as they have reached a certain level or threshold of proficiency in the language. Once acquired, CALP can be accessed and used via any language, again once the threshold level of proficiency in the language has been reached.

The concept of threshold in Cummins's model may have important implications for LEP students faced with the task of learning mathematics and other academic subjects. If LEP students already possess a threshold proficiency in CALP (in mathematics, for example, learned through their first language), they have a basis on which to develop CALP for mathematics through their second language. Hence their chances to succeed in academic tasks, in this case mathematics tasks, are enhanced, given enough time and motivation to learn their second language.

However, it may be the case that LEP students who have little or no CALP in their first language will have considerable difficulty developing CALP through their second language. Although it is not explicitly stated by Cummins, their difficulties may have to do not only with learning L2 skills but also with learning the cognitive, academic content expressed through the second language. Thus the threshold that LEP students must reach is both a certain minimal level of language skills and a certain minimal knowledge of the academic area.

Dawe's work (1983, 1984) with bilingual students in mathematical reasoning appears to agree with research conducted by Mestre, Gerace, and Lockhead (1982) with Hispanic engineering students in college algebra courses. These researchers report that Hispanic students were much more likely than non-minority students to misinterpret word problems in English and that slower reading speed and comprehension contributed significantly to a greater number of problems not being completed (and consequently ''missed'') in the word problem tests they administered. Mestre (1984) recommends that problem-solving instruction for Hispanics (and other LEP students) should therefore include extensive practice emphasizing speed and accuracy in translating the language of word problems into mathematical notation. He argues that LEP students who are given a chance to grapple with problems that demand considerable linguistic processing would learn how to get information from a problem and set it up correctly.

In summary, the role of language in learning is not yet clear, although it is likely that its role is crucial in the following ways:

1. There appears to be a high correlation between reading skills and mathematics achievement, particularly when the tasks involve reading

texts or solving word problems. Preliminary research evidence appears to indicate that this correlation may be even stronger for LEP students performing tasks in their second language.

2. On a deeper level, language works as a mediator for mathematical thinking and metacognition. Whether the thinking defines the language or the language defines the thinking remains to be answered. Probably both occur. The important point is that mathematical thinking, mediated by linguistic processes, is a prerequisite for mathematics achievement.

3. LEP students who must learn mathematics through their second language must reach a minimal level (Cummins's threshold) of proficiency in the cognitive, academic skills required of mathematics and in the language skills used to express the mathematical skills.

4. The language used in mathematics is intricately connected to the mathematical concepts, processes, and applications it expresses. Therefore, mathematics instruction, particularly for LEP students learning in their second language, should integrate mathematics and language skills.

LEARNING A SECOND LANGUAGE THROUGH MATHEMATICS

Another aspect of the relationship between language and mathematics is critical for LEP students. Mathematics instruction for LEP students can be a source of opportunities to acquire and learn English, their second language. In other words, mathematics can be a language learning experience in both the mathematics and the language class.

Recent research and practical experience appear to suggest that the forms, functions, and uses of language can be best acquired and learned in context. Second language acquisition theory, notably that of Krashen (1982), points to the importance of context to provide language experiences, or input, that students can comprehend. It seems obvious that the language input students need most in school must come from experiences in their academic subject courses.

Traditionally, mathematics has not been one of the subject areas educators use to provide L2 experiences and practice for LEP students. It is possible that the myth that mathematics requires minimal language proficiency may have kept mathematics from being a logical choice as the academic content base of L2 activities. Perhaps the fact that many language teachers feel unprepared and reluctant to get involved with any topic related to mathematics has also affected the ''popularity'' of choosing mathematics content.

It is essential, however, that the classroom environment in which language is taught through mathematics content be carefully structured so that L2 acquisition can occur. For both the language and the mathematics classroom, this means that instructional activities should promote L2 development through a natural, subconscious process in which the focus is not on language per se but on *communicating* the concepts, processes, and applications of mathematics.

Mohan (1986) points out that an instructional environment that promotes L2 (and L1) development must be carefully structured to provide students with a range of opportunities to communicate subject matter. His general framework for teaching language and content suggests that activities based on mathematics content make use of graphics, manipulatives, and other hands-on concrete experiences that clarify and reinforce meanings in mathematics communicated through language.

It is not enough, however, to include instructional activities that provide linguistic and nonlinguistic enforcement for communicating mathematical ideas. As with any instruction, teachers must constantly monitor their students for comprehension, which may require special attention in mathematics given the cognitive complexity of many mathematics tasks and the tendency for mathematics to be a silent, individual activity (Cazden, 1979). Teachers therefore need to provide both quality input tailored to the language and mathematics levels of their students *and* ample opportunity for students to respond (i.e., *talk*), again commensurate with their level of language and mathematics proficiency. Given the cognitive demands of mathematics tasks, teachers must also provide students with extensive and varied experiences in which to apply the mathematical thinking techniques and the metacognitive behaviors (i.e., the self-monitoring of mathematical processes) they will need to develop to be mathematics achievers.

Whenever possible, instructional activities in the mathematics classroom should be built on students' real-life experiences and prior knowledge of mathematics, and offer situations in which students can interact with the teacher and fellow students (both LEP and English-speaking). Such activities stimulate both L2 acquisition and learning. Wilson, DeAvila, and Intili (1982) and DeAvila and Duncan (1984) have shown that when LEP students are provided with a classroom environment organized around interactive activities, they can acquire both mathematics and English simultaneously. DeAvila and Duncan's program provides hands-on experiments that foster critical thinking skills for mathematics and science. Because the activities naturally emphasize process, they lend themselves well to promoting verbal interaction. Similar evidence for the simultaneous development of language and mathematics and science can be found in studies by Kessler and Quinn (1980, 1984), Quinn and Kessler (1984), and Rodriguez and Bethel (1983).

Affective factors also play a crucial role in the language acquisition process described here. Many students, not just LEP students, decide for one reason or another that they "are not good in mathematics." For many LEP students faced with the formidable task of learning mathematics through a second language, mathematics instruction can be doubly traumatic. Mathematics teachers can do much to reduce the trauma by giving LEP students opportunities to experience success in mathematics through activities they can understand.

Positive experiences in mathematics build on themselves and can consequently lower anxiety in language learning. The result is that LEP students find themselves learning mathematics, while at the same time they are acquiring language skills used both in everyday communication and in the academic setting of mathematics.

Results from the work of Hayes and Bahruth (1985) and Hayes, Bahruth, and Kessler (1985) bear out this observation. These researchers report extraordinary progress in fifth-grade LEP students' English reading skills as a result of extensive experience in reading and writing their own mathematics word problems. Both studies emphasize that students' success was due not only to exposure to great quantities of interesting and relevant language input but also to the students' changes in attitudes toward school and learning.

INSTRUCTIONAL STRATEGIES

The background that teachers need in order to develop strategies and activities that integrate language and mathematics skills for LEP students has been presented in the previous sections. In this section, suggestions are given for the development of instructional activities in the mathematics classroom.

Language-Based Strategies for the Mathematics Classroom

The mathematics curriculum at any grade level is generally composed of four basic areas: concepts, computation, applications, and problem solving. For the purpose of illustrating the differences in language requirements that exist in these four basic mathematics areas, following are two short lessons:

Lesson 1: Statistics—The Concept of Mean

TEACHER: We have on the board two lists of numbers; let's say the numbers represent scores on tests. Add the scores in the first list or distribution; after you have obtained a sum, divide the total by the number of scores in the list. Let's see, first what is the total?

STUDENT 1: (Gives the correct total.)

TEACHER: Now, what is the result of the division?

STUDENT 2: (Gives the correct quotient.)

TEACHER: Repeat the same operation with the second list or distribution. (Answers are checked before proceeding.) Please tell me where in each distribution the final quotient is located. (Students locate the quotient or "average" on the board.)

TEACHER: Give me a word or expression that tells where this number is in the distribution of scores.

STUDENT 3: Middle.

STUDENT 4: Center.

STUDENT 5: The other scores are around this answer.

TEACHER: I see we pretty much agree that this result or quotient is somewhere in the center of each distribution. We call this number a *measure of central tendency*. We know that the calculations we did had to do with the average of each of the distributions. Can someone give me a definition of "average"? *(The students give a number of plausible definitions.)* In statistics, this average has a special name. It is called the *mean*.

Lesson 2: Statistics—The Computation of Standard Deviation

TEACHER: *(The students have previously been presented with the concept of standard deviation.)* Now we are ready to learn the sets involved in the computation of the standard deviation of the distribution.

First, subtract the mean of the distribution from each of the scores in the distribution.

Second, square each of these differences.

Third, add these squares.

Fourth, divide the sum of the squares by the number of scores in the distribution.

Fifth, take the square root of this quotient. *(The students have followed each of the steps and have responded with answers to each as the teacher developed the algorithm.)*

In analyzing these two sample lessons, mathematics teachers can readily distinguish the mathematics content: Lesson 1 deals with the development of a concept, in this case, the idea of arithmetic mean; Lesson 2 covers the presentation of the algorithm to compute the standard deviation. As for the language demands of the two lessons, teachers can observe a fairly clear difference in the "scripts" for each lesson. Generally, Lesson 1 contains a larger percentage of natural language, whereas Lesson 2 emphasizes the technical vocabulary and structures of the mathematics register. The nature of the mathematics content in each lesson defines the kind of language used to teach it. The introduction of a concept requires the teacher to communicate ideas in language familar to the students (i.e., through natural language) to facilitate comprehension. In the development of algorithmic procedures, the instructor assumes understanding of the concept and uses very technical language from the mathematics register to present the steps involved in the computation of the standard deviation.

Second Language Approach to Mathematics Skills (SLAMS)

Mathematics teachers can start with general observations on the language content of mathematics tasks (such as the ones just given) and from them develop an expanded mathematics/language approach for LEP students that includes a language component. Cuevas (1981, 1984) has developed such an approach called Second Language Approach to Mathematics Skills (SLAMS), which incorporates language development activities into the "regular" mathematics lessons planned by teachers. This approach was initially developed for grades K through 12 but can be applied to any level of mathematics instruction. It is based on the assumption that in order for a student to master the mathematics concepts presented in class, the language of the concepts must be addressed and mastered. It is also assumed that by teaching the language together with the content, understanding of the material will be facilitated (Cuevas, Mann & McClung, 1985).

The approach is composed of two strands, one focusing on mathematics content and the other emphasizing related language skills. The activities developed for each strand are based on identified instructional objectives from the mathematics curriculum.

The Content Strand

The content strand encompasses strategies for analysis and diagnosis of mathematics skills, followed by preventive or prescriptive activities. Since this approach follows a standard diagnostic-prescriptive model for teaching, its components are described only briefly here.

1. *Analysis of Concept/Skills:* This component deals with what needs to be taught, that is, the basic mathematics concepts and skills determined by the instructional objectives. At this point, the teacher may also wish to analyze prerequisite skills necessary for mastery of the objectives.
2. *Diagnosis:* This process encompasses assessment (formal and informal) of the level of skills mastery and/or the extent and nature of mathematical errors. Diagnosis must involve data-collection activities in which the teacher focuses on patterns of behavior. These patterns are essential for the instructional decisions made in the next components of the diagnostic-prescriptive process. As a result of the analysis of the instructional objective(s), the teacher needs to ask: "Does the student have the prerequisite skills necessary for mastery of the mathematics objective(s)?" For example, before teaching how to apply the basic arithmetic operations to problem situations dealing with money, the teacher needs to know to what degree the students have mastered the operation(s) they are being asked to use.

3. *Preventive Strategies:* This component addresses the activities designed to review or reinforce skills that are prerequisite to the mathematics objective(s) being taught.
4. *Lesson:* On the basis of the student's strengths and weaknesses, the teacher develops instructional activities designed to teach selected mathematics concepts or to develop certain skills. In constructing these activities, care should be taken to select from various approaches such as the use of manipulatives, small-group work, individual tasks, and tutorial sessions with other students as tutors.

As is common in a diagnostic-prescriptive approach, an assessment is made of the level of student mastery of the mathematics content presented in class. The cycle is then repeated or other activities are designed if remediation is necessary.

The Language Strand

The language strand of the SLAMS model follows a path parallel to the content strand. The components of the language strand include:

1. *Analysis of the Language Used:* For this component, teachers need to be aware that at least two languages are present in the mathematics curriculum: the objective language, or mathematics register, and the natural language. Vocabulary and other terms the teacher feels are important in the communication of ideas to the student must be identified. For example, in a word problem such as, "If Marta buys three pencils at $0.15 each, how much change will she receive from $1.00?" students need to determine which terms and what syntactic and other textual clues indicate the correct sequence of operations.
2. *Diagnosis of Language Skills:* On the basis of the language skills identified in the first component, the teacher must answer the following questions:
   a. Does the student recognize the symbols/terms that pertain to the skill?
   b. Can the student pronounce them? Write them?
   c. Can the student define the terms used?
   d. Is the student knowledgeable of the structures used so that ideas and relationships are understood?
3. *Preventive Language Strategies:* Many LEP students have received mathematics instruction in their native language and are proficient in the mathematics register of that language. Preventive language activities could focus on:
   a. A review of the mathematics content, presented this time in the students' native language.
   b. Structured language activities designed to increase the students' level of competence in the English-language skills needed to master the mathematics content in English.

4. *Lesson:* Instructional language activities for mathematics should involve listening comprehension, verbal production, and reading and writing of the language features identified by the teacher. *These activities must be incorporated as an integral part of the mathematics content lesson.*

The mathematics/language approach of SLAMS outlined here is recommended for mathematics teachers in general. The approach provides a framework for adapting activities the teacher needs to develop to focus on the language needs of LEP students. As can be seen in Figure 22.1, mathematics teachers must analyze each mathematical task into mathematics and language skills. Instructional activities that integrate both kinds of skills must then be devised for the prescriptive and evaluation phases of the approach.

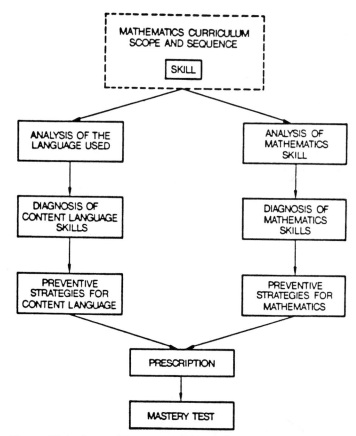

Figure 22.1. *Second Language Approach to Mathematics Skills (SLAMS) Instructional Model*

CLOSING REMARKS

This chapter has provided mathematics educators with background information and instructional strategies that address the educational needs of LEP students. To this end, a brief overview of the nature of the language used in mathematics was given, as well as the role language plays in mathematics teaching and learning. On the basis of this information, suggestions for the adaptation or development of instructional strategies that integrate mathematics and L2 learning in the mathematics classroom were illustrated. The underlying goal has been to assist teachers in the communication of mathematical content to students in order to develop mathematical and L2 skills.

FOLLOW-UP QUESTIONS AND ACTIVITIES

1. Dale and Cuevas talk about the "myth" that perpetuates the idea that mathematics requires minimal language proficiency. In what ways is this common misconception a myth?

2. Although the authors mention the importance of building instructional activities in mathematics on students' real life experiences, they do not develop this idea to any great extent. How might you incorporate real-life experiences into any activities you might develop? Share your ideas with a small group.

3. What about culture? How might aspects of the cultures represented by your students be brought into mathematics instruction? Give specific examples.

4. Develop a sequence of language-based mathematics activities based on the SLAMS model. Clearly indicate the specific type of course and students for whom the activities are intended. Tell how you would relate to the prior knowledge and to the cultures of your students during the implementation of your lessons.

23

Multicultural Art Projects

Jo Miles Schuman *Burns Park School, Ann Arbor, Michigan*

Editors' Introduction

Although this chapter's emphasis is on the development of multicultural art projects, it is easy to see how students' language needs might be served in the process. It is highly likely that students will be drawn into meaningful communication by the excitement of self-expression through art. Jo Schuman offers means by which art pieces from many cultures can become part of the classroom environment and the focus for numerous art projects. She gives us tips about where to find such pieces, assuring us that we do not need to be world travelers to obtain them; they can be obtained in local secondhand shops just around the corner. Of special interest is the author's warning about the literal copying of art forms. Students themselves should be encouraged to be creators and not slaves to art forms. Even though the chapter is written with elementary students in mind, its ideas can be adapted to all age levels.

BEGINNING THE PROJECT

Where does one begin? There are many beginnings. The study may start spontaneously, through a news clipping that describes art from another culture; through something a child or parent or teacher sees or does or brings to class; or perhaps through research on a particular culture that is part of a social studies unit. Whatever sparked the study, if children are to engage in an art project, showing them an actual piece of art brings the highest motivation and involvement.

Children feel a certain magic about the real thing. You hear their breath draw in, see their eyes widen, sense their respect and wonder when they can see and maybe touch an Inuit sculpture of smooth black stone, an intricate and vibrantly colored painting on amate paper from Mexico, or a hand-stamped and embroidered adinkra cloth from Ghana. Nothing can really substitute for this exciting experience.

From "A Method for Teaching Multicultural Art Projects" by J. Schuman, 1981, in J. Schuman, Art From Many Hands *(pp. 1–6). Copyright 1981 by Davis Publications. Adapted by permission.*

Giving children this experience is not as difficult as it might seem. Is there a secondhand shop in your community? You can find surprising things there—a seventy-five-cent clay animal from Mexico with lovely hand-painted designs (it does not matter if there are small chips); a backstrap loom from Guatemala, which shows young students how cloth is created; an old Polish wycinanki design for two dollars, a treasure to be shared (Figure 23.1). These are chance finds, but as tourism grows, such small, inexpensive things become easier to find even if one cannot travel oneself.

Most cities have an increasing number of art import shops. Although larger items can be prohibitively expensive, smaller handcrafted pieces are often within a teacher's budget. Many shops are willing to lend items to a school for one day if they are assured that the pieces will not be harmed. They may require a refundable deposit against loss or damage.

We often live in a community without ever tapping its human resources. Has someone in your community traveled abroad? Are there foreign visitors to your town—students or business representatives who may have art objects to show or skills to teach? Are there Americans with ethnic backgrounds in your area who have knowledge of a traditional craft? Invite to the classroom a Japanese student who can demonstrate ink painting, a Chinese visitor who

Figure 23.1. *Items Found in Secondhand Shops*
A weaving on a backstrap loom from Guatemala, a plate and a papier mâché bird from Mexico, a gold-leafed lacquerware owl from Burma, a Navajo silver and turquoise bracelet, and a toy papier mâché beast of burden from Japan.

Figure 23.2.
Vee-Ling Edwards shares her knowledge of calligraphy with Dan, a fifth-grade student.

can show the growth of a language through calligraphy (Figure 23.2), a Native American who can demonstrate beadwork, or a Polish American who has learned to cut wycinanki designs. Many people are willing and happy to give this valuable experience to your students, but you will have to search for them—they do not advertise these special skills. In most cities there are international organizations that might help you. You can also inquire at universities, which often have students and faculty from many countries.

Perhaps the art you wish to see can be found only in a museum or art gallery. Then you have to take the class to the art. Make arrangements in advance with the people in charge and ask a guide to explain the artwork to the children. Take paper and pencils so that the students can sketch and bring home their impressions.

Failing an actual object, pictures are the next best thing. The public libraries are rich resource places. Most art books are beyond the budget of public schools, but public libraries often have a number of books with beautiful color illustrations for those with the curiosity to find them and the muscle to carry them home. If teachers request it, libraries will sometimes purchase or borrow books that are not in their own collections.

MATERIALS

Once you have chosen an art project, think about materials. Is the same material available, or can you create a substitute? If you are studying Pueblo clay pottery and the school is lucky enough to have a kiln, you can work directly in clay. Or you could even create your own outdoor kiln in the Pueblo manner. However, if you have seen an exhibit of African masks and sculpture carved from wood, you will realize that wood is not a practical medium to use at the elementary level. Papier mâché would be a good substitute. Children's enthusiasm is greatest when their materials are as close to the original as possible, but their imagination is boundless and can fill great gaps. Children are realistic and know that making sculpture of pure gold is impossible in the classroom, but they are delighted to see their cardboard sculptures (inspired by ancient pre-Columbian art) transformed by an application of gold paint.

The budgets of most public schools require that materials be as inexpensive as possible. Most indigenous art uses materials that are found naturally in the environment. The school usually has paper, glue, paints, and other basic art supplies. But look further into your community for other, sometimes free, often more exciting materials. Look at the land where you live, at what grows there naturally and by cultivation; look at the industries, the stores, inside the homes.

In some areas, children can dig clay, an act that brings them to the source of their material. Slate for use in rock engravings can be found naturally in some areas. Sand can be colored and used for sand painting. Native grasses and weeds can be used for weaving and basketry. In many cultures, jewelry is made from natural objects that are often available: seeds, bones, shells, and feathers.

Visit the industries in your area. Sheets of aluminum, which are excellent for making African repoussé panels or Mexican tin figures, are waste material from offset printing. Iron foundries throw away large hunks of manmade sandstone, which is a perfect medium for young children to use for their own sculpture when they are studying Inuit carving. Look into the stores and services in your community. Round, three-gallon containers from the ice cream store can be used as segments in a totem pole. Old rubber inner tubes can be cut into shapes and used for making prints.

Use waste products from the home. Cartons, boxes, and tubes can be bases for papier mâché sculpture. Aluminum TV dinner trays can be cut up and made into tin sculpture. Leftover balls of yarn become fine weavings.

TRYING IT OUT

After finding the inspiration (in the form of art pieces or illustrations) and the materials, go through the project yourself before presenting it to the class. There may be pitfalls in directions or construction that you cannot foresee unless you go through the steps first. The method may be too tedious or require a skill level too high for the age level you have in mind. (Sometimes, however, especially with older students, encountering difficulties and overcoming them together is a valuable part of the problem-solving aspect of the art process.)

In a few cases there may be dangers in the art materials that are not immediately apparent. In going through the steps first, the teacher encounters these and makes the process safer before presenting it to the class. For instance, taping the overly sharp edges on cut aluminum or learning the safest possible way to set up hot wax for batiking can help prevent accidents from occurring.

TO COPY OR CREATE?

Do you want replicas of ethnic art, or do you want to use an art form as a basis for inspiring the child's own creativity? This is an important question, and the answer will vary according to the purpose of the project. My feeling is that only *rarely* should an art form be literally copied. If the group is studying a particular culture and wants to get as close to it as possible so the children can participate vicariously in an aspect of that culture, then the answer may be yes, make replicas. For instance, if the group is studying Indonesia, they may choose to make shadow puppets. Children enjoy doing research; choosing a story; learning its meaning in that culture; and using the particular shapes, symbols, and colors for each character. Children have some freedom to choose which characters to re-create. They can put on a performance, complete with instrumental accompaniment, for their schoolmates. The feeling created by attempting to make and use authentic puppets and simulating the rhythm of musical instruments is a valuable experience.

Even in this situation it is not a good idea to be rigid. Most children will find challenge enough in re-creating an intricate shadow puppet. However, an especially creative child may use the inspiration to create his or her own character, using his or her own symbols. This is how new forms are created within all societies, and sometimes they are then perpetuated by tradition. Such an innovation should be acceptable within the classroom, too.

My own predilection, whenever possible, is to use the art form in question as a method of exploring new ways of seeing and of expressing *oneself.* Except for the previously mentioned ''re-enactment,'' which can be very rewarding, most children get little satisfaction from a copy—it falls short of reality and has too little of themselves in it. Children should learn the method and especially the *spirit* in which the art form was made and then use this knowledge to create their own art work. For example, in making amate paper cutouts, authentic bark paper cutouts are shown (Figure 23.3). The Otomí Indian method of making the paper is explained, and the method we will use to simulate it. Then we talk about traditional Mexican designs. We look at examples in *Design Motifs of Ancient Mexico* by Jorge Enciso. We talk about

Figure 23.3.
This two-headed bird-of-the-mountain design by a fifth-grade student was inspired by the Otomí Indian cutouts. It is the student's own personal expression, not a copy.

how some of these designs spring from natural forms (birds, lizards, flowers, and people), even though they are not realistically drawn, and how others are based on geometric shapes (zigzags, triangles, squares, and so on). The children are encouraged to make imaginative designs based on a natural form or an abstract shape of their choice. The resulting designs, because of the materials and the original inspiration, have the spirit of the Otomí Indian work but are as varied as the children themselves and are very much their own personal expressions.

It is not expected that students will be able to create pieces of art as fine as the examples shown them, which are usually the result of years of training and tradition. But when they work with materials with their own hands, students appreciate the skills of those artisans even more. At the same time, they enjoy the creative process themselves and gain some confidence in their own abilities. Exposing students to art from all over the world brings them the wonder of art in all its many forms, expands their knowledge of what art is, and shows them the variety of ways design problems can be solved.

FOLLOW-UP QUESTIONS AND ACTIVITIES

1. Schuman states that "Only *rarely* should an art form be literally copied." What are the issues surrounding the rigid reproduction of art forms? How

important are these issues for children? For teenagers and adults? Are there differences pertaining to age level? Explain.

2. With a small group, answer the following questions:

> Are there stores in your neighborhood at which art pieces from around the world can be purchased at reasonable prices? Make a list. Describe the kinds of art that each store might be likely to sell.
>
> Are there people living in your neighborhood who might serve as multicultural resources for your art classes? List possibilities along with the specific art form that each might be able to share with your students.
>
> Explore the area where you live for indigenous materials for art projects. What did you discover? Name ways in which these materials might be used in an art class.

3. For what reasons does the author stress the importance of going through the steps of an art project first before introducing it to your students? What might happen if you do not?

4. Design a multicultural art project for a class of your own. Describe it to a small group and ask for their input. If possible, bring in the art objects you might present as examples. Discuss several strategies you might use to aid language development through the activities described (see especially Chapter 10 for ideas).

24

Using Low Organized Games in Multicultural Physical Education

Marianne Torbert and Lynne B. Schneider   Temple University

EDITORS' INTRODUCTION

Marianne Torbert and Lynne Schneider combine their expertise to present both theoretical and practical aspects of low organized games for multicultural physical education. They stress cooperation as opposed to competition, equalization as opposed to elimination, inclusion as opposed to exclusion, choices as opposed to mandates, and success (every player a winner) as opposed to failure. By focusing on bonding and autonomy simultaneously, students are encouraged to become respected members of the group without losing individual integrity.

"Play may be the key to open many doors." (Torbert, 1982). Eric Erikson and Jean Piaget have taught us that play is a child's way of processing life. Robert White of Harvard beautifully summarized the process when he said, "Play may be fun, but it is also a serious business in childhood. During these hours the child steadily builds up his (her) competence in dealing with the environment" (1959). Well-planned play can be a potentially powerful means through which alternatives can be experienced.

Low organized games/activities can be carefully selected, modified, and/or created to focus on *any* desired objective or purpose, whether it be for processing or building competencies. If we wish participants to experience and process specific behavioral alternatives, then it becomes necessary for us to reflect on this objective and determine what type of play would enhance these experiences. We must accept as much responsibility as possible to ensure that growth and development can occur.

Our focus here will be upon Positive and Effective Multicultural Interaction, which we refer to as PEMI. To accomplish PEMI we feel our selected

This article is reprinted with permission from the Journal of Physical Education, Recreation and Dance, *Volume 57, September, 1986 (pp. 40–44). The Journal is a publication of the American Alliance for Health, Physical Education, Recreation and Dance, 1900 Association Drive, Reston, VA 22091.*

Figure 24.1
Play is not only the "serious business of childhood," it is also the serious business of our profession. (Photo by Carol Sonstein. Used by permission of Marianne Torbert.)

games/activities and the atmosphere in which these are offered must support opportunities for inclusion of individuals who differ from one another. To accomplish this, we need to select activities in which choices, self-determination (autonomy), and differences are not only acceptable but can become sources of growth. Individual differences can thus become a source from which participants can gain alternatives from which they can broaden their behavioral choices. These growth-producing situations may then lead to a "bonding" in which an increase in positive interactions increases feelings of acceptance, belonging, ability to make valuable contributions, and positive relationships.

An example of how a traditional game might be evaluated and changed will help illustrate this. Most people are familiar with the party game, Musical Chairs, which is an elimination game. This game, which is usually selected and perpetuated by a well-meaning adult, encourages a "me-me" or "me-first" orientation and the blatant exclusion of others. The adult has probably assumed that "common," "traditional," "familiar," and "good" are synonymous and if asked to examine what is really happening to individuals involved might question, "How could so many be so wrong for so long?"

After years of tradition, Orlick (1978) took issue with this game and created Cooperative Musical Chairs in which no one is eliminated. Chairs are removed, but everyone has to find means to allow all participants to sit on fewer and fewer remaining chairs. What a revolutionary change! But success should never deter us from looking even further. Although blatant elimination has been conquered, there are still subtle eliminations that could occur. What if a chair broke, someone got physically squashed, or if the speedy little child said to one who arrived to the chair later, "Don't sit on me, you're too fat!"?

Perhaps Orlick had considered this when he created Cooperative Musical Chairs, or some had started to substitute the game of Islands (Team on a T-Shirt, or All Aboard) (Torbert, 1980) for Musical Chairs.[1] But traditions die hard. Children's parties continue to perpetuate Musical Chairs without a clear awareness that inclusion or exclusion experiences can be joyfully or traumatically experienced by the participants. If we prefer to perpetuate a "we" rather than a "me" world, perhaps we need to examine the experiences we are offering our children.

There is probably at least one reader who is thinking that the foregoing is irrelevant and that children are not so deeply affected by the experiences of simple games. If you are one of these doubters, we challenge you to select ten adults and ask them if they had any feelings of exclusion or discomfort in physical education during their first twelve years of school. If, as Erikson, Piaget, and White have indicated, a child processes and learns to deal with life through play, we may have to consider this aspect of life more carefully. If we wish to support PEMI, our first step is to carefully examine all that is happening to all the players, all the time. Do the affects and effects match our objectives, or must we reevaluate and accept the responsibility to select, modify, and/or create accordingly? Play is not only the "serious business of childhood," it is also the serious business of our profession. We should be the first to recognize and the last to ignore its relevance. The interactions that occur within the play experience can either help generate alternatives and PEMI, or they can perpetuate elimination, exclusion, rejection, and the inability to effectively interact with those who are different from oneself. As Combs and Snygg (1959) indicated in their work, our behaviors are a product of our perceptions, which are a product of our experiences and how we process them.

We have selected four low organized games to examine in relation to factors that might contribute to PEMI. We encourage readers to try these games.

---

[1] See *Follow Me: A Handbook of Movement Activities for Children* by M. Torbert, 1980. May be ordered from The Leonard Gordon Institute for Human Development Through Play, 3306 Midvale Avenue, Philadelphia, PA 19129.

Chaotic Team Juggle

Equipment

Make 8 to 15 "trash" balls. A trash ball is simply a *soft, loosely* packed wad of paper (newspaper is good) about the size of a head of cabbage and held together by one or two rubberbands. If available, you may want to wrap an old plastic bag around each paper wad before securing it with rubberbands.

Before passing out the soft trash balls (one for about every three players), indicate that each participant with an object may throw it to anyone else *if* the thrower can first get eye contact with an intended receiver. Inform players that their challenge will be to keep as many balls as possible going at once. If a ball hits the floor, a player may pick it up and start again. A good throw is frequently based on a good follow-through toward one's target. Let the group try this challenge for a while. It may become chaotic, so it will be important to have a signal to stop this action. One technique we have used is to hold a large trash bag and encourage players to shoot a basket.

Comments

There is so much equipment involved in this activity that players are continually looking for anyone who is without an object so that they can get rid of their object to receive another. This reduces the chance of a player being or feeling left out. Eye contact, as a requirement for a throw, seems to support a subtle bonding effect between players.

Because of the difference between a trash ball and a regulation ball, everyone will occasionally miss a throw or a catch. This creates an almost natural equalization among the participants in which missing is less embarrassing because everyone does it. Also, missing is rarely noticed by others who are really too busy to care.

If someone feels a need to "buy out" (this activity can become rather stressful for some), that person can avoid eye contact with others until he or she is ready to buy back in. The softness of the objects thrown also helps eliminate potential fear, failure, and injury since it allows for the impact force to be absorbed, thus reducing these subtle exclusion factors.

The game is so much fun that we have had to develop the special ending mentioned above. We call this "living basketball" because the leader or players holding the large trash bag can move to help make more baskets. The group encourages and cheers for each shooter, which creates a very nice sense of camaraderie and group unity.

Nonelimination Snatch the Flag

Equipment

Old socks, a torn-up bed sheet, or anything that can become a flag.

All players put a strip of cloth in the back of their waistbands. The objective is to try to snatch as many flags as possible while trying to keep their own. If players lose their flag, they stay in the game and continue to snatch flags. Try this and see what happens.

Comments

This nonelimination game creates a special "interactive challenge" (Torbert, 1983) where all players grow from each other's involvement. Players who have lost their flags are not eliminated but remain in the game with only one intent—to get a flag. This increases the challenge for the highly skilled; it encourages those who have lost their flag to focus intensely upon those who still have their flag and the successful techniques used by those who are able to keep their flag. To our delight we have found that a great deal of learning occurs during this highly motivating process. Out of this type of interactive challenge, where players' differences (in this case, levels of skill) actually facilitate each other's growth, we find a special group cohesiveness and bonding occurring.

The game gets very exciting, with strategic collaboration developing among those who have lost their flags. If we find the game getting too rough before sufficient skill has developed, to prevent injuries we simply stop the episode before the last flags are snatched, and go through a somewhat elaborate process indicating all kinds of ways players have won.

Rag Hockey

Equipment
Rags or carpet pieces; newspaper; beanbags.

This is a fascinating game in which all tend to be handicapped or made "more equal" because they must stand on rags or carpets and move by using a cross-country skiing or twisting motion. Sticks can be made from rolled newspaper; a bean bag puck encourages players to place their stick on the bean bag and use a flinging motion that leads to "flattening the arc" (an effective hockey technique) and discourages wild backswings.

Optional
All players can start with a rag/carpet under each foot. Then if a team scores, the opposing team can select any player on the scoring team to become a "twister"—a player who places both feet on just one rag/carpet, which forces him or her to use a twisting motion to move. We have found that we incorporate rules only as they help more to participate effectively.

Comments
We have found players consider it an honor and a compliment to be selected to become a "twister." This selection process tends to equalize teams and players.

Because the space needed to play is greatly reduced, we have found more individuals can be involved (and needed) in the same space. Children of all sizes, both sexes, and mixed skill abilities seem to play this game together successfully.

Other games/activities can also be tried on rags/carpets. This can allow for additional abdominal and cardiorespiratory involvement.

Frantic Ball

Equipment
One tennis ball or nerf ball for every two or three players.

Frantic Ball has much the same flavor as Chaotic Team Juggle except that the objects are tennis balls moved on the floor by using the feet. All balls must be kept moving and no ball can be lifted from the ground. The group works as a single team.

Each time a ball stops or is lifted a "hectic" (a whistle) is called. During play all stopped balls must be put back into motion and are a continuing part of the play. Five hectics and the "frenzie" (timed episode) is over. The team competes against the clock, trying to increase the length of each frenzie. If only a small space is available, the balls can be played off the walls.

Comments

Since some cultures are soccer oriented while others are throwing oriented, Chaotic Team Juggle and Frantic Ball may allow for a sense of intercultural sharing.

All can enter at their capability level and participate to their best ability level. Again, because there is so much going on, all are needed, but there remains an element of privacy since no one will probably notice if anyone misses. Over time players seem to find ways to use their combined abilities to cover for each other in relatively effective ways.

The small ball encourages the use of the feet in ways that lead to good soccer technique and future success. It seems that when all members of a group are able to feel a sense of growth and improvement their ability to enjoy each other and accept differences in each other increases. The skills being gained in these activities contribute to opportunities for future group interactions.

Since the entire group is *the* team and the competition is against the clock, a growing sense of unity develops.

In searching for games that could allow each player to experience PEMI and to "steadily build up his or her competence in dealing with the environment" (White, 1959), two key components seem to be very important—bonding and autonomy. Bonding is a magical quality of unity that can occur over time among players. Games that encourage collaboration, identification, equalization, orchestration of individual differences, challenges for all at their personal level, the elimination of elimination, taking the focus off failure, new definitions of winning, and inclusion seem to increase the occurrence of this quality of interaction. The second more subtle factor that seems to be necessary to enhance PEMI is autonomy (self-determination, self-legislating). When each player is allowed to make personal choices/decisions; is allowed some opportunity to be self-determining; feels accepted and respected for himself or herself and his or her contributions; can be actively involved in interactive challenges; is allowed privacy when needed; is allowed some opportunity to buy in and out; is able to belong without having to lose "self"; is able to have a positive sense of self; is intrinsically motivated; and has a sense of inclusion, individual integrity can be maintained and each player has more opportunity to contribute positively to group interactions.

As these two components are incorporated or increased within a given activity, the activity's PEMI potential seems to also increase. Thus our task may become one of analysis and selection or construction in relation to factors that encourage bonding and autonomy.

For those who may be serious about becoming change agents through the use of low organized games, we have included a list as a partial comparison between what has sometimes been and what could be. Notice how much the possibility for bonding and autonomy increases between the ''has been'' to the ''could be'' columns.

What Has Sometimes Been	*What Could Be*
Everyone for Self/Star Player (King of the Mountain)	Collaboration/Problem-Solving Focus—Everyone Growing at His or Her Own Level
Conformity/Standardized/ Everyone the Same	Respect and Orchestration of Differences and Uniquenesses
Tradition/Assumption/Habit Usually Determined Course of Action	New Alternatives Generated, Examined, and Evaluated by Leaders and Players
Other/Outer Controlled	Inner/Self-Control
And Then There Was One	No Elimination—Instead, Equalization = Challenging for All
Single Way to Play/Perform	Choices, Generating Alternatives Encouraged
Exclusion/Elimination/''Survival of the Fittest''	Inclusion—Each at His or Her Own Level
Chosen Last/Not Good Enough	Every Player Contributes to Other Players' Growth Regardless of Ability Level = ''Interactive Challenge''
Embarrassment from Failure	Focus is Taken off Failure and Placed on ''Challenge'' and Improvement
Embarrassment in Front of Others; Can Lead to Self-Elimination	Privacy When Needed—Opportunity to Try Again; Perseverance Encouraged
I'm a Failure	I Can Do It!
Score/Outcome = Only Focus	Process Becomes Relevant; Growth and Development of Players = Focus
Limited Leadership	Shared Responsibility
Only Some Belong	Sense of Belonging for All

One Winner	Every Player a Winner
Pecking Order/Hierarchy	Horizontal Interaction
Self-Esteem for a Few	Positive Self-Concept for as Many as Possible
Extrinsic Motivation Dominant	Intrinsic Motivation = New Focus
Elitist Sports for a Limited Number of Players	Play for All
Someone Else Makes Most of the Decisions	Individual Choices and Decision Making Increased

In conclusion, we hope we have allowed you to consider means by which we could collectively select, modify, and create low organized games to become experimental models to generate experiential alternatives that could increase inclusion, bonding, autonomy, and the celebration of differences to support our goal of PEMI.

FOLLOW-UP QUESTIONS AND ACTIVITIES

1. Torbert and Schneider quote White (1959): "Play may be fun, but it is also the serious business of childhood." What does this mean? In what ways may play also be *serious business* for older children and adults?

2. What are low organized games? In what ways may they further language development in language minority students? How about cultural learning? Even though the authors do not develop the aspect of cultural learning, can you think of ways in which it, too, may be incorporated?

3. How can *success* be redefined as it pertains to low organized games? In what other ways, other than in such games, can success be stressed over failure in physical education?

4. Find a low organized game to share with a small group. In what ways does it promote the following:

    Cooperation (versus competition)
    Equalization (versus elimination)
    Inclusion (versus exclusion)
    Choices (versus mandates)
    Success (versus failure)
    Language development
    Cultural learning

25

Music as Multicultural Education

JACK P. B. DOBBS *Dartington College of Arts, United Kingdom*

EDITORS' INTRODUCTION

Jack Dobbs champions music, not only for the enjoyment it can bring, but as a means by which greater awareness and sensitivity to other cultures can be developed. He believes that through music students may be brought out of their sometimes limited world views and given positive encounters with various musical styles, themes, structures, rhythmic groupings, and the like from around the world. Not only does he advocate exposing students to a variety of musical experiences; he also feels that they should be introduced to societal perceptions about those experiences and how they relate to other art forms within a given culture. Hence, students might be encouraged to extend their interest in and perhaps even pursue serious study of another culture. Although language development is not directly addressed in relation to music, one can conceive of several means by which such development may be promoted through discussion and sometimes by the music itself when it contains lyrics in the target language.

If we believe that music is essentially concerned with living and life, music cannot be separated from education. Its elements are present in an embryo state in all children. And from them music elicits responses on various levels, whatever the children's cultural backgrounds and irrespective of whether they are intellectually gifted or suffering from a mental or physical handicap.

Music is not an international language, but it is a universal medium of expression for the deepest feelings and aspirations that belong to all humanity. It provides this medium through various means—traditional and folk music, jazz, the works of individual composers, and the popular music that speaks so powerfully for and to the young.

Many young people are being educated musically without our help. The music to which they listen, emanating from radios, record players, televisions, and concert stages, is not of one uniform type, and much of it shows influences from many cultures. They take it all in their stride. Some of it they like; some they reject. What to an older generation were "exotic" sounds imported from foreign parts do not seem strange or bizarre to the young. The sounds are a natural part of their auditory experience. This is not entirely a new phenomenon. A friend who grew into adolescence with George Harrison was introducing the sitar into his song "Within You, Without You," told me recently that she had not thought of that sound as "exotic." It was just one of the many fascinating sounds to be enjoyed.

A lot of music making and listening, then, is going on out of school. How far is this accepted and extended in the activities of the classroom? Can we fit yet another area of music into an already crowded music scheme? Or does our music education require a type of conceptual approach that is not based on thinking about the addition of extras but on the recognition that there are many manifestations of music, all of which can be drawn on freely to illuminate basic elements of any scheme of music education. If the latter is true, where do we begin?

START WITH SOUND

The impact of all music is made directly by the experience of sound, whatever the system through which that sound is conveyed. And so it is sound *per se* that must be the starting point for music education. The differences between the various systems can be understood and cherished later, as can the context in which they were conceived and the reasons for their creation. So let us start with sound and silence, rather than system, letting our children investigate sounds and themselves as sound producers. Sound is our common property, and the savoring of a single sound is the beginning of musical wisdom. As we experiment with sounds—of the children's own environment, of human voices, of instruments (homemade, purchased, electronic, or acoustic), of whatever sort we wish to include in our soundscape—we begin also to explore pitch, rhythm, timbre, texture, and structure.

As children's imagination catches fire, they become creators, making from the raw material satisfying patterns and structures, working together, whatever their cultural backgrounds. The more we place emphasis on creation rather than imitation, re-creation, or transmission, the quicker any prejudices we may have about the validity of certain music systems will disappear.

It is at this stage that the wealth of the world's music—folk, high art, popular—can be of such value in helping to extend pupils' musical experience. In a multicultural society such as ours there are many resources already at hand. They are all to be welcomed. The sounds and sound producers of the minority groups, together with the natural sounds of their homelands, still retained in the memories of the older members of their families, can be shared in the classroom. This always depends on the teacher's sensitivity to the origins and associations of those sounds within the cultures from which they come.

We can learn from each other, not allowing ourselves to be blown off our indigenous feet but being refreshed by new sources of inspiration—and that means new sources of life. This can happen only if we ensure that all those minority groups are encouraged to make their own music, to share it with others, and to know its value, both for itself and for its contribution to the total pattern of music making.

UNDERSTAND STYLES

Having absorbed the sounds that make up the music, children can be helped in trying to understand the styles of the music itself. This may force us as teachers to question some of our own preconceptions. Is there, for example, as we sometimes suggest, a correct style of singing voice that all children should aim to produce in the classroom? If so, what is it? As we listen to voices of a cathedral choir, Cathy Berberrian, members of the Peking Opera, and Mick Jagger is the answer quite as straightforward as we had thought—or are we beginning to discover something about style and appropriateness?

WHAT CAN STUDENTS GAIN?

What then, are we hoping that our children will gain as they move away from their home base and meet the music of other cultures?

1. Students will gain new musical experiences and an extension of their means of expression through the enlargement of their vocabulary as they use scales, rhythmic groupings, tone colors, textures, and structures that before were unfamiliar to them.
2. Students will achieve an appreciation of diversities and, at a deeper level, of similarities.
3. Students will participate in different ways of making music together. In the West we shall particularly benefit from group music making that depends on interaction between the members of the group— listening to and relating to each other or to an instrumental leader within the group instead of following the visual directions of a conductor or printed notation. In so doing there will be a development of their aural perception through an approach more akin to that used in folk, jazz, rock, and other popular forms of music. Spontaneity and improvisation will play more important roles, and composer and performer will often be the same person.

4. Students will come to understand the influences of nonindigenous music on twentieth-century composers, popular music, jazz, and rock. Students who wish to study these musics in depth need to know about their sources and the social situations that gave them birth.

5. Students will see the relatedness of the arts. That divisions between music, dance, and other arts are less strong or are nonexistent in many cultures provides a lesson to those of us who perpetuate these divisions by our specialist approaches.

6. Social involvement and audience participation with direct emotional expression will restore to music its function of bringing together people from varying backgrounds in celebrations, seasonal festivities, and other domestic rituals.

7. Pupils will gain the intellectual stimulus that working within new systems gives and may later wish to embark upon the serious study of a nonindigenous culture in order to become scholars in their own chosen area.

8. Students will develop tolerance and respect, leading to an attitude that, it is hoped, will find expression in their relationship with people of other races, cultures, and geographic areas.

This, then, is music education for all schools—not just those in areas with a concentration of pupils from nonindigenous cultures. Perhaps it is even more important in isolated rural areas from which young people will of necessity go to industrial areas in search of work. If they have had no contact with people from different cultures and are hardly aware of their existence, they will take with them a limited view of life. Attitudes bred in isolation can easily succumb to persuasive racist propaganda.

If music education is to meet more adequately the needs of our own age and environment, we must decide what there is in our tradition to which we must hold fast and determine what human and material resources are required to effect necessary change.

We certainly need many more musicians and teachers from nonindigenous cultures to play key roles in music education. We also need indigenous teachers prepared for new thinking and processes of working. But changed attitudes, good will, tolerance, and understanding are not enough. In order for their attitudes to be translated into practical reality, teachers need material resources and a knowledge of other musics that is the result of experience, practice, and involvement.

I am not referring to the training of musicologists. I am asking, rather, for a broadening and deepening of the education of all musicians. Nor is this a concern for initial training only. In-service courses must be established to develop a new orientation for all teachers. More is required than lectures on multicultural music. These may be informative, but they do not always lead to practical action. There must be opportunities for all musicians and especially music teachers to be immersed in the music of nonindigenous cultures as part of their everyday training. For this purpose we need centers where music of specific cultures is performed within as appropriate a setting as possible. There must be close links between the centers to avoid duplication, and a regular flow of performing musicians from the centers to other colleges and institutions where teaching about the music is given.

Wherever possible, the music must be live. When this is not possible, we shall have to rely on tapes, records, videos, and films made by the carriers of the traditions represented. This is where close cooperation with ethnomusicologists is important, so that the resources are authentic and are not diluted. The songs that are sung, the instruments that are used, and the music that is played on them all need the careful scrutiny of the ethnomusicologist, especially where there is no practicing member of the tradition at hand. It is equally important for the ethnomusicologist to understand the aims and intentions of the music teachers and limitations within which they have to work. One of the most valuable contributions ethnomusicologists can make is to help bring about an understanding of the culture from which a music comes, its significance to those who make it, and its function in their society. At later stages we also need more opportunities for exchange visits, so that young people can experience the music in its home setting. Music is not just an art to be practiced within the education of a multicultural society. It is, in itself, a truly multicultural education.

FOLLOW-UP QUESTIONS AND ACTIVITIES

1. Dobbs, who is from the United Kingdom, states that music should not be used as a means of being "blown off our indigenous feet." What does he mean? Why might the word *indigenous* as used elsewhere in this chapter *not* be appropriate in the United States context? What term might be better? Why?

2. Of all the benefits of music as multicultural education listed on page 366–367, which do you feel are most important? Would you add any to the list?

3. Do you agree with the author that lectures about music are not enough to bring about its potential benefits? If so, why not? What alternatives are there to the lecture method that may be more effective in music as multicultural education?

4. Dobbs suggests that more musicians (and teachers) from minority cultures in your area play key roles in music education. Think of possible resources in your own community. With a small group, make a list of such resources.

5. If you were to choose a piece of music containing English lyrics to present to your class for discussion, what factors would you consider in making your selection? Refer to Chapter 10 for guidelines.

6. Choose a musical genre closely associated with a specific cultural group in your area. Learn as much as you can about that particular genre and the culture of which it is a part. Present it to a small group for feedback. Include in your presentation the music's significance to and function in that culture. If possible use a resource (a recording or live musicians) to demonstrate the form. Include also several prelesson activities (to explore prior knowledge, awaken interest, etc.) and postlesson activities (to ensure comprehension, to extend meaning, etc.) so that both cultural awareness and language will be promoted.

26

Serving Language Minority Students in Business Education

JOAN E. FRIEDENBERG *National Center for Research in Vocational Education*

EDITORS' INTRODUCTION

Language minority students often are excluded from business education programs for a variety of reasons: (1) They may lack awareness of available programs, (2) they may fail to pass required entrance examinations, (3) their special needs may not have been taken into account by those in charge. In this chapter, Joan Friedenberg describes some of the more salient policies and strategies associated with successful business education programs in order that others may learn from them and ultimately offer language minority students greater access to this important and dynamic field.

Limited English Proficient (LEP) persons are more likely than the national average to be enrolled below the expected grade level, to drop out of school, to be unemployed, or to be underemployed (Rezabek, 1981). LEP persons face difficulties in seeking, keeping, and advancing in jobs due to their limited English skills, cultural differences, low levels of education, and discrimination (National Commission for Employment Policy, 1982).

Business education can be a viable option for many LEP persons. In addition to the relatively healthy number of positions available in business and office careers, our increasing contact with international markets makes bilingual word processing capabilities, for example, quite desirable. Yet many business education programs, both secondary and postsecondary, do not provide adequate access or services to LEP persons. Many programs require entrance tests in English, which exclude LEP persons from participating. Others allow LEP students to enroll but do not provide them with the services needed to help them succeed.

From ''Serving Limited English Proficient Students in Business Education'' by J. Friedenberg, 1988, in Journal of Education for Business, March, 1988, pp. 245-247. Adapted with permission of the Helen Dwight Reid Educational Foundation. Published by Heldref Publications, 4000 Albemarle St., NW, Washington, DC 20016. Copyright © 1988.

BILINGUAL VOCATIONAL TRAINING PROGRAM

Since 1976, the Office of Vocational and Adult Education (OVAE) of the U.S. Department of Education has funded a modest number of bilingual vocational training (BVT) programs throughout the United States each year. Probably the most important contribution made by these federal programs is the development of the BVT model. This model is often considered to be the most effective instructional delivery system for LEP vocational students. It consists of the following seven components:

1. Target recruitment specifically to LEP students (examples: produce promotional materials in the potential trainees' native language and advertise in the native language mass media).
2. Institute intake and assessment procedures that are appropriate and nonexclusionary (examples: test vocational interest and aptitude in the native language, test for English language proficiency, and native language proficiency).
3. Adapt vocational instruction so that students do not have to be proficient in English before learning a trade (examples: use bilingual instruction and materials, simplify English). (See Chapter 10 for additional ideas.)
4. Provide vocational English as a second language (VESL) instruction that is taught by a trained ESL instructor and focuses specifically on the student's vocational areas (examples: offer auto mechanics ESL, data entry ESL, food services ESL).
5. Offer counseling and support services that take the special needs of LEP students into account (examples: refer students to appropriate agencies that provide immigration counseling and social and health services in the native language, offer bilingual and culturally sensitive personal and professional counseling).
6. Promote job development and placement geared to the special needs of LEP individuals (examples: foresee and counsel employability problems resulting from cultural differences, prepare employers for LEP and culturally different employees).
7. Coordinate the previous six elements so that each supports the other (example: make sure that the VESL and vocational instruction are coordinated so that the VESL instructor is teaching the vocabulary and grammar used in vocational classes).

BILINGUAL BUSINESS EDUCATION PROGRAMS

During the 1986–1987 funding period, ten of the nineteen BVT programs funded nationwide offered bilingual training in business and office careers. For example, Maricopa Technical Community College in Phoenix, Arizona, offered bilingual data entry programs in Spanish, Vietnamese, and Chinese. Asians for Job Opportunities (AJOB) and Adelante, Inc., both in Berkeley, California, offer bilingual word processing and clerical courses for speakers of Spanish, Chinese, Japanese, Korean, Vietnamese, Khmer, Hindi, and Tagalog. Two bilingual teachers, one who speaks Spanish and one who speaks Chinese, work with the majority of the students. Instructors who speak the other six languages are on staff and are called on as needed to tutor LEP students. Chinatown Resources Development Center (CRDC) of San Francisco offers a general clerical program for speakers of Chinese; Metropolitan State College in Denver, Colorado, offers an on-the-job bilingual training program for Indo-Chinese. In the Colorado program, a bilingual counselor accompanies the trainees and assists with tutoring as well as job-related problems. New Opportunities for Waterbury, Inc. in Waterbury, Connecticut, provides clerical training in Spanish and English. Salt Lake Skills Center in Salt Lake City, Utah, offers courses in computer operations, accounting, and data entry for speakers of Spanish and Vietnamese. In the Salt Lake program, bilingual teacher aides work with an English-speaking teacher. Chinatown Manpower Project, Inc., in New York City, has offered bilingual (Chinese) instruction in general clerical, data entry, and automated bookkeeping for over five years. HACER, Inc., also in New York City, offers computer-related clerical courses in Spanish. The Community College of Rhode Island offers word processing and data entry courses for speakers of Spanish. The Employment and Training Center in Arlington, Virginia, offers a bilingual clerical program to speakers of Vietnamese and Spanish.

PROGRAMS WITHOUT FEDERAL FUNDING

Many research efforts have been undertaken to investigate the problems and practices in implementing the BVT model in the federally funded BVT programs. However, little research has been undertaken on whether programs without special federal funding are using the model. The National Center for Research in Vocational Education at Ohio State University conducted a one-year study of secondary and adult vocational programs in seven areas of the United States with large numbers of LEP persons but no federal BVT funding. The results indicate that although most programs do not recruit, assess, counsel, or instruct LEP vocational students appropriately, a few individual programs demonstrate some outstanding practices in working with LEP students (Friedenberg, 1987). These outstanding practices are found in business education as well as in other vocational programs. For example, a high school typing class in Southern California with Chinese, Vietnamese, and Spanish-speaking, as well as English-speaking students has an ethnic Chinese teacher from Vietnam who speaks English, Chinese, and Vietnamese, and a Spanish-speaking bilingual aide. This class provides instruction, handouts, and tests in four languages. An adult typing class in South Florida with Haitian, Hispanic, and English-speaking students plays multicultural background music (from Haiti, Latin America, and the U.S.) while students practice typing. This helps them become accustomed to outside noise while they work, as well as conveys acceptance of them and their cultures. A high school data entry class in Southeastern Michigan with English, Arabic, and Spanish-speaking students has an English-speaking teacher and two bilingual advocates (Spanish/English and Arabic/English) who come into the classroom as needed to tutor LEP students in their native languages.

Successful strategies that were found in other vocational classes but that could easily be applied to business education include the following:

Simplifying the English on tests

Translating tests

Providing bilingual dictionaries

Using more demonstration and visual aids

Frequently reviewing the names of equipment

Using bilingual peer tutors

Speaking English more carefully

Spending time after hours to tutor LEP students

Getting the audio portions of slides and tapes translated

Learning and using a little of the students' native languages to greet and praise them

Translating handouts

Ordering textbooks in other languages to use as reference

Bringing bilingual retired persons in from the community to tutor and to act as role models

Labeling the equipment around the room in English

Labeling the equipment around the room in their native language

Getting instruction translated onto a cassette tape.

CONCLUSION

LEP students are underrepresented in business education. Until school districts and adult programs have clearer policies for serving LEP students effectively, how they fare in business education as well as in other vocational programs will be determined by individual teachers. Learn more about LEP students by reading more professional resources, seeking out appropriate presentations and workshops, and calling on the National Center for Research in Vocational Education for help. Welcome LEP students into your classes, and use every resource and technique you can to help them.

FOLLOW-UP QUESTIONS AND ACTIVITIES

1. In what ways can VESL instruction promote both content and language learning simultaneously? What about cultural learning? Although Friedenberg doesn't develop the cultural aspect, can you think of ways in which it, too, may be incorporated?

2. Is business education strictly a secondary/adult field? Can any of its goals and objectives be served in elementary schools?

3. Why is it important that language minority students not be excluded from business education because they are speakers of another language?

4. Which strategies might you incorporate from this chapter into a program of your own? Describe a specific unit you might teach and explain how you would use these strategies. Share your ideas with a small group for their feedback.

References

Acton, W. (1979). *Second language learning and perception of difference in attitude.* Unpublished doctoral dissertation, University of Michigan.

Adler, P. S. (1972). *Culture shock and the cross cultural learning experience: Readings in intercultural education* (Vol. 2). Pittsburgh: Intercultural Communication Network.

Allen, H. (1979). *Elementary science activities for every month of the year.* West Nyack, NY: Parker.

Allen, V. (1976). *Children as teachers: Theory and research on tutoring.* New York: Academic Press.

Allen, V. (1985, December). *Language experience techniques for teaching subject content to elementary level limited English proficient students.* Paper presented at the Second Annual LAU Center Conference, Columbus, OH.

Alvarez, L. P. (1986). *Home and school contexts for language learning: A case study of two Mexican-American bilingual preschoolers.* Unpublished doctoral dissertation, Stanford University.

Anastasi, A. (1976). *Psychological testing* (3rd ed.). New York: Collier-Macmillan.

Anderson, J. R. (Ed.). (1981). *Cognitive skills and their acquisition.* Hillsdale, NJ: Erlbaum.

Anderson, J. R. (1983). *The architecture of cognition.* Cambridge: Harvard University Press.

Anderson, J. R. (1985). *Cognitive psychology and its implications* (2nd ed.). San Francisco: Freeman.

Anderson, J. R., Eisenberg, N., Holland, J., Weiner, H. S., with Rivera-Kron, C. (1983). *Integrated skills reinforcement: Reading, writing, speaking, and listening across the curriculum.* White Plains, NY: Longman.

Andrini, B. (1989). *Cooperative learning and mathematics: A multi-structural approach.* San Juan Capistrano, CA: Resources for Teachers.

Applebee, A. N. (1981). *Writing in the secondary school: English and the content area.* Urbana, IL: National Council of Teachers of English.

Asher, J. (1982). *Learning another language through actions. The complete teacher's guide.* Los Gatos, CA: Sky Oaks Productions.

Atwell, N. (1987). *In the middle: Reading and writing with adolescents.* Portsmouth, NH: Heinemann, Boynton/Cook.

Au, K. (1980). Participation structures in a reading lesson with Hawaiian children. *Anthropology and Education Quarterly, 11,* 91–115.

Au, K., & Jordan, C. (1981). Teaching reading to Hawaiian children: Finding a culturally appropriate solution. In H. Trueba, P. Guthrie, & K. Au (Eds.), *Culture and the bilingual classrooms: Studies in classroom ethnography.* New York: Newbury House.

Ausebel, D. A. (1963). Cognitive structure and the facilitation of meaningful verbal learning. *Journal of Teacher Education, 14,* 217–221.

Baker, K., & de Kanter, A. (1981). *Effectiveness of bilingual education: A review of the literature.* Washington, DC: Office of Planning and Budget, U.S. Department of Education.

Banks, J. A. (1977). Developing racial tolerance with literature in the black inner city. In Joyce & Ryan (Eds.), *Social studies and the elementary teacher,* Bulletin 53. Washington, DC: National Council for the Social Studies.

Banks, J. A. (1988). *Multiethnic education: Theory and practice* (2nd ed.). Boston: Allyn & Bacon.

Banks, J. A., with Clegg, A. A., Jr. (1985). *Teaching strategies for the social studies* (3rd ed.). White Plains, NY: Longman.

Bateson, G. (1972). *Steps to an ecology of mind.* New York: Ballantine Books.

Bausell, R., Moody, W., & Walzl, F. (1972). A factorial study of tutoring versus classroom instruction. *American Educational Research Journal, 9,* 592–597.

Beck, I. L. (1981). Reading problems and instructional practices. In T. G. Waller & G. E. MacKinnon (Eds.), *Reading research: Advances in theory and practice* (Vol. 2). New York: Academic Press.

Bejarano, Y. (1987). A cooperative small-group methodology in the language classroom. *TESOL Quarterly, 21*(3), 483–504.

Bereiter, C., & Scardamelia, M. (1981). From conversation to composition: The role of instruction in a developmental process. In R. Glaser (Ed.), *Advances in instructional psychology* (Vol. 2), pp. 1–64. Hillsdale, NJ: Erlbaum.

Bierman, K., & Furman, W. (1981). Effects of role and assignment rationale on attitudes formed during peer tutoring. *Journal of Educational Psychology, 73*(1), 33–40.

Blocksma, M., & Blocksma, D. (1983). *Easy-to-make spaceships that really fly.* Englewood Cliffs, NJ: Prentice Hall.

Bloom, B., & Krathwohl, D. (1977). *Taxonomy of educational objectives: Handbook I: Cognitive domain.* White Plains, NY: Longman.

Blount, B. (1977). Ethnography and caretaker-child interaction. In C. Snow & C. Ferguson (Eds.), *Talking to Children.* Cambridge: Cambridge University Press.

Boggs, S. (1972). The meaning of questions and narratives to Hawaiian children. In C. Cazden, V. John, & D. Hymes (Eds.), *Functions of language in the classroom* (pp. 299–327). New York: Columbia University, Teachers College Press.

Bonham, F. (1965). *Durango street.* New York: Dutton.

Brinton, D., Snow, M. A., & Wesche, M. B. (1989). *Content-based second language instruction.* New York: Newbury House.

Brodkey, D. (1983). An expectancy exercise in cohesion. *TESL Reporter, 16*(3), 43–45.

Brown, H. D. (1980). The optimal distance model of second language acquisition. *TESOL Quarterly, 14,* 157–164.

Brown, H. D. (1987). *Principles of language learning and teaching* (2nd ed.). Englewood Cliffs, NJ: Prentice Hall Regents.

Bruck, M. (1984). The feasibility of an additive bilingual program for language-impaired children. In M. Paradis & Y. Lebrun (Eds.), *Early bilingualism and child development.* Amsterdam: Swets and Zeitlinger.

Bruner, J. (1975). Language as an instrument of thought. In A. Davies (Ed.), *Problems of language and learning.* London: Heinemann.

Burak, A. (1987). Russian speakers. In M. Swan & B. Smith (Eds.), *Learner English: A teacher's guide to interference and other problems.* Cambridge: Cambridge University Press.

Burling, R. (1970). *Man's many voices.* New York: Holt, Rinehart & Winston.

Bye, M. P. (1975). *Reading in math and cognitive development.* Unpublished manuscript. (ERIC Document Reproduction Service No. ED 124 926)

Byers, P., & Byers, H. (1972). Non-verbal communication and the education of children. In C. Cazden, V. John, & D. Hymes (Eds.), *Functions of language in the classroom* (pp. 3–31). New York: Columbia University, Teachers College Press.

California Literature Institute Participants. (1985). *Literature for all students: A sourcebook for teachers.* Los Angeles: UCLA Center for Academic Interinstitutional Programs.

California State Department of Education. (1984). *Studies on immersion education: A collection for United States educators.* Los Angeles: Evaluation, Dissemination and Assessment Center, California State University.

California State Department of Education. (1986). *Beyond language: Social and cultural factors in schooling language minority students.* Los Angeles: Evaluation, Dissemination and Assessment Center, California State University.

Canale, M., & Swain, M. (1980). Theoretical bases of communicative approaches to second language teaching and testing. *Applied Linguistics, 1,* 1–47.

Cantoni-Harvey, G. (1987). *Content-area language instruction: Approaches and strategies.* Reading, MA: Addison-Wesley.

Carin, A. A., & Sund, R. B. (1985). *Teaching science through discovery* (5th ed.). Columbus, OH: Merrill.

Carlson, S., & Bridgeman, B. (1983). *Survey of academic writing tasks required for graduate and undergraduate foreign students (TOEFL Research Report #15).* Princeton, NJ: Educational Testing Service.

Carlson, S., Bridgeman, B., Camp, R., & Waanders, J. (1985). *Relationship of admission test scores to writing performance of native and nonnative speakers of English (TOEFL Research Report #19).* Princeton, NJ: Educational Testing Service.

Carmichael, L., Hogan, H. P., & Walter, A. A. (1932). An experimental study of the effect of language on visually perceived form. *Journal of Experimental Psychology, 15,* 73–86.

Carrell, P. L. (1986). Text as interaction: Some implications of text analysis and reading research for ESL composition. In U. Connor & R. B. Kaplan (Eds.), *Writing across languages: Analysis of L2 text* (pp. 55–72). Reading, MA: Addison-Wesley.

Carrell, P. L. (1987, March). *Readability in ESL: A schema perspective.* Paper presented at the TESOL Convention, Miami, FL.

Carrell, P. L., & Eisterhold, J. C. (1983). Schema theory and ESL reading pedagogy. *TESOL Quarterly, 17*(4), 553–572.

Cazden, C. B. (1979). Curriculum/language contexts for bilingual education. In E. J. Briere (Ed.), *Language development in a bilingual setting* (pp. 129–138). Los Angeles: National Dissemination and Assessment Center, California State University. (ERIC Document Reproduction Service No. ED 224 661)

Cazden, C. B. (1985). Classroom discourse. In M. C. Wittrock (Ed.), *Handbook of research on teaching* (3rd ed.). New York: Macmillan.

Cazden, C. B., & Legrett, E. (1981). Culturally responsive education: Recommendations for achieving Lau Remedies II. In H. Trueba, P. Guthrie, & K. Au (Eds.), *Culture and the bilingual classroom.* New York: Newbury House.

Celce-Murcia, M. (1987, May). *New concerns in English as a foreign language.* ATESL Plenary speech at the 39th Annual NAFSA Convention, Long Beach, CA.

Celce-Murcia, M., & Larsen-Freeman, D. (1983). *The grammar book.* New York: Newbury House.

Celce-Murcia, M., & Hawkins, B. (1985). Contrastive analysis, error analysis, and interlanguage analysis. In M. Celce-Murcia (Ed.), *Beyond basics: Issues and research in TESOL.* New York: Newbury House.

Chamot, A. U. (1981). Applications of second language acquisition research to the bilingual classroom. *Focus, 8.* Wheaton, MD: National Clearinghouse for Bilingual Education.

Chamot, A. U. (1985). English language development through a content-based approach. In *Issues in English language development* (pp. 49–55). Wheaton, MD: National Clearinghouse for Bilingual Education.

Chamot, A. U. (1987a). *America: the early years.* Language development through content. Reading, MA: Addison-Wesley.

Chamot, A. U. (1987b). *America: after independence.* Language development through content. Reading, MA: Addison-Wesley.

Chamot, A. U. (1987c). *Teacher's guide: America: the early years/America: after independence.* Language development through content. Reading, MA: Addison-Wesley.

Chamot, A. U. (1988). *Mathematics, Book A.* Language development through content. Reading, MA: Addison-Wesley.

Chamot, A. U., & O'Malley, J. M. (1986a). *A cognitive academic language learning approach: An ESL content-based curriculum.* Wheaton, MD: National Clearinghouse for Bilingual Education.

Chamot, A. U., & O'Malley, J. M. (1986b). Language learning strategies for children. *The Language Teacher, 10*(1), 9–12.

Chamot, A. U., & O'Malley, J. M. (1987). The cognitive academic language learning approach. *TESOL Quarterly, 21,* 227–247.

Chamot, A. U., & Stewner-Manzanares, G. (1985). *A summary of current literature on English as a second language.* Rosslyn, VA: InterAmerica Research Associates.

Chang, J. (1987). Chinese speakers. In M. Swan & B. Smith (Eds.), *Learner English: A teacher's guide to interference and other problems.* Cambridge: Cambridge University Press.

Chavez, J. (1984). *The lost land: The Chicano image of the Southwest.* Albuquerque: University of New Mexico Press.

Cheng, D. (1948). *Acculturation of the Chinese in the United States: A Philadelphia study.* Foochow, China: Fukien Christian University Press.

Chihara, T., & Oller, J. W. (1978). Attitudes and proficiency in EFL: A sociolinguistic study of adult Japanese speakers. *Language Learning, 28,* 55–68.

Chimombo, M. (1987). Towards reality in the classroom. *ELT Journal, 41,* 204–210.

Chipman, S., Sigel, J., & Glaser, R. (Eds.). (1985). *Thinking and learning skills: Relating learning to basic research* (Vols. 1–2). Hillsdale, NJ: Erlbaum.

Cicirelli, V. (1972). The effect of sibling relationship on concept learning of young children taught by child-teachers. *Child Development, 43,* 282–287.

Clarke, M. A. (1976). Second language acquisition as a clash of consciousness. *Language Learning, 26,* 377–390.

Clarke, M., Losoff, A., McCracken, D., & Rood, D. S. (1984). Linguistic relativity and sex/gender studies: Epistemological and methodological consideration. *Language Learning, 34,* 47–67.

Clemens, S. L. (1986). *The adventures of Tom Sawyer.* New York: Penguin.

Clement, J. (1981). *Algebra word problem solutions: Thought processes underlying a common misconception.* Unpublished manuscript. Amherst, MA: Dartmouth College, Department of Physics and Astronomy, Cognitive Development Project.

Cloward, R. (1967). Studies in tutoring. *Journal of Experimental Education, 36*(1), 14–25.

Cohen, A. D., & Aphek, E. (1981). Easifying second language learning. *Studies in Second Language Acquisition, 3*, 221–236.

Cohen, E. (1984). Talking and working together. In P. Peterson, L. Wilkinson, & M. Hallinan (Eds.), *The social context of instruction*. New York: Academic Press.

Cohen, E. (1986). *Designing group work: Strategies for the heterogeneous classroom*. New York: Columbia University, Teachers College Press.

Cohen, E., & DeAvila, E. (1984). *Learning to think in math and science: A program for linguistic and academic diversity*. Report to National Curriculum Dissemination Network. Palo Alto, CA: Stanford University.

Cohen, E., & Lotan, R. (1987). *Application of sociology to science teaching: Program for complex instruction*. Report 7–CERAS–17. Stanford, CA: Center for Educational Research at Stanford.

Cole, R. (1987). Some interactional aspects of ESL instruction for preliterates. In C. Cargill (Ed.), *A TESOL professional anthology: Culture*. Lincolnwood, IL: National Textbook Company.

Collier, J. (1973). *Alaskan Eskimo education*. New York: Holt, Rinehart & Winston.

Collie, J., & Slater, S. (1987). *Literature in the language classroom: A resource book of ideas and activities*. New York: Cambridge University Press.

Combs, A., & Snygg, D. (1959). *Individual behavior: A perceptual approach*. New York: Harper & Row.

Condon, E. C. (1973). *Introduction to cross cultural communication*. New Brunswick, NJ: Rutgers-The State University.

Condon, J. (1984). *With respect to the Japanese: A guide for Americans*. Yarmouth, ME: Intercultural Press.

Condon, J. (1986). . . . So near the United States. In J. M. Valdes (Ed.), *Culture bound: Bridging the cultural gap in language teaching* (pp. 85–93). Cambridge: Cambridge University Press.

Condon, J., & Yousef, F. (1975). *An introduction to intercultural communication*. Indianapolis, IN: Bobbs-Merrill.

Connor, U., & Kaplan, R. B. (1987). *Writing across languages: Analysis of L2 text*. Reading, MA: Addison-Wesley.

Connor, W. (Ed.). (1986). *Mexican American in comparative perspective*. Washington, DC: Urban Institute.

Cortes, C. (1986). The education of language minority students: A contextual interaction model. In California State Department of Education, *Beyond Language: Social and Cultural Factors in Schooling Language Minority Students* (pp. 3–33). Los Angeles: Evaluation and Dissemination and Assessment Center, California State University.

Crandall, J. (Ed.). (1987). *ESL through content-area instruction: Mathematics, science, social studies*. Englewood Cliffs, NJ: Prentice Hall Regents/Center for Applied Linguistics.

Crandall, J., Dale, T. C., Rhodes, N. C., & Spanos, G. (1985, October). *The language of mathematics: The English barrier*. Paper presented at the Delaware Symposium on Language Studies VII. University of Delaware, Newark, DE.

Crandall, J., Dale, T. C., Rhodes, N. C., & Spanos, G. (1989). *English skills for algebra*. Englewood Cliffs, NJ: Prentice Hall Regents/Center for Applied Linguistics.

Cuevas, G. J. (1981, April). *SLAMS: A second language approach to mathematics learning*. Paper presented at the annual meeting of the National Council of Teachers of Mathematics, Toronto.

Cuevas, G. J. (1984). Mathematics learning in English as a second language. *Journal for Research in Mathematics Education, 15,* 134–144.

Cuevas, G. J., Mann, P., & McClung, R. M. (1985, August). *Language orientation to mathematics teaching.* Paper presented at the annual meeting of the American Psychological Association, Los Angeles.

Cummins, J. (1979a). Cognitive/academic language proficiency, linguistic interdependence, the optimum age question and some other matters. *Working Papers on Bilingualism, 19,* 121–129.

Cummins, J. (1979b). Linguistic interdependence and the educational development of bilingual children. *Review of Educational Research, 49*(2), 222–251.

Cummins, J. (1980). The exit and entry fallacy of bilingual education. *NABE Journal, 4*(3), 25–59.

Cummins, J. (1981). The role of primary language development in promoting educational success for language minority students. In California State Department of Education, *Schooling and language minority students: A theoretical framework* (pp. 3–49). Los Angeles: Evaluation, Dissemination and Assessment Center, California State University.

Cummins, J. (1982). Tests, achievement, and bilingual students. *Focus, 9.* Wheaton, MD: National Clearinghouse for Bilingual Education.

Cummins, J. (1983a). *Heritage language education: A literature review.* Toronto: Ministry of Education, Ontario.

Cummins, J. (1983b). Language proficiency and academic achievement. In J. Oller, Jr. (Ed.), *Issues in language testing research.* New York: Newbury House.

Cummins, J. (1983c). Conceptual and linguistic foundations of language assessment. In S. S. Seidner (Ed.), *Issues of language assessment: Vol. 2. Language assessment and curriculum planning* (pp. 7–16). Wheaton, MD: National Clearinghouse for Bilingual Education.

Cummins, J. (1984a). *Bilingualism and special education: Issues in assessment and pedagogy.* Clevedon, England: Multilingual Matters.

Cummins, J. (1984b). *Bilingualism and special education: Issues in assessment and pedagogy.* San Diego: College-Hill.

Cummins, J. (1986). Empowering minority students: A framework for intervention. *Harvard Educational Review, 56*(1), 18–36.

Cummins, J., & Das, J. (1977). Cognitive processing and reading difficulties: A framework for research. *Alberta Journal of Educational Research, 23,* 245–256.

Cummins, J., Swain, M., Nakajima, K., Handscombe, J., Green, D., & Tran, C. (1984). Linguistic interdependence among Japanese and Vietnamese immigrant students. In C. Rivera (Ed.), *Communicative competence approaches to language proficiency assessment: Research and application.* Clevedon, England: Multilingual Matters.

Curtain, H. A., & Martinez, L. S. (1990). Elementary school content-based foreign language instruction. In A. M. Padilla, H. H. Fairchild, & C. M. Valadez (Eds.), *Foreign language education: Issues and strategies* (pp. 201–202). Newbury Park, CA: Sage.

Damen, L. (1987). *Culture learning: The fifth dimension in the language classroom.* Reading, MA: Addison-Wesley.

Dannequin, C. (1977). *Les enfants baillinnes.* Paris: CEDIC, Di FFUSION Nathan.

Das, J., & Cummins, J. (1982). Language processing and reading disability. In K. Gadow & I. Bialer (Eds.), *Advances in learning and behavioral disabilities: A research annual.* Greenwich, CT: JAI Press.

Davidson, R. G., Kline, S. B., & Snow, C. E. (1986). Definitions and definite noun phrases: Indicators of children's decontextualized language skills. *Journal of Research in Childhood Education, 1,* 37–48.

Dawe, L. (1983). Bilingualism and mathematical reasoning in English as a second language. *Educational Studies in Mathematics, 14,* 325–353.

Dawe, L. (1984, August). A theoretical framework for the study of the effects of bilingualism on mathematics teaching and learning. Paper presented at the Fifth International Congress on Mathematical Education, Adelaide, Australia.

DeAvila, E., & Duncan, S. (1984). *Finding out/descubrimento: Teacher's guide.* San Rafael, CA: Lingametrics Group.

DeAvila, E., Duncan, S., & Navarrete, C. J. (1987). *Finding out/descubrimiento: Teacher's resource guide.* Northvale, NJ: Santillana.

Deen, J. (1986). *An analysis of students' questions in a cooperative learning setting.* Unpublished manuscript, University of California, Los Angeles.

Deen, J. (1987). *An analysis of classroom interaction in a cooperative learning and teacher-centered setting.* Unpublished master's thesis, University of California, Los Angeles.

Delgado-Gaitan, C. (1982). *Learning how: Rules for knowing and doing for Mexican children at home, play, and school.* Unpublished doctoral dissertation, Stanford University.

Department of Education and Science. (1975). *A language for life: Report of the Committee of Inquiry appointed by the Secretary of State for Education and Science under the chairmanship of Sir Alan Bullock, F.B.A.* London: Her Majesty's Stationery Office.

Derry, S. J., & Murphy, D. A. (1986). Designing systems that train learning ability: From theory to practice. *Review of Educational Research, 56,* 1–39.

Díaz, S., Moll, L., & Mehan, H. (1986). Sociocultural resources in instruction: A context-specific approach. In California State Department of Education, *Beyond language: Social and cultural factors in schooling language minority students* (pp. 187–230). Los Angeles: Evaluation, Dissemination and Assessment Center, California State University.

Dolciani, M., & Wooten, W. (1970). *Modern algebra: Structure and method* (Book 1) (rev. ed.). Boston: Houghton Mifflin.

Donaldson, M. (1978) *Children's minds.* Glasgow, Scotland: Collins.

Doushaq, M. H. (1986). An investigation into stylistic errors of Arab students learning English for academic purposes. *ESP Journal, 5*(1), 27–39.

Dumont, R. V., Jr. (1972). Learning English and how to be silent: Studies in Sioux and Cherokee classrooms. In C. Cazden, V. John & D. Hymes (Eds.), *Functions of language in the classroom* (pp. 344–369). New York: Columbia University, Teachers College Press.

Durkheim, E. (1897). *Le suicide.* Paris: F. Alcan.

Ebel, R. L. (1977). *The uses of standardized testing.* Bloomington, IN: Phi Delta Kappa Foundation.

Edelsky, C., Hudelson, S., Flores, B., Barkin, F., Altweger, B., & Jilbert, K. (1983). Semilingualism and language deficit. *Applied linguistics, 4,* 1–22.

Edwards, H., Wesche, M. B., Krashen, S., Clément, R., & Kruidenier, B. (1984). Second language acquisition through subject matter learning. *Canadian Modern Language Review, 41*(2), 268–282.

Eisenberg, A. (1982). *Language acquisition in cultural perspective: Talk in three Mexicano homes.* Unpublished doctoral dissertation, University of California, Berkeley.

Ellis, R. (1984). *Classroom second language development.* Oxford: Pergamon Press.

Encisco, Jorge. (1947). *Design Motifs of Ancient Mexico.* New York: Dover.

Enright, D. S., & McCloskey, M. L. (1985). "Yes, talking!: Organizing the classroom to promote second language acquisition. *TESOL Quarterly, 19*(3), 431-453.

Enright, D. S., & McCloskey, M. L. (1988). *Integrating English.* Reading, MA: Addison-Wesley.

Erikson, F. (1982). *The counselor as gatekeeper: Social interaction in interviews.* New York: Academic Press.

Erickson, M., & Cromack, T. (1972). Evaluating a tutoring program. *Journal of Experimental Education, 41*, 27-31.

Escobedo, T. H. (Ed.). (1983). *Early childhood bilingual education: A Hispanic perspective.* New York: Columbia University, Teachers College Press.

Fader, D., Duggins, J., Finn, T., & McNeil, E. (1976). *The new hooked on books.* New York: Berkeley.

Falk, J. (1988). *More science activities.* New York: Galison Books.

Fathman, A. K., & Quinn, M. E. (1989). *Science for language learners.* Englewood Cliffs, NJ: Prentice Hall Regents/Center for Applied Linguistics.

Feeley, J. T. (1983). Help for the reading teacher: Dealing with the limited English proficient (LEP) child in the elementary classroom. *Reading Teacher, 35*(7), 650-655.

Finnan, C. (1980). *Community influence on occupational identity development: Vietnamese refugees and job training.* Paper presented at American Anthropological Association Meetings.

Firsching, J. T. (1982). Speaker expectations and mathematics word problems. *The SECOL Review, 3*, 35-47.

Flaugher, R. (1978). The many definitions of test bias. *American Psychologist, 33*(7), 671-679.

Fletcher, P., & Garman, M. (Eds.). (1979) *Language Acquisition.* Cambridge: Cambridge University Press.

Ford Foundation. (1984). *Hispanics: Challenges and opportunities.* New York: Ford Foundation.

Ford, M. (1979). *The development of an instrument for assessing levels of ethnicity in public school teachers.* Unpublished doctoral dissertation, University of Houston.

Foster, G. M. (1962). Traditional cultures. New York: Harper & Row.

Foster, P. (1972). Attitudinal effects on fifth graders of tutoring younger children. *Dissertation Abstracts International, 33*, 5-A, (University Microfilms No. 2235).

Frechette, E. (1987). Some aspects of Saudi culture. In C. Cargill (Ed.), *A TESOL professional anthology: Culture.* Lincolnwood, IL: National Textbook Company.

Frederiksen, J. R., Weaver, P. A., Warren, B. M., Gillotte, H. P., Rosebery, A. S., Freeman, B., & Goodman, L. (1983). *A componential approach to training reading skills* (Report No. 5295). Cambridge, MA: Bolt, Beranek & Newman.

Freedman, G., & Reynolds, E. (1980). Enriching basal reader lessons with semantic webbing. *The Reading Teacher, 33*, 677-684.

Freire, P. (1970). *Pedagogy of the oppressed.* New York: Seabury.

Friedenberg, J. (1987). *The condition of vocational education for LEP students in selected areas of the United States.* Columbus, OH: National Center for Research in Vocational Education.

Friedenberg, J. E., & Bradley, C. H. (1984). *The vocational ESL handbook.* New York: Newbury House.

Fry, E. B. (1968). A readability formula that saves time. *Journal of Reading, 11*, 513-581.

Frye, N. (1964). *The educated imagination.* Bloomington: Indiana University Press.

Fulwiler, T. (Ed.). (1987). *The journal book.* Portsmouth, NH: Boynton/Cook, Heinemann.

Gadda, G., Peitzman, F., & Walsh, W. (1988). *Teaching analytical writing.* Los Angeles: UCLA Center for Academic Interinstitutional Programs.

Gaies, S. (1985). *Peer involvement in language learning.* Englewood Cliffs, NJ: Prentice Hall Regents/Center for Applied Linguistics.

Gamberg, R., Kwak, W., Hutchings, M., & Altheim, J. (1988). *Learning and loving it.* Portsmouth, NH: Heinemann.

Gardiner, J. R. (1980). *Stone Fox.* New York: Harper & Row.

Gardner, R. C., & Lambert, W. E. (1972). Attitudes and motivation in second language learning. New York: Newbury House.

Garvey, C. (1977). *Play.* Cambridge: Harvard University Press.

Genesee, F. (1986). The baby and the bathwater or what immersion has to say about bilingual education—Significant immersion instructional features. *NABE Journal, 10*(3), 227–254.

Genesee, F. (1987). *Learning through two languages: Studies in immersion and bilingual education.* New York: Newbury House.

Gilles, C., Bixby, M., Crowley, P., Crenshaw, S. R., Henrichs, M., Reynolds, F. E., & Pyle, D. (1988). *Whole language strategies for secondary students.* New York: Richard C. Owens.

Gleason, H. A. (1961). *An introduction to descriptive linguistics* (rev. ed.). New York: Holt, Rinehart & Winston.

Goelman, H., Oberg, A., & Smith, F. (Eds.). (1984). *Awakening to literacy.* Portsmouth, NH: Heinemann.

González, A. (1983a). *Classroom cooperation and ethnic balance: Chicanos and equal status.* Unpublished manuscript, California State University, Fresno, Psychology Department.

González, A. (1983b). *A cooperative/interdependent technique for the bilingual classroom and measures related to social motives.* Unpublished manuscript, California State University, Fresno, Psychology Department.

González, P. C. (1981). Second language learning in a social studies classroom. *The Social Studies,* November/December, 254–260.

Goodlad, S., & Hirst, B. (1989). *Peer tutoring: A guide to learning by teaching.* London: Kogan Page; New York: Nichols.

Goodman, K. S. (1982). Acquiring literacy is natural: Who skilled cock robin? In. F. Gollasch (Ed.), *Language and literacy: Selected writings of Kenneth S. Goodman* (Vol. 2). Boston: Routledge & Kegan Paul.

Goodman, K., Goodman, Y., & Flores, B. (1979). *Reading in the bilingual classroom: Literacy and biliteracy.* Rosslyn, VA: National Clearinghouse for Bilingual Education.

Gossard, J. (1986). Using read-around groups to establish criteria for good writing. In C. B. Olson (Ed.), *Practical ideas for teaching writing as a process* (pp. 132–135). Sacramento: California State Department of Education.

Graham, J. G. (1987). English language proficiency and the prediction of academic success. *TESOL Quarterly, 21,* 505–522.

Graham, L. (1958). *South town.* Chicago: Follett.

Graham, L. (1965). *North town.* New York: Crowell.

Graham, L. (1969). *Whose town?* New York: Crowell.

Green, P. S., & Hecht, K. (1985). Native and nonnative evaluation of learner's errors in written discourse. *System, 13*(2), 77–97.

Guiora, A. Z. (1981). Language, personality and culture or the Whorfian hypothesis revisited. In M. Hines & W. Rutherford (Eds.), *On TESOL '81.* Washington, DC: TESOL.

Gunnarson, B. (1978). A look at content similarities between intelligence, achievement, personality, and language tests. In J. Oller & K. Perkins (Eds.), *Language education: Testing the tests*. New York: Newbury House.

Hall, D., Hawkey, R., Kenny, B., & Storer, G. (1986). Patterns of thought in scientific writing: A course in information structuring for engineering students. *ESP Journal, 5*(2), 147–160.

Hall, E. T. (1959). *The silent language*. New York: Doubleday.

Hall, E. T. (1966). *The hidden dimension*. New York: Doubleday.

Hall, E. T. (1976). How cultures collide. *Psychology Today, 10*, 66–78.

Halliday, M. A. K. (1975). Some aspects of sociolinguistics. In E. Jacobsen (Ed.), *Interactions between linguistics and mathematical education: Final report of the symposium sponsored by UNESCO, CEDO and ICMI, Nairobi, Kenya, September 1–11, 1974* (UNESCO Report No. ED-74/CONF.808, pp. 25–52). Paris: United Nations Educational, Scientific and Cultural Organization.

Hannah, G. G. (1982). *Classroom spaces and places*. Belmont, CA: Pitman Learning.

Harris, M. (1971). Learning by tutoring others. *Today's Education, 60*, 48–49.

Harrison, P. A. (1983). *Behaving Brazilian: A comparison of Brazilian and North American social behavior*. New York: Newbury House.

Hatch, E., Gough, J. W., & Peck, S. (1985). What case studies reveal about system, sequence, and variation in second language acquisition. In M. Celce-Murcia (Ed.), *Beyond basics: Issues and research in TESOL* (pp. 37–59). New York: Newbury House.

Hauptman, P. C., Wesche, M. B., & Ready, D. (1988). Second language acquisition through subject-matter learning: A follow-up study at the University of Ottawa. *Language Learning, 38*(3), 439–482.

Hawkins, B. (1988). *Scaffolded classroom interaction and its relation to second language acquisition for minority language children*. Unpublished doctoral dissertation, University of California, Los Angeles.

Hayden, D., & Cuevas, G. (1990). In D. J. Short & G. Spanos (Eds.), *Pre-algebra lexicon*. Washington, DC: Center for Applied Linguistics.

Hayes, C. W., & Bahruth, R. (1985). Querer es poder. In J. Hansen, T. Newkirk, & D. Graves (Eds.), *Breaking ground: Teachers relate reading and writing in the elementary school*. Portsmouth, NH: Heinemann.

Hayes, C. W., Bahruth, R., & Kessler, C. (1985). *To read you must write: Children in language acquisition*. Paper presented at the First International Conference on Second/Foreign Language Acquisition by Children, Oklahoma City, OK.

Heath, S. B. (1982a). Questioning at home and at school: A comparative study. In G. Spindler (Ed.), *Doing the ethnography of schooling: Educational anthropology in action*. New York: Holt, Rinehart & Winston.

Heath, S. B. (1982b). What no bedtime story means: Narrative skills at home and school. *Language in Society, 11*(2), 49–76.

Heath, S. B. (1983a). A lot of talk about nothing. *Language Arts, 60*(8), 999–1007.

Heath, S. B. (1983b). *Ways with words: Language, life and work in communities and classrooms*. Cambridge: Cambridge University Press.

Heath, S. B. (1984). Linguistics and education. *Annual Review of Anthropology, 13*. Palo Alto, CA: Annual Reviews.

Heath, S. B. (1985a). Being literate in America: A sociohistorical perspective. In J. A. Niles (Ed.), *Issues in literacy: A research perspective—Thirty-fourth Yearbook of the National Reading Conference*. Rochester, NY: National Reading Conference.

Heath, S. B. (1985b). Intelligent writing in an audience community. In S. W. Freedman (Ed.), *The acquisition of written language: Revision & response*. Norwood, NJ: Ablex.

Heath, S. B. (1985c). Language policies: Patterns in retention and maintenance. In W. Connor (Ed.), *Mexican Americans in comparative perspective*. Washington, DC: Urban Institute.

Heath, S. B. (1986). Sociolinguistic contexts of language development. In California State Department of Education, *Beyond language: Social and cultural factors in schooling language minority students* (pp. 143–186). Los Angeles: Evaluation, Dissemination and Assessment Center, California State University.

Helmus, T. M., Toppin, E. A., Pounds, N. J., & Arnsdorf, V. E. (1988). *The United States yesterday and today*. Englewood Cliffs, NJ: Silver, Burdett & Ginn.

Henry, G. H. (1978). *Teaching reading as concept development: Emphasis on affective thinking*. Newark, DE: International Reading Association.

Herber, H. L. (1978). *Teaching reading in the content areas* (2nd ed.). Englewood Cliffs, NJ: Prentice Hall.

Herbert, D. (1980). *Mr. Wizard's supermarket science*. New York: Random House.

Herman, M. E. (1983). *Fabulas bilingues*. Lincolnwood, IL: National Textbook Company.

Hill, R. W. (1979). *Secondary school reading: Process, program procedure*. Boston: Allyn & Bacon.

Hinds, J. (1983). Contrastive rhetoric: Japanese and English. *Text, 3*, 183–195.

Holt, D. (1986). *Creating a community in the second language classroom*. Unpublished manuscript, California State Department of Education, Sacramento.

Honeyfield, J. (1977). Simplication. *TESOL Quarterly, 4*, 431–440.

Horan, J., DeGirolomo, M., Hill, R., & Shute, R. (1974). The effect of older-peer participant models on deficient academic performance. *Psychology in the Schools, 2*, 207–212.

Horowitz, D. (1986). What professors actually require: Academic tasks for the ESL classroom. *TESOL Quarterly, 20*, 445–462.

Horwitz, E. (1986). Adapting communication-centered activities to student conceptual level. *Canadian Modern Language Review, 42*(4), 827–840.

Houston, J. W. (1975). *Farewell to Manzanar*. New York: Bantam.

Hsu, F. (1949). *Under the ancestors' shadow*. London: Routledge & Kegan Paul.

Hsu, F. (1955). *Americans and Chinese*. London: Cresset Press.

Hsu, F. (1983). Chinese kinship and Chinese behavior. In F. Hsu (Ed.), *Rugged individualism reconsidered*. Knoxville: University of Tennessee Press.

Hu, C. (1960). *China: Its people, its society, its culture*. New Haven, CT: Human Relations Area Files.

Hu, H. (1944). The Chinese concepts of face. *American Anthropologist, 46*, 45–64.

Hume, E. (1985). Vietnam's legacy: Ten years after: A series. *The Wall Street Journal*, March 21, pp. 1, 15.

Hunter, K. (1969). *The soul brothers and sister Lou*. New York: Scribner.

Immigration and Naturalization Service, U. S. Department of Justice. (1987). *United States history 1600–1987*. Washington, DC: Government Printing Office.

Iwatake, S. (1978). Bridging the Asian cultural gap. In D. Ilyin & T. Tragardh (Eds.), *Classroom practices in adult ESL*. Washington, DC: TESOL.

Jackson, G., & Cosca, C. (1974). The inequality of educational opportunity in the Southwest: An observational study of ethnically mixed classrooms. *American Educational Research Journal, 10*, 219–229.

Jacob, E., & Mattson, B. (1987). *Cooperative learning: A way to instruct heterogeneous classes of language minority students.* Unpublished manuscript, Center for Applied Linguistics, Washington, DC.

James, M. O. (1987). ESL reading pedagogy: Implications of schema-theoretical research. In J. Devine, P. L. Carell, & D. E. Eskey (Eds.), *Research in reading in English as a second language* (pp. 175–188). Washington, DC: TESOL.

Jenkins, S., & Hinds, J. (1987). Business letter-writing: English, French, and Japanese. *TESOL Quarterly, 21,* 327–349.

Johns, A. (1986). The ESL student and the revision process: Some insights from schema theory. *Journal of Basic Writing, 5*(2), 70–80.

Johns, A. (1987). On assigning summaries: Some suggestions and cautions. *TECFORS, 10*(2), 1–5.

Johnson, D. (1983). Natural language learning by design: A classroom experiment in social interaction and second language acquisition. *TESOL Quarterly, 17*(1), 55–68.

Johnson, D. W., & Johnson, F. P. (1987). *Joining together: Group theory and group skills.* Englewood Cliffs, NJ: Prentice Hall Regents/Center for Applied Linguistics.

Johnson, D.M., & Roen, D.H. (Eds.). (1989). *Richness in writing.* White Plains, NY: Longman.

Johnson, T. D., & Louis, D. R. (1988). *Literacy through literature.* Portsmouth, NH: Heinemann.

Johnston, J., & Johnston, M. (1990). *Content points A: Science, mathematics & social studies.* Reading, MA: Addison-Wesley.

Johnston, J., & Johnston, M. (1990). *Content points B: Science, mathematics & social studies.* Reading, MA: Addison-Wesley.

Johnston, J., & Johnston, M. (1990). *Content points C: Science, mathematics & social studies.* Reading, MA: Addison-Wesley.

Jordan, C. (1978). Teaching learning interactions and school adaptations: The Hawaiian case. In *A multidisciplinary approach to research in education: The Kamehameha early education program* (pp. 31–38) (Technical Report No. 181). Honolulu: Kamehameha Schools/ Bishop Estate, Center for Development of Early Education.

Kagan, S. (1980). Cooperation-competition, culture, and structural bias in classrooms. In S. Sharan, P. Hare, C. Webb, & R. Hertz-Lazarowitz (Eds.), *Cooperation in education* (pp. 197–211). Provo, UT: Brigham Young University Press.

Kagan, S. (1986). Cooperative learning and sociocultural factors in schooling. In California State Department of Education, *Beyond language: Social and cultural factors in schooling language minority students* (pp. 231–298). Los Angeles: Evaluation, Dissemination and Assessment Center, California State University.

Kagan, S. (1988). *Cooperative learning resources for teachers.* Laguna Nigel, CA: Resources for Teachers.

Kaplan, R. B. (Ed.). (1983). *Annual Review of Applied Linguistics, 3,* New York: Newbury House.

Katsaiti, L. (1983). *Interlingual transfer of a cognitive skill in bilinguals.* Unpublished master's thesis, University of Toronto.

Kessler, C., & Quinn, M. E. (1980). Positive effects of bilingualism on science problem-solving abilities. In J. E. Alatis (Ed.), *Current issues in bilingual education: Proceedings from the Georgetown University round table on languages and linguistics.* Washington, DC: Georgetown University Press.

Kessler, C., & Quinn, M. E. (1984, March). *Second language acquisition in the context of science experiences.* Paper presented at the TESOL Convention, Houston, TX. (ERIC Document Reproduction Service No. ED 248 713)

Kessler, C., & Quinn, M. E. (1985). Positive effects of bilingualism on science problem-solving abilities. In J. E. Alatis & J. J. Staczek (Eds.), *Perspectives on bilingualism and bilingual education.* Washington, DC: Georgetown University Press.

Kessler, C., & Quinn, M. E. (1987). ESL and science learning. In J. Crandall (Ed.), *ESL through content-area instruction* (pp. 55–88). Englewood Cliffs, NJ: Prentice Hall Regents/Center for Applied Linguistics.

Kessler, C., & Quinn, M. E. (1988, March). Cooperative learning in ESL science classes. Paper presented at the TESOL Convention, Chicago, IL.

Kessler, C., Quinn, M. E., & Hayes, C. W. (1985, October). *Processing mathematics in a second language: Problems for LEP children.* Paper presented at the Delaware Symposium on Language Studies VII, University of Delaware, Newark, DE.

Khalil, A. (1985). Communicative error evaluation: Native speakers' evaluation and interpretation of written errors of Arab EFL learners. *TESOL Quarterly, 19,* 335–351.

King, D., & Watson, D. (1983). Reading as meaning construction. In B. Busching & J. Schwarts (Eds.). *Integrating the language arts in the elementary school.* Urbana, IL: National Council of Teachers of English.

Klosterman, R. (1970). The effectiveness of a diagnostically structured reading program. *The Reading Teacher, 24,* 159–162.

Knight, L., & Hargis, C. (1977). Math language ability: Its relationship to reading in math. *Language Arts, 54,* 423–428.

Koch, K. (1970). *Wishes, lies, and dreams: Teaching children to write poetry.* New York: Perennial/Harper & Row.

Koch, K. (1973). *Rose, where did you get that red?* New York: Vintage.

Koch, K., & Farrell, K. (1981). *Sleeping on the wing: An anthology of poetry with essays on reading and writing.* New York: Vintage.

Kohlberg, L., & Mayer, R. (1972). Development as the aim of education. *Harvard Educational Review, 42,* 449–496.

Krashen, S. D. (1982). *Principles and practice in second language acquisition.* Oxford: Pergamon Press.

Krashen, S. D., & Terrell, T. (1983). *The natural approach: Language acquisition in the classroom.* Oxford: Pergamon Press.

Kroll, B. (1982). *Levels in error in ESL composition.* Unpublished doctoral dissertation, University of Southern California.

Kroll, B. (1987, April). *Graduate students in ESL writing classes.* Paper presented at the meeting of the Conference on College Composition and Communication, Atlanta, GA.

Lado, R. (1957). *Linguistics across cultures.* Ann Arbor: University of Michigan Press.

Lambert, W. E. (1967). A social psychology of bilingualism. *Journal of Social Issues, 23,* 91–109.

Lambert, W. E., & Tucker, G. R. (1972). *Bilingual education of children: The St. Lambert experiment.* New York: Newbury House.

Lampe, P. E. (1984). Mexican American labeling and mislabeling. *Hispanic Journal of Behavioral Sciences, 6*(1), 77–85.

Langer, J. (1986). *Children reading and writing: Structures and strategies.* Norwood, NJ: Ablex.

Laosa, L. (1980). Maternal teaching strategies and cognitive styles in Chicano families. *Journal of Educational Psychology, 72,* 45–54.

Laosa, L. (1984). Sociocultural diversity in modes of family interaction. In R. W. Henderson (Ed.), *Parent-child interaction: Theory, research, and prospect.* New York: Academic Press.

Lapp, D., & Flood, J. (1978). *Teaching reading to every child.* New York: Macmillan.

Larson, D. N., & Smalley, W. A. (1972). *Becoming bilingual: A guide to language learning.* New Canaan, CT: Practical Anthropology.

Lay-Dopyera, M., & Dopyera, J. (1987). *Becoming a teacher of young children* (3rd ed.). New York: Random House.

Lee, D., & Allen, R. V. (1963). *Learning to read through experience.* New York: Appleton-Century-Crofts.

Leiderman, P. H., Tulkin, S. R., & Rosenfeld, A. (Eds.). (1977). *Culture and infancy: Variations in the human experience.* New York: Academic Press.

Levine, D. (1982). The educational backgrounds of Saudi Arabian and Algerian students. In L. Samovar & R. Porter (Eds.), *Understanding intercultural communication.* Belmont, CA: Wadsworth.

Lewis, G. (1974). *Linguistics and second language pedagogy: A theoretical study.* The Hague: Mouton.

Lim, P. L., & Smalzer, W. (1990). *Noteworthy: Listening and notetaking skills.* New York: Newbury House.

Lindstrom, M. (1981). *Native speaker reaction to second language errors in academic prose.* Unpublished master's thesis, Colorado State University.

Liu, H. (1959). The traditional Chinese clan rules. *Monographs of the Association for Asian Studies VII.* Locust Valley, NY: J. J. Augustin.

Loftus, E. F. (1976). *Language memories in the judicial system.* Paper presented at the NWAVE Conference, Georgetown University.

Long, M. (1981). Input, interaction, and second-language acquisition. *Annals of the New York Academy of Sciences, 379,* 259–278.

Long, M., & Porter, P. (1985). Group work, interlanguage talk, and second language acquisition. *TESOL Quarterly, 19*(2), 207–228.

Loughlin, C. E., & Suina, J. J. (1982). *The learning environment: An instructional strategy.* New York: Columbia University, Teachers College Press.

Macnamara, J. (1970). Bilingualism and thought. In J. J. Alatis (Ed.), *Proceedings from the Georgetown University round table on languages and linguistics.* Washington, DC: Georgetown University Press.

Maley, A. (1986). *Xanadu—''A miracle of rare device'': The teaching of English in China.* In J. M. Valdes (Ed.), *Culture bound.* Cambridge: Cambridge University Press.

Manning, M. M., & Manning, G. L. (1979). *Reading Instruction in the Middle School.* Washington, DC: National Education Association.

Martin, A. (1983, March). *ESL students' perceptions of L1–L2 differences in organizing ideas.* Paper presented at the TESOL Convention, Toronto, Canada.

Mason, G. E., Blanchar, J. S., & Daniel, D. B. (1983). *Computer applications in reading* (2nd ed.). Newark, DE: International Reading Association.

Matalene, C. (1985). Contrastive rhetoric: An American writing teacher in China. *College English, 47,* 789–808.

McGroarty, M. (1989). The benefits of cooperative learning arrangements in second language instruction. *NABE Journal, 13,* 127–143.

McGroarty, M., & Galvan, J. L. (1985). Culture as an issue in second language teaching. In M. Celce-Murcia (Ed.), *Beyond basics: Issues and research in TESOL* (pp. 81–95). New York: Newbury House.

Mead, M. (1951). Columbia University research in contemporary cultures. In H. Guetzkow (Ed.), *Groups, leadership and men.* Pittsburgh, PA: Carnegie-Mellon University Press.

Mehan, H. (1973). Assessing children's school performance. *Recent Sociology, 5,* 240–263.

Mehan, H. (1979). *Learning lessons: Social organization in the classroom.* Cambridge: Harvard University Press.

Merritt, M. (1982). Distributing and directing attention in primary classrooms. In L. C. Wilkinson (Ed.), *Communicating in the classroom.* New York: Academic Press.

Mestre, J. P. (1984). The problem with problems: Hispanic students and math. *Bilingual Journal,* Fall, 15–20.

Mestre, J. P., Gerace, W. J., & Lockhead, J. (1982). The interdependence of language and translational math skills among bilingual Hispanic engineering students. *Journal of Research in Science Teaching, 19,* 399–410.

Mevarech, R. (1985). The effects of cooperative mastery learning strategies on mathematical achievement. *Journal of Educational Research, 78*(6), 372–377.

Michaels, S. (1981). "Sharing time": Children's narrative styles and differential access to literacy. *Language in Society, 10*(3), 423–442.

Milk, R. (1985). The changing role of ESL in bilingual education. *TESOL Quarterly, 19*(4), 657–672.

Mohan, B. A. (1979). Cultural bias in reading comprehension tests. In *On TESOL '79* (pp. 171–177). Washington, DC: TESOL.

Mohan, B. A. (1986). *Language and content.* Reading, MA: Addison-Wesley.

Mohatt, G., & Erickson, F. (1981). Cultural differences in teaching styles in an Odawa school: A sociolinguistic approach. In H. Trueba, P. Guthrie, & K. Au (Eds.), *Culture and the bilingual classroom: Studies in classroom ethnography.* New York: Newbury House.

Monk, B., & Burak, A. (1987). Russian speakers. In M. Swan and B. Smith (Eds.), *Learner English.* Cambridge: Cambridge University Press.

Montgomery, G. T., & Orozco, S. (1984). Validation of a measure of acculturation for Mexican Americans. *Hispanic Journal of Behavioral Sciences, 6*(1), 53–63.

Morris, R. W. (1975). Linguistic problems encountered by contemporary curriculum projects in mathematics. In E. Jacobsen (Ed.), *Interactions between linguistics and mathematical education: Final report of the symposium sponsored by UNESCO, CEDO and ICMI, Nairobi, Kenya, September 1–11, 1974* (UNESCO Report No. Ed–74/CONF.808, pp. 25–52). Paris: United Nations Educational, Scientific and Cultural Organization.

Moskowitz, G. (1978). *Caring and sharing in the foreign language class: A sourcebook on humanistic techniques.* New York: Newbury House.

Munro, J. (1979). Language abilities and maths performance. *Reading Teacher, 32,* 900–915.

Murdock, G. P. (1961). The cross-cultural survey. In F. W. Moore (Ed.), *Readings in cross cultures.* New Haven, CT: HRAF Press.

Naiman, N., Fröhlich, M., Stern, H. H., & Todesco, A. (1978). *The good language learner.* Unpublished manuscript, Ontario Institute for Studies in Education, Toronto, Canada.

National Commission for Employment Policy. (1982). *Hispanics and jobs: Barriers to progress.* Washington, DC: National Commission for Employment Policy.

Navarrete, C., & Rivera, O. (1983). *Science and math learning activities.* Albuquerque, NM: APS Curriculum Center.

Nemerouf, A., & Williams, R. J. (1986). *Masters of words, makers of meaning: Designs for teaching writing.* Los Angeles: UCLA Center for Academic Interinstitutional Programs.

Neves, A. (1983). *The effect of various input on the second language acquisition of Mexican American children in nine elementary school classrooms.* Unpublished doctoral dissertation, Stanford University.

Neville, M. H., & Pugh, A. K. (1982). *Towards independent reading.* London: Heinemann.

Niedermeyer, F. (1970). Effects of training on the instructional behaviors of student tutors. *Journal of Educational Research, 64*(3), 119–123.

Northcutt, L., & Watson, D. (1986). *S.E.T.: Sheltered English teaching handbook.* Carlsbad, CA: Northcutt, Watson, Gonzales.

Ochs, E. (1983). Cultural dimensions of language acquisition. In E. Och & B. Schieffelin (Eds.), *Acquiring conversational competence* (pp. 185–191). London: Routledge and Kegan Paul.

Ogbu, J. U., & Matute-Bianchi, M. E. (1986). Understanding sociocultural factors: Knowledge, identity and school adjustment. In *Beyond language: Social and cultural factors in schooling language minority students* (pp. 73–142). Los Angeles: Evaluation, Dissemination and Assessment Center, California State University.

Oller, J. W. (1979). *Language tests at school.* London: Longman.

Oller, J. W. (1981). Research on the measurement of affective variables: Some remaining questions. In R. W. Andersen (Ed.), *New dimensions in second language acquisition research* (pp. 14–27). New York: Newbury House.

Oller, J. W. (1982). Gardner on affect: A reply to Gardner. *Language Learning, 32,* 183–189.

Oller, J. W. (1983a). *Issues in language testing research.* New York: Newbury House.

Oller, J. W., Jr. (1983b). Story writing principles and ESL teaching. *TESOL Quarterly, 17*(1), 39–53.

Oller J. W., Baca, L. L., & Vigil, A. (1978). Attitudes and attained proficiency in ESL: A sociolinguistic study of Mexican-Americans in the Southwest. *TESOL Quarterly, 11,* 173–183.

Oller, J. W., Hudson, A., & Liu, P. F. (1977). Attitudes and attained proficiency in ESL: A sociolinguistic study of native speakers of Chinese in the United States. *Language Learning, 27,* 1–27.

Olsen, L. (1988). *Crossing the schoolhouse border: A California tomorrow policy research project.* San Francisco: California Tomorrow.

Olson, C. B. (Ed.). (1986). *Practical ideas for teaching writing as a process.* Sacramento: California State Department of Education.

Olson, D. (1977). From utterance to text: The bias of language in speech and writing. *Harvard Educational Review, 47,* 257–281.

Olson, D. (1984). "See! Jumping!" The antecedents of literacy. In H. Goelman, A. Oberg, and F. Smith (Eds.), *Awakening to literacy.* Portsmouth, NH: Heinemann Educational Books.

O'Malley, J. M. (1985). Learning strategy applications to content instruction in second language development. In *Issues in English language development* (pp. 69–73). Wheaton, MD: National Clearinghouse for Bilingual Education.

O'Malley, J. M., Chamot, A. U., Stewner-Manzanares, G., Küpper, L., & Russo, R. P. (1985). Learning strategies used by beginning and intermediate ESL students. *Language Learning, 35,* 21–46.

O'Malley, J. M., Chamot, A. U., Stewner-Manzanares, G., Russo, R. P., & Küpper, L. (1985). Learning strategy applications with students of English as a second language. *TESOL Quarterly, 19,* 557–584.

O'Malley, J. M., Chamot, A. U., & Küpper, L. (1986). *The role of learning strategies and cognition in second language acquisition: A study of strategies for listening comprehension used by students of English as a second language.* Rosslyn, VA: InterAmerica Research Associates.

O'Malley, J. M., Chamot, A. U., & Walker, C. (1987). Some applications of cognitive theory in second language acquisition. *Studies in Second Language Acquisition, 9*(3), 287–306.

Orasanu, J. (Ed.). (1985). *Reading comprehension: From research to practice.* Hillsdale, NJ: Erlbaum.

Orlick, T. (1978) *The cooperative sports and games book.* New York: Pantheon Books.

Ostrander, S., & Schroeder, L. (1979). *Superlearning.* New York: Dell.

Oxford, R. L. (1990). *Language learning strategies: What every teacher should know.* New York: Newbury House.

Pardo, E. (1984). *Acquisition of the Spanish reflexive: A study of a child's over-extended forms.* Unpublished doctoral dissertation, Stanford University.

Parker, D. (1986). *"Sheltered" English: Method and technique.* Presentation at California Immersion/Second Language Institute, University of California, Santa Barbara.

Parker, O. D., & Educational Services Staff, AFME. (1986). Cultural clues to the Middle Eastern students. In J. M. Valdes (Ed.), *Culture bound.* Cambridge: Cambridge University Press.

Pearn, M. (1978). *Employment testing and the goal of equal opportunity: The American experience.* London: The Runnymede Trust.

Peñalosa, F. (1975). Sociolinguistic theory and the Chicano community. *Aztlan, 6*(1), 1–11.

Perfetti, C. (1985). *Reading ability.* New York: Oxford University Press.

Philips, S. (1972). Participant structures and communicative competence: Warm Spring children in community and classroom. In C. Cazden, V. John, and D. Hymes (Eds.), *Functions of language in the classroom* (pp. 370–394). New York: Columbia University, Teachers College Press.

Philips, S. (1974). Warm Spring Indian time: How the regulation of participation affects the progression of events. In R. Bauman & J. Sherzer (Eds.), *Explorations in the ethnography of speaking.* Cambridge: Cambridge University Press.

Philips, S. (1983). *The invisible culture: Communication in classroom and community on the Warm Spring Indian Reservation.* White Plains, NY: Longman.

Piaget, J. (1926). *The language and thought of the child.* New York: Harcourt, Brace.

Piaget, J. (1968). *Six psychological studies.* New York: Random House.

Poole, A. (1971). *Final project report: Cross-age teaching* (No. 68–06138–0). Ontario-Montclair School District, Ontario, CA: Poole-Young Associates.

Poppe, C. A., & VanMatre, N. A. (1985). *Science learning centers for the primary grades.* West Nyack, NY: Center for Applied Research in Education.

Porter, P. (1983). *Variations in the conversations of adult learners of English as a function of the proficiency level of the participants.* Unpublished doctoral dissertation, Stanford University.

Quinn, M. E., & Kessler, C. (1984, December). *Bilingual children's cognition and language in science learning.* Paper presented at the Inter-American Seminar on Science Education, Panama.

Rabinowitz, M., & Chi, M. T. (1987). An interactive model of strategic processing. In S. J. Ceci (Ed.), *Handbook of cognitive, social, and neuropsychological aspects of learning disabilities* (Vol. 2), (pp. 83–102). Hillsdale, NJ: Erlbaum.

Readance, J. E., Bean, T. W., & Baldwin, R. S. (1981). *Content area reading: An integrated approach.* Dubuque, IA: Kendall/Hunt.

Reder, S. (1981). *A Hmong community's acquisition of English.* Research report. Portland, OR: Northwest Regional Educational Laboratory.

Reder, S., Green, K. R., & Sweeney, M. (1983). *Acquisition and use of literacy in the Hmong community of Newton.* Portland, OR: Northwest Regional Educational Laboratory.

Reid, J. (1988). *The process of composition* (2nd ed.). Englewood Cliffs, NJ: Prentice Hall.

Renault, L. (1981). Theoretically based secondary language reading strategies. In C. W. Twyford, W. Diehl, & K. Feathers (Eds.), *Monographs in language and reading studies: Reading English as a second language: Moving from theory.* Bloomington: Indiana University, School of Education.

Resnick, L. (1987). Learning in school and out. *Educational Researcher, 16,* 13–20.

Rezabek, D. (1981). *Horizon: An overview of vocational education and employment training services for limited English proficient persons in California.* Sacramento: California State Department of Education.

Richard-Amato, P. (1988). *Making it happen: Interaction in the second language classroom.* White Plains, NY: Longman.

Richard-Amato, P. (1989, March). *Using reaction dialogues to develop writing skills in ESL.* Paper presented at the TESOL Convention, San Antonio, TX.

Richard-Amato, P. (1990). *Reading in the content areas: An interactive approach for international students.* White Plains, NY: Longman.

Richards, J. C. (1980). Conversation. *TESOL Quarterly, 14*(4), 413–432.

Richards, J. C. (1984). The secret life of methods. *TESOL Quarterly, 18,* 7–23.

Richmond, K. (1987). Cross-cultural coping: Suggestions for Anglo teachers of ESL to native Americans. In C. Cargill (Ed.), *A TESOL Professional Anthology: Culture.* Lincolnwood, IL: National Textbook Company.

Rigg, P. (1981). Beginning to read in English the LEA way. In C. W. Twyford, W. Diehl, & K. Feathers (Eds.). *Monographs in language and reading studies: Reading English as a second language: Moving from theory.* Bloomington: Indiana University, School of Education.

Rivera, C. (1984). *Language proficiency and academic achievement.* Clevedon, England: Multilingual Matters.

Robertson, D. (1971). The effects of inter-grade tutoring experience on tutor attitudes and reading achievement. *Dissertation Abstracts International, 32,* 6A, 3010.

Robinson, F. P. (1962). *Effective reading.* New York: Harper & Row.

Rodriguez, I., & Bethel, L. J. (1983). An inquiry approach to science and language teaching. *Journal of Research in Science Teaching, 20,* 291–296.

Rosenblatt, L. M. (1976). *Literature as exploration.* New York: Noble & Noble.

Rubin, J. (1981). Study of cognitive processes in second language learning. *Applied Linguistics, 11,* 117–131.

Rumelhart, D. E. (1981). Schemata: The building blocks of cognition. In J. T. Guthrie (Ed.), *Comprehension and teaching: Research reviews.* Newark, DE: International Reading Association.

Russell, R., & Ford, D. (1983). Effectiveness of peer tutors vs. resource teachers. *Psychology in the Schools, October,* 20.

Rust, S. P., Jr. (1970). The effect of tutoring on the tutor's behavior, academic achievement, and social status. *Dissertation Abstracts International, 30,* 11–A, 4862.

Sanchez, R. (1984). *Chicano discourse: Socio-historic perspectives.* New York: Newbury House.

Sandburg, C. (1928). *Abe Lincoln grows up.* New York: Harcourt, Brace.

Sapiens, A. (1982). *Instructional language strategies in bilingual Chicano peer tutoring and their effect on cognitive and affective learning outcomes.* Unpublished doctoral dissertation, Stanford University.

Sato, C. (1981). Ethnic styles in classroom discourse. In M. Hines & W. Rutherford (Eds.), *On TESOL '81*. Washington, DC: TESOL.

Savignon, S. J. (1983). *Communicative competence: Theory and practice*. Reading, MA: Addison-Wesley.

Saville-Troike, M. (1976). *Foundations for teaching English as second language*. Englewood Cliffs, NJ: Prentice Hall.

Saville-Troike, M. (1977). The cultural component of bilingual teacher education programs: Theories and practices. In J. F. Fanselow & R. L. Light (Eds.), *Bilingual, ESOL and foreign language teacher preparation: Models, practices and issues*. Washington, DC: TESOL.

Saville-Troike, M. (1984). What *really* matters in second language learning for academic achievement? *TESOL Quarterly, 18,* 199–219.

Sawyer, J. (1976). *The implications of passive and covert bilingualism for bilingual education*. Paper presented at the Southwest Area Language and Linguistics Workshop, San Antonio, TX.

Scarcella, R. (1983). Discourse accent in second language performance. In S. Gass & L. Selinker (Eds.), *Language transfer in language learning*. New York: Newbury House.

Scarcella, R. (1990). *Teaching language minority students in the multicultural classroom*. Englewood Cliffs, NJ: Prentice Hall Regents.

Scarcella, R., & Lee, C. (1988, March). *Korean ESL writing difficulties*. Paper presented at the 1988 TESOL Covention, Chicago, IL.

Schieffelin, B. (1979). Getting it together: An ethnographic approach to the study of the development of communicative competence. In E. Ochs & B. Schieffelin (Eds.), *Developmental pragmatics* (pp. 73–108). New York: Academic Press.

Schieffelin, B. (1983). Talking like birds: Sound play in a cultural perspective. In E. Ochs & B. Schieffelin (Eds.), *Acquiring conversational competence*. London: Routledge and Kegan Paul.

Schieffelin, B., & Ochs, E. (Eds.). (1986). *Language socialization across cultures*. Cambridge: Cambridge University Press.

Schumann, J. H. (1976). Social distance as a factor in second language acquisition. *Language Learning, 26,* 135–143.

Schwartz, T. (Ed.). (1976). *Socialization as cultural communication: Development of a theme in the work of Margaret Mead*. Berkeley: University of California Press.

Scruggs, T., & Osguthorpe, R. T. (1986). Tutoring intervention within special educational settings: A comparison of cross-age and peer tutoring. *Psychology in the Schools, April, 23.*

Seelye, H. (1974). *Teaching culture: Strategies for foreign language educators*. Skokie, IL: National Textbook Company.

Shackle, C. (1987). Speakers of Indian languages. In M. Swan & B. Smith (Eds.), *Learner English*. Cambridge: Cambridge University Press.

Shaver, J., & Nuhn, D. (1968). Underachievers in reading and writing respond to a tutoring program. *The Clearinghouse, 4(3),* 236–239.

Shaver, J., & Nuhn, D. (1971). The effectiveness of tutoring under-achievers in reading and writing. *Journal of Educational Research, 65,* 107–112.

Shepherd, D. L. (1982). *Comprehensive high school reading methods* (3rd ed.). Columbus, OH: Merrill.

Short, D., Seufert-Bosco, M., & Grognet, A. (1991). *Of the people: U.S. history*. Englewood Cliffs, NJ: Prentice Hall Regents/Center for Applied Linguistics.

Short, D., Crandall, J., & Christian, D. (1989). *How to integrate language and content: A training manual.* Los Angeles: UCLA Center for Language Education and Research. (ERIC Document Reproduction Service No. ED 305 824)

Shuy, R. (1978). Problems in assessing language ability in bilingual education programs. In H. Lafontaine, H. Persky, & L. Golubchick (Eds.), *Bilingual education.* Wayne, NJ: Avery Publishing Group.

Shuy, R. (1981). Conditions affecting language learning and maintenance among Hispanics in the United States. *NABE Journal, 6,* 1–18.

Shuy, R. (1984). Linguistics in other professions. In *Annual Review of Anthropology, 13,* Palo Alto, CA: Annual Reviews.

Silberman, C. E. (Ed.). (1973). *The open classroom reader.* New York: Random House.

Sinatra, R., & Stahl-Gemake, J. (1983). *Using the right brain in the language arts.* Springfield, IL: Thomas.

Sinclair, J., & Coulthard, M. (1975). *Towards an analysis of discourse: The language of teachers and pupils.* New York: Oxford University Press.

Shaver, J., & Nuhn, D. (1971). The effectiveness of tutoring under-achievers in reading and writing. *Journal of Educational Research, 65,* 107–112.

Skinner, D. (1981). *Bi-modal learning and teaching: Concepts and methods.* Unpublished manuscript, Hispanic Training Institute.

Skutnabb-Kangas, T., & Toukomaa, P. (1976). *Teaching migrant children's mother tongue and learning the language of the host country in the context of the socio-cultural situation of the migrant family.* Helsinki: The Finnish National Commission for UNESCO.

Slavin, R. (1983). *Cooperative learning.* White Plains, NY: Longman.

Smith, B. (1987). Arabic speakers. In M. Swan & B. Smith (Eds.), *Learner English: A teacher's guide to interference and other problems.* Cambridge: Cambridge University Press.

Smith, F. (1975). *Comprehension and learning: A conceptual framework for teachers.* New York: Holt, Rinehart & Winston.

Smith, F. (1978). *Understanding reading* (2nd ed.). New York: Holt, Rinehart & Winston.

Smith, V., & Reid, J. (1983). Audience expectation exercises for ESL writing classes. *Curriculum Clearinghouse Newsletter, 3*(2), 18.

Smyth, D. (1987). Thai speakers. In M. Swan & B. Smith (Eds.), *Learner English: A Teacher's Guide to Interference and Other Problems.* Cambridge: Cambridge University Press.

Snow, C., & Ferguson, C. (Eds.). (1977). *Talking to children.* Cambridge: Cambridge University Press.

Snow, M. A., & Brinton, D. (1988). Content-based language instruction: Investigating the effectiveness of the adjunct model. *TESOL Quarterly, 22*(4), 553–574.

Snow, M. A., Met, M., & Genesee, F. (1989). A conceptual framework for the integration of language and content in second/foreign language instruction. *TESOL Quarterly, 23,* 201–217.

Sperling, S. K. (1977). *Poplollies and bellibones: A celebration of lost words.* New York: Clarkson Potter.

Stark, I., & Wallach, G. (1980). The path to a concept of language disabilities. *Topics in Language Disorders, 1,* 1–14.

Stein, N. (1982). What's in a story? Interpreting the interpretation of story grammars. *Discourse Processes, 5,* 319–336.

Stevick, E. (1976). English as an alien language. In J. F. Fanselow & R. H. Crymes (Eds.), *On TESOL '76.* Washington, DC: TESOL.

Stone, J. (1989). *Cooperative learning and language arts: A multi-structural approach.* San Juan Capistrano, CA: Resources for Teachers.

Stover, L. E. (1962). *Face and verbal analogues of interaction in Chinese culture.* Unpublished doctoral dissertation, Columbia University.

Sue, S. (1983). Ethnic minority issues in psychology: A reexamination. *American Psychologist, 38,* 583–592.

Sue, S., & Padilla, A. (1986). Ethnic minority issues in the United States: Challenges for the educational system. In California State Department of Education, *Beyond language: Social and cultural factors in schooling language minority children* (pp. 35–72). Los Angeles: Evaluation, Dissemination and Assessment Center, California State University.

Swain, M. (1985). Communicative competence: Some roles of comprehensible input and comprehensive output in its development. In S. Gass & C. Madden (Eds.), *Input in second language acquisition* (pp. 235–253). New York: Newbury House.

Swain, M., & Lapkin, S. (1982). *Evaluating bilingual education: A Canadian case study.* Clevedon, England: Multilingual Matters.

Swales, J. (1987). Utilizing the literatures in teaching the research paper. *TESOL Quarterly, 21,* 41–68.

Swan, M., & Smith, B. (Eds.). (1987). *Learner English: A teacher's guide to interference and other problems.* Cambridge: Cambridge University Press.

Szynal-Brown, C., & Morgan, R. (1983). The effects of reward on tutors' behaviors in a cross-age tutoring context. *Journal of Child Psychology, 36*(2), 196–208.

Tepper, E. L. (Ed.). (1980). *Southwest Asian exodus: From tradition to resettlement—understanding refugees from Laos, Kampuchea and Vietnam in Canada.* Ottawa: Canadian Asian Studies Association.

Terdy, D. (1986). *Content area ESL: Social studies.* Palatine, IL: Linmore Publishing.

Tharp, R., & Gallimore, R. (1988). *Rousing minds to life: Teaching, learning and schooling in social context.* New York: Cambridge University Press.

Thomas, E. L., & Robinson, H. A. (1982). *Improving reading in every class* (3rd ed.). Boston: Allyn & Bacon.

Thompson, I. (1987a). Japanese speakers. In M. Swan & B. Smith (Eds.), *Learner English.* Cambridge: Cambridge University Press.

Thompson, I. (1987b). Turkish speakers. In M. Swan & B. Smith (Eds.), *Learner English.* Cambridge: Cambridge University Press.

Thonis, E. W. (1981). Reading instruction for language minority students. In California State Department of Education, *Schooling and language minority students: A theoretical framework* (pp. 147–181). Los Angeles: Evaluation, Dissemination and Assessment Center, California State University.

Topping, K., & Whiteley, M. (1988). Sex differences in the effectiveness of peer tutoring. *Paired Reading Bulletin, 4,* 16–23.

Torbert, M. (1980). *Follow me: A handbook of movement activities for children.* Englewood Cliffs, NJ: Prentice Hall.

Torbert, M. (1982). *Secrets to success in sport and play.* Englewood Cliffs, NJ: Prentice Hall.

Torbert, M. (1983, Fall). Have we sold low organized games/activities short? *PaJOHPERD (Pennsylvania Journal of Health, Physical Education, Recreation, and Dance), 3.*

Tritch, D. (1984). *Logical connectors and scientific register.* Unpublished manuscript, University of Texas, San Antonio.

Trueba, H., Guthrie, P., & Au, K. (Eds.). (1981). *Culture and the bilingual classroom: Studies in classroom ethnography.* New York: Newbury House.

Vacca, R. T. (1981). *Content area reading.* Boston: Little, Brown.

Van Allen, R., & Halvoren, G. (1961). *The language experience approach to reading instruction.* Boston: Ginn.

Vann, R., Meyer, D., & Lorenz, F. (1984). Error gravity: A study of faculty opinions of ESL errors. *TESOL Quarterly, 18,* 427–440.

Varonis, E., & Gass, S. (1983, March). *"Target language" input from nonnative speakers.* Paper presented at the TESOL Convention, Toronto, Canada.

Vuong, L. D. (1982). *Master frog in the brocaded slipper.* Reading, MA: Addison-Wesley.

Vygotsky, L. S. (1962). *Language and thought.* Cambridge: MIT Press.

Vygotsky, L. S. (1978). *Mind in society: The development of higher psychological processes.* Cambridge: Harvard University Press.

Wagner, D. A., & Stevenson, H. W. (Ed.). (1982). *Cultural perspectives on child development.* San Francisco, CA: Freeman.

Wardhaugh, R. (1976). The contexts of language. New York: Newbury House.

Wayman, J. G. (1985). Reaching and teaching the gifted child. *Challenge, 4*(1), 2–4.

Webb, N. (1982). Student interaction and learning in small groups. *Review of Educational Research, 52*(3), 421–445.

Webb, N., & Kenderski, C. (1985). Gender differences in small-group interaction and achievement in high- and low-achieving classes. In L. Wilkinson & C. Marrett (Eds.), *Gender influences in classroom interaction* (pp. 209–236). Orlando, FL: Academic Press.

Weeks, T. (1983). Discourse, culture and interaction. In B. Robinette & J. Schachter (Eds.), *Second language learning.* Ann Arbor: University of Michigan Press.

Weik, M. H. (1967). *The jazz man.* New York: Atheneum.

Weinstein, C. E., & Mayer, R. E. (1986). The teaching of learning strategies. In M. C. Wittrock (Ed.), *Handbook of research on teaching* (3rd ed.) (pp. 315–327). New York: Macmillan.

Wells, G. (1981). *Learning through interaction.* Cambridge: Cambridge University Press.

Wendelin, K. H., & Greenlaw, M. J. (1984). *Storybook classrooms: Using children's literature in the learning center.* Atlanta, GA: Humanics Limited.

Wenden, A. (1985). Learner strategies. *TESOL Newsletter, 19*(5), 1–7.

White, R. W. (1959). Motivation reconsidered: The concept of competence. *Psychological Review, 66*(5), 297–333.

Whorf, B. (1956). Science and linguistics. In J. Carroll (Ed.), *Language, thought, and reality: Selected writings of Benjamin Lee Whorf.* Cambridge: MIT Press.

Wilkinson, A. C. (Ed.). (1983). *Classroom computers and cognitive science.* New York: Academic Press.

Wilkinson, A., Barnsley, G., Hanna, P., & Swan, M. (1980). *Assessing language development.* London: Oxford University Press.

Willetts, K. (Ed.). (1986). *Integrating language and content instruction.* CLEAR Educational Report #5. Los Angeles: UCLA Center for Language Education and Research. (ERIC Document Reproduction Service No. ED 278262).

Willetts, K., & Crandall, J. (1986). Content-based language instruction. *ERIC/CLL News Bulletin, 9*(2). Washington, DC: ERIC Clearinghouse on Languages and Linguistics.

Wilson, B. E. A., DeAvila, E., & Intili, J. K. (1982, April). *Improving cognitive, linguistic and academic skills in bilingual classrooms.* Paper presented at the annual meeting of the American Educational Research Association, New York.

Wilson, L., & Wilson, M. (1987). Farsi speakers. In M. Swan & B. Smith (Eds.), *Learner English: A teacher's guide to interference and other problems.* Cambridge: Cambridge University Press.

Wong-Fillmore, L. (1976). *The second time around: Cognitive and social strategies in second language acquisition*. Unpublished doctoral dissertation, Stanford University.

Wong-Fillmore, L. (1985). When does teacher talk work as input? In S. Gass & C. Madden (Eds.), *Input in second language acquisition* (pp. 17–50). New York: Newbury House.

Wong-Fillmore, L., Ammon, P., McLaughlin, B., & Ammon, M. (1985). *Learning English through bilingual instruction*. Final report to National Institute of Education, Contract #400–80–0030.

Zeigler, N., Larson, B., & Byers, J. (1983). *Let the kids do it* (Books 1 and 2). Belmont, CA: David S. Lake Publishers.

Zubrowski, B. (1981). *Drinking straw construction*. Boston: Little, Brown.

Index

Academic information-processing skills, 159–160

Academic language learning, 50. *See also* Second language learning

Academic proficiency, conversational vs., 20–21, 156

Academic prose. *See also* Writing
evaluation of, 219–220
use of contrastive rhetoric in, 212–213
using authentic writing tasks to develop, 213–215
using rhetorical and syntactic conventions to develop, 215–219

Academic success, 106–107, 111

Accounts, 121

Acculturation
culture shock as stage of, 80–83
explanation of, 79–80
role of social studies in, 288
stages of, 81

Achievement tests, 258, 266, 267. *See also* Testing

Acton, William, 85–86

Adaptation, 81

Adjunct Approach, 64–65

Adjunct classes, 12, 145

Adler, Peter, 80–81, 83

Advance organization, 55

Advertising industry, 87

African Americans
introducing literature about, 195
view of questioning, 133

Age, feedback patterns and, 136–137

Allen, Van, 48, 178

American Indians. *See* Native Americans

Americans, world view of, 76

Anderson, J. R., 43–44

Anomie, 81, 86

Answering
pauses before, 127, 135, 153
as type of feedback, 127, 133–135
during verbal review, 233–234

Anticipation guides, 157, 308–309

Arabs, gender problems with, 137

Art projects
aims of, 353–354
beginning, 349–351
materials for, 352
pretesting, 352–353

Asians. *See also* Chinese Americans; Indo-Chinese Americans; Japanese; Laotians; Thai people; Vietnamese
complementing and criticizing, 129, 130
difficulty in stating opinions by, 134
use of pausing by, 135
view of volunteering answers, 134

Assignment planning, 161

Assimilation, 81

Attitudes
explanation of, 77–79
language success and, 78, 81
negative, 77, 79

Audiotapes
recording lectures of talks on, 149
used as reading learning strategy, 191

Auditory representation, 56

Autonomy, 45, 361

Bahruth, R., 343

Ballads, 194

Basic Interpersonal Communicative Skills (BICS), 16–18

Bateson, Gregory, 82

Biethnicity, 96